People of the Wachusett

PEOPLE OF THE WACHUSETT

Greater New England in History and Memory, *1630–1860*

DAVID JAFFEE

Cornell University Press

Ithaca and London

First published 1999 by Cornell University Press

Printed in the United States of America

Library of Congress Cataloging-in-Publication Data

Jaffee, David.
    People of the Wachusett : greater New England in history and memory, 1630–1860 / David Jaffee.
        p. cm.
    Includes bibliographical references and index.
    ISBN 0-8014-3610-9 (alk. paper)
    1. New England—History—Colonial period, ca. 1600–1775. 2. New England—History—1775–1865. 3. Cities and towns—New England—History. 4. Land settlement—New England—History. 5. Frontier and pioneer life—History. 6. New England—History, Local.
    I. Title.
F7.J34   1999
974'.02—dc21   99-14578

Cornell University Press strives to use environmentally responsible suppliers and materials to the fullest extent possible in the publishing of its books. Such materials include vegetable-based, low-VOC inks and acid-free papers that are recycled, totally chlorine-free, or partly composed of nonwood fibers. Books that bear the logo of the FSC (Forest Stewardship Council) use paper taken from forests that have been inspected and certified as meeting the highest standards for environmental and social responsibility. For further information, visit our website at www.cornellpress.cornell.edu.

Cloth printing   10   9   8   7   6   5   4   3   2   1

To my mother and the memory of my father

Contents

Illustrations and Tables   ix
Acknowledgments   xi

Introduction: New England Begins   1

PART I. TOWN SETTLEMENT IN THE SEVENTEENTH CENTURY   23

1. Indians, English, and Missionaries: The Plantation of Nashaway   25
2. "Indian-Fighters" and Town Founders:
   The Resettlement of the Wachusett, 1675–1725   73

PART II. TOWN SETTLEMENT IN THE EIGHTEENTH CENTURY   101

3. Lancaster and Its Offspring: Serial Town Formation
   Enters the New Century   103
4. Narragansett No. 2: Reproducing Families and Farms   127

PART III. THE CREATION OF GREATER NEW ENGLAND   163

5. New England Moves North: The South Shore of Nova Scotia   165
6. Town Founding and the Village Enlightenment:
   Walpole, New Hampshire   200

Epilogue: The Myth of Town Settlement   239

Notes   251
Bibliographical Essay   291
Index   296

Illustrations and Tables

MAPS

1. William Wood's map of New England   11
2. Settlement of New England, 1620–1675   15
3. The Wachusett   31
4. Indian tribal territories of New England, 1630   36
5. Champlain's map of Malle Barre (Nauset Harbor, Cape Cod, Massachusetts)   39
6. Lancaster's home lots on the Eastern Neck, about 1653   49
7. Lancaster's home lots west of the Nashaway River, about 1653   50
8. Indian villages of southern New England, after 1674   62
9. Settlement in New England and New York, 1676–1713   75
10. John Foster's map of New England   77
11. Lancaster and its contiguous communities   108
12. Settlement of New England and New York, 1713–1743   116
13. Fitchburg and its early settlers, 1764   118
14. Worcester County towns, circa 1774   130
15. Narragansett No. 2 lots, drawn from the Proprietors' Plan of 1734   133
16. Planter Nova Scotia, 1767   166
17. Chester Township, circa 1766   176
18. Settlement patterns and economic activity in northeastern America, circa 1800   189
19. The Green Mountain frontier, circa 1750   203
20. Cheshire County, as surveyed by Benjamin Bellows Jr., 1767   214
21. Walpole town center, 1780 and 1810   220

ix

FIGURES

1. Town foundings in New England, 1630–1650   10
2. Town foundings in New England, 1714–1740   115

PLATES

1. Henry Willard house, Lancaster, Massachusetts, built in 1680s,
   photographed about 1893   84
2. Caleb Sawyer house, Westminster, Massachusetts, built in 1690s,
   drawn about 1893   84
3. Samuel Willard house, Lancaster, Massachusetts,
   built about 1727   106
4. Fairbanks Moor house, Westminster, Massachusetts,
   built in 1737   147
5. Nathan Wood house, Westminster, Massachusetts,
   built in 1756   148
6. Levi Willard house, or the "Mansion House,"
   Lancaster, Massachusetts, built about 1750   149
7. Moses Gill house, Princeton, Massachusetts   150
8. Broadside by Nova Scotia governor Charles Lawrence   169
9. Simple frame and Cape Cod houses, late eighteenth century   183
10. Tall clock with an Asa Sibley eight-day movement,
    sold uncased, 1790   224
11. Bliss and Horswell easy chair, Charlestown,
    New Hampshire, 1798   224
12. Bow-front sideboard, Windsor, Vermont, circa 1798   225
13. Front page of the *Farmer's Weekly Museum*, April 5, 1796   230

TABLES

1. Members of the Nashaway Company   42
2. Lancaster and its garrison families, 1676–1711   83
3. David Page's land holdings, 1748–1763   123
4. Population of Westminster, 1737–1800   146
5. Landholdings in Westminster, 1751–1865   151
6. Land usage in towns of Massachusetts, 1771   152
7. Average farm holdings of livestock in towns of
   Massachusetts, 1771   153

Acknowledgments

This project has roots reaching back years ago when I discovered a cache of documents that eventually came to form the core of this book. Beyond the physical documents, however, I owe my greatest debts to the people who have helped me along the way. Bernard Bailyn's powerful example of how history can be done and why it matters led me into studying early American history and continues to inspire my work. His enthusiasm for my early results and his probing of my analysis and my writing pushed the project and me to greater heights. While at Harvard, I was fortunate also to get to know Stephen Botein, whose subtle practice of the historical craft has remained with me long after his premature death robbed the world of his gentle but acute mind. Christopher Jedrey and Fred Anderson, fellow historians of New England, shaped this project from the very beginning. I am grateful as well to Chris Appy, Gary Gerstle, and Mark Hirsch. Early in my Wachusett labors I was introduced to the riches of the American Antiquarian Society, which I consider the spiritual as well as archival base for this project. There, Nancy Burkett, John Hench, Joanne Chaison, Gigi Barnhill, and Marie Lamoreaux have been both supportive and patient.

Financial support came from numerous grants and fellowships. The American Antiquarian Society gave me a Frances Hiatt and a Kate B. and Hall J. Peterson fellowship. I received a grant from the Charles Warren Center for Studies in American History, a CBS Bicentennial Fellowship, and a Frank Knox Memorial Fellowship at Christ's College, Cambridge. Support also came from the Henry Huntington Library and the Newberry Library. The Smithsonian Institution provided a postdoctoral fellowship at the National Museum of American History, where Gary Kulik and Barbara Smith furnished guidance in the world of material culture studies. A Fulbright lectureship at the University of Tokyo gave me a fascinating environment to work in, as well as introduced me to some wonderful graduate students and colleagues, including Yasuo Endo, Masako Notoji, and Hiroshi Yoneyama, who made my year in Japan an intellectual as well as cultural experience and helped me to see the United States in a broader perspective. At the City College of New York several PSC–CUNY research grants afforded me monies for valuable travel and research. In the humanities division we have been fortunate in generous support for scholarly activity from our deans, Paul Sherwin and Martin Tamny. CCNY colleagues and friends Susan Besse, David Johnson, Larry Kaplan, Lou Masur, Geraldine Murphy, Darren Staloff, and Judith Stein have offered intellectual succor, especially during the recent statewide political assaults on public education for working people in New York.

I am grateful for the efforts and interest of librarians and archivists at the Massachusetts Archives, the New Hampshire Historical Society, the New Hampshire State Library, the Lancaster Town Library, the Fitchburg Public Library, the Fitchburg Historical Society, the Public Archives of Canada, the Bancroft Library (Berkeley), the Walpole Historical Society, the Massachusetts Historical Commission, and the Public Archives of Nova Scotia. Warren Leon and Cynthia Robinson were generous with their companionship and hospitality during my many visits to Worcester County; Warren listened to me talk about the Wachusett, and Cynthia shared her expertise on New England public history. In Nova Scotia, Jack Crowley and Marion Binkley were similarly generous. Conversations about the project with Joyce Appleby, Bill Cronon, Bob Gross, Michael Lapp, Elise Marientstras, Elizabeth Mancke, Marcus Rediker, Daniel Scott Smith, and Joe Wood provided guidance and helped shape the final effort. Fred Anderson, Chris Clark, Tom Dublin, Ann Fabian, Peter Mancall, Terry Murphy, and Alan Taylor were each gracious in reading the entire manuscript and providing invaluable advice, some of them more than once. Barbara Smith, Lou Masur, Elizabeth Mancke, Elise Marienstras, and Steve Nissenbaum read parts of the manuscript and also helped guide its development. Commentators and audiences at the Institute of Early American History and Culture Conference, at the University of Tokyo and the University of Paris, and at the Planter Studies Conference provided invaluable sounding boards. Furthermore, I have been lucky to have "The Reading Group" since my arrival in New York—John, Betsy, Jeanie, Herb, Ann, David, Peter, the two Joshes—to illuminate all the pitfalls that publications can fall into. Roy Rosenzweig has been a friend since the days of our early trips to AAS.

My editor Peter Agree was interested in the project for a long time and was a constant supporter of it. Grey Osterud helped a weary author go the final distance with the manuscript and restore my original intellectual enthusiasm. Finally, Barbara Brooks was an intrepid companion throughout, from Lancaster to Louisbourg, as well as a partner in the many other more important things in life. She conveyed to me that there were other kinds of history and other places in the world to live. Our daughter, Isadora, was generous in allowing me computer time in our busy household. Finally, my mother, Dorothy Brown Jaffee, instilled in me a passion for books, and my late father, Eugene Victor Jaffee, infected me with a sense of curiosity about all matters cultural. I hope this book, which they long awaited, helps to acknowledge my enormous debt to them.

D. J.

Introduction

> The scene is a novelty in the history of man. The colonization of a wilderness
> by civilized men, where a regular government, mild manners, arts, learning,
> science, and Christianity have been interwoven in its progress from the begin-
> ning, is a state of things of which the eastern continent and the records of past
> ages furnish neither an example, nor a resemblance.
> Timothy Dwight, *Travels; in New-England and New-York* (1821–22)

Timothy Dwight, a nineteenth-century minister who traveled
throughout New England and New York, placed colonization at the center
of the story of New England. The concept of serial town settlement—if not
that phrase—held a key to his understanding of the history of the region.
He defined a town-centered landscape as the essence of New England's past,
firmly embedding commerce in his contemporary tale, and envisioned the
continuation of serial town settlement as the means of navigating the loom-
ing perils of the new nation's future.

This book is a cultural history of the frontier, examined in terms of serial
town settlement.[1] By the phrase "serial town settlement" I refer to the
process of the continual creation and replication of towns across the landscape, the sequential founding of new towns based on a model understood
by New England's settlers and supervised by the colonial authorities.
Through this process Europeans colonized the New England region and
New Englanders commercialized their cultural life in the seventeenth and
eighteenth centuries. The process of serial town settlement includes the
establishment and expansion of towns as well as the crafting of narratives
of local history that place town founding at their center.[2] Serial town settlement created New England.

The significance of the New England town is well known and needs no
further promotion; but serial town settlement points beyond the founding
of individual towns to suggest how town settlement created a regional and
national culture. Colonization provided a vehicle for the transmission and
transformation of New England culture, while stories about colonization
gave shape and meaning to New England life.

New Englanders colonized their region by establishing towns. When those towns reached demographic maturity and there were no longer any available niches in the local economic hierarchy, or when the consensual community became riven by cultural conflict, the "budding" process began and a new town was established. The movement from old settlement to new was bound together by the social process of town formation, while the writing and telling of local history served up luminous examples of town founders and constituted a medium in which cultural changes could be validated. As they transplanted and transformed their culture across the region, settlers were guided by internalized social strictures, the intervention of the colonial authorities, and the work of cultural mediators such as ministers and missionaries.

The New England town has long been the basis for our thinking and rethinking about the American past. Genteel nineteenth-century antiquarians and early twentieth-century institutional historians focused on the towns of the region in constructing a national history and professional historiography. The revolutionary developments of "the new social history" meant that we came to know enormous amounts about the everyday lives of English migrants to the eastern coastal "little communities" of early modern British North America.[3] More recently, attention has moved inland to the second generation of towns where war was a constant feature of life.[4] Also, New England rural communities in the postrevolutionary period have been laboratories for debates on the transition to capitalism in the northern United States.[5]

Our understanding of early American frontiers, too, has changed in recent years. Practitioners of the "new western history" have urged us to forgo the national boundaries of the United States and see the North American frontier as a fluid congeries of encounters between various peoples.[6] Ethnohistorians have rewritten early American history to envision an Indian New World, where syncretic cultural exchanges occurred across the permeable and shifting cultural border between Europeans and Indians in the Northeast.[7] Scholars of Puritanism have contextualized their texts in light of this vast social history and challenged the notion of a monolithic Puritan ideology.[8] Still, each of these powerful new formulations too often remains within a rich but discrete body of scholarship. In this book I attempt to bridge many of these artificial divides: those between Puritan and Indian villagers, eastern and western towns, colonial and postrevolutionary communities, New England and Nova Scotia, and, perhaps most significant, those between social and cultural history.

This book explores these grand themes through a regional study of inland New England, starting with the Wachusett in northern Worcester County, Massachusetts, and tracing the founding of new towns by Wachusett people. In Part 1, I look at the mid-seventeenth-century founding of Lancaster and its resettlement and expansion after Metacom's War; in Part 2, at the hiving off of that large township and the granting of new townships in the region in the early eighteenth century; and finally in Part 3, at their offspring within the region as well as in northern New England and Nova Scotia in the Revolutionary Era. Within that broad scope I emphasize two significant groups in the process: the citizen-founders of the towns, who, although not the leading lights of colonial New England history, played important roles in the settlement process, and the local historians, including some well-known writers such as Mary Rowlandson as well as others whose voices have remained relatively obscure but who nonetheless defined the culture of this region.

Frederick Jackson Turner saw the frontier as a safety valve and a democratizing influence that created a geographic region in which social mobility was possible for the most able and industrious of the settlers, no matter how impoverished their origins.[9] Serial town formation, the central means of New England colonization, is an equally influential but much more complex process. The frontier can still be seen as a safety valve, because the ability to found new towns on recently vacated lands prevented land morselization (the division of holdings into ever smaller parcels), a resort to wage labor, and class division in the older towns. But the implications of the process are anything but democratic, for serial town settlement tended to retard social change by promoting the replication of a conservative, largely consensual, agrarian order. The changes that took place over time—the increasing scope of land speculation, for example—represent intensification of characteristics evident from the start, not innovations. This process was adaptive and evolutionary and in no way conformed to either a declension of the social order or a democratizing model of development. New methods of town founding were grafted onto the model initially formulated by the colonial government's General Court during the first decade of New England's expansion.

This achievement was no singular progress through the wilderness, as some contemporary and later historians have imagined. Town founding had haphazard beginnings; it took form in the first days of the Great Migration—the massive influx of Puritan colonists from England in the 1630s—with the decisions to avoid clustering migrants around one or two coastal settlements. Puritan leaders and settlers improvised a way to contain the enormous growth of their population by creating separate, bounded communities through a sort of budding process that opened up new niches in the agrarian society of British North America. The impetus to extend English settlement to the inland Wachusett in the 1640s came from two unlikely sources: Indian initiatives in securing access to desired English traders and their goods, and English efforts to locate industrial sites.

The two villages and two village cultures occupied the Wachusett for some time. Joint occupancy had unintended consequences for the native inhabitants of the Wachusett. The Puritan demographic success pushed

English and Indian villagers closer together physically but farther apart culturally, a situation which undermined their common goal of peaceful coexistence. Protestant missionaries and Indian "superintendents" introduced a variant of the New England town to the Nipmuc people that was intended to "civilize" them and enable them to enter into full membership in town society. Christian Indians altered the economic and spiritual forms that were introduced, promoting their own syncretic form of cultural exchange across the porous frontier of mid-seventeenth-century New England. Peaceful encounters with Indians were an everyday occurrence and significant part of the colonizing experience for English townspeople in their first half-century of settlement. By the close of the seventeenth century, however, colonization led to war.

War was only the most visible of a variety of problems that settlers of the Wachusett confronted at the turn of the century. Serial town settlement proved to be a resilient system that responded effectively to internal and external challenges in the eighteenth century. Legislative debates posed a stark choice between continuing the familiar, familial mode of granting authority to numerous farmer/proprietors or passing the initiative to a few larger proprietors to effect settlement. The House of Representatives' vision of family proprietorship won out and offered standardized town grants to meet the challenges of the post-1713 land rush. Townspeople pushed into the contested borderlands of the English, French, and Algonquian peoples in the early eighteenth century. Colonists spilled out from their original core around Lancaster, first to found a layer of towns northwest of the outpost and then to inch their way up the Connecticut River valley.

In its eighteenth-century variant, town founding did not fall away precipitously from a once careful and communal process but rather fostered the full-blown development of central Massachusetts. This extensive mode of colonization created a regional system that connected old and new townships and retained control in a proprietary system that had survived a challenge by British imperial officials. The business of town founding expanded and extended into new areas where Indian fighting was a necessary and almost continuous concomitant of colonization. The expansion of English settlement gave wider scope for migrating families to use familiar strategies to secure independence for the next generation and to secure a competency on the "near frontier" of Worcester County.

There were significant continuities in serial town settlement in colonial New England, both from above and from below. Provincial leaders and ordinary farmers used the legal instrument of proprietary control and other flexible institutions of town life, including the established system of allocating land and the Congregational church. Farmers maintained the goal of family settlement from below, and legislative oversight came from above. All groups were guided by expectations that "bounded communities" of a certain demographic and geographic size would be sustained and that upon reaching certain well-defined limits, new towns would be created and the settlement process would begin anew. Ideological statements about the New England way of life kept those ideals visible. Tensions and conflicts within the system could be mediated at both the local and the colonial levels. Although colonial townspeople often conceptualized change as decline, change did come to the process of town settlement. As the pace of town grants accelerated after 1713, bureaucratic procedures were set in place to produce a standardized grant. The greater distances between the older and newer foundings made the eighteenth-century terrain appear discontinuous to contemporaries. Certainly, mass proprietorship made for a more bureaucratic process. Speculation as a means of accumulating land and capital was built into the system of serial town settlement. Greater attention was paid to material comfort and genteel adornment, most distinctly in the "rebuilding" of the Wachusett housing, a refinement that widened the social differentiation within prospering towns. Extending colonization beyond the Massachusetts core area into northern New England and Nova Scotia made the spectrum of settlement possibilities far wider and variant outcomes more possible; this divergence eventually produced a gulf when Nova Scotian Planters were cut off from their southern cousins.

Town founders were entrepreneurial from the start as a result of the English migrants' craving for land and their limited material resources upon arrival. Entrepreneurship was intended, however, to secure a competency rather than accumulate a fortune. Some town founders cast large shadows on the landscape. Fur traders and Indian mediators, such as Simon Willard and John Prescott in the seventeenth century, and surveyors and militia leaders, such as Benjamin Bellows a century later, sometimes wielded substantial power. The immense and intense effort to establish a family farm and wrest a living from the hard-scrabble soil of New England required commercial activity from the start of settlement. The post-1713 flood of town settlements gave greater room for individual initiative and also fostered an intensification of commercial activities when town lands gave out and regional migration stalled; seasonal by-employment became full time and laboring stages in the life cycle more permanent. Commercial villages appeared in the region; indeed, towns founded in the eighteenth century were transformed more rapidly than older communities. The commercialization of the countryside had deep roots in the Wachusett's agricultural past, but also depended upon the emerging infrastructure of turnpikes and bridges, rural storekeepers and artisans that prompted greater market exchange. The New England village, the historian Stephen Nissenbaum has written, was compatible with capitalism, not in conflict with it. Its subsequent memorialization as a refuge from industrial society came from the mid-nineteenth century construction of a mythic colonial age of homespun.[10]

We can better understand colonization and commercialization by looking at the people of the Wachusett as town founders and village historians.

These venturesome conservatives undertook a long process of colonization, accompanied by warfare. Looking beyond the town to the process of serial town settlement makes sense of the extensive mobility in the Massachusetts colonial system and recognizes the efforts of ordinary settler-citizens in constructing that system. Over time the Indians were transformed from neighbors into "others," but porous boundaries continued to exist between the different peoples of the region. Commercialization in the original area, with its indigenous industrial roots, was successfully transplanted to the upper Connecticut River Valley by the 1790s. Individuals and groups, once they were embarked upon commercial activities that drew them away from older patterns of sociability, could find themselves enmeshed in new social relationships with constricting consequences, but they often seized upon new opportunities to realize familiar strategies of family settlement until the original bounds of the social system were transformed. Tensions were present at every level of society—from family to farm to town—however, a certain amount of internal tension could be sustained, and challenges could lead to complex innovations. The binary categories of community and commerce do not fit the experience of the people of the Wachusett. We must turn away from the Puritans' own stories as well as those Turnerian stories of the frontier that have seeped into the "new social history" which posit an original Puritan cohesiveness followed by eighteenth-century declension and the emergence of the Yankee. Instead, we should conceptualize the individual and collective stories of town founders as evidence of resiliency and conservative innovation rather than of loss and decline. Colonization and commercialization went together, produced by the accumulated actions of countless town founders.

History making also made New England. Towns were given form through the efforts of town founders, who created local institutions, and village historians, who organized the haphazard memories of colonization into coherent patterns that provided social meaning for the townspeople, present and future. Whether one considers Edward Johnson's 1653 *History* with its town-by-town narration of progress through the wilderness—with all its metaphorical overtones—or the vivid story of John Winthrop gazing upon the Wachusett as the future site for the expansion of Massachusetts Bay, early accounts of town settlement made sense of the messy experience of colonization and willed themselves onto the landscape. Local history produced a localistic culture; it legitimated social change in an early modern culture that saw change as declension. Mary Rowlandson's heroic lamentations about her "removes" from civilization, published after the social fabric had been rent by war with the Indians and frontier towns had been pushed back to the coast, allowed settlers to confront the abyss of Metacom's War and still continue colonization. Eighteenth-century orations memorialized Indian fighters; ministers celebrated Lancaster's centennial with paeans to economic development.

After the War for Independence regional self-definition became paramount for the Worcester County historian Peter Whitney and others who fashioned local and state histories for the new nation-state. Vernacular culture found odd champions. In their widely read satires, the literati of Walpole, the federalist Walpole Wits, created an idealized New England town—deferential in the past, disordered in the present—as part of a cultural strategy to oppose democratizing trends in their society. Ironically, they furthered that very process by their own literary entrepreneurship. Even migrants north to the British military colony of Nova Scotia, when looking for their own identity amid the confusions of the Revolutionary era, resorted rhetorically to New England's historical mission of town settlement. In the mid nineteenth century, centennial orators placed the New England town at the center of a new mythic age of homespun; they cleared the way for the consolidation of a new northern middle-class culture around the unbroken transmission of a common Puritan village inheritance. Throughout the region's long history, print culture in New England defined the experimental community to itself and the world at large. Stories about settlement constituted the history of New England and enabled the past to be transmitted to future generations. The production and consumption of local history linked the new to the old, even as the shape of settlement was transformed.[11]

Watertown: "This Great Town"

The Puritans embarked upon their migration with conservative intentions; they sought to preserve their customary way of life and replicate a localistic, town-centered culture based on English village life. Ironically, in their effort to transplant traditional institutions, the migrants created new social formations that looked very little like the ones they had left behind. "The town was among the more intentionally innovative structures created by the Massachusetts settlers," the historian Stephen Innes declared in *Creating the Commonwealth*.[12] The settlement of Watertown in the 1630s and its subsequent generation of new towns demonstrates how the Puritans created serial town settlement as part of an adaptive process of finding their way in a new environment. Neither the New England town nor the process of serial town settlement was an immediate, singular creation.

Before the Puritans began the Great Migration, the Massachusetts Bay Company had proposed a headright system of allocating land (a system in which colonists received a land grant for each arrival they sponsored, one similar to that of the Virginia Company). Such a system would have facilitated the recruitment of settlers but would not have promoted the type of community formation that the leaders espoused. Once relocated, leaders and residents felt their way toward town-based settlement by the mid-

1630s. Settlers quickly dispersed from Salem, Charlestown, and Cambridge, forcing their leaders to abandon the idea of a single settlement. By the fall of 1630 seven separate settlements in Massachusetts Bay Colony ranged from Salem in the north to Dorchester in the south, with Boston, Medford, Charlestown, Roxbury, and Watertown lying between them.[13]

Watertown, the first inland town, began the process of westward movement that would result in the colonization of the Wachusett in the 1640s. An entry point for numerous transatlantic voyagers, Watertown also served as the original home for the Wachusett's first generation of settlers. Watertown residents' early need to relieve the pressures of land and population fostered the process of serial town settlement, which they improvised during the 1630s.

In July 1630 Sir Richard Saltonstall, the nephew of the lord mayor of London and a prominent organizer of the Massachusetts Bay Company, and the Reverend George Phillips led forty families four miles up the Charles River to found Watertown. Before leaving Charlestown they observed a day of fasting and prayer, after which the family heads subscribed to the church covenant. Upon arrival to the new site, land was quickly allocated in "small lots," or home lots, located throughout the entire town. The haphazard land system and the richness of the site led residents to disperse, which caused concern among the colony's magistrates. Edward Johnson described Watertown's location as a "fruitful plat . . . scituated upon one of the Branches of the Charles River." The town was "watered with many pleasant Springs, and small Rivulets" that "hath caused her inhabitants to scatter," made religious ceremonies "very thin," and left "this great Town . . . to shew nothing delightful to the eye in any place." Entrepreneurial settlers recognized the town's commercial potential; some residents began a fishery, while others, by 1634, had constructed a mill. The pattern of dispersed settlement made it difficult for the townspeople to gather to conduct town business.[14] Organizing town affairs took time. Dispersal of the residents was compounded with religious division in the early years, as the Elder Richard Browne's latitudinarian positions split the ranks of parishioners. In 1634 the residents agreed to choose three persons as selectmen "for the ordering of the civil affairs." That and several visits by John Winthrop placated the roiled religious waters and restored comity to the community.

Realizing a compact and communal mode of settlement proved impossible. The small size of land allotments, nine quick divisions of land, and an active land market left the settlers free to consolidate their holdings and farm their land independently. The General Court's directives to regroup around the meetinghouse proved ineffective. At the same time, despite the settlers' dispersal and the active land market, Watertown created a relatively egalitarian social structure: the top tenth of the taxpayers owned less than one-third of the land. Yet, maintaining what the residents considered to be an ideal economic and social order meant refusing to allocate land to newcomers and holding onto large reserves for the second generation of the founders' families. Average land holdings of one-third of the male household heads rose to two hundred acres by 1647, only 6 percent of which was under cultivation.

Framed by these decisions to restrict access to land, Watertown already seemed to its residents to be overpopulated by 1635. The freemen decided that "there be too many inhabitants in the Towne" and the town itself was "in danger to be ruinated." But the system of land distribution in New England remained quite open because of the relative ease with which the General Court granted townships after 1635, when massive amounts of land became available on the colony's borders. A spate of new towns appeared during the next fifteen years (see figure 1 and map 1). In 1634, John Oldham led one group from Watertown a great distance to plant another Watertown (later renamed Weathersfield), the first town in Connecticut. Thirty-six residents of the original Watertown, claiming "straitness of accomodation [sic] and want of meadow," petitioned the General Court for a town grant further inland. The court answered favorably; it charged three organizers "to remove and settle a plantation," which they named Sudbury, next door to the parent community. It offered the town founders only quite general directives: land allotments should follow "men's estates" and family size and migrants would have to commit to the new community—they could sell their improved holdings in Watertown, but unimproved lands had to be left behind.[15]

Sudbury's settlers did not need detailed instructions for they sought not to make a new order but only to recreate the old order in a new place. The three organizers included Brian Pendleton, an early town officer of Watertown; Peter Noyes, who arrived after the ranks of the Watertown grantees had been closed; and the Reverend Edmund Brown, who was on the lookout for a new parish. The early settlers of Sudbury consisted of two main groups: a few Watertown residents with substantial land grants but without access to the town's leadership and a majority of residents with neither land nor proprietary status in the older town. The ranks of the leaders expanded; three organizers became seven commissioners, who parceled out the small house lots that were laid out along the three roads radiating from the meetinghouse. Sudbury was organized on an expanding open-field system (small strips in common fields), different from Watertown's layout (individual farmsteads, individual meadow lots, and large common fields for pasturage).

Sudbury's expansion brought change and conflict. Within a decade, members of the rising, younger generation challenged the town founders, who attempted to maintain the original hierarchy by restricting access to land. Sudbury's inhabitants had created a new economic and social order with fresh places for families, but the colonists' expectation of ample land for all, coupled with their demographic success, meant that population outstripped land supplies within a generation, and conflict rent the consensual commu-

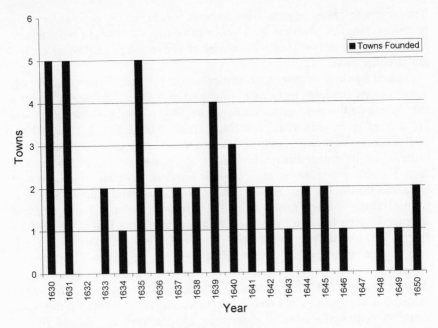

Figure 1. Town foundings in New England, 1630–1650.
Data from William Francis Galvin, *Historical Data Relating to Counties, Cities, and Towns in Massachusetts*, 5th ed. (Boston, 1997).

nity.[16] Sudbury's successful petition to the General Court resulted in an additional two-mile-wide grant on its western border that only exacerbated the conflict when the time came to divide up the bonus. The younger sons, led by John Ruddock, wanted to open up new places in town by distributing the new lands to individual farmers and maintaining the unrestricted grazing of cattle on the common pasture. Traditionalists controlling the town's offices, on the other hand, replaced the original distribution plan, which was to offer "every man . . . a like quantity of land," with a plan that would determine new allotments of land and pasturage according to the size of existing meadow grants. This system would deny younger sons access to the town's pasture land. The two sides squared off, town meetings became contentious, and the entire roster of town officers was swept from office in 1656. Only the formation of another new town, Marlborough, could restore comity within Sudbury's town bounds.[17]

When a General Court committee sustained the traditionalists, the younger generation, led by some substantial citizens of Sudbury, petitioned colonial authorities for a new town in 1656. Their petition was articulated in the conventional language of family settlement. They claimed that "God hath been pleased to increase our children, which are grown to men's estates," that the "fathers should be glad to see them then settled before the

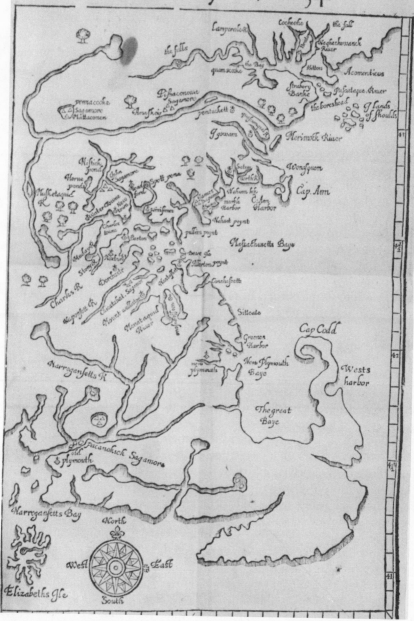

The South part of New-England, as it is Planted this yeare, 1634.

Map 1. William Wood's map of New England. This is the first printed map made by a colonist. As three thousand settlers streamed into Massachusetts Bay, Wood's map showed thirteen English towns and three remaining Indian villages (shown as sets of three triangles). On the north shore Indian and English residents lived in close proximity. Wood paid great attention to representing inland Massachusetts, and this was the first time that the Merrimack River appeared on a map. (Reprinted from *New England's Prospect* [London, 1634], inscribed, "The South part of New-England, as it is Planted this yeare, 1634." Courtesy of the Massachusetts Historical Society, Boston.)

Lord take us away from hence," and that "God having given us some considerable cattle so that we are so straightened that we cannot so comfortably subsist as could be desired." Thus, the growth of families and herds led them to seek a township, "a place which lyeth westward." The General Court, even as it sustained the traditionalists in the maintenance of the Sudbury hierarchy, also recognized the expansive forces which led to the conflict and gave the new petitioners Marlborough. Like Sudbury's original petitioners, the founders of Marlborough included the landless as well as those with substantial holdings in the parent township. Those Sudbury grantees that relocated sought to expand their holdings in Marlborough in order to provide for the future needs of their offspring and to obtain economic and political rewards for themselves.[18]

The movement from Watertown to Sudbury to Marlborough reveals how town founding and serial town settlement were linked in a process of simultaneous population dispersal and clustering. Drawing from the general principles of religious and social community that fueled their migration, the New Englanders organized themselves into a town-based culture, but they had equally important expectations of family farms. As families and towns matured, pressure built up for the founding of new communities. The availability of town grants from ample colony supplies allowed a centrifugal movement out to the borders of their townships and then beyond into new ones. This extensive mode of development of agrarian society across the landscape by means of the replication of town settlement is the defining feature of life in colonial New England.[19]

The Puritans' desire for what the historian T. H. Breen has called "persistent localism," strengthened by material factors, determined that town formation would be a decentralized process. The General Court bestowed general guidelines upon the town founders that grew looser over time. The grantees were left free to determine the method of land allocation and the structure of social and economic life in their new community. And as we have discovered through a generation of social histories of individual communities, towns varied enormously, from the layout of their field systems to the distribution of property and even the level of social conflict. But the shared cultural values of the early generations were such that the formation of a town followed certain general precepts and stages.[20]

While diverse reasons prompted colonists to petition the General Court for a town grant, the court always granted land to a limited number of proprietors who were responsible for the development of the town. The Massachusetts Bay government devolved authority for the establishment of the town upon these "undertakers," as they were sometimes called, whose experience as Indian traders or suppliers of capital made them especially suited for the onerous tasks of surveying the land, dealing with the Indians, and encouraging migrants. The historian John Martin's study *Profits in the Wilderness* emphasizes the entrepreneurial role of these town founders, who furthered regional development in exchange for land and milling privileges in new townships. Forces external and internal to the settlement constrained entrepreneurial initiative. Colonial statutes placed legal restraints upon town founders' speculative activities, while the good will of prospective settlers determined the success of their investment of time and money. The colonial authorities licensed entrepreneurially minded proprietors, who might never move to the new town, to engage in speculative activities that created an economic and social infrastructure for the anticipated settlers. Paradoxically, harnessing individual economic initiative advanced Puritan communalism.[21]

Migrants were enticed to leave older, more developed communities for the hard work of new settlements, lured by the possibility of owning ample land and by new opportunities for social and political advancement. Family concerns often prompted the move to a new town, while kinship ties facilitated migration. Giles Firmin of Ipswich wrote to John Winthrop about the considerations involved in moving to a new plantation in 1639:

> my father in law Ward since his sonne came over, is very desirous that wee might sett downe together, and so that he might leave us together if God should remove him from hence, because that it cannot be accomplished in this Towne, is very desirous to gett mee to remove with him to a new Plantation, after much perswasion used considering my want of accommodation heere (the ground the Town having given mee lyinge 5 miles from mee or more). . . . So I humbly request your favour, that you would bee pleased to give us the libertye of choosinge a plantation; . . . wee thinke it will be either Pentuckett, or Quichichchek, by Shawshin: soone as the season will give us leave to goe, wee shall informe your worship which we desire; and if that by the Court of elections we cannot gather a company to begine it, wee will let it fall.[22]

Migration was a family-based system; kinship ties were both its means and its end. Migrants became settlers when they could achieve the goal of securing a competency for their family—a comfortable allotment of land and other resources—and the prospect of passing on that achievement to their children. Small amounts of land devolved to early settlers as the bulk of the town's lands remained undivided. The ranks of the settlers matched those of the proprietors, those who received land grants. The original proprietary right (and its size) determined access to later divisions of land. Early settlers would be able to settle many of their children on the future allotments of land that accrued to them from their original grants. The relatively open nature of the proprietary structure for the earliest arrivals came at the expense of latecomers. Later settlers could not achieve the status of grantees, who received automatic allotments as divisions were made.[23]

Other institutions bolstered town settlement. After gathering at the site to establish church and town, residents organized schools and roads. Town officials sponsored essential services by granting municipal monopolies, tax abatements, and land to millers and other artisans. Numerous communal rituals such as militia musters, fall harvest, house raisings, weddings, and funerals, created and re-created shared cultural values. "Seating the meetinghouse" gave physical form to the local status hierarchy to the town; minute distinctions were made between young and old, rich and poor, male and female.[24]

Change and conflict could be accommodated in this social system even if it was ideologically suspect among the Puritans. A man's position in the life cycle held great significance in determining his wealth and position in these preindustrial agrarian towns. Young men waited for their elders to pass land on to them. They provided labor for the farm household during the years while they waited; they cleared forested lands and brought in the crops. Wealth reached its apogee in midlife, before men began to pass on land and goods to sons and daughters. Most male inhabitants had the opportunity to hold town office at some point in their lives. In Sudbury, over one-half of the grantees became selectmen in the first decade and a half of the town's history. Although the office of selectmen went to the older and more established residents, younger men held lesser offices, such as fence viewer or hogreeve.[25]

Towns also followed a life cycle. The relatively egalitarian pattern of landholdings in the first decade of Watertown's history was maintained by closing the door to those who followed the early founders and their descendants, who had inherited or purchased grantee rights. In the next phase, newcomers arrived, who could only receive farms by purchasing land through the market, so the ranks of proprietors and inhabitants diverged. Such an inegalitarian system maintained the ideal of farmsteads where a competency could be achieved, preventing peasant morselization, while ensuring that those who were closed out of a competency in one town would move on to a new settlement where they might achieve proprietary status. A delicate balance always existed between the twin goals of family settlement and social hierarchy. The two-tiered system of landholding occasionally caused local conflicts, such as Sudbury's generational strife in 1656. However, conflict was dissipated by the opening of newer proprietorships in the numerous towns that were founded between 1630 and 1675 in New England (see map 2).[26]

In this final phase of town settlement, when latecomers found access to land too restricted, they moved on to found new towns where they could enter at the ground floor. The "Great Reshuffling," as Virginia DeJohn Anderson has called it, of population that accompanied the Great Migration enabled the creation of the communal town-based system of settlement so that all could find niches in the agrarian order. This phenomenon continued throughout the colonization of New England. Townspeople sought to create and maintain consensual communities; when the growing population began to threaten the available economic opportunities and familiar social relationships, they responded by planning a new settlement. This splintering process occurred within a town's borders when outlying districts, popu-

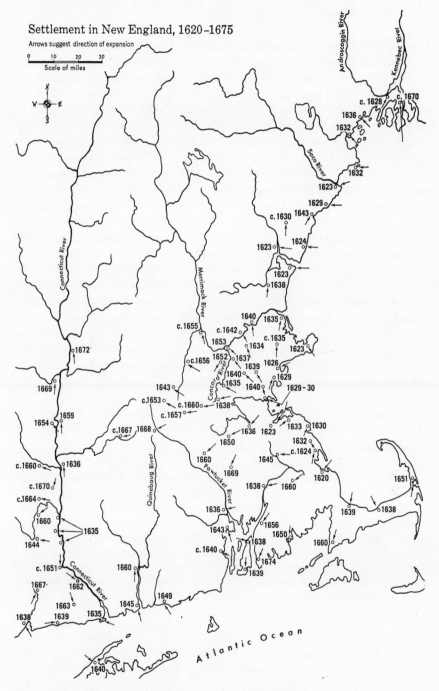

Map 2. Settlement of New England, 1620–1675. English colonization moved out from Massachusetts Bay in several directions; settlers moved west along the Merrimack River and the Nashua, its tributary. Also, clusters grew around Rhode Island, Plymouth, and the lower Connecticut River. (Reprinted from Douglas Edward Leach, *The Northern Colonial Frontier, 1607–1763* [New York, 1966], p. 34. By permission of the University of New Mexico Press. Courtesy of Cornell University Libraries.)

lated by those moving out to later divisions of land, found themselves too distant from the meetinghouse and too remote from the town's concerns. Often, early town grants were quite large (50 to 100 square miles). John Winthrop declared that the General Court's intention in making such large grants of land was to allow a natural process of development and fission to take place. "When the Townes should be increaced by their children & servantes growinge vp &c," they might have a "place to erecte villages, where they might be planted, & so the lande improved." Winthrop expected this demographic and economic process to create new towns, multiplying the number of towns as well as the number of people given lands of their own. Members of a parent community could also form a new and adjoining town, such as in the case of Sudbury, or migrants from several established towns could come together in a new area, as was the case in Lancaster.[27]

This process of serial town settlement, despite some variations, took place often enough to create a distinctive form of town and landscape in New England. The homogeneous, town-centered culture left a distinct mark upon the land. Settlement was essentially contiguous, with the whole area organized into towns where clustered villages were spaced unevenly but with a general regularity every few miles, wherever the terrain and soil allowed.[28] When later observers such as Timothy Dwight located the site and source of a regional culture, the New England town took center stage. But first, that critical institution needed to find its chronicler, its first historian of the New England town.

Edward Johnson, Town Founder and Local Historian

> To begin, this Town, as all others, had its bounds fixed by the General Court, to the contense of four miles square (beginning at the end of Charles Town bounds). The grant is to seven men of good and honest report, upon condition, that within two years they erect houses for habitation thereon, and so go on to make a Town thereof, upon the Act of the Court; these seven men have power to give and grant out lands unto any persons who are willing to take up their dwellings within the said precinct, and to be admitted to all common priviledges of the said Town, giving them such an ample portion, both of Medow and Upland, as their present and future stock of cattel and hands were like to improve, with eye had to others that might after come to populate the said Town; this they did without any respect of persons, yet such as were exorbitant, and of a turbulent spirit, unfit for a civil society, they would reject, till they come to mend their manners; such came not to enjoy any freehold.
>
> Edward Johnson, *A History of New England* (1654)

Edward Johnson, town founder and village historian, published the first history of New England in 1654, his intended title, *A History of New England, or The Wonder-Working Providence of Zion's Saviour in New*

England. Johnson offered the first explicit rendition of the process of town founding; he glorified the "peopling" of New England and upheld the critical role of the "planting" of towns and churches in the wilderness.[29] In his history he gave order to the chaotic events of the first two decades of Massachusetts Bay, evoking typological and providential significance, while anchoring it with numerous stories of town foundings. Out of the process of serial town settlement, which he knew intimately from personal experience, Johnson created a myth of settlement, a providential order for a chosen people. His was a settler's history of New England, rather than a story about pilgrims or migrants from England, as were the works of his historian-contemporaries William Bradford and John Winthrop. *Wonder-Working Providence,* recently called "the literary masterpiece of first-generation New England," was part of the communal self-fashioning of New England in the period when events in North America and abroad were leading the settlers in Massachusetts Bay to see themselves as a unique people embarked upon an errand to found towns and churches across a vast wilderness.[30]

Johnson was neither a prominent magistrate nor a minister, the usual occupations of seventeenth-century historians, but a local notable living in a series of struggling new settlements that inched westward from the seaboard. Born in Canterbury, England, in 1598, trained perhaps as a joiner, he rose in military service on both sides of the Atlantic. Johnson knew the details of New England town life intimately from his positions as a founder of Woburn, its town clerk, and the keeper of the records, where he enlivened the mundane details of land transactions and road byways with his own verse and anecdotes. Johnson devoted a majority of the chapters of his only book to recounting the establishment of particular towns and their churches, forty-three in all, interweaving these stories with the more momentous material on Indian wars and antinomian threats in the churches that dominates the other histories.[31]

History was critical to New England's self-definition. New England was as much an idea created in stories told about its past as it was a place mapped on the ground by settlers. Providential history charted the progress of God's larger design to Puritan believers. Johnson's *Wonder-Working Providence* commemorated the planting of towns and churches as the central event and process in the making of New England. But the history that he produced was also a highly stylized, carefully structured narrative that was self-conscious in its artifice and powerful as mythmaker in fostering a cohesive society. Johnson added an epic quality, a militant solidarity, and a utopian urgency to the discourse of local history.

Through the "divinely given" word of Christ's Herald—"purity, peace, and plenty"(24)—Johnson announced the three-part structure that orders his providential history: the establishment of pure churches, peaceable towns, and gardens of plenty in the wilderness.[32] At the very beginning of the work, Johnson's "Christ" proclaimed the divinely decreed destiny of

New England, binding its creation to its consummation, reconnecting the reader with the original purpose of the mission, and thereby creating a persuasive myth of colonization. His rhetoric was meant to stir the imagination of the colonists and inspire faith in the Commonwealth.[33] Johnson incorporated images of the divine mission that were familiar to Puritans and used rhetorical structures that involved his implied readers dramatically. He gave his vivid narrative epic grandeur by including prophetic sacred history.

Johnson's text fused the military metaphor with the errand into the wilderness. The sacred army of the Puritans swept across the Atlantic, establishing churches and doing battle with the Antichrist to prepare for the day and the place of Christ's triumphant return to earth. Here in New England, settlers were soldiers of Christ, not the poor pilgrims or migrants of Bradford's or Winthrop's histories. In Johnson's account they were personally charged to do battle: "See then you store your selves with all sorts of weapons for war, furbish up your Sword, Rapiers, and all other piercing weapons. As for great Artillery, seeing present means falls short, waite on the Lord Christ, and hee will stir up friends to provide for you; and in the meane time spare not to lay out your coyne for Powder, Bullets, Match, Armes of all sorts, and all kinds of Instruments for War" (33). The providential dimension of Johnson's account helped author and reader discern the larger pattern of God's plan in historical events and locate analogies or types from Biblical texts in the colonial past and present. "Here the Reader is desired to take notice of the wonderful providence of the most high God toward these his new-planted Churches" (209). Johnson also employed color, strong imagery, and a plain style. He depicted countless, easily forgotten, ordinary events of colonization and in so doing, united the mythic and the everyday in this settlers' history.[34]

The truly important work, according to Johnson and many of his fellow settlers, was settlement. The "cultural work" of *Wonder-Working Providence* was the identification of the New England way as the establishment and expansion of individual congregations of "pure" churches. The founding of towns in the "wilderness condition," an endlessly repeatable experience, had trained up a spiritual army. "Their own wilderness would be like the Biblical Sinai in which the children of Israel were led by God and purified," as literary critic Ormond Seavey wrote, "or like the wilderness in which Christ resisted the temptations of spiritual pride and worldly sustenance and power." The settlement process would never end; colonists would never leave the desert entirely behind, as Johnson keenly observed, because their economic, religious, and cultural values required a continual experience of settling in the wilderness. Increasing population and a localistic culture demanded new town foundings; the need for continual and collective transformation necessitated the perpetuation of the wilderness condition of the first settlement indefinitely. So Johnson devoted himself to telling (or perhaps retelling) the story of town settlement: the reasons for the founding, significant geographical details and statistical measures of material development, and a versified account of the minister whose godly qualities portend spiritual order and success. He was less concerned with identifying the particularities of each settlement than with representing *the* New England town.[35]

In his description of Concord's settlement, Johnson celebrated the beginnings of town foundings, the "Epitome of the manner how they placed downe their dwellings in this Desart Wildernesse" (111). The migrants battle a series of hardships along their arduous journey towards successfully planting a new town and church that symbolized, as literary critic Stephen Arch wrote, "New England's larger success in establishing purity and uniformity out of the swamps and thickets and woods of human error." While Johnson gave the settlers practical guidance in their attempts to purchase land from the Indians in the story of Captain Simon Willard's experience, Johnson also emphasized the need for providential faith in planting a town in the wilderness. He described the migrants as bewildered travelers searching "sometimes they know not whether," with their compasses leading them awry, moving along Indian paths so narrow that one can search for days without ever stumbling upon a "known way" (113). To illuminate the "directing Providence of Christ," Johnson interrupted the Concord story to recount the three-day ordeal of a female servant who got lost between towns. Only the Lord's efforts, not the colonists', could resolve her woes. The journey to Concord seemed interminable. The settlers' hardships were not over even when they reached the site. At first without shelter, exposed to the rain and snow, with food in short supply, these "poor servants of Christ," even in their "poore Wigwames, they sang Psalms, and pray, and praise their God" (114). Their faith brought manna from the heavens in the form of bountiful supplies of fish, which could be used as fertilizer to produce enormous yields of Indian corn. Johnson recounted the difficulty of transplanting English agriculture to the New World; livestock perished in the wilderness, and little grain was available except Indian corn. Colonists substituted venison and raccoons for lamb, pumpkin and squash for apples and pears; the "Indian bread" they made was "a sore affliction for some stomachs" (115). "Thus this poor people," Johnson noted, "populate this howling Desart, marching manfully on (the Lord assisting) through the greatest difficulties, and forest labours that ever any with such weak means have done" (115). The "Desart" was both a literal and symbolic wilderness, a school for the soldiers of Christ. The hardships and physical suffering of the early days purified the soul. Amid this catalogue of afflictions, the historian reminded his readers of the beneficial fruits of "wildernesse work" for the chosen people of Concord (and New England), "then very healthy more then now they are" (114–15); settlers enjoyed spiritual health, for everyone—the pastors and people, the men of estates and those without—all suffered and gathered together in church fellowship, "and verily the edge of their appetite was greater to spirituall duties at their first comming in time of wants, than afterward" (114).[36]

Peace was Johnson's concern in Book 2, which describes how civil government created order by "looking after such as were like to disturb the peace of this new erected government" (175).[37] The "Bulwarkes and Walles" in New England would be the establishment of institutions—"planting Towns and Churches in N.E."—to ensure the peace and purity that represented the workings of civil government (212). Since he was town clerk of Woburn, Johnson related the founding of his own community, not as an individual or group journey to the site of the town, as in the case of Concord, but as a detailed chronicle of the steps by which Woburn came into being. He narrated the birth of a new New England town as the process became regularized in the 1640s. Charlestown was the parent community of Woburn, which was formed from the Charlestown church and named after the English home of its surveyor Captain John Sedgwick. Here Johnson emphasized a narrative of settlement, bounded by local institutions and clear borders. The General Court issued the grant to a supervisory committee, specifying a four-mile-square tract adjoining Charlestown. Johnson and the other six supervisors were entrusted with the power of granting lands up to a well-ordered number of sixty families, excluding from that distribution those "as were exorbitant, and of a turbulent spirit, unfit for a civil society" (213). Lands were distributed according to family size and livestock holdings. This plan ensured that the social structure would balance concerns for a competency for all early settlers with the possibility of reserves for the next generation, but it also recognized and rewarded prominent families who had larger herds. "Thus was this Town populated," concluded Johnson, "and after this manner are the Towns of New England peopled" (214).

Woburn's geography was also keenly appraised. Describing its well-watered lands, its rivers, streams, and springs, its meadows amply distributed throughout the township, and the possibilities of trade in masts, tar, and iron ore, Johnson displayed an eye toward agricultural improvement and the production of commodities. The planting of the church and the securing of a minister took center stage, "it being as unnatural for a right N.E. man to live without an able Ministery, as for a Smith to work his iron without a fire" (214). To deflect English charges about the colonists' antinomian methods, Johnson carefully described the communal rituals around which authority was established in New England towns and churches. The gathering of the Woburn church with the members' declaration of the Church covenant and the subsequent ordination of the Reverend Thomas Carter took place before the leading ministers and magistrates of the Massachusetts Bay colony. Johnson celebrated the successful planting of another New England church by recounting the increase in church members in Woburn and the increase of churches throughout the colony.

The story of Woburn's settlement, the establishment of its institutions, and the progressive improvement of parishioners and herds contrasted significantly with Book 1's tale about the harsh journey through the thickets of underbrush to plant a church. Yet, in *Wonder-Working Providence*, "wildernesse work" is as much a symbolic process as a physical one.[38] Johnson rejoiced in the transformation of New England: "This remote, rocky, barren, bushy, wild-woody wilderness, a receptacle for Lions, Wolves, Bears, Foxes, Rockoones, Bags, Bevers, Otters, and all kind of wild creatures, a place that never afforded the Natives better then [sic] the flesh of a few wild creatures and parch't Indian corn incht out with Chestnuts and bitter Acorns, now through the mercy of Christ becom a second England for fertilness in so short a space, that it is indeed the wonder of the world" (210). The transformed landscape was an index of the spiritual state of the community, not simply a domesticated space won from the wilderness. As many scholars have noted, Johnson conflated the Biblical wilderness and the New England forest, the literal and figural wilderness, history and myth. For Johnson, God's garden was a well-ordered collection of New England towns and Congregational churches; "wigwams, huts, and hovels" gave way to "orderly, fair, and well-built houses" surrounded by orchards and gardens, mounting acres of tillage, and large numbers of livestock (211).

Plenty posed problems, however. The greatest danger to the Puritan "retreate" into the wilderness was neither physical hardships nor the external threats but the internal failings brought about by a life of material success. Yet Johnson did not adopt the elegiac tone of Bradford's *Of Plymouth Plantation*, which recounted how prosperity brought about spiritual decay in the colony. Johnson told in Book 3 about the passing of the first generation leaders, the "suddain forgetfulness of the Lords former received mercy" (254), and the sending of an army of caterpillars that fell upon the farmers' fields, leaving them "like winter-wasting cold, bare and naked" (253). Johnson turned these distresses into necessary rebukes, and the *Wonder-Working Providence* concluded on an optimistic, indeed a triumphalist note, announcing the chosen people defeating the Antichrist and ushering in the Millennium.[39]

With the millennium came an end to history. Johnson's mythic role for New England lay in the future, outside of history and geography. Seeking to escape the sense of historical contingency that bedeviled the histories of Bradford and Winthrop, he championed a state of stasis, an indefinite preservation of New England's special destiny, which would come by constantly repeating the process of purification through town settlement. The travails of Concord's settlers and each subsequent story of "wildernesse work" trained up a spiritual army.

Such a history of settlement contained several problems. Of course, as Johnson's narrative and those of his contemporary historians demonstrated, material prosperity and spiritual coldness accompanied the process of serial town settlement. Stasis, a precarious achievement, would always threaten to dissolve into development and dispersal.[40] Johnson answered these textual and cultural dilemmas by fashioning a new myth of settlement, creating new stories for New Englanders about New England. He wrote amid the cultural crisis of the 1640s when the old stories no longer fit. The meaning of New England increasingly relied upon the creation of an identity for the colony of immigrants separate from Old England, which grew ever more distant in time and space. The historical and literary framework within which local histories were written as well as the physical process of serial town settlement changed over time, but the larger contours of both the historical genre and the settlement process remained central to the meaning of New England. Both activities remained critical for the creation (and re-creation) of the region's special destiny and were mutually reinforcing. Edward Johnson, town founder and village historian, served as an agent of change by authorizing change through his use of the past. Evoking tradition, ironically, became the means by which change was legitimated in New England society. By articulating a new and powerful myth of town settlement, Johnson incorporated town founding into the discourse of local history, irretrievably binding the two together. The history of New England emphasizes stories about town settlement and the "conversion of literal facts into memory," and stories about colonization lay at the center of the meaning of New England.[41]

I TOWN SETTLEMENT IN THE SEVENTEENTH CENTURY

Town settlement in the seventeenth-century Wachusett involved three groups with competing visions of the New England town: Indian villagers seeking trade, English colonists seeking land, and Puritan missionaries seeking souls. These divergent goals eventually led to conflict between the Indians and the colonists, but for a generation the English and Indians were interdependent. During the 1640s, colonization burst out from the Massachusetts Bay area in all directions, following the river valleys and inching westward into inland Massachusetts; migration into the Wachusett proceeded along the Merrimack River and its tributaries. The plantation of Nashaway, the first European outpost in the Wachusett, was sponsored by an irregular group of English industrialists and religious dissenters from the Puritan Commonwealth, who sought to extract commodities for the metropolitan marketplace. As enterprising colonists looked west for furs and lands, they transformed the settlement of Nashaway into the town of Lancaster. During the early seventeenth century, towns varied markedly in the background of their settlers, the size of their grants, and the land system they created. These variations diminished over time as town founders followed Edward Johnson's strictures and the precepts of the General Court to reconstruct an orderly way of life.

English settlement in the seventeenth-century Wachusett was not a simple, unidirectional process. Colonial expansion led to war with the native inhabitants in 1675, when a pan-Indian alliance sought to reclaim territory and assert autonomy. In what became known as Metacom's or King Philip's War, Indians destroyed inland settlements and set back English colonization for a decade, but after the English achieved victory, they removed the Indians and transferred their lands to the Bay Colony. War between the French, Indians, and English continued intermittently for the next half-century, but the English resettled inland New England. The hazards of frontier life forced both practical and ideological revisions in the models of town settlement. Settlers improvised defensive measures, such as garrison living, and then turned them into offensive measures, advancing into the borderlands between competing groups to found new towns. War and colonization became inextricably connected, both in the town settlement process and in the collective memory of New England.

I Indians, English, and Missionaries: The Plantation of Nashaway

Morning dawns, Glooscap puts on his belt and leads off, and they follow. About the middle of the forenoon they reach the top of a high mountain. From thence they can discern another mountain away in the distance, the blue outlines of which are just in sight above the horizon: the men conclude that it will take them at least a week to reach it. They push on; and to their astonishment, at about the middle of the afternoon they have reached the top of this second mountain. From the top of this they are directed to look around; and lo! all is familiar to them. They are perfectly acquainted with hill and forest, lake and river; and Glooscap says to them, there is your native village. Then he leaves them and returns. They go on, and before sunset are at home.

Silas Tertias Rand, "Glooscap and his Four Visitors" (1894)

The Gouernor & some Company with him, went vp by Charles river about 8 miles about Watertown, & named the 1: brooke on the north side of the river . . . beauer brooke . . . .

Thence they came to another highe pointed rocke, having a faire assent on the west side, which they called mount Feake, from one Robert Feake, who had married the Governors daughter in lawe. On the west side of mount F: they went vp a verye highe rocke, from whence they might see all ouer neipnett, & a verye high hill due west about 40: miles off.

John Winthrop, *History of New England,* January 27, 1632

In the Algonquian village story above, four warriors led through the woods by the giant mythical character Gluskap ("Glooscap") experience a magical natural world. They see their "native village" a week's journey away yet find themselves home "before sunset" as a result of Gluskap's intervention. These pilgrims return personally transformed by their encounter with the animate powers of the forest. The Gluskap myths about the giant culture hero allowed for the existence of magical transformations, with easy passage between town and wilderness, animal and human.

This is in stark contrast to the way the Concord pioneers saw the land. When John Winthrop went fifteen miles inland and stood on Mount Wataquidock, he and his party were the first Europeans to gaze "over neipnett," or Nipnett, the inland region that circled Mount Wachusett, the "verye high hill due west." The Europeans' exploration and visual occupation of the landscape began the process of settlement, which led to the placing of townships upon the land until the area became filled with New England towns. Winthrop's view of the landscape drew clear lines between nature and civilization; the raw wilderness would become the cultivated town. In this way the two societies, Indian and European, encountered each other across an enormous cultural gulf.[1]

For the Nashaway people of the Wachusett, like the other Algonquians of the Northeast, the woods were inhabited not only by humans but also by other animate beings and human-like forms with magical power. Where Europeans saw inanimate objects, the Indians saw persons and beings. The word *manitou,* which the colonists translated as God or gods, actually referred to animate manifestations of spiritual power. Roger Williams learned the names of thirty-seven "Manitoo," but that number was flexible. One European classification of Indian deities ranged from the great southwest god, Cautantowwit, who created and ruled humankind, to the giant, humanlike culture hero named Gluskap. No sharp nature-culture divide separated the animal and human world in the Algonquian worldview.[2]

The figure of Gluskap, the culture hero who gave the world its present shape, was responsible for the Indians' descent from their animal ancestors in Algonquian mythology. In addition to altering animals, Gluskap modified the elements and created the landscape. This ageless, chameleon-like character assumed many shapes and forms and names. The Nashaways and all other southern New England Indian peoples, the anthropologist William Simmons believes, knew the helpful and industrious giant as Maushop, the local representation of the broader northeastern giant culture hero. "They have many strange Relations of one Wetucks," Roger Williams wrote, "a man that wrought great Miracles amongst them, and walking upon the waters, &c. with some kind of broken Resemblance to the Sonne of God." Living in a family setting, Gluskap taught lessons about cooperation and the dangers of social disorder. He did battle with his enemies the giant man-eating birds who represented forces, nonpersons, outside the social order that threatened by their hunger to engulf the Indian band and its values. One tale about a giant frog that once held all the world's water in his belly provided the Algonquians with an explanation of the origins of land "ownership" and a model of social organization. When the frog refused to share the valuable resource, Gluskap killed him and created the earth's waterways. Those who rushed to drink, unable to curb their thirst, were transformed into water animals. The survivors, in remembrance of their relatives, borrowed animal names and picked hunting territories along the streams and rivers that Gluskap had created. The Gluskap legends drew little narrative content from historical events, except for one event: the coming of the Europeans. This event marked the end of Gluskap's family life, his departure, and the cessation of his magical transformations of the land and its beings. Those who sought his magical powers after the colonists' arrival were forced to undertake an arduous journey towards the west. Gluskap and other animate beings and powers are encountered deep in the forest, a liminal space where "reality becomes fluid." Paradoxically, although those outside the village or camp are isolated, power comes to them as they journey alone in the forest.[3]

In the tale related above, "Glooscap and his Four Visitors," which one might consider an Indian's *Pilgrim's Progress,* four warriors go in quest of the being Gluskap who can transform the fruit of the forest into bountiful feasts and the plain folk of the woods into godlike creatures. The warriors discover a "man apparently about forty years old" seated in a large wigwam, attended to by a "very aged woman" who is addressed as mother, along with another man identified as the younger brother. They enjoy their host's hospitality for about a week as they rest after their arduous journey. This man's generosity exemplifies the centrality of hospitality because, according to folklorist Irving Hallowell, "other-than-human persons share their power with human beings." Then the visitors observe their host transform his mother into an active and young woman. "The men look on the transformation in utter bewilderment." He gives them a tour of his environs, "tall trees with luxuriant foliage . . . air . . . balmy and sweet." When he finally inquires about the purpose of their journey, they inform him that they are in search of Gluskap.[4]

The man then dramatically identifies himself as Gluskap and asks what they want him to do for them. They each tell him about their dreams of personal transformation. The first visitor says that he is a "wicked man" and wishes to be pious and holy; another Indian who is very poor desires "to be rich"; the third one says, "I am despised and hated by my people, and I wish to be loved and respected." Gluskap assents to all these requests. But when the final pilgrim asks for a long life, Gluskap shakes his head and responds that he will see what he can do. He outfits his visitors with "new and stunning robes" from his medicine bag and gives them three small boxes, which he instructs them not to open until they return home. The robes are an important element in the story, since in myth, clothing can act as a protective mechanism, power being lodged in dress: when one puts on the clothing of a powerful person, one assumes that person's power. Ready to depart, the warriors express doubt that they can make it back home, for "it took them one whole summer, a whole winter, and half another summer to come." But for Gluskap such expanses of time and space present no problem. "He smiles, and tells them he knows that way well" and agrees to guide them back to their home village." Gluskap leads them to the top of the mountain described in the passage above, where they can faintly make out a distant peak, a week's journey away. "They go on," and because of Gluskap's powers, "before sunset [they] are at home."[5]

The warriors return from their journey filled with a sense of the wonder of the wilderness. Yet "no one knows them, for their new and splendid robes have so changed their appearance for the better." They reveal their identities and open their boxes. The explorers stand forth, armed with the magical charms of Gluskap; one becomes "fragrant," another assumes stature as a legendary hunter, and the third attains wisdom and piety. The fourth visitor, however, is left behind in the form of a black and gnarled tree, a victim of his overreaching desire for immortality.[6]

The Indians' mythic search reveals a being whose magical powers existed in harmony with nature—hill and forest, lake and river—and who improved its fruits rather than exploited them. This anthropomorphic conception of nature makes the visitors' journey from settlement into the wilderness simple, and Glooscap's natural wisdom grants them an easy return to civilization. The structure of Algonquian stories, their language, and their very subject matter, all focus on transformative properties. Forms are constantly changing; even death is not necessarily permanent. The universe is unpredictable; the stories instruct humans and other persons on how to accumulate power, how to use it, and how it can be lost.

When the Nashaways wandered the Wachusett they passed through a landscape where spiritual and natural forces converged and mingled like the two branches of the Nashua River. The legends "convey a self-contained magical world where the ancestors, landscape, weather, sounds, and sea creatures are alive in distinctly Indian ways," writes William Simmons. Gluskap legends remained at the center of Algonquian history, with syncretic reworkings from historical events and the teachings of Christian missionaries. The stories the Nashaways told themselves about villages and culture-heroes served as vehicles of moral education and the socialization of the young. The teller of tales passed along information about local social structure and maintaining the social order when relating the way Gluskap helped the warriors. The legends revealed values that had emerged from Algonquian past experience, embodying a kind of social history.[7]

The Puritans' vision of nature and spirit differed radically from that of the Indians. When John Winthrop spelled out his views concerning title to the land, he saw no source for Indian claims. All men had a natural right to make use of any part of the earth that another had not possessed before him. Indians had no rights "for their whole bodye have no artes Cattle or other menes to subdue and improve any more of those lands that they plant with Corne." And Winthrop articulated the fundamental basis for European possession: "God Gave the earth etc. to be subdued." The Europeans' superior social organization and technology placed their claims and needs far above those of the "primitive" Indians. Little in New England's harsh, treacherous terrain held the Puritans in awe.[8]

English and Indian alike were localistic societies, and both relied upon myth to connect the past, present, and future. But whereas Algonquian kinship units rejected authoritarian integration and required individual responsibility, the European colonists relied on institutional authority to organize their expanding societies. Each culture's myths recorded its tribal values while also providing a vehicle for historical change. Puritan stories about the founding of "Towns and Churches" starkly separated the civilized settlements from the wilderness and offered a confident vision of the landscape of expectation, filled with the providential power of transformation that John Winthrop felt as he gazed from Mount Wachusett. In contrast, for the Nashaways and other Algonquians, telling tales about Gluskap's magical transformations, about acquiring power as well as losing it, made humans part of the natural world, not above it.[9]

Initial contacts between these two peoples, both on the coast and then farther inland in the Wachusett, began on several fronts: commercial exchange of local furs and European commodities; diplomatic encounters between Indian and English leaders; and Christian conversions to bolster Indian faith and Puritan certitude.[10] But residents of the two Nashaways of the Wachusett—the Indian village and the English one—improvised amidst the larger forces of social and cultural change without following the models provided by their more powerful Indian and European neighbors. These people seldom appear in the historical record; their inland location and relatively sparse settlement communities gave them a more marginal status. What did emerge from these unusual beginnings was an Anglo-American frontier where Nashaways and Puritans were neighbors. The Wachusett was different from the coastal region, where natives and newcomers confronted one another on an imperial stage.

The Wachusett's Natural History

The Wachusett region has three histories: a natural history of the land; a native history of the Nashaways and their relationship with the region; and finally, the main focus of this book, the providential history of the Puritans, who transformed all before them into a mosaic of New England towns. The early part of this providential history of the Wachusett shows how the Indians and the English were drawn together in this setting, then were pushed apart by their divergent cultures.

The Wachusett is part of the larger region of central Massachusetts that includes all of Worcester County and the northwestern corner of Middlesex County. This central uplands region of Massachusetts, also known as the Worcester Plateau, contains rugged terrain and numerous waterways. The general uniformity in elevation is only pierced by monadnocks—isolated mountains such as Mount Wachusett (2006 feet above sea level). Three river valleys divide the larger region. The Nashua River valley, where the first settlers—Indian and then European—occupied the land, dominates the Wachusett in the northeastern portion of Worcester County. The Merrimack River valley and the coastal lowlands bound the inland region of the Wachusett on the east. To the west, the plateau slopes until it meets the Connecticut River valley. The Wachusett obstructs east-west travel because, while the numerous watercourses connect to the surrounding bays and river valleys, none completely traverses the region. Overland connections proved the most significant mode of travel and communication for all the Wachusett's residents.[11] (See map 3.)

Topography and water dominate the Wachusett's complex geological history. The bedrock foundation consists of north-south oriented bands of slatelike rocks, which affect soil patterns. The orientation of hills and valleys often follows structural patterns in the bedrock. Glacial forces and erosion created the landscape that John Winthrop observed. Mount Wachusett, the "verye high hill due west," anchors the chain of monadnocks that govern the complex drainage system. The monadnocks are remnants of the great Appalachian chain that stretched from the St. Lawrence River to Alabama about 250 million years ago. Originally the larger region was extremely mountainous, with several thousand feet of rock above the present land surface. But subsequent geological erosion removed these overlying rocks and left just a few exposed points. The word "monadnock" is derived from the Indian word meaning "the hill that rises above."[12]

Glacial retreat created a particularly rich site for agriculture. About 17,500 years ago the melting of the ice sheet covering the area smoothed the land's contour and left a variety of land forms. While the ice-deposited till generally reflects the deeper bedrock foundations, many low-lying scattered hills are mounds of till known as drumlins. With their deep soils, gentle contours, and moisture-retaining qualities, these hills make ideal farm sites. Early English settlers chose areas rich with drumlins, only later moving on to the valleys to pursue manufacturing activities. The deposits from glacial lakes created another significant landform in the Wachusett. The Nashua valley contains extensive sediments from the melting of these glacial lakes, leaving valuable, stoneless agricultural land with a gentle terrain. Over the millennia, rivers cut their channels through the landscape and created alluvial areas with flat, fertile land that proved attractive to agriculturists. Finally, as the glaciers ground down everything in their path, they left a sandy, porous soil cover which promoted a rich natural growth of forest. Birch, beech, maple, and hemlock surrounded the earliest settlers and satisfied English farmers' needs for wood for almost two hundred years.[13]

The Wachusett's waterways played a significant role in every phase of settlement. The swiftly flowing streams, fed by numerous ponds and lakes and

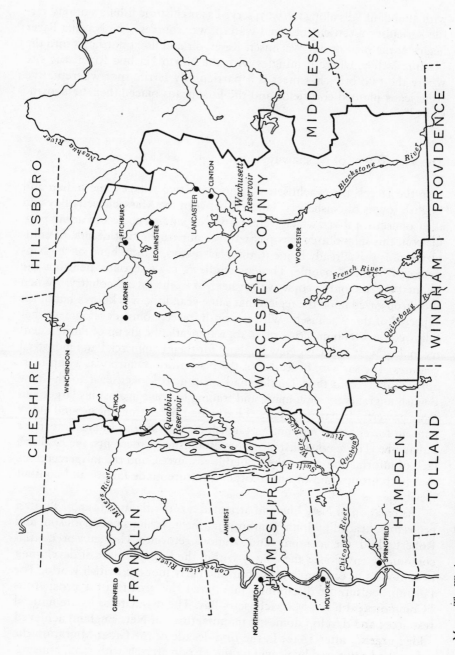

Map 3. The Wachusett. (Reprinted from John Donald Black and George William Westcott, *Rural Planning of One County: Worcester County, Massachusetts* [Cambridge, Mass., 1959], p. 13. By permission of Harvard University Press. Courtesy of Cornell University Libraries.)

with abundant falls along the way, served as prehistoric fishing stations, fertile agricultural settlements, and waterpower sources. The Nashua River begins at the present-day Wachusett Reservoir and flows northeast into the Nashua Valley, where it mingles with the North Nashua River; the site where the two branches meet is a particularly fertile spot where native Americans planted cornfields and the Europeans placed their first townships.[14]

The Two Towns of Nashaway

In the 1640s, the Wachusett was home to two villages: the Indian and English towns of Nashaway. Located between the Massachusetts Bay and the Connecticut River, which were the two expanding nodes of Puritan population, this inland area was passed over during the first decade of colonization. It was already home to the Nashaways, a local band of the Nipmuc or "Nipnett" people; Thomas Dudley's 1631 account mentions the Nipnett as "the only people we yet hear of in the inland country." When Winthrop gazed upon the region that same year, little was known but much expected of the Wachusett. With the push for economic development that followed the economic crisis of 1640, a transatlantic group of Puritan gentry looked west to inland New England for their commercial and industrial ventures. The sachem, or leader, of the Nashaways (which was a considerably weaker band than Dudley had imagined) looked east to the new English migrants for diplomatic and trading leverage against his larger and more powerful Indian neighbors.[15] Extracting riches from the ground didn't pan out for either group, but an English Nashaway was founded near the Indian one. The region's distance from established settlements, the English's lack of information about the available resources, and the misperceptions that both groups had of one another's culture made failure and conflict inevitable.

The creation of New England attracted a transatlantic group of Puritan projectors, headed by John Winthrop Jr., the governor's polymath son, and Robert Child, the economic and religious reformer. This entrepreneurial community envisioned the colony within the larger project of developing new models of economic growth in the early modern British world. The Puritan "culture of discipline" facilitated the growth of a prosperous "Commonwealth" in Massachusetts Bay. The mandate to locate natural resources and develop domestic manufactures in New England achieved added urgency after 1640. In the first decade of the Great Migration the colony had prospered by providing the 13,000 arrivals with food, housing, and other local supplies in return for English credit and specie. With the advent of the English Revolution, however, immigration was disrupted, prices for goods plummeted, credit constricted, and the supply of imported commodities dried up. Providing domestic supplies of salt, iron, and other sources of exchange, part of Winthrop and Child's project from the start of settlement, became even more urgent. Provincial authorities encouraged an economic development policy with such legislation as the 1641 Act for Encouraging Mines, which promised investors control of their mineral finds and the right "to purchase the interest of any Indians in such lands where such mines shall be found." The first decade of English migration disrupted Indian communities, most significantly the coastal Massachusett people. But inland peoples such as the Nashaway found a changing balance of power when their powerful new neighbors developed diplomatic and trading relationships. The Wachusett was isolated no longer.[16]

John Winthrop Jr., entered the Wachusett to extract riches from the mines below the surface. From his arrival in Massachusetts Bay, Winthrop had been busy attempting to develop colonial industries, the fur trade and saltworks. In 1640 he searched New England for potential mineral sites, stating in a petition to the General Court that "these plantacions much abounding with rocklike hills [were] the nurceries of mynes and mineralls." Robert Child offered to "helpe forwarrd the digging of some good mine, if you have found any in the country." Winthrop reported success to Child in 1641; a blacklead or graphite deposit had been found at Tantiusques (near Sturbridge, Massachusetts). Winthrop was hopeful of extracting silver from the graphite, the former a rare mineral in Britain, but even the graphite itself was of value: "The common uses of black-lead," Child wrote in one of his treatises on agricultural improvement, "first to make black-lead pens for Mathematicians &c. 2. for Painters and Limners. 3. For those that work in Copper to make their hammers go glib. And lastly, if any great pieces be found, to make Combes for them, because they discolor grey hairs, and make black hair of a Ravenlike or glittering blackness, much desired in Italy, Spain, &c."[17]

Samuel Eliot Morison called Child one of "the best educated men among the early settlers of New England." Born into a Kentish gentry family, Child completed his studies at Cambridge and moved on to Leyden and Padua for medical studies. During his European travels, Child found his interest aroused less by medicine and more by scientific agriculture, chemistry, and metallurgy. When he arrived in Massachusetts Bay in 1640 he made a careful survey of the new English colony's resources, met all the Bay notables, and visited many of the towns. Child formed a lasting friendship with the governor's son, John Winthrop Jr., who shared his interest in science as well as a desire for the economic development of New England. Both men turned to new efforts at diversifying the colonial economy by extracting wealth from the Wachusett's soil.[18]

Winthrop engaged Stephen Day, an English locksmith and the Bay Colony's first printer, to direct the project. He explored the site and secured title from the local band of Nipmucs with his co-signer Thomas King of

Watertown. Day wrote to Winthrop that he would "speedily goe up with other men . . . unto Tautauues the blacklead hill" to work with his men "upon the digging up of Blacklead."[19] Yields of silver from the blacklead were disappointing, Child cautiously reported from England, but he added: "I am unwilling to beate you out of your great hopes; may I hope/I shall not discourage you from digging lustily." An unexpected market was found for the ore; the local Indians used it to adorn their faces. Winthrop gave up on the distant operation in Nipmuc country (south central Massachusetts) and later concluded that development without settlement was impossible. "Plantations in their beginnings have work ynough & find difficulties sufficient to settle a comfortable way of subsistance, there being buildings, fencings, clearings and breakinge up of ground, lands to be attended, orchards to be planted, highways & bridges & fortifications to be made, and all things to doe, as in the beginninge of the world."[20] The New England town served the English as a flexible instrument for their industrial, trading, colonizing, and missionary activities.

Winthrop moved on to an even larger industrial project: a New England ironworks, which would have great significance to European settlement of the Wachusett. Winthrop envisioned a sophisticated plant that integrated several stages of iron production and required large amounts of capital and skilled workers. While Child provided technical advice and served as liaison in England, Winthrop returned to Massachusetts with men and money in 1641. He had located several sites of iron ore during his prospecting, including Nashaway, but the focus became Braintree. The colony provided substantial support for the eagerly awaited venture. The English owners that dominated the company of undertakers grew impatient and replaced Winthrop as resident manager. While production and sales increased, Massachusetts authorities were dissatisfied with the overseas control, mounting costs, and unruly ironworkers. Eventually, the company went into bankruptcy, Winthrop moved on to Connecticut, and many of the Bay Colony's entrepreneurial ironworkers became involved in the founding of Nashaway.[21]

The next Wachusett prospector took more interest in the riches scampering on the ground. In 1643 Showanon, the sachem of the Nashaways, traveled to Watertown to negotiate the sale of a load of beaver pelts. Showanon discussed the possibilities of trade in the Wachusett with a young fur trader, Thomas King, and invited him to set up a trading station there. Showanon must have reasoned that having a local outpost would facilitate trade, and perhaps offer the Indians direct access to trading partners rather than working through intermediaries. Trade and the exchange of goods were significant activities in Indian life. As Roger Williams noted, "amongst themselves they trade their Corne, skins, Coates, Venison, Fish, etc." Inside Indian villages such trade was similar to the widespread practice of gift giving. Often adjacent groups balanced their varying supplies of resources by exchange. Ritualized exchange between bands signified alliances. A sachem such as Showanon would have paid tribute to a stronger sachem as part of a diplomatic relationship. But, as the historian William Cronon writes, "most exchanges, whether internal or external to a village were articulated in the language of gift giving." The wampum and fur trade with Europeans entered into Indian culture within this pattern of localized trade for personal needs or group prestige. The exchange of goods involved in both ritual behavior and trade activity was embedded in the deeper structure of reciprocity that characterized Indian relationships. While the impetus to engage in such activities was the maintenance of cultural balance, historian Neal Salisbury reminds us that "to judge from the early colonial evidence, genuine enthusiasm, even a kind of cosmopolitanism, was at least as important as fear of adverse consequences in motivating Indians to enter into exchange."[22]

The Nashaways, members of the Eastern Algonquian culture group, were affiliated with the larger confederations of New England Indian peoples, but their exact ties are disputed by historians and anthropologists. (See map 4.) Some authorities place the Nashaways with the Pennacook, a confederation of Eastern Abenakis located in northern New England. I will follow the convention that sees the Nashaways as part of the Nipmucs, a weak group of inland peoples who at the time of European contact relied upon the neighboring Massachusett for diplomatic and military strength. Nipmuc culture centered on inland fresh-water resources, and the Nashaways, the people of Nipnett or "fresh water country," resided along the inland waterways of central Massachusetts.[23] They occupied three permanent villages and many temporary sites throughout the Wachusett. Their villages were located at Weshakim, between the two ponds of present-day Sterling; Nashaway, just north of the convergence of the north and south branches of the Nashua River; and the foot of Mount Wachusett, where they had their stronghold. Showanon, who was sachem in the 1640s, resided in Weshakim, the largest settlement, which had three hundred inhabitants. Sachems exercised their authority by virtue of personal presence rather than by inherited or legal office. Showanon's influence extended to the two other settlements, which each contained about two hundred inhabitants.[24]

Although the three villages were home sites for them, the Nashaways inhabited various other locales during the year as well: fishing stations, wild-plant collecting areas, marshes frequented by migrating waterfowl, and deer-hunting territories. Their seasonal cycles were related to different food sources and determined where the Nashaways might be found. Villagers came together in the spring to plant their crops in the cleared fields which adjoined their cluster of huts. In the summer, families moved away from the villages to sites along the numerous waterways of the Wachusett. Autumn brought a return to the villages for harvest. During the winter, hunters maintained huts "where they know the deer usually doth frequent,"

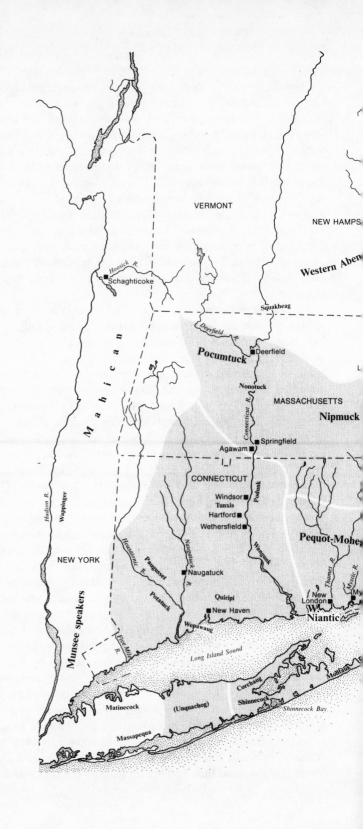

Eastern
Abenaki

MAINE

Saco R.

Saco Bay

Casco Bay

Pascataway
Dover ■   Accominta
          ■ ■York Village

Penacook ■

Ipswich   *Cape Ann*
Agawam
          ■ Gloucester

Naumkeag ■
Saugus ■ ■ Salem

Charles R.   *Massachusetts Bay*
Nonantum ■ ■ Boston
Newton ■   *Neponset R.*
     ■ Milton ■ Weymouth
Massachusett   Wessagusset
Neponset ■ Stoughton
     ■ Brockton   ■ Marshfield

Cape Cod

Plymouth ■

■ Middleboro   *Cape Cod Bay*

Pawtuxet
■ Providence
ODE
AND
agansett
     ■ Bristol
                    ■ Barnstable
Coweset
Narragansett
Bay

Pokanoket

Merrimack R.
Concord R.
Seekonk R.

Dutch I.

Conanicut I.   *Buzzards Bay*

Elizabeth Is.

Nantucket Sound

kapaug
sland Sound
     Martha's Vineyard

Nantucket I.

Block I.

Atlantic Ocean

0   10   20
└─────┴─────┘ Miles
┌──┬──┬──┐ Kilometers
0 10 20

Map 4. Indian tribal territories of New England, 1630. (Reprinted from Bert Salwen, "Indians
of Southern New England and Long Island: Early Period," in Bruce Trigger, ed., *Handbook of
North American Indians*, vol. 4, *Northeast* [Washington, D.C., 1978], p. 161. By permission
of the *Handbook of North American Indians* and the Smithsonian Institution. Courtesy of
Cornell University Libraries.)

as William Wood observed in the 1630s. The fishermen, he noted, camped near the rivers, the natives were "experienced in the knowledge of all baits, and diverse seasons; being not ignorant likewise of the removal of fishes, knowing when to fish in rivers."[25] In the spring the cycle began again, with Indian settlements near rivers where fresh-running streams provided runs of salmon and alewives and where fertile soil allowed for horticulture.

Indians' houses were well suited to these frequent changes of residence. Portable round houses, about fourteen to sixteen feet in diameter, were intended for two families and were formed by a circle of poles tied at the top and covered with overlapping shingles, woven mats, or strips of bark. Frames were left behind and mats rolled up and carried to the new site. Multipurpose tools that could be fashioned on the spot and discarded after use discouraged the accumulation of cumbersome material possessions. "Although every proprietor knowes his own," wrote Thomas Morton, "yet all things, (so long as they will last), are used in common amongst them."[26]

The Nashaways' "large corne fields" were located where the North and South Branches of the Nashua came together. In addition, the river's ample stock of fish supplied an important part of the Indian diet. Samuel de Champlain's map of 1605 illustrates the typical village structure, with Indian wigwams set up alongside both the corn fields and fish traps that provided the major portion of the native diet. (See map 5.) Southern New England's native peoples such as the Nashaways had developed a gendered division of labor where women's horticulture produced corn, beans, and squash (about 65 percent of caloric intake), which were supplemented by men's hunting and mixed-gender fishing.[27]

Despite their itinerancy, the Nashaways of Nipmuc country occupied permanent villages, traveled through a well-defined region adjacent to their settlements, and held an attachment to the locality. All of Nipmuc country was partitioned into large areas identified by place names; these in turn were divided and subdivided, so that even specific groves and meadows had names. The Indian villagers chose names for their communities that aptly described the terrain around them: Wachusett, "near the mountain"; Nashaway, "the place between"; and Weshakim, "the springs." At first the Europeans adopted many of these place names, yet they shed them slowly for the more familiar names of English shires or their provincial leaders. In this way, Nashaway became Lancaster, Wachusett became Princeton (after Thomas Prince), and finally in 1729, all of Nipmuc country became the county of Worcester.[28]

As Showanon and other Indian leaders initiated trade relationships with their new neighbors, they introduced dramatic changes in village society. Trade was removed from its structure of reciprocity and gift giving; it became solely an economic relationship, a change which had serious consequences. Europeans in the fur trade insinuated themselves into the local system of village exchange and linked it to the wider Atlantic economy. The

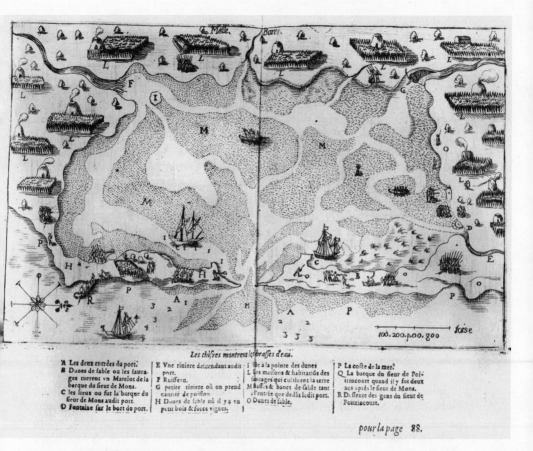

Les chiffres montrent les brasses d'eau.

A Les deux entrées du port.
B Dunes de sable ou les sauuages tuerent vn Matelot de la barque du sieur de Mons.
C les lieux ou fut la barque du sieur de Mons audit port.
D Fontaine sur le bort du port.

E Vne riuiere descendant audit port.
F Ruisseau.
G petite riuiere où on prend cantité de poisson.
H Dunes de sable où il y a vn petit bois & force vignes.

I Isle à la pointe des dunes.
L Les maisons & habitatiõs des sauuages qui cultiuent la terre
M Bassis & bancs de sable tant à l'entrée que dedãs ledit port.
O Dunes de sable.

P La coste de la mer.
Q La barque du sieur de Poitrincourt quand il y fut deux aus apiés le sieur de Mons.
R Dissente des gens du sieur de Poitrincourt.

pour la page 88.

Map 5. Champlain's map of Malle Barre (Nauset Harbor, Cape Cod, Massachusetts). Champlain voyaged south from New France along the coast of New England. His charts of the harbors depicted numerous Indian villages and corn fields. This 1605 map shows individual houses (wigwams with smoke holes) surrounded by cornfields (L on the map) along with a French and Indian skirmish (B) and a fish trap (G). A decade later the English found abandoned villages after epidemics swept the coastal Indian communities. (Reprinted from Samuel de Champlain, *Les Voyages du Sieur de Champlain Xaintongeois* [Paris, 1613]. Courtesy of the American Antiquarian Society.)

"wampum revolution" accelerated this process of commercialization. Wampum, strings of white and purple shell beads, were highly valued objects that represented personal power and wealth. Their exchange occurred at ritual moments within the process of gift giving. Dutch merchants were the first to recognize the possibility of making this one medium of exchange, among the many others, into a singular item of currency in a translocal trading system. What was once a symbol of prestige became a medium of exchange, and this led the Indians to a greater dependence upon Europeans. European merchants created a regional economy, becoming the

vital links between southern wampum producers and northern fur suppliers. The pursuit of fur-bearing animals further commercialized Indian cultural patterns. Previously, hunting had occupied a certain place in the seasonal cycle of Indian subsistence, as the northern Indians "killed animals
only in proportion as they had need of them." European trade introduced
Indians to new trade goods around which cultural constructions of prestige
could be fashioned. This shift drew Indians into the expansionist cycle of
the Atlantic economy.[29]

King was interested in Showanon's invitation to set up a trading station
in the Wachusett; he soon set off on an exploratory trip to the Wachusett,
traveling along the Charles River valley, passing through Sudbury, and then
crossing over toward the Nashua River. King must have liked what he saw,
for he returned to Watertown to secure a business partner, Henry Symonds
of Boston, who was then building a tidal mill on the marshes of the bay. In
1643 the two purchased from Showanon a tract of land, measuring ten
miles by eight miles, which began where an Indian trail crossed the Nashua.
The English promised not to disturb the Indians' fishing, hunting, or planting places, which represented the Indian conception of settlement. This
extensive tract eventually became the towns of Lancaster, Clinton, Bolton,
Harvard, and Sterling.[30] Ownership of land in a Nashaway community
conformed to the Algonquian conception of land as integral to the nurtur-
ing environment, part of a universally shared cosmic order, rather than a
commodity to be parceled out in individual allotments. Each settlement,
composed of thirty to fifty families, held claim to the area around the village
where its houses and fields lay and where its residents settled in spring and
autumn, and also to the hunting and fishing stations in the immediate locale
where the residents scattered during their seasonal sorties. As sachem,
Showanon assigned areas for temporary use to the various bands of villagers. But land was not transferred to an individual in fee simple or sold to
families in private transactions. Instead, according to one authority, land
was an inheritance from one's ancestors, to be held in trust by the tribal
chief for future generations. In return for tribute, the chief allowed his people to share in the bounty of the land. In their treaties with the Europeans,
the Indians made their first dealings with the settlers in terms of their own
conceptions of land use, and this arrangement caused significant problems.
In the Indians' view, a stranger could be admitted to a territorial allotment,
and the idea that the Europeans would demand exclusive possession did not
occur to them. The Nashaways, like other Indian groups, eventually came
to realize that these so-called temporary arrangements with whites entailed
the irrevocable loss of their land.[31]

The English traders built a trucking, or trading, house on the east slope of
George Hill where two Indian trails from the west met up with the Bay Path
to Boston at a crossing of the Nashua River. Early business must not have
proved profitable to the English entrepreneurs, for when King died in

December of 1643, he left little property and £18 of debts owed him from his Indian customers. Symonds died about that time, also burdened with debt, demonstrating the tenuous nature of business as colonists searched for commercial opportunities to sustain the Bay Colony's solvency.[32]

While the trading outpost stood empty, the political leader of the Nashaways allied himself with the colony's leaders in Boston. On March 7, 1644, Showanon and Wassamegon, another Nipmuc sachem, joined three Massachusett sachems at a formal ceremony before Winthrop and the entire General Court; they placed themselves, their subjects, and their lands under the jurisdiction of the English colony, "to bee governed & protected by them, according to their just lawes & orders, so farr as we shalbee made capable of understanding them." The sachems then responded to a series of questions that had become a familiar text to the coastal sachems who appeared before the court to acknowledge English sovereignty and receive protection after the Pequot War of 1637, when the English had organized a coalition to crush the Pequots of southeastern New England. After that time, powerful confederacies had allied themselves with the various colonial regimes on mutually advantageous terms, and weaker bands, such as the Nashaways, had attempted to bypass Indian intermediaries and form direct trading links with European traders as well as place themselves under English diplomatic protection. As was traditional practice, the five sachems who met with the court in March of 1644 presented wampum to seal their agreement with the General Court, and the colonial officials gave each sachem a red coat and "a potful of wine" to share in exchange for their entry into an alliance with the new European power against their traditional enemies.[33]

Political and social authority in Indian villages derived from a fluid set of personal relationships, in a manner similar to the native Americans' mobile system of settlements within the region. Political leaders were responsible for group concerns beyond the family or individual: hunting, intragroup justice, and intergroup trade and diplomacy. The consent of the governed and consultation with other village notables circumscribed sachems' political power. While leaders often came from a particular line of descent, as William Wood noted, if the sachem's "fair carriage bear him not out the better," the villagers "will soon uncepter him." The principle of reciprocity structured the relationship of leaders and followers. The territorial rights of the band were vested in the person of the sachem, who assigned plots to families and received portions of the harvest in return. Sachems often lived well off their tribute, but they were careful to reciprocate with regular presents to their followers. Sachems also were placed in hierarchical relationships with their more powerful neighbors. Showanon's position as sachem of a weak inland group had forced him to seek Pennacook aid against Mohegan raids from the west. The entry of new powerful eastern neighbors prompted his allegiance to shift again. In this way, English authority reached into the villages of the Wachusett.[34]

Thomas King and Henry Symonds's solitary trading hut represented the European presence in the Wachusett at the beginning of 1644. But the Nashaway Company, a group of enterprising colonists more interested in iron ore than beaver skins, banded together that year. Exactly how King and Symonds's interests passed to the new company is unclear, but they did. The Nashaway Company's members, a mix primarily of Boston and Watertown residents (see table 1), were mostly involved in commercial or artisanal production with over half of them specializing in iron working. They were led by Nathaniel Norcross and Robert Child, both of whom were graduates of Cambridge University and residents of Watertown. Norcross was looking for a parish, while Child continued Winthop's quest for marketable commodities. The General Court acknowledged their predecessors' land purchase, but stipulated that any additional purchases would have to be granted by them. The General Court's reference to "Undertakers," a term reserved for iron works rather than agricultural settlement, acknowledged their industrial orientation. The new members of the Nashaway Company agreed to initiate the plantation and sent three farmers from Watertown—Richard Linton; his son-in-law, Lawrence Waters; and John Bell—to make preparations for "the general appearance of the Company."³⁵

Prospective settlers at Nashaway had to contend with both physical barriers and religious unorthodoxy in their isolated outpost. In June of 1645 they complained to the General Court about the "utter impossibilyte to

Table 1. Members of the Nashaway Company

Name	Residence	Occupation	Notes
Nathaniel Norcress	Watertown	Minister	Returned to England
Robert Child	Watertown	Gentry	Returned to England
Steven Child	Cambridge	Printer	Locksmith; active in settlement
John Prescott	Watertown	Miller, smith	Only member to settle in Nashaway
Harmon Garrett	Charlestown	Smith	
John Hill	Boston	Smith	Associate of Henry Symonds
John Fisher	Medfield		
John Davis	Boston	Joiner	
John Chandler	Boston		Married Symonds' widow
Isaac Walker	Boston	Trader	
John Cowdall	Boston	Trader	Bought trucking house
James Cutler	Watertown		Married King's widow
Samuel Bitfield	Boston	Cooper	
Matthew Barnes	Braintree	Miller	
John Shawe	Boston	Butcher	
Samuel Rayner	Cambridge		Known to be in Nashaway in 1651
George Adams	Watertown	Trader, glover	Took up land

Source: Complied from data collected in Duane Hamilton Hurd, *History of Worcester County* (Philadelphia, 1889), vol. 1, p. 3.

plant at Nashaway" without "a convenient way made for the transportation of our cattel and goods over Sudbury River and Marsh." They insisted to the court that the settlement's slow progress came from the perilous passage to the remote site. Although Sudbury was directed to complete its bridge, little appears to have been done. In 1646 John Winthrop attributed the difficulties of John Prescott (the only member of the Nashaway Company to become a settler) in reaching the plantation as divine retribution for the pioneer's association with the dangerous heretic Robert Child: "Prescott another favourer of the Petitioners lost a horse & his ladinge in Sudbury River & his wife & children being vpon another horse were hardly saved from droninge."[36] Child and Prescott had allied themselves with the growing movement to support religious toleration in the colony, a movement that would culminate in a pamphlet war and petition to Parliament, the Remonstrance of 1646, which challenged the colonial magistrates' authority. Adding to Winthrop's concern, the seven prospective settlers desired the status of a congregation. The magistrates denied their request—these seven "who were no members of any churches"—and advised them to go and build houses first and take along colonists who did belong to other churches, as previous town founders had done. But the settlers ignored these proscriptions, and, as Winthrop almost gleefully reported, they lost their prize settler, the Reverend Norcross. "But the persons interested in this plantation, being most of them poor men, and some of them corrupt in judgment, and others profane, it went on very slowly, so as that in two years they had not three houses built there, and he whom they had called to be their minister left them for their delays." Similar suspicions characterized the General Court's subsequent oversight. The association of Nashaway's town founders with challenges to the Congregational establishment cast a shadow of irregularity over all residents of the plantation.[37]

With only Prescott and three fellow Watertowners on site but more settlers expected, the nonresident company members turned to the critical issue of laying out lands. Several agents were deputized to set out lots to "all the Planters," with the General Court's approval "provided they sett not their houses too farr asunder & the greater lotts to be proprtionable to mens estates & charges." Allotments of land in new towns were related to a town founder's economic stature, along with his contribution to the expenses of starting a settlement. The court maintained supervisory powers by charging "none to have their material allotment confirmed before he hath taken the Oath of Fidelity" and by appointing Simon Willard and two others as commissioners to lay out the lots.[38]

The system of mixed public and private powers that marked New England town settlement—the devolution of public authority to private proprietors—faltered in the case of Nashaway. In the fall of 1647, the grantees of Nashaway having "acted nothing as undertaken yet nor laid out any lands," expressed to the General Court "their utter unwillingness" to go forward with the Wachusett settlement. The General Court, despite its numerous doubts about the regularity of the Nashaway plantation, now resolutely determined not "to destroy the said plantation, but rather to encourage it," stated its intention to procure new proprietors, and in the interim decided to supervise the distant plantation itself. The undertakers had gone in several directions: Robert Child had fled the colony after his harsh rebuke by the court, Norcross had gone back to England, several company members had died, and others must have lost interest after the iron industry did not pan out. Of the original company members, only John Prescott removed to the Wachusett.[39]

Indeed, the very year that the company members relinquished their grant Prescott indicated his determination to proceed by purchasing Thomas King's original trading post and an adjoining twenty acres of land and by entering the fur trade. Prescott had made several stops in the overseas British colonies after leaving Yorkshire in 1638. In his two years in Barbados, he accumulated some land. He moved on to Boston in 1640 and then made his way to Watertown where he pursued his trade as a blacksmith, accumulated an estate of 126 acres, and raised a family of six. At the age of forty-nine Prescott sold his holdings in the parent settlement and committed himself to Watertown's newest offspring, the plantation of Nashaway. Perhaps his support of Robert Child's Remonstrance made his exit from Watertown appealing; perhaps it was impossible for him to settle all his children near him in Watertown. Whatever circumstance prompted his migration, John Prescott became the commercial and industrial pioneer of the new town, taking over the role of town founder from the hesitant company members.[40]

John Eliot, the third member of Nashaway's first generation of town founders, entered the Wachusett in 1648. Eliot had begun his missionary career two years earlier. He had been jolted into action by the Pequot War. His response differed from that of most colonists; Eliot decided to learn the Algonquian language. Initial promoters of colonization had hoped that the example of the colonists' "good life and orderlie conversion maie wynn and incite the natives of the country to knowledge and obedience of the . . . Christian fayth."[41] The colony's leaders embarked upon a more aggressive plan when this policy of exemplary civility produced few results. Showanon's 1644 visit to John Winthrop had brought his promise "from time to time to bee instructed in the knowledg & worship of God." The sachems also, it appears, had learned to parrot back an English minister's text that included several of the Ten Commandments:

   1. Quest. To worship ye onely true God, who made heaven & earth, & not to blaspheme him. An. We do desire to reverence ye God of ye English, & to speake well of him, because wee see hee doth better to ye English than other gods do to others.
   2. Not to swear falcely. An. They say they know not wt swering is among ym.

3. Not to do any unnecessary worke on ye Saboth day, especially whin ye gates of Christian townes. An. It is a small thing to ym; they have not much to do any day, and they can well take their ease on yt day.

4. To honor their parents and all their supiors. An. It is their custome so to do, for the inferiors to honor their supiors.

5. To kill no man whout just cause & just authority. An. This is good, & they desire so to do.

6. To comit no unclean lust, as fornication, adultery, incest, rape, sodomy, buggery, or bestiality. An. Though sometime some of ym do it, yet they count that naught, & do not alow it.

7. Not to steale. An. They say to yt as to ye 6th quere.

To suffer their children to learn to reade Gods word, yt they may learn to know God aright, & worship him in his owne way.

They say, as oportunity will serve, & English live among ym, they desire so to do. That they should not bee idle.

To these they consented, acknowledging ym to bee good.[42]

Faced with mounting criticism from England for the slow progress of conversion, the General Court passed legislation in the fall of 1646 that aimed at establishing a systematic missionary effort. Laws were passed for the founding of towns "for the incuragement of the Indians to live in an orderly way amongst us." They forbade natives to "pawwaw." And it was decreed that two ministers were to be sent to preach to the Indians. That summer John Eliot began his ministry with a friendly sachem. The Indian audience responded to Eliot's preaching in Algonquian of some simple Biblical truths with a series of questions about what caused thunder, where winds came from, and why the tides operated regularly. Eliot retired for some additional preparation.[43] These Indians' interest in Eliot was sparked by internal political and social changes within Indian bands. Eliot was the latest in a line of patrons who supplied trade goods and information about the new neighbors, possession of which brought prestige to its native holder. Eliot served as a cultural mediator between English and Indian societies. When Eliot was invited to resume his lectures in 1646 in the "wigwam of one Waban, a new sachem near Watertown," this new sachem near Wachusett was challenging a more established leader. Waban's embrace of Christianity, perceived to be an alliance with the powerful English missionary, attracted new supporters and increased the size of his band.[44]

By 1648 Eliot moved his mission west; the missionary reported that Showanon, flanked by powerful leaders on other side of his position in central Massachusetts, "doth embrace the Gospel & pray unto God." The Roxbury minister had been out to Nashaway four times that summer, his message received with great enthusiasm, but the distance meant that he could visit only occasionally, and his native followers "are troubled and desire I should come oftener, and stay longer when I come." Eliot targeted potential converts at the Nashaways' seasonal fishing run at the falls of the Merrimack, where the gatherings of Indians "are like Faires in England." Eliot found the 1649 trip almost impossible, so he hired John Prescott, "that hardy man of Nashaway," to beat a path through the forest. As they traveled by Showanon's Nashaway village, the sachem "commanded twenty armed men" to ensure Eliot's safety because of troubles between the Narragansett and Mohegans. Despite Eliot's pleasure at this apparent display of the natives' "good affection" to him and his work, he wrote that he "took some English [men] along with me also."[45]

The emerging missionary strategy in the 1640s saw the sachems as critical to any effort at conversion. Daniel Gookin recognized that "when a sachem or sagamore is converted to the faith, and yields himself up to embrace the gospel, it hath a great influence upon his subjects." The missionaries attacked and undermined the local authority of those who refused English entreaties. One sachem charged that Eliot's preaching of the punishment waiting in Hell was intended "to scare us out of our old customs, and bring us to stand in awe of them." The English attempted to replace Indian spiritual leaders by proper Christian ones. Shamans or "powwows" wielded spiritual authority; they were believed to be able to cure illness, control the elements, foretell the future, and bewitch their band's enemies. Shamans were distinguished from other Indians because it was believed that the god Hobbamock had entered their bodies during a vision or dream, making available to them his extensive powers. Shamans offered greater access to the spirit world, and villagers, who prized the powers they had, sought their advice. Yet their authority could easily be challenged by the sudden appearance of ill-fated events or the emergence of more powerful claimants to divine communication. A good relationship with spiritual forces was critical for maintaining village solidarity. So a shaman's powers were important for communal matters as well as divine-human relationships.[46]

In 1650 Eliot celebrated his initial successes in the Wachusett, reporting that many embraced the gospel and "Pauwauing [powwowing] was wholly silenced." But the great distance and intermittent supervision let Satan back into the native villages of Nashaway, and later Eliot wrote that "I learn to my grief there hath been Pauwauing again with some of them." Backsliding was regarded as a constant danger to missionaries' slow and hard-won successes. But in the context of cultural exchange between the English and the Indians, backsliding indicated native resistance to the intended English eradication of their culture, as well as the syncretic nature of Indians' borrowing of material and cultural goods from the Europeans on their own terms. To solidify and advance the conversion campaign, Eliot recognized the superiority of clustering the native Americans in a new version of the New England town, "the praying town," which would have a clear advantage over his solitary visits to distant native villages where backsliding threatened to eradicate his work. Eliot conceived of the new conversion program as a two-stage process: stationing the "savages" as townspeople would "civilize" them; converting them to Christianity would follow, completing their transformation.[47]

Residents of the Wachusett's only English town also wrestled with questions of religious orthodoxy. The General Court, still suspicious of the godly path of Nashaway's irregular settlers and hesitant to infringe upon proprietors' property rights, rebuked the residents for petitioning for permission to tax the nonresident landowners in 1650. The place is not "fitt" to make a plantation without a minister, the court thundered: the residents would be summoned back east if the situation were not remedied by the next session of the court.[48] Reports from the western outpost raised further doubts about irregular beliefs circulating in the new plantation. In 1651 Samuel Phillips, a Harvard student and minister's son who had visited Nashaway, answered the inquiries of a prominent Cambridge resident, George Whaley, about his impressions of the new town's location and its people. Phillips gave full and detailed responses to both questions, commenting that some Nashaway residents held the opinion "that all things were [held in] common . . . as in the apostles time," including "men's wives." Whaley later identified Elizabeth Hall, whose husband was in England, as the holder of these heretical views. Hall brought a slander suit against Whaley that forced him to retract this last comment and she joined her husband back in England.[49]

At the close of 1652 the nine heads of households in Nashaway gathered in John Prescott's house to covenant together and ask the General Court to recognize their community as a New England town called Prescott, in honor of their leader. In agreeing to the petition, the court considered the growing numbers of settlers at the site, twenty-five miles from any other English town, as well as indications that "others intend to goe and settle there." The General Court's 1653 grant specified the geographic bounds of the town, according "to a deede of the Indian Sagamore," as well as the social, political, and religious institutions that were the defining features of a New England town. All landholders were required to take the oath of fidelity, maintain a "godly ministry," and lay out roads from Sudbury to bring the pioneers within the ranks of the established eastern coastal communities. The court selected six "prudentiall men" led by John Prescott to order the town's affairs and the planters' allotments until "the place be so farre settled with able men" that the court would grant "full liberties of a township." The General Court objected to naming the town after John Prescott, who sympathized with the Bay Colony's critic, Robert Child, and proposed West Town instead. The residents of Nashaway rejected this alternative; they honored their founder by calling the town Lancaster, the English county where Prescott had been born.[50]

The Wachusett contained the institutional skeleton of its first English settlement by 1653. Nashaway had left behind its origins as mining camp and fur-trading post; it was well on its way to becoming a fully functioning agrarian village in the proper mould of a New England town. As settlers arrived, they were sited in two groups of house lots separated by the North River and its fertile intervale (see maps 6 and 7). On the eastern neck, Ralph Houghton bought Prescott's recently constructed house and awaited the arrival of his brother John from Watertown. Lawrence Waters, one of the original Nashaway settlers from Watertown, sold his house and moved closer to the river. The rest of Nashaway's pioneers resided across the stream. John Prescott and his family occupied the original trading post, and the remainder of the western residents huddled around this site. Philip Knight built a house on a lot purchased from Stephen Day, and when Thomas Sawyer, a blacksmith, married Mary Prescott they settled next to him. Daniel Hudson, a brick maker from Watertown, completed this compact settlement. Magistrates and settlers shared a vision of their future community in the Wachusett, but only about fifty residents, a few houses, and some scattered fields existed at the bend of the Nashua River. Over the next decade Prescott's pioneers on the margins of the Bay Colony would affirm the hierarchical social structure of older settlements and fill their ranks with the right sort of settlers.[51]

Lancaster Grows

Migrants arrived slowly in the 1650s, deterred by the institutional difficulties and inland location that placed the plantation of Nashaway at some distance from its increasingly mature parent towns to the east. In 1653 the General Court had recognized that the town was in the process of establishing the basic structures required for entry into ranks of Bay Colony communities. Life must have been very different in this isolated outpost of English settlement, set apart from the New England communities that clustered together along the Massachusetts coast and the Connecticut River. In the Wachusett, English townspeople lived in close geographical proximity to the Nashaway and were involved with the Indians both economically and socially.

Land was critical for establishing a New England town. The slowly gathering residents of Lancaster gradually reconstructed a familiar agrarian world. Decisions about land allotments gave shape to a town's economic hierarchy as well as made explicit the unspoken assumptions about status in a seventeenth-century community. John Prescott assumed the leading role in building a commercial infrastructure, but Lancaster's selectmen recognized the critical importance of attracting additional town founders to fill in the bare outlines of settlement. Their moderate success caused setbacks in Lancaster's progress toward political autonomy. However, the pace of European settlement, slow as it might be, went steadily in one direction. Showanon and the Nashaway peoples, the other villagers in the Wachusett,

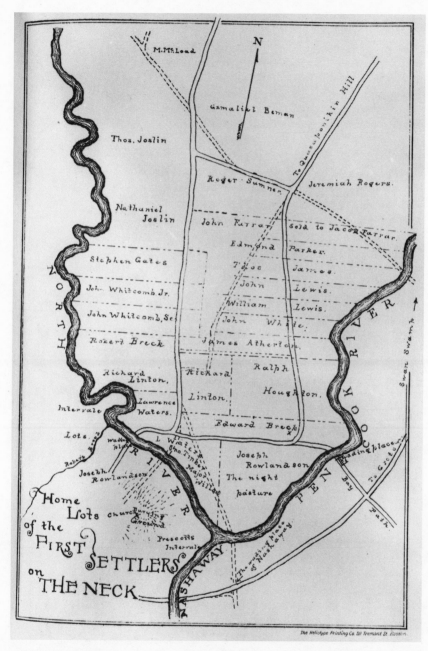

Map 6. Lancaster's home lots on the Eastern Neck, about 1653. (Reprinted from Henry Stedman Nourse, *The Early Records of Lancaster, Massachusetts, 1643–1725* [Lancaster, 1884], after p. 244. Courtesy of the American Antiquarian Society.)

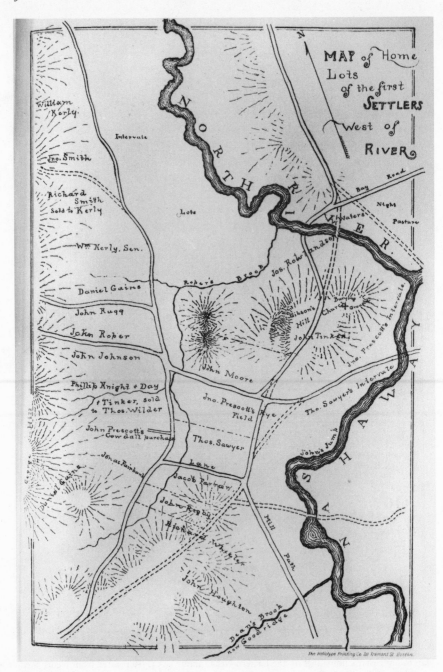

Map 7. Lancaster's home lots west of the Nashaway River, about 1653. (Reprinted from Henry Stedman Nourse, *The Early Records of Lancaster, Massachusetts, 1643–1725* [Lancaster, 1884], after p. 244. Courtesy of the American Antiquarian Society.)

could only watch their invited guests build more houses, lay out more fields and fences, and move ever closer to their own village at Weshakim.

The General Court's 1653 town grant proposed vague but familiar outlines for the expected institutional structure. The settlers came together "to covenant and bind ourselves" in agreements about Lancaster's people and lands. Church matters led the list. The first allotments were for church lands, to entice and support the requisite minister. The community pledged itself to build a public meetinghouse and a minister's house and to pay a ministerial tax to be levied upon the house lots. Only those with sound religious principles were to gain entry to the plantation. The anticipated economic and social hierarchy would be rooted in the soil. In 1643 home lots and intervale land had been distributed without regard to family size or wealth; the goal in those early days was to entice migrants and to keep the settlers clustered around the bend in the river. Handing out equally sized home lots to early settlers was the standard practice in the first wave of New England town foundings; later allotments would be sized variably, according to family size, social status, and assessed wealth. Lancaster, busy solidifying its irregular beginnings, would abandon equal amounts "to Rich and poore," and base its new divisions of land on status where "equalite of estates" meant unequal allocations of land. "Whereas Lotts are now laid out for the most part Equally to Rich and poore, Partly to keep the Town from Scaterring to farr, and partly out of Charite and Respect to men of meaner estate, yet the Equalite (which is the Rule of God) may be observed, we Covenant and Agree, that in a second Devition and so Through all other Devitions of Land the matter shall be drawn as near to equalite of estates as we are able to doe." The exception to the rule, offering "gifts of land" to lure leading figures to settle in Lancaster, only reinforced the construction of the desired hierarchy of town founders.[52]

All residents signed and affirmed these laws, ritually binding members to the community. The earliest signatures were even dated before the court's town grant. Edward Breck, a Dorchester selectmen for many years, signed first and was chosen by the court as one of the "Prudentiall" men. The covenant also required the settlers, "for the better preserving of peace and love," to settle controversies by arbitration. Entry into Lancaster was limited to thirty-five families, to ensure adequate supplies of land for the earliest settlers. By the end of the 1650s, fifty-nine men had signed the covenant. The largest contingent, twelve, came from Dorchester, six each from Sudbury and Hingham, and the rest from nine different localities.[53]

The minister, Joseph Rowlandson, arrived in 1654. A fresh graduate of Harvard College, Rowlandson had drawn the ire of college officials for posting a scandalous and satirical broadside upon the Ipswich meetinghouse lashing out at locals for ridiculing his father's frequent court appearances. Joseph came to town with his destitute father and mother; within two years he married Mary White, the daughter of John White, his richest parishioner. The White family had migrated to New England in 1639; they passed through crowded Salem and then Wenham before arriving in the new town in 1653. Rowlandson's alliance with the largest Lancaster landowner, as well as his own ministerial position, gave Joseph and Mary instant social stature in the Puritan town; Mary White became Mistress Rowlandson. Rowlandson's position was still not secure, however; a series of contentious disputes about his salary and land grants occurred throughout the 1650s. These disputes seemed to pit earlier settlers, those involved in the Nashaway fur trade, who chafed at court regulation, against the newer arrivals, such as the Rowlandson-White clan, who had larger landholdings and relied upon court support.[54]

The General Court's incorporation act of 1653 established a provisional township directed by a committee of six "Prudentiall Men" charged to organize the town's affairs until sufficient population existed to warrant the full privileges of a New England town. The very next year, with twenty families in town and two of the prudential men no longer resident, the residents requested that authority be transferred to the town itself. The court obliged. At the first town meeting, called in January 1654, twenty-five men were designated townsmen, male residents with the ability to hold town meetings and choose selectmen. However, the residents of Lancaster found that, while their numbers had grown, only three freemen (adult male church members entitled to colony-wide vote) were actually present in town. "The scarcitie of freemen," they petitioned the General Court, meant that they could not choose selectmen according to Massachusetts Bay law. So they asked for the revocation of local autonomy and requested the court to appoint another committee to "put us into such a way of order as we are Capable of." The court appointed Edward Johnson, Simon Willard, and Thomas Danforth as commissioners. These commissioners came to Lancaster in September 1657, met at John Prescott's house, and inquired about the town's condition. Their decision on the long-running Rowlandson dispute sided with the newcomers. They set the minister's salary at fifty pounds a year and instructed the townspeople to include their minister in all subsequent land allotments. Rowlandson immediately became entitled to eighty-two acres of land. Town leaders also quickly disciplined Mary Gates for making a saucy reproach during a church meeting (in which she criticized the new minister for disputing her mother's word). Religious authority was an important pillar of community order.[55]

The commissioners chose five selectmen to manage the long list of orders that they issued concerning town rates, land allotments, highways, and admissions to town. Those selectmen, leading figures such as John Tinker, John Prescott, William Kerley, and Ralph Houghton, quickly found their authority questioned and the extent of their power unclear, so that it became "hard to repell the boilings" among the town's population. They requested that their power be clarified and extended to include the ability to levy some small penalties for breach of their orders, "or lese it is a sword-toole and no edge." The commissioners quickly agreed with the request. The town records noted that over the next six years the selectmen had frequent meetings, which the commissioners subsequently approved.[56]

The native Nashaways were also having difficulty during the 1650s. Showanon's death in 1654 precipitated a squabble over his successor that demonstrated the changing balance of power in the Wachusett. Hearing of the sachem's death, the General Court ordered John Eliot and Increase Nowell to go "and by way of perswasion and counsell, not by compulsion, to prevayle with them for the choyce of such a one as may be most fitt." Showanon had been a good friend to the English; he had received Eliot in his village and protected the minister on his travels in the Wachusett; he had journeyed to Thomas King in Watertown to invite him to the Wachusett for trade; and he had joined other sachems in Boston to acknowledge English diplomatic power. The colonial authorities were anxious to secure an equally friendly successor. The choice was between Shoshanim (called "Sam" by the English), a "debaust" and "drunken" fellow, according to English accounts, and "no friend of the English," and Matthew, who was described as "very hopefull to learne the teachings of Christ." The English emissaries did their best to have Matthew chosen as sachem and described their intervention as "a good service to the countrie." Indian communities had become split between those who sought accommodation with the English and those advocating traditionalist goals. Matthew, it was clear, would continue Showanon's policy of accommodating the English presence in the Wachusett. In the end, the English got their pick when Matthew won out. Showanon had been a member of the first generation of town founders, the initiators of intercultural contact, converts to Christianity who counseled the avoidance of warfare with the English. When his Pennacook counterpart, the sachem Passaconoway died in 1660, he advised his subjects "not to make war" with the English: although "you may do them much mischief," Passaconoway warned, the Pennacooks would "all be destroyed and rooted off the Earth" in a war against the English, for the newcomers' military advantage was overwhelming. Some native leaders of the older generation still hoped for a trading relationship or military and political alliance with the English to suit tribal diplomatic goals in the 1650s, but many of the younger generation would begin to agitate for English removal in the 1660s.[57]

Lancaster residents continued to spread out from their original cluster at the bend in the Nashua River. With a diet of ground cereals, they needed their own mill, a significant local institution in early modern agrarian villages. When the Springfield mill owned by John Pynchon experienced difficulties in 1675, for example, he relayed the townspeople's feelings to Governor Leverett: "our People are under great discouragement, Talke of Leaving the Place . . . [We need] Provisions, I meane Bread, for want of a mill is difficult." "John Prescott blacksmith," as he was called in colonial documents, armed with the artisanal and entrepreneurial bent that initially led him to join the

Nashaway Company, built and ran a gristmill in Lancaster.[58] New England towns secured needed capital improvements and commercial development by granting monopolies to leading town founders, such as Pynchon and Prescott, who invested their own capital and expertise. Indeed, the very proprietary system of town founders was one such monopoly. Lancaster granted Prescott seventy acres of land, a five-pound loan for the purchase of irons for the mill, and a seven-year abatement of taxes. In addition, he would get, as was customary, a proportion of the ground product in exchange for the use of their equipment. Prescott contracted with a Charlestown artisan to build the gristmill, which opened a little over four months later.

In 1657 Prescott approached his neighbors at a militia training day to inquire about adding a saw mill to the commercial and artisanal enterprises in town. The eight militia days a year required the presence of every able-bodied male resident between sixteen and sixty, making these events an efficient arena for transacting town business. Prescott offered to set up a sawmill "for the good of the town," as he stated it, if he should receive "according to his desire" more land and another tax abatement. Since the town was growing but had no local source of sawn lumber, the offer met with quick approval. Prescott agreed to supply the inhabitants with "boards and other sawing." The miller obtained another grant of one hundred and twenty acres to add to his growing industrial complex on the town's southern border. With his grist- and saw-milling operations, which enjoyed a monopoly in the growing but isolated township, Prescott secured a new and expanding source of income at a time when his other main commercial enterprise, the fur trade, was beginning to contract.[59]

But Lancaster's position in central Massachusetts, at great distance from the mosaic of multiplying settlements that stretched out from Massachusetts Bay, still offered opportunities for English traders. The town had attracted prominent traders such as Stephen Day, an original prospector and Nashaway Company member, and John Tinker, a prominent fur trader pursuing the diminishing supplies of animals westward through the Merrimack River basin to the bend in the Nashua River. But the town's biggest catch was Simon Willard, whose move through the Merrimack Valley to its westernmost settlement in 1658 illustrates the changing fortunes of Indians and English as well as Lancaster's growth. The growing numbers of inhabitants drawn west by the new town's opportunities proved favorable for Lancaster's development as a New England town. But it spelled trouble for their original hosts, neighbors, and trading partners—the Nashaways.

The Other Nashaway: "A Great People in Former Times"

Europeans had settled the Wachusett for trade. Thomas King's acceptance of Showanon's invitation led to an active fur trade that filled the ranks of the infant community with enterprising town founders, whose primary occupation involved trading animal pelts. The fur trade quickly moved inland after 1633, when supplies of beaver around Massachusetts Bay were depleted. The greatest rush for commerce came in the settlements along the broad banks of the Connecticut River. William Pynchon, the founder of Springfield, Massachusetts, was the leading merchant in the western Bay Colony. Simon Willard dominated the trade in northeastern Massachusetts, securing posts along the Merrimack River and initiating contacts with Indians to the north. Willard had participated in the founding of Concord in 1635 and Chelmsford, at the southernmost bend in the Merrimack River, in 1652; he moved to Lancaster, situated on its tributary, the Nashua, in 1658. Both men, and their lesser trading companions, became close to the Indian peoples in their regions. Willard was able to introduce John Eliot to natives living along the Merrimack River as far north as Concord, New Hampshire. By 1640 fur traders had pushed the colonization process well inland.[60]

Fur traders became town founders, not just as initiators of English settlement, but because they were men of substantial capital and social standing. The General Court closely regulated the fur trade from its beginning. In 1636 it formalized the granting of monopolies by authorizing a standing committee to farm out the fur trade "to such persons as they shall think meete, for a tearme of three yeares," with a yearly rent to be collected and taxes levied on the annual catch. Colonial connections, not local ties, determined who would be awarded one of the licenses. The large amount of capital required for entry into the trade was far beyond the reach of most settlers. Men such as Willard and Pynchon, who were prominent in the Bay Colony, became the dominant traders in their respective regions. But a second rank of Englishmen entered the trade in the Wachusett in the brief, flush days of the inland fur trade. Lancaster's first trader, Thomas King, who built his trucking house on George Hill, had seventy-three pounds of debts due to him from his Indian trading partners upon his death in 1644. The presence of middling traders in Lancaster indicates the profits available from the inland commerce in pelts in the 1650s. John Prescott bought King's trading post in 1645 and continued to trade with his Indian neighbors. His extensive contacts with the Nashaways and his prominent position in the Wachusett must have facilitated his participation in the fur trade, even as he diversified into the milling business. John Tinker moved to Lancaster in 1656 and took over Prescott's trading post. Tinker had been trading at Windsor, Connecticut, until the Pynchons drove him out of the Connecticut River trade; moving to Boston in 1654, he worked briefly the dwindling Bay trade. In 1657 he purchased the fur-trade monopoly for Nashaway and Groton for £8. Returns must have been good, for the next year he was taxed £64 for his Lancaster and Groton catch. As Tinker came to assume a leading role in Lancaster, he was made a selectmen and town clerk. But he must have foreseen the fur trade's decline, for after a time, he moved to New London, Connecticut, where he went into the liquor business.[61]

Meanwhile, Simon Willard, the preeminent trader on the Merrimack River and its tributaries, was making his way west following the declining supplies of beaver. He transferred his operations to Chelmsford in 1655 and purchased exclusive rights to trading "at Merrimack" for £25 a year. Chelmsford settlers, excluded from this business by the colony's monopoly policy, petitioned the court for permission to engage in the fur trade, citing the difficulties of securing supplies "in this Remoat Corner of the Wilderness." But the General Court, recognizing the value of granting temporary monopolies to private individuals to promote economic development, declined to change its policy. Profits in the Merrimack trade remained substantial as late as 1658. Willard paid more in tax than his western counterpart, Pynchon, who suffered an unusually small catch worth £530 that year. Willard's average yearly gross trade has been estimated to be approximately £800 during the 1650s. Another estimate puts the entire Merrimack River valley trade at greater than two thousand pounds of beaver divided among several traders in 1657, at a time when the catch was already waning. What Prescott might have secured as the only trader in Lancaster cannot even be guessed. However, Chelmsford residents continued their trade with local native peoples, whereby "the Indians obtained food in winter . . . better utensils, and, too often, rum." Willard's role in supervising Lancaster's political affairs gave him personal knowledge of the potential of the Wachusett, and he may have found it attractive to move to a site with fewer competitors and more plentiful beaver. In Lancaster Willard occupied Lawrence Waters's home lot, the site of the first house built in the plantation. He purchased Tinker's land and trading post in 1659 and bought the rights to the Lancaster and Groton fur trade. Later, Willard built an imposing brick and stone structure that stood out from his neighbor's frame houses, and the Willard family put down roots in the Wachusett.[62]

Lancaster's traders abused their native trading partners, selling them guns and liquor in exchange for skins. Immediately before his arrival in Lancaster, John Tinker was fined "for selling now & then a gill of strong waters to ye Indians." More likely than not, he continued these practices in the Wachusett, far from the eyes of the colonial authorities. George Adams, located just north of the trading post, overstepped the colony's laws regarding selling liquor and guns. The court found him guilty in 1653 of "selling two gunnes and strong waters" to the Indians and sentenced him to be "severely whipt the next lecture day at Boston." Cyprian Stevens, who married Simon Willard's daughter Mary, was convicted of selling powder and shot and three gallons of "Strong liquors" to a party of Indians hunting "up in the woods near Watchuset." Even Stephen Day, an indefatigable early proprietor of Nashaway who was once lauded by colonial authorities for his role in promoting the plantation to English and Indians alike at his Cambridge home, was admonished for defrauding the Nashaways.[63]

By the 1660s the fur trade had sharply declined. Both the Indians and the English of the Wachusett, without access to waterways reaching deep into the interior for fresh supplies of beaver, quickly found the animals disappearing. English entrepreneurs such as Prescott and Tinker continued to prosper by selling their stake in the fur trade and moving into other kinds of commercial ventures with steady returns, such as milling or distilling. Those like Willard, who did not, were reduced to petitioning the General Court for allotments of land in lieu of trading revenues. The General Court gave Willard a large farm on the banks of the Nashua River. The Nashaways had fewer alternatives, however, and for them the precipitous decline of the trade had disastrous consequences. Throughout the Wachusett as in other areas where Indians had been trading partners in the regional New England economy, the end of the fur trade deprived them of a meaningful role. No longer able to exchange furs for goods such as textiles, knives, guns, kettles, and liquor that English suppliers offered from their trading hut in Lancaster, they had little left to trade but their land—a finite commodity, and the basis of their economic and cultural life. The era of interdependency in the Wachusett gave way to a new period of dependency.[64]

Nashaways faced mounting pressure to alienate their land. Traders customarily advanced trade goods to their Indian suppliers each season; those hunters, with depleted stocks of beaver, found themselves with huge debts and few ways of paying except by selling land. Willard approached the General Court for satisfaction in the form of a land grant when a Pawtucket Indian could not meet his £44 debt in 1658. The English had never recognized the Indian conception of land ownership, a cultural misunderstanding present in Showanon's original deed to Thomas King. Lancaster's generous boundaries meant that the native Nashaway and the English newcomers did not come into direct conflict over land usage for some time. Yet in the 1660s a growing number of settlers acquired Indian lands and pushed ever closer to the Nashaway villages by the waters of Weshakim. John Prescott, in addition to his growing mill complex to the south, petitioned the General Court for a farm "in some place undisposed of" for services rendered in colonial business, and the court responded in 1659 by bestowing upon him one hundred acres adjoining the western borders along Weshakim. Stephen Day purchased land from Matthew, the new sachem. George Adams received sixty acres in 1670 from the common fields, land south of Weshakim and close to the town borders, as compensation for an earlier grant never laid out. Prescott also enlarged his holdings by buying property from individual Nashaways, who sold off portions of Nashaway land. In 1672 Prescott appeared with a deed of sale from James Quanapohit for another one hundred acres along his previous grant at Weshakim. "The ancient Planter," Prescott, asked the court "to confirm the Indian grant to him," which it duly did.[65]

The combination of increasing geographical proximity and decreasing economic interdependence led to conflict between the two peoples. The folklore of the early days of Lancaster features numerous tales of contests between John Prescott and the Nashaways. One story tells of how Prescott used an imposing suit of English armor to retrieve a stolen horse. When Indians stole one of his horses, he left his home clad in this garment and overtook the thieves. Surprised by the lone warrior, they approached him with their weapons. Prescott bid them draw closer and strike him a blow, but when their tomahawks glanced off his helmet, the astonished Indians asked Prescott to give them the hat with its supposed magical qualities and hit them in return. The helmet proved too big for their leader, and Prescott's blows forced it down over his ears and bruised his skin. This series of events left the marauders amazed, and they returned the Englishmen's horse and hastened away with his supernatural headpiece. Even if apocryphal, this anecdote captures the English assumption of superiority.[66]

In the 1660s the Nashaways faced increasing pressure on their village lands, a threat to their economic system with the decline of the fur trade, and claims of political sovereignty. Intertribal warfare, however, posed the greatest threat to the Indian villages in the Wachusett. The Mohawks, the easternmost of the Iroquois nations, began a decade of military assaults on their neighbors that extended as far east as the Nashaway settlements. The Mohawks, a French observer claimed in 1659, were "insolent in disposition, and truly warlike, they have had to fight with all their neighbors." Mohawks frequently came into conflict with New England groups in the early seventeenth century; their intermittent incursions into the Connecticut and Merrimack River valleys established their influence over Algonquians in western New England. But the disruptions in trading relationships pushed the Mohawks to attempt to tighten their control over supplies of wampum and trade goods such as guns. Like their Algonquian neighbors, the Iroquois had incorporated commerce with the Europeans into their culture; indeed, the Mohawk term for Europeans, Asseroni, meant "axmaker." The oversupply of wampum in the northeast caused havoc in the Iroquois' trade with the Dutch, as it did in the Algonquians' trade with the English. The Mohawks, well situated on the borders of the French, Dutch, and English empires, sought to control militarily the access of other groups to reliable European trading partners. Furthermore, with their population diminished in the 1650s by war and disease, the Mohawks carried out a series of "mourning wars," which involved the taking of captives in order to replenish their strength.[67]

Mohawk attacks against the Abenakis and the western New England Algonquians began in 1662. The Nashaways, among others, appealed to their English allies because, as Major Willard informed the Council in November of 1663, "the Mohawks lately come down and slaine severall of the Confederate Indians who are in confederacy with us." Nashaway pleas met with little success; Willard was told to furnish all of the "Confederate Indians with powder and shott not exceeding three barrells." The following month the Mohawks struck Squakeag, in the Connecticut River valley. The next summer the members of a Mohawk-led peace delegation to the

Pocumtucks were murdered by those opposed to a truce. This provocation, whatever its cause, escalated the conflict. The Mohawks retaliated by destroying the Pocumtuck fort and village and killing and scattering its inhabitants. Mohawk forays continued throughout southern New England. Indians' expectations of reciprocity between Puritan and Algonquian were dashed further when a Mohawk raid took a heavy toll among the Nash-aways, and there was no English response. Finally in 1669, the Nashaways joined other Algonquians in mounting a large force of six to seven hundred men against the Mohawks. They marched two hundred miles to lay siege unsuccessfully to a Mohawk fort and suffered heavy casualties upon their retreat. The Nashaways were left disillusioned with the meager military aid that their English allies had provided. "Driven from their planting fields through fear," Gookin reported, "and from their fishing and hunting places, yea they durst not go into the woods, to seek roots and nuts to sustain their lives." These troubles gradually weakened their society and reduced their numbers. By 1672, Gookin estimated that the Nashaways, "a great people in former times," numbered about fifteen families, having been "consumed by the Maquas' wars and other ways."[68]

In 1672, the increasing stability of Lancaster, the Wachusett's other town, gained it status as a full town, as the General Court had promised two decades earlier. For some time the selectmen issued lengthy orders and held frequent meetings, with the commissioners' subsequent approval. By 1663 the residents conducted their own town meetings called by the selectmen. One such meeting petitioned the committee to return governance to the town's hands. The committee members fully "concure and consent" to "the ratifying of what is," an acknowledgement that the town had achieved the requisite numbers of residents and institutional legitimacy. The General Court approved the transfer of political power to the town and its well-known leaders in 1672. The creation and maintenance of political authority had not been a straightforward process in the twenty years after the township had been granted, but resembled the haphazard formation of planta-tion itself in the 1640s. But Lancaster's growing number of families had suc-ceeded in constructing the economic and social structure necessary to gain recognition as a New England town.[69] Those same developments put them on a collision course with their Nashaway neighbors, whose own situation was becoming increasingly difficult during those years.

Daniel Gookin's Indian Work

Daniel Gookin, town founder, Indian superintendent, and village historian extended the project of colonization and conversion to the Wachusett.[70] As a town founder, Gookin, functioned as a cultural mediator. Familiar through his Indian work with native leaders and their communities, he took a sympathetic view of the Christian Indians, a stance that would marginalize him during the hysteria of Metacom's War. His political connections sent him off on General Court missions that intertwined public and private business, providing him with numerous land grants and town proprietorships in the new settlements on the New England frontiers. His alliance with John Eliot gave him expertise with both the Puritan and the Christian towns being founded in this era of English-Indian interdependency and coexistence. And Gookin became the Christian Indians' historian as he attempted to bring them into the recounting of the Puritan errand into the wilderness.[71]

The Gookin family had taken advantage of the global scope of British colonization. Daniel Gookin was born in 1612 in Ireland, another of England's colonial ventures, where his father Daniel had purchased an estate. The Gookins were lesser English gentry living in Ireland, and his father later bought another plantation in Virginia. When his father died in 1629, Daniel and his brother moved to this New World property, Marie's Mount. He purchased his own plantation in a newer area of the Virginia colony near the Nansemond River. But Gookin's apparently staunch Congregationalist beliefs brought him into conflict with Governor Berkeley and forced his removal to the Massachusetts Bay town of Roxbury about 1643. He became the neighbor and friend of John Eliot, who was just about to embark upon his Indian missionary activities. Gookin, whom Eliot called "my only cordial assistant," joined in the mission of Christianizing and civilizing the Indians. In 1648 Gookin moved to Cambridge and began his ascent in the colony's political hierarchy by assuming a town militia post and being elected to the General Court, first as a deputy and then as an assistant. He remained in the General Court for almost thirty years. In 1656, the court appointed him as the first Indian superintendent to oversee the new legal system for praying Indians in 1657.[72]

The New England town was the focus of Gookin's work and of his historical writings. Resettlement in praying towns was intended to turn Massachusett and Nipmuc people into civilized Christians. Gookin provided a unique portrait of the Christian Indian communities in his *Historical Collections of the Indians in New England* (1674), the second volume of an intended larger *History of New England*: "BOOK II. Treateth of the Indians, natives of the country: their customs, manners, and government, before the English settled there: also their present state in matters of religion and government; and in especial of the praying Indians, who have visibly received the gospel; mentioning the means and instruments that God hath used for their civilizing and conversion, and the success thereof through the blessing of God." He planned his eight-volume *History* "to draw some rude delineaments of God's Work in this Land," including discussions of the bounties of the lands, the manners and customs of the Indians, the planting of New England, the forms of civil government, the towns and their people, the remarkable providences they experienced, and the religious order. But, bogged down in the grand opus, Gookin sent off a shorter version, *Indians Converted, or Historical Collections of the Indians in New England* (its original title), to England in 1674 or 1675. The historian described the seven old and the seven new praying towns, town by town, with immediacy and insight through a narrative of the tour that he conducted with Eliot in 1673 and 1674. Through his town founding and history-writing, Gookin attempted to represent the Christian Indians within the Puritan cultural myth of the workings of divine will in human affairs. He wrote about the planting of towns and churches, not by the erasure of Indians as Edward Johnson did, but by their incorporation in the history of New England. His *Historical Collections* provides an account of serial town settlement on the eve of Metacom's War: the move from old to new praying towns, the factions within Indian communities, the reception of the English message, and its transformation by the Indian respondents.[73]

About 1,100 natives lived in fourteen praying towns when Eliot and Gookin visited them. (See map 8.) The Indian superintendent noted the mixed success in transplanting English material culture in Natick, the oldest and most populous of the communities, the fruits of two decades of missionary efforts. Eliot had supervised the layout of family lots, the construction of the meetinghouse and frame homes, and the clearing and planting of fields and orchards. By 1673, the staples of English agriculture, fences and flocks of livestock, had appeared. Some Indian farmers even planted orchards or prepared shingles, following the missionary directive to participate in the colonial economy. The town and a few houses displayed the "English manner," but many residents clung to their traditional dwellings, the warmer and more transportable wigwams. In Nashobah, another praying town, Gookin complained, they had planted and harvested orchards of apples, but instead of trading for profit, the townspeople drank up the produce. Eliot's strategy clustered the Indians into towns so the program of spiritual transformation could begin. Eliot offered a Massachusett translation of the Bible, Indian preachers, and a new set of rituals, including Sabbath worship services and daily prayer. Christian Indian preachers asked listeners to look inside and confront their own essentially evil nature. These new European constructs of time, spirituality, and cosmology diminished Indian notions of identity. Eliot and Gookin's program offered both opportunities and dangers for praying Indians. Under enormous demographic and economic pressure, coastal Algonquian peoples used English patronage to reconstitute themselves as distinct villages and communities in the middle decades of the seventeenth century. Conversion to Puritanism was less complete than the missionaries desired; Christian Indians displayed a syncretic faith composed of traditional and Christian elements. The creation of the praying towns not only worked toward conversion but also anchored Indians to a compact settlement site, forcing them to abandon their mobile ways and leave vast amounts of land open for English development.[74]

Map 8. Indian villages of southern New England, after 1674. The map includes Nashaway and the Indian pray-ing towns, both new and old, that John Eliot and Daniel Gookin visited on the eve of Metacoms War. (Indian settlements are marked with circles, English towns with rectangles.) Old praying towns, to the east, were Nat-ick, Punkapog, Hassanamesitt, Okommakamesit (Marlborough), Wamesit or Pawtuckett, Nashobah, and Magunkaquog. New ones were in central Massachusetts; they include Manchage, Chabanakongkomun, Maanexit, Quantisset, Wabquissit, Packachoog, and Waeuntug. (Reprinted from Laura E. Conkey, Ethel Bosse-vain, and Ives Goddard, "Indians of Southern New England and Long Island: Late Period," in Bruce Trigger, ed., *Handbook of North American Indians*, vol. 4, *Northeast* [Washington, D.C., 1978], p. 178. By permission of the *Handbook of North American Indians* and the Smithsonian Institution. Courtesy of Cornell University Libraries.)

In September 1674 Eliot and Gookin journeyed to the Wachusett in an effort to extend English legal sovereignty into Nipmuc villages and construct new praying towns. At their deepest progress, forty-four miles from Boston, Gookin held court at Pakachoog, near Worcester, with Wattasacompanum, ruler of the Nipmucs, as his "chief assistant." He clothed sachems with "the authority of the English government," charged ministers to root out "idolatry and powowing," and chose constables at these sessions. Then he attempted to bring Nashaway and Weshakim, nonpraying towns, into the fold. Gookin sent Jethro, a Christian Nipmuc and Natick teacher, to Weshakim as minister, along with a lengthy letter to Shoshanim, the new Nashaway sachem, Matthew's successor, exhorting him to "abstain from drunkenness, whoredom, and powowing." But Gookin's business was not done, despite the fall of night. A visitor from "Weshakim near Nashaway" spoke up with impassioned words. A group of his people wished to take up Christianity but was blocked by a faction in the village, "very wicked and much addicted to drunkenness." He appealed to Gookin for power to help in suppressing the disorder in his town. Seeing the opportunity to further his temperance crusade, Gookin inquired whether this pilgrim would like to be a constable and apprehend drunkards. Suddenly, the Nashaway man grew cautious. He replied that he must talk first with his friends, "and if they chose him, and strengthened his hand," he would return to the English commissioners for "a black staff and power." The two English men retired for the night. They returned east the next morning, however, without bringing Weshakim or Nashaway into the fold of praying towns.

Social isolation was a serious question for Christianized Indians and led to internal political maneuvering. In Eliot's *Indian Dialogues,* the missionary presented a fictional Indian who professed interest in Christianity but objected to leaving his friends, for "if I should forsake our former ways, all my friends would rise up against me like a stream too strong for me to stand against." In existing Indian communities, the addition of outside English magistrates and Christian ministers altered the power structure; local leaders who did not accept English direction found their authority superseded by those who did. This English strategy often led to rifts between traditionalists and Christian Indians and to struggles for the leadership of divided villages.[75]

Gookin's "Indian work," his efforts at town founding and history writing, went together. He intended to reduce the Indians to civility and incorporate them into the Puritan errand into the wilderness by securing them in New England towns and inscribing them in the narrative of redemption. Gookin faced resistance from both land-hungry English settlers and Indian traditionalists; even the Christian Indians split into pro- and anti-English factions. The Indian superintendent's vision did not take hold, either in joint English-Indian occupancy of New England or in rewriting the Indians into the founding of a Christian nation. Gookin's next foray into writing history, *An Historical Account of the Doings and Sufferings of the Christian Indians of New England,* recounted the travails of the Christian Indians during Metacom's War.

Shoshanim and Metacom's War

Matthew, the Nashaway sachem, died about 1673 and was succeeded by Shoshanim (Sam). He harbored no love for the English, whose presence in the Wachusett had caused the Nashaway to lose economic and political power. He led the Nashaways into what became known as Metacom's or King Philip's War. The Nashaways and the other Indian groups who joined the original Wampanoag warriors led by Metacom (King Philip) were bound together by a series of festering grievances and long-term threats to the continuation of their way of life in southern New England. According to the historian Neal Salisbury, the war was "a loose-knit uprising" of Indian bands who occupied lands along both sides of Narragansett Bay northwestward through Nipmuc country and on to the Connecticut River: "This was the region in which the worlds of indigenous exchange and European exchange had flourished together in the 1640s and 1650s and then began to be undermined." The Indians of southern New England were threatened not just by the overall advance of English towns but also by their own growing economic dependency from the declining fur trade, the loss of their material base from land sales, Puritan missionaries' religious intervention, and the weakening of political structures by factionalism. In the 1660s, a new generation of English settlers ominously pressed upon Indian resources that had seemed endless only a few decades earlier. In 1671 Metacom bitterly described the transformation that had taken place since his father's generation: "When the English first Came, their [the Wampanoags'] kings father was as a great man and the English as a litell Child, he Constraened other indians from ronging the English and gave them Coren and shewed them how to plant and was free to do them ani good and had let them have a 100 times more land, than now the king had for his own peopell." The accession of a group of native American sachems such as Shoshanim of the Nashaways and Metacom of the Pokanoket in Plymouth, who no longer welcomed English settlers, was accompanied by a resistance movement that sought to restore a system of reciprocity between the two peoples.[76]

Metacom's experience paralleled that of the Nashaway sachem. His father Masasoit, chief sachem of the Wampanoags, had been a good friend to the Plymouth Colony. But his brother Wamsutta (Alexander) and later Metacom (Philip) himself had had to deal with the problems brought by expanding English settlements that pushed Wampanoags onto more marginal lands. Closer proximity between the two peoples gave rise to disputes over trampled Indian crops and wayward English cattle. Metacom attempted to restrain land sales; he rejected Eliot's overtures; he cast out John Sassamon, a Christian Indian educated at Harvard; and he decided to oppose English encroachments. War was narrowly averted in 1671. Four years later, when Sassamon's body mysteriously appeared in a frozen pond, the English took swift revenge, which precipitated the outbreak of hostilities in June 1675. The resulting war emptied Lancaster and drove back serial town settlement in the interior for a generation.[77]

Wampanoag warriors attacked frontier Swansea in June and all New England was gripped in panic. War had been anticipated for some time. Blundering English diplomatic overtures to the powerful Nipmucs of inland Massachusetts were followed by Indian ambushes and the siege and destruction of Brookfield, the only other English town in central Massachusetts, in July. The local Nashaways joined the conflict in late August; they attacked Lancaster in an effort to roll back English settlement, an effort begun before Metacom's arrival in Nipmuc country. The pan-Indian campaign widened along the western frontier terrifying settlers from Cape Cod to the upper Connecticut River. The Indians' military tactics gave them the upper hand; native warriors possessed an intimate knowledge of the terrain and were skilled in the art of ambush. English forces struggled to follow their foes in the forest. As William Hubbard put it, it was "one thing, to drill a Company in a plain Champagne and another to drive an enemy through the desert woods." By winter only five English towns remained in the west. An intercolonial force of over one thousand men went on the offensive; they attacked the powerful, neutral Narragansetts at their winter stronghold in the swamps of Rhode Island. English soldiers burned the village and slaughtered warriors and noncombatants alike. The surviving Narragansetts fled to Nipmuc country where the combined Indian forces wintered; some quartered around Mount Wachusett, while Metacom approached the Mohawks for an alliance. Instead of allying with Metacom, the Mohawks, supported by New York authorities, attacked his forces. The English began to try new tactics, striking at villages and food supplies and utilizing pro-English Indian troops and spies.[78]

Although the natives split into pro- and anti-English factions, the colonists became unqualified Indian haters. Attacks by some Indians brought down suspicion on all, even on Christianized Indians from neighboring praying villages. Massachusetts Bay colonists marched Concord's Indians down to Boston to be interned on Deer Island. Eliot, Gookin, and Willard advocated a lenient Indian policy and opposed selling Indian captives into slavery, but their voices were drowned out by the colonists' indiscriminate hatred of Indians. By the time the three men visited the "bleak and cold" island in Boston harbor, there were over five hundred Christian Indians there, who "lived chiefly upon clams and shell-fish" supplemented with meager rations of corn, and whose wigwams were "poor and mean."

The first generation of town founders and cultural mediators witnessed the tragic end of joint occupancy of the region that winter.[79]

Lancaster's residents spent the winter of 1675–76 huddled in their gloomy garrison homes with rumors rife about the Indian forces camped twelve miles from town. Two Christian Nipmuc men agreed to go deep into Nipmuc country for information. James Quanapohit, a Nashaway resident, informed Major Gookin at his Cambridge home about the planned Indian offensive led by Monoco, his former comrade-in-arms, against five frontier towns, Lancaster being the first strike.

> Next morning I went to one-eyed John's wigwam. He said he was glad to see me; I had been his friend many years and had helped him kill Mohaugs; and said, nobody should meddle with me. . . . He said, if any body hurt me they should die. . . . And this Indian told me they would fall upon Lancaster, Groton, Marlborough, Sudbury, and Medfield, and that the first thing they would do should be to cut down Lancaster bridge, so to hinder their flight, and assistance coming to them; and they intended to fall upon them in about twenty days time from Wednesday next.

The colonial authorities ignored Quanapohit's warning. In Lancaster the agitated townspeople sent the Reverend Rowlandson and his brother-in-law Henry Kerley to Boston for more troops. When the second spy pounded upon Daniel Gookin's door in Cambridge with the news that a troop of four hundred Nipmucs were set to fall upon Lancaster the next morning, Gookin dispatched orders for squads to hasten from Concord and Marlborough.[80]

Monoco and his men attacked "about sun-rising," according to Mary Rowlandson's rhetorically inflamed eyewitness account. Rowlandson watched the attack as it began, first against the other garrisons then finally against hers:

> At length they came and beset our House, and quickly it was the dolefullest day that ever mine eyes saw. . . . From all which places they shot against the House, so that the Bullets seemed to fly like hail; and quickly they wounded one man among us, then another, and then a third. . . . Some in the house were fighting for their lives, some wallowing in their blood, the House on fire over our heads, and the bloody Heathens ready to knock us on the head, if we stirred out. . . . But out we must go, the fire increasing, and coming along behind us, roaring, and the Indians gaping before us with their Guns, Spears and Hatchets to devour us.

With "Bullets flying thick," Mary Rowlandson fled the burning house with her child in her arms. Her eldest sister lay dead over the threshold, the Indians set upon her brother-in-law, and a blow to the head killed her nephew. When the English troops arrived they found the Rowlandson garrison in flames, about fourteen townspeople dead, and twenty-three residents swept off into captivity, including Rowlandson and her family.[81]

Attacks followed on exposed English outposts all along the frontier. Shoshanim and Monoco fell upon Medfield, sixteen miles southwest of Boston, burned houses and left a note on the bridge across the Charles River, which they had destroyed: "Know by this paper, that the Indians that thou hast provoked to wrath and anger, will war this twenty-one years if you will; there are many Indians yet, we come three hundred at this time. You must consider the Indians lost nothing but their life; you must lose your fair houses and cattle." Settlers along a wide range of old and new frontier towns feared for their lives. The various bands of Indians pursued a loosely organized, multifront offensive: the Nipmucs and Nashaways in the Wachusett, the Narragansetts and Wampanoags to the southeast in the Plymouth and Rhode Island colonies, other forces along the Connecticut River valley, and another group in the northern Merrimack Valley. Lancaster's beleaguered residents, with their provisions spent and overwhelmed by fear, petitioned the General Court to allow them to leave "this plantation. We are in danger eminent, the enemy laying above us, nay on both sides of us." The Indians burned the abandoned town only weeks after the initial attack.[82] By late March, the Indian offensive had successfully cleared out the outer ring of frontier settlements, such as Lancaster and Groton, where the English had slowly inched their way west for over a generation. Crowded coastal towns filled with refugees. To compound their problems, with the settlement line collapsing and spirits sagging, an epidemic swept through southern New England and carried off prominent colonial leaders, including John Winthrop Jr., Connecticut's governor, and Simon Willard, a Massachusetts Bay military leader, both of whom had played influential roles in the exploration and colonization of the Wachusett.[83]

At this point, the tide turned. The Indians, who had a relatively small population base, were significantly affected by the loss of warriors even in victorious battles. Mary Rowlandson, encamped with her captors near Mount Wachusett, watched the somber return of warriors after a successful attack upon Sudbury. "Yet they came home without that rejoycing and triumphing over their victory, which they were wont to shew at other times, but rather like Dogs (as they say) which have lost their ears. . . . When they went, they acted as if the Devil had told them that they should gain the victory: and now they acted, as if the Devil had told them they should have a fall."[84] A new group of aggressive English military leaders struck deep into the Indian homelands; New England men such as William Turner and Benjamin Church, advocates of unorthodox "Indianizing" tactics that had been initially rejected by colonial authorities, were handed command at the low point of the war. In April, with Indian supply lines stretched to the breaking point, English attacked the Indian soldiers at their seasonal fishing runs; isolated bands gave themselves up. Indian forces began to splinter.[85] Church had great success that summer; his forest operations called for scattered movements to avoid ambush and reliance upon native allies. As enemy losses mounted, attention shifted to hunting people down, especially the elusive leaders of the rebellion.[86]

The war produced numerous captives and refugees on both sides. The Indians often secured prisoners to replace warriors lost in battle; when the war began to draw to a close and the rebellion appeared to be lost, they used their prisoners as pawns for ransom or to gain advantage in negotiations. Gookin dispatched interned Indians from Deer Island to inquire about English prisoners. Astonished, he received one written reply from Jethro, the very constable he had dispatched to Weshakim in 1674, demanding twenty pounds for Mary Rowlandson. All spring English captives throughout New England were released, and Mary Rowlandson was reunited with her husband Joseph in May.[87] The Indian leaders with whom she had lived were hunted down that summer. Shoshanim begged for clemency: "do you consider it again: we do earnestly entreat you, that it may be so by Jesus Christ. O let it be so: Amen Amen," offering his signature, X Sam Sachem. The Council replied that those "treacherous persons who began the war" should not expect any mercy. An allied Indian killed Metacom; Shoshanim and several other sachems surrendered. Increase Mather recorded their fate: "Sept 22. This day Sagamore Sam was hanged at Boston. . . . The Same day 3 other Indians, hanged, viz the Sagamore of Quaboag, one eyed John and Jethro. They were betrayed into the hands of the English by Indians." Metacom's and Shoshanim's widows and children, along with several hundred other Indians, were sold into slavery in the West Indies, as were hundreds of other Indians.[88] The war, the costliest in U.S. history in terms of loss of life proportionate to the population, challenged some of Puritanism's certitudes and halted the process of town formation. Two raids upon Lancaster had emptied the town of English settlers for several years, driving the refugees back to the coastal communities temporarily. But for the Nashaways and other Indian combatants, Metacom's War had far more dire consequences. The conflict permanently ended joint occupancy of the region, produced an Algonquian diaspora out of southern New England, and cleared the way for the continued expansion of English settlement throughout the Wachusett.

Mary Rowlandson's Removes

> On the tenth of February 1675, Came the *Indians* with great numbers upon *Lancaster;* Their first coming was about Sun-rising; hearing the noise of some Guns, we looked out; several Houses were burning, and the Smoke ascending to Heaven. There were five persons taken in one house, the Father, and the Mother and a sucking Child, they knockt on the head; the other two they

took and carried away alive. . . . Thus these murtherous wretches went on, burning, and destroying before them.

Mary Rowlandson, *The Sovereignty and Goodness of God, Together with the Faithfulness of His Promise Displayed; Being a Narrative of the Captivity and Restoration of Mrs. Mary Rowlandson* (1682)

Mary Rowlandson's Indian captivity narrative, *The Sovereignty and Goodness of God,* the first example of this important American literary genre, was also the first historical work about the Wachusett. Rowlandson's task, as urged upon her by her ministerial sponsors, was "to control the meaning of the war by the use of the Puritan method of typology or exemplification."[89] Instead, Rowlandson exposed the social tensions that existed within the colony between the Boston ministerial elite, who disapproved of the dispersal of population, and the frontier settlers, who were busy founding new towns. Her narrative revealed ambiguities that undermined orthodoxy's strictures about the necessity of a communal setting for salvation and about the dangers of the wilderness encircling Puritan society. Most important, Mary Rowlandson's successful survival "in her wilderness condition" actually sanctioned towns such as Lancaster and promoted the expansion of settlement in the next generation.[90]

Ministers had been quick to employ the travails of Metacom's War as an indictment of the unorthodox behavior of those living in the outlying settlements. Increase Mather's *Brief History of the War with the Indians in New England* appeared just after Metacom's death; he saw the war as a judgment sent upon the second generation for not following "the blessed design of their Fathers." Mather provided a vivid parable of the massacre of "old Wakely" and his family by Indians in Maine. Seeking worldly gain, Wakely led his family beyond the protection of the church to a "Plantation where there was no Church, nor Instituted Worship, only to perish on the exposed frontier, where God sent Indians to destroy him." Mather's son and successor as leading ministerial spokesman, Cotton Mather, soon followed with a clearer condemnation of those migrating to the margins of New England: "Do our Old People, any of them Go Out from the Institutions of God, Swarming into New Settlements, where they and their Untaught Families are Like to Perish for Lack of Vision. They that have done so, heretofore, have to their Cost Found, that they were got unto the Wrong Side of the Hedge, in their doing so. Think. Here should this be done any more?" Rowlandson countered with the perspective of the godly folk who remained on the right side of the "Hedge."[91]

Rowlandson's account of her capture from Lancaster in February 1675 and her three-month captivity was broken down into "twenty removes" within the wilderness, an ordeal during which she gave a recitation of the afflictions that befell her; she ignored exact chronology and geography. Her narrative paralleled the Puritan conversion experience: a sudden descent, a lengthy wandering, and a final ascent into salvation, with the individual all the while burdened by anxiety over his or her sinfulness and the hope of God's grace. Rowlandson drew upon the genres of the sermon, the historical narrative, and the spiritual autobiography to compile her folk narrative of the perils of settlement on the precarious, exposed frontier of Massachusetts Bay.[92]

Students of American Puritanism in recent years have come to recognize the critical role of exemplaristic typology, "the exercise of perceiving persons and events not in terms of their singularity but as specimens of abstract spiritual types recurring through history." The Puritan orthodoxy achieved its cultural authority by ideological power, a power that became immanent in the interpretation of experience. Rowlandson's captivity and deliverance became paradigmatic of the New England story. Her efforts to find a pattern in her afflictions paralleled the postwar New England project of exerting control over unsettling events. The opening pages of Rowlandson's captivity narrative depicted a providential drama taking place within a binary world where Puritan ideology opposed society to the wilderness, the civilized to the savage. "History," Sacvan Bercovitch has argued, "is invoked to replace historicism." Experience was subordinated to idea.[93]

Rowlandson's vision of the region outside Lancaster evoked little of a landscape filled with native villages or natural wonders; she focused instead on the sinful environment she observed, which reflected the Puritan conception of the wilderness as a physical type of hell. Her "first remove" dropped her into the netherworld of the Indian camp. "This was the dolefullest night that ever my eyes saw." She recounted the "roaring, and singing and danceing, and yelling" of "those black creatures in the night," which made her dwelling place "a lively resemblance of hell." Rowlandson endured this and subsequent removes by recourse to the solace of Scripture and the memory of family. She remembered the family gathering around the hearth on the Sabbath, "relations and neighbors with us, found in prayer and song." When plagued with "heart-aking thoughts" about her "poor Children," she would open her Bible, which served as a "sweet Cordial to me."[94]

Yet, this narrative of afflictions contained unstable tendencies. Rowlandson's narrative continually broke out of the rigid schemas she employed, as the struggle for survival cracked open the process of exemplification to reveal the real. In several cases concerning food, the wilderness, and the Indians, Rowlandson moved beyond Puritan categories and certitude. "The first week of my being among them, I hardly ate anything; the second week, I found my stomach grow very faint for want of something; and yet it was very hard to get down their filthy trash: but the third week, though I could think how formerly my stomach would turn against this or that, and I could starve and die before I could eat such things, yet they were sweet and savory to my taste."[95] Her series of removes and her entry into the Indian economy through the productive work of sewing things to be traded revealed the vacant "wilderness" to be the site of an extensive network of roads and byways and commercial exchange. Finally, her struggle for survival necessitated an involvement with her captors that resulted in a representation of particular Indians that differs dramatically from her earlier, emblematic diabolical savage. Rowlandson's explosion of abstract types comes across in her individual characterizations, such as the detailed portrait of the Wampanoag clan matron, Weetamoo: "a severe and proud Dame she was, bestowing every day in dressing herself neat as such time as any Gentry of the land: powdering her hair, and painting her face, going with Neck-laces, with Jewels in her ears, and Bracelets upon her hands: When she had dressed herself, her work was to make Girdles of *Wampom* and *Beads*."[96]

Rowlandson's narrative ambiguities opened up a space for personal agency in the workings of salvation. Salvation becomes possible outside the community of saints. Within a narrative form intended to decry those who strayed beyond the "hedge" of the covenanted community, a subversive message about the solitary soul who achieved spiritual enlightenment in wilderness emerged.

> *I can remember a time, when I used to sleep quietly without workings in my thoughts, whole nights together, but now it is other wayes with me.* When all are fast about me, and no eye open, but his whoever waketh, my thoughts are upon things fast, upon the awfull dispensation of the Lord towards us . . . through so many difficulties . . . returning us in safety. . . . I remember in the night season, how the other day I was in the midst of thousands of enemies, & nothing but death before me: It was then hard work to perswade myself, that ever I should be satisfied with bread again. But now we are fed *with the finest of Wheat* and, as I may say, *with honey out of the rock*.[97]

Even after Mary Rowlandson is redeemed and returned to society, she cannot or will not reenter the society of believers. She no longer can "sleep quietly without workings in my thoughts." While all others "are fast [asleep] about me," spiritually unawakened, Rowlandson's thoughts are upon her wilderness work, her journey in the forests of the Wachusett "in the midst of thousands of enemies" where her experiences set her off from her Puritan peers.[98] While she had then doubted "that ever I should be satisfied with bread again," her awful experience in the Wachusett had served to privilege her and her narrative, "but now, we are fed *with the finest of Wheat*." Her enterprising struggle for survival and her unceasing mourning of lost relatives allowed Rowlandson to break through her culture's dominant mode of representation. Rowlandson's *Sovereignty and Goodness of God* got away from the ministers' designs. The captivity narrative shaped and promoted an American rhetoric of self-creation that was uniquely created by women as the genre developed in the next century and a half. The subsuming of the *type* by the *real* exploded the binary categories of Puritan ideology in this one narrative and increasingly led to a more ambiguous rendering of the wilderness. "In the process, the logic of the captivity figure helped to transform the Puritan colonists' image of the American wilderness," according to the literary historian Tara Fitzpatrick, "from a savage wasteland haunted by demonic adversaries to the 'fresh, green breast' from which European settlers might draw their virtuous sustenance."[99]

English settlers in the Wachusett would utilize the conventions of self-righteousness contained in Rowlandson's narrative, this document of Puritan typology, to ward off the continued Indian blows during a half-century of warfare in the region. But they also took to heart its more subversive promise of personal salvation in the wilderness. The narrative figure of Mary Rowlandson, created in an effort to maintain communal boundaries, instead transgressed them and legitimated individual ventures into the wilderness. In eighteenth-century sermons and orations, the frontier became less a token of the New England spiritual pilgrimage than the locus of political strife during the European wars of empire. Frontier settlements shielded eastern towns; Cotton Mather praised their residents for their heroism, rather than scorning them for being beyond "the Hedge" of settlement. In the next generation, as the locals moved from warding off Indian attacks to mounting offensive sorties in the north, local historians celebrated Indian fighters as the new heroes.

Lancaster is an unusual but significant place to begin a New England history. Historians have used the coastal peoples' experiences—both Indian and English—to conceptualize life in seventeenth-century New England. Inland, things were different. The English residents of the Wachusett, fifty miles from the bay with the Nashaways as their only neighbors, were far from the center of New England's dominant social and religious practice. It is important to see the Indians and English together and to think about the history of New England as an interdependent experience, for that was how life was lived along both sides of the inland frontier. Without the prevailing models of the coastal peoples, the people of the Wachusett improvised in their interactions and in their construction of community. Their inland position gave them more time and freedom for those efforts. Historians have recently reacquainted us with the importance of commercial activity for the growth of the Puritan Commonwealth, revising the previous emphasis on religious motives. That commercial orientation should not be overstated. Town founders in Massachusetts Bay were entrepreneurs from the very start of settlement; however, the hegemonic social and cultural structures of Puritan life pushed towns and townspeople toward the center, severely constraining outliers—whether people or places. Even Lancaster—despite its origins as a mining camp and trading post established by suspect entrepreneurs and religious reformers and, later, as a frontier town neglected by the colonial magistrates and scorned by the leading clerics—became a community of families and farms.

2 "Indian-Fighters" and Town Founders: The Resettlement of the Wachusett, 1675–1725

> I hope the Reader will pass a favourable Censure upon an Old Soldier, yet telling of the many Rancounters he had led, and yet to come off alive. It is a pleasure to Remember what a great Number of Families in this and the Neighboring Provinces in New-England did during the War, enjoy a great measure of Liberty and Peace by the hazardous Stations and Marches of those Engaged in Military Exercises, who were a Wall unto them on this side and on that side.
>
> Benjamin Church,
> *Entertaining Passages Relating to Metacom's War* (1715)

Colonel Benjamin Church—land speculator, military hero, and author—wrote a history of Metacom's War that occasionally mentioned acts of "divine providence," but the focus of which was Church himself. He wrote history that departed from the tales of ministers and ministers' wives who emphasized "afflictions" endured by pious Puritans, giving instead enthusiastic accounts of town founding and Indian fighting.[1]

Church had been born at Plymouth in 1639, the son of a carpenter, and he pursued his father's trade in several towns. Both father and son were active town founders. They relocated several times, took up claims in new settlements, built houses and cleared farms, and then sold out to newcomers and sought opportunities on newer frontiers. The onset of Metacom's War found Church beyond the bounds of English settlement, the only white settler at Sogkonate, near the Rhode Island border.

> For in the year 1675 that unhappy and bloody Indian War broke out in Plymouth Colony, where I was then building, and beginning a Plantation, at a Place called by the English, Little Compton. I was the first English Man that built upon the Neck, which was full of Indians. My head and hands were full about setting a New Plantation, where nothing was brought to; no preparation of Dwelling House, or Out-Housing or Fencing made. Horses and Cattel were

to be provided, Ground to be clear'd and broken up; and the uttermost Caution to be used, to keep my self free from offending my Indian neighbors.

Church's arduous labors were interrupted by a military commission sent from Plymouth. Enlisting the local Indians, he adopted the native style of warfare to improve English military fortunes. The cessation of hostilities and the removal of Indians from southern New England allowed Church to exploit opportunities around New England; he founded several new settlements and pursued the remaining rebel Indians in Maine.[2]

At the close of this colorful career in 1715, Church dictated his "Entertaining Passages" to his son, Samuel. Church offered his own story as the centerpiece of a narrative related "to the Former and Later Wars of New-England, which I myself was not a little concerned in." His description of the conflict, despite asides to the "almighty power," focused on the foibles of the English commanders and the valor of the fighting soldiers, both Indian and English, while the figure of Church, stalking like a native through the forest, dominated the story of "hazardous Stations and Marches." In his informal autobiographical sketch, Church remembers the "pleasures not afflictions" that the war provided; as he invoked the Mathers' familiar image of the wall or "hedge" to protect civilization from nature, he left no doubt that this barrier was the product of human endeavor, not divine decree.[3] Church's pioneer work in combining town founding and Indian fighting was taken up by a new generation. These settlers ventured into a contested borderland after Metacom's War, well beyond the hedge of the older core settlements, and continued to people the landscape, founding towns during an era of intermittent Indian and French warfare.

Indian fighters became the town founders and culture heroes of the early eighteenth century. The people of the Wachusett had pushed the remaining native population of New England well back from settled areas and founded new frontier towns on the borders of the colony. But a successful resettlement after the devastation of Metacom's War was followed by several more decades of warfare, which slowed the pace of expansion as settlers were periodically driven back to eastern towns. Challenges and conflicts erupted in and around Lancaster. These settler-soldiers followed Benjamin Church's example, however, and they marched into the wilderness armed for combat. Indian fighting became a popular enterprise. Colonization accompanied warfare for the generation of settlers that followed Metacom's War. (See map 9.) At the close of a half-century of conflict, local historians chose Indian fighters as their new culture heroes.

War and Colonization

War as part of daily life is not what comes to mind when we think about colonial New England, but it was a constant experience for New England

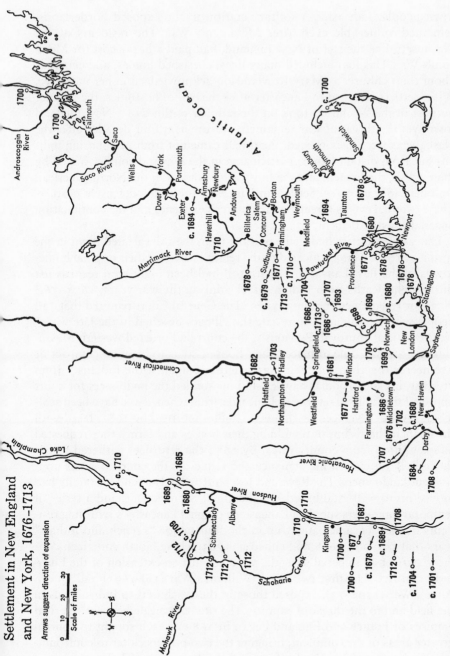

Settlement in New England and New York, 1676–1713

Arrows suggest direction of expansion

Scale of miles
0   10   20   30

Map 9. Settlement in New England and New York, 1676–1713. New England expanded as town founders resettled frontier townships and then moved into the borderlands after Metacom's War; the potential for conflict increased between French, English, and Indian. Colonists moved up the river valleys—the Connecticut River and Hudson River—and along the coast of Maine as demographic pressure built up in the older towns. (Reprinted from Douglas Edward Leach, *The Northern Colonial Frontier, 1607–1763* [New York, 1966], p. 116. By permission of the University of New Mexico Press. Courtesy of Cornell University Libraries.)

townspeople. Lancaster, a solitary station in the exposed borderlands, remained vulnerable even after Metacom's War. The residents of the Wachusett, like the rest of New England, had paid a heavy cost for Metacom's War. This loss included many lives, cherished homes, and certitude about their culture, as Mary Rowlandson acknowledged in her narrative. When settlers returned to Lancaster after the end of hostilities, the frontier outpost in the Wachusett took on the familiar outlines of a New England town, yet the threat of war remained. For the next four decades after the Nashaways were dispossessed, the threat came not from neighboring Indians but from distant bands, participants in the imperial conflict waged by the English, the French, and the Indians for control of the North American continent (See map 10). Settlers in Lancaster took on a defensive posture. These external events threatened Lancaster's existence and the continuation of serial town settlement.[4]

Lancaster's settlers had fled eastward from their devastated town in the spring of 1676. Many relocated to the relative safety of their original hometowns in the Bay. Lancaster's death toll had been high; vital records list thirty-eight deaths from Indian attacks during the war years, 1675–76.[5] Plans for resettlement began in 1679. The General Court required that "all people who are intended to resetle the villages deserted in the late warr" receive official approval. Previously, the court had ordered western Massachusetts townspeople to place "their houses, so as to be more compact & live neerer together, for their better deffence against the Indians." John Prescott, his son, Thomas Sawyer, and his son led the petitioners for court approval that fall "to returne to Lancaster from whence wee have been scattered." About seventeen or eighteen families returned by 1681; faced with the financial hardships of rebuilding their houses and farms, they requested an exemption from county rates. By 1684 the returnees gathered to tax themselves for church maintenance and requested the court to assess nonresident landowners. The Reverend Joseph Rowlandson and his family had moved on to well-established Weathersfield, Connecticut, and a series of temporary ministers supplied Lancaster's pulpit.[6] Lancaster's returning residents quickly became caught up in the four major "French and Indian" wars that began in 1688 and ended in 1763. These North American conflicts, part of an imperial struggle, were not just an extension of the European conflict. The first two, King William's War (1689–97) and Queen Anne's War (1702–13), exposed those in the Wachusett to Indian raids in the field and to the threat of capture. The titanic struggle between the rival empires of France and England began in 1689 as each sought to control greater areas of the continent, bringing the two powers closer to confrontation and diminishing the buffer zone between them. The accession of William and Mary of Orange to the English throne in the Glorious Revolution of 1688 brought England into the War of the League of Augsburg against France.[7]

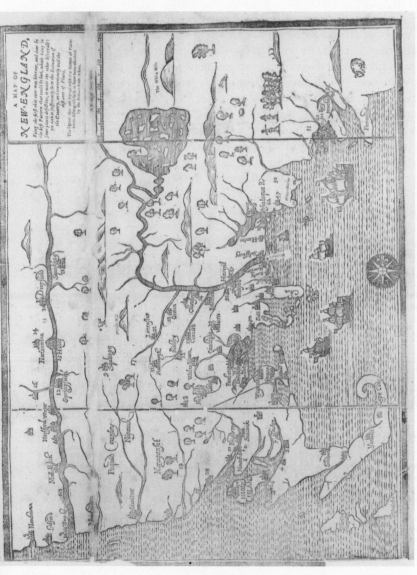

Map 10. John Foster's map of New England. This map accompanied Hubbard's history of Metacom's War. The map, basically a war map, showed the extent of colonization at the onset of the war and indicated those English communities "assaulted by the Indians" (Lancaster appears as 21). In contrast to Wood's earlier map, Indian towns and villages no longer appear as part of New England, even though Foster's focus is directed west into the inland areas of Massachusetts Bay, a region where the defeated Nashaways and other Indians had lived. (Reprinted from William Hubbard, *A Narrative of the Troubles with the Indians in New-England* . . . [Boston, 1677]. Courtesy of the American Antiquarian Society.)

In North America the Iroquois had already lashed out at the French even before the European conflict erupted. The Iroquois, linked to the English by the "Covenant Chain," wanted to maintain their strategic position between the two rival European colonial powers; they struck French settlers close to Montreal as well as Indians allied with the French. In turn, French-backed Indian warriors attacked English towns along the Connecticut River valley in the summer of 1688. As word of Europe's war arrived in the summer of 1689, each side planned major campaigns against the enemy's center of settlement. The new French governor, Frontenac, aimed to conquer New York; as winter approached he attacked the northern English frontier—the upper Hudson, New Hampshire, and coastal Maine. This three-pronged offensive created panic across New England. The English colonists responded quickly with a more united front and an offensive of their own, unlike their initial response in Metacom's War. Sir William Phips led an expedition against French Acadia and captured Port Royal on the west coast of Nova Scotia. But the invasion of Quebec failed, and King William's War degenerated into a war of Indian raids similar to Metacom's War. French-allied Indians with coureurs de bois struck English towns, travelling far across the borderlands. Indians from northern New England joined these attacks. Their ranks included Nipmucs and groups from other tribes that had been defeated in the previous Indian war and dispersed to the north in the Algonquian diaspora. Residents of interior towns such as Lancaster and Deerfield were once again embattled.[8]

Peace vanished in the Wachusett, and intermittent warfare generated constant fear. Captain Francis Nicholson reported in Lancaster that "the people were very much afraid"; they apparently took little resolve from Nicholson's hearty charge "that they had the happinesse of being subjects of a victorious King who could protect them from all their enemies." Distant British military power offered faint protection for isolated "out towns" like Lancaster. The news about the European conflict only intensified settlers' fears about the peril of "being surprised by the Indians." After they addressed the colonial authorities in Boston in July of 1689, the governor and General Court approved new militia officers and sent a small scouting party.[9]

Settlers adapted to life on the besieged frontier; they created a new form of compact settlement, with certain costs picked up by the colony as the price for their exposed position. "The settlement of a new country could never be effected," Thomas Hutchinson wrote, "if the inhabitants should confine themselves to cities or walled towns." So they gathered together in garrisons, a residential pattern to which Lancaster's residents adhered for the next generation. Hutchinson described this new form:

> in every frontier settlement there were more or less garrison houses, some with a flankart at two opposite angles, others at each corner of the house; some

houses surrounded with pallisades, others, which were smaller, built with square timber, one piece laid horizontally upon another, and loop holes in every side of the house; and, besides these, generally in any more considerable plantation, there was one principal garrison house, capable of containing soldiers sent for the defense of the plantation and the families near, whose homes were not fortified.[10]

These fortified dwellings provided for a greater level of defense than the ordinary farmhouse for settlements under attack. Fortifications varied, as Hutchinson made clear, but most had massive doors, shuttered windows, and ample water or sand to put out fires. Colonists could shoot at their attackers through windows and special firing ports, or "loop holes" in the walls of the structure. Indians would not accept heavy casualties in direct assaults on well-defended houses, and the threat of outside relief prevented lengthy sieges. Defensive measures saved numerous English lives. However, garrison occupants often watched helplessly as their homes and fields went up in smoke. Lancaster's garrisons filled up with returning and new settlers. John Prescott's and Joseph Rowlandson's prewar fortified posts were joined by six additional stockades.[11]

The town's two hundred and fifty settlers lived with the fear of Indian attack and the hardships of garrison life. Many wanted to flee the Wachusett, reported the local commander, Major Thomas Henchman, when local hunters sighted a company of about three hundred Indians near Mount Wachusett in the summer of 1692. He beseeched his superiors for reinforcements. The day's hard work at farming rendered his sentries unfit for the night's constant garrison duty, but he feared they would be "made a sacrifice" if they returned to their homes. His fears proved well founded when Peter Joslin returned from his fields to find his wife and three children slain by Indian raiders and his wife's sister and another son taken captive. Such events continued to make life in the frontier treacherous for years: in 1695, Abraham Wheeler was ambushed at his distant homestead when he returned from garrison duty. Jonathan Houghton's 1694 petition to the court for assistance listed the heavy burdens of life on the borders of English settlement: the memory of the past destructive war with the Indians, the recent violent deaths in town, and the constant necessity of remaining sequestered in garrisons "where neither men nor women can doe but very little towards the support of their family," while getting bread required putting their lives in peril. They had become impoverished by rebuilding their town after Metacom's War, and their scanty resources were going to maintain the town's numerous garrisons.[12]

The war in Europe came to an inconclusive end with the Treaty of Ryswick, signed on September 30, 1697. Skirmishing in the North American borderlands dragged on. A general assault on Lancaster, feared for so long, finally took place after formal hostilities ceased. The town's new minister, John Whiting, and twenty-five other settlers were killed, five settlers were taken captive, and two garrison homes were lost. The remaining residents again turned to the court, lamenting that the "heathen Indian enemy" had killed so many "in a cruel and barbarous manner" and took away their minister, and they requested military and financial assistance to repair from the losses of "such a Wasting, and desolating War."[13]

Neither the war nor the subsequent uneasy peace resolved the conflict. King William's War was the prelude for the series of eighteenth-century French and Indian wars that terrorized settlers along the frontiers of British North America—both north and south. The English outposts lay open to attack and destruction, and their residents were slain and captured. The strategy of the colonists shifted from defensive actions in their settlements to making offensive forays into the wilderness, a lesson New Englanders had learned in Metacom's War. English and Indians participated in joint raiding parties, a lesson borrowed from the French. Frontier residents in Lancaster learned to protect the settlement through defensive measures while simultaneously founding new towns out in the borderlands.[14]

When Queen Anne's War broke out in Europe in the spring of 1702, peace along the New England frontier rested upon the eastern Indians' and the Iroquois' professed neutrality. The Iroquois, formerly the staunch allies of the English, but now disillusioned after heavy losses inflicted by the French, withdrew to the sidelines in the Anglo-French imperial confrontation. Iroquois neutrality prevented New France from threatening New York, so New England bore the brunt of French and Indian attack. As long as French border raids threatened Deerfield, Lancaster, and other exposed settlements, the war was defensive in character, intended to preoccupy English colonial authorities with their own frontier and forestall any invasion of Canada. Raids on the Maine towns of Wells and Saco alarmed all of New England, especially the frontier towns.[15]

Frontier settlers withdrew again from their homes and fields into the relative safety of the garrison houses. The attack on Deerfield, the northwesternmost Massachusetts town, in the winter of 1703 demonstrated the dangers of living in the borderlands. An unusually large force of two to three hundred French and Indians—regular army and coureurs de bois, Mohawk and Abenaki warrior—swept across three hundred miles of snow-covered forests and ice-bound riverways to stage a well-planned surprise attack. Inside the palisaded fort the residents and garrison soldiers slept. In the raid, 56 English died and 109 were captured—almost three-fifths of the town's population. The Deerfield minister's family was dragged off, initiating a lengthy drama played out across the English-Indian-French border and inspiring a famous Puritan captivity narrative, *The Redeemed Captive*. All New England lay in shock after the assault on the Connecticut River towns. Cotton Mather's graphic writing focused on the dangers of living on the margins of English society: "Ever now and then, we hear of some, who in Planting their *Corn,* alas, have their *Fields watr'd with their Blood:* Some, who while *Mowing their Grass,* are Cut down by the *Scythe* of a *Bloody Death:* Some, who stepping forth to look their *Cattel,* have themselves become *Sheep for the Slaughter."* [16]

The French and their Indian allies dictated the battlefield in both Queen Anne's War and King William's War by making sudden offensive strikes. Gathered behind their palisades, the English settlers placed themselves in a defensive posture. The garrison house, privately constructed and operated, but available as a public refuge, remained at the core of the system of town defense. And the New England town served as the essential source of military personnel and the unit of organization. Lancaster's eleven small forts were scattered around the town. Colonial military officers commanded the soldiers and families under their protection. Massachusetts reported nineteen hundred soldiers stationed in frontier towns to reinforce the local citizenry by the summer of 1704. The court threatened those residing in certain designated frontier towns with harsh penalties for withdrawal, to prevent any rollback of the settlement line as had occurred in Metacom's War. Each town was required to raise a company of men between the ages of sixteen and sixty to serve in the local militia, the backbone of the colony's military force. Troops held training exercises in town a few days a year, practicing close-order drill and other staples of European battlefield tactics. The New England militia system, rooted in local town life, proved far more potent in fielding a fighting force than its Chesapeake counterpart; the critical difference, the historian John Shy writes, was that "the clustering of manpower and the cohesive atmosphere in the town community gave New England greater military strength." [17]

Colonial leaders pursued more offensive policies to prosecute the war and combat Indian raids. English soldiers tracked down hostile Indians in search-and-destroy missions, and called for volunteers to range beyond the line of settlement to search "all the Usuall places of the Indians abode." The government offered bounties for scalps: ten pounds for a scalp to an impressed soldier in the regular service, twenty pounds to a volunteer, and fifty pounds to a volunteer serving without pay during Queen Anne's War. Benjamin Church advanced along the Atlantic coast and threatened French settlements; but his threat to let loose a thousand Indians upon the Canadian frontiers to commit "barbarities upon poor helpless women and children," as the French-allied Indians had done in Deerfield, came to naught. Major offensives against Nova Scotia and Quebec failed dismally. [18]

Skirmishing at the outsettlements marked Queen Anne's War. Seven hundred French and Indians descended from Canada in the summer of 1704; one group aimed at Northampton, but with reports that the English were "thick as the trees in the woods," they assaulted Lancaster instead. The attack fell upon six garrisons, but the town's defenses held, fortified by the colony's garrison troops, until assistance came. The enemy's losses were heavy. As the raiders retreated, they burned Lancaster's meetinghouse and substantial numbers of dwellings and livestock. In late October alarm rose again with the ambush of a Lancaster traveler on his way to Groton. Residents of the Reverend Gardner's garrison searched for the reported party of Indians near Simon Willard's remote Still River village on the town's outskirts. They returned without any sign of the enemy, and the Reverend Andrew Gardner, who had taken over his slain predecessor's house and lands, stood watch that evening while the weary scouts slept. When he left the watch house to warm himself by the fire, he inadvertently awakened a man who, "surprised with an excess of fear," fired upon the minister. Gardner stumbled through the door and died within the hour. Lancaster again had no minister. The town appealed to the General Court, supplying graphic details of garrison life. "Near half our time . . . [was] spent in actual service . . . by ranging the woods after when Rumours and Alarms have happened." Constant patrols gave settlers "little peace day or night," and many had been "greatly impoverished" by Indian raids. The court again abated the town's taxes and supplied forty pounds toward rebuilding the meetinghouse.[19]

The condition of war reoriented the town defensively. Many settlers relocated on their second division lots eastward of the town's exposed western flank. The old village cluster yielded its preeminent position to newer settlements that appeared alongside the increasing number of garrisons. War, however, did not stem the growth of the town. Lancaster's residents held their station and even increased their numbers during wartime. Population rose from both natural increase and migration. There were seventeen families in Lancaster after Metacom's War; by 1688 there were fifty families, or about 275 residents; and by 1708 (during Queen Anne's War) the population passed its pre–Metacom's War totals of approximately 300 to 350. The town's population increased by a phenomenal 35 percent over the next three years (see table 2). By 1711 the population stood at 458.[20]

Changes can also be seen in the housing, reflecting the rebuilding of the town and its expansion under military siege. What little is known about prewar Lancaster's homes indicates the typical seventeenth-century single-story dwellings had one or two rooms. The town's destruction was complete in Metacom's War; as the settlers returned, they rebuilt sturdier and more substantial homes that were clustered on the eastern side. One of the first to resettle, John White Jr., a prosperous farmer, built on the Neck. Although the irregular window placement suggests an early, small building, the completed structure was a large double-pile house (that is, one that is two rooms deep) with five bays. Other two-story structures went up in the Still River neighborhood on the second division lands to the east, houses such as Henry Willard's double-pile structure, which only later reached full size through the addition of a lean-to on the rear of the house and other elements (see plate 1). About 1685 Benjamin Willard built an end-chimney,

Table 2. Lancaster and its garrison families, 1676–1711

Year	Garrisons	Families	Polls	Soldiers	Residents
1676	2	50			300–350
1682		17–18			100
1688		50			275
1692	8			74	
1704	11			95	
1708			79		356
1711	27	83			458

Sources: (1676) Abijah R. Marvin, *History of the Town of Lancaster* (Lancaster, 1879), p. 156; (1682) Joseph Willard, *An Address in Commemoration of the 200th Anniversary of the Incorporation of Lancaster* (Boston, 1853), p. 100; (1688) Willard, *Address*, p. 102; (1692) "Manuscript Garrison List," printed in Henry Stedman Nourse, *Lancastriana: A Supplement to the Early Records and Military Annals of Lancaster, Massachusetts* (Lancaster, 1900), p. 23; (1704) "Garrison List," printed in Marvin, *Lancaster*, p. 156; (1708) Willard, *Address*, p. 101; (1711) "Garrison List," Massachusetts Archives 71:876, printed in Henry Stedman Nourse, *Early Records of Lancaster, Massachusetts, 1643–1725* (Lancaster, 1884), p. 173.

Note: A blank means no information available.

three-bay saltbox with a lean-to that faced west towards the Nashua River valley, but its entry was on the southern face opposite its massive chimney. At the close of the century, Caleb Sawyer, the grandson of John Prescott, built a moderately sized one-story house, a form more typical in the next century, with its more open asymmetrical room plan, its chimney off-center and not aligned with the entry leading into the front room (see plate 2). These middling family dwellings, built at the turn of the century, had small, open plans without formal entry lobbies, often constructed in stages from smaller core structures.[21]

War brought numerous hardships to the Wachusett: raids on isolated homesteads, constant scouting expeditions, and strained resources from support of garrisoned troops. Lancaster's residents suffered heavily from the generation of Indian warfare that began with Metacom's War. Ephraim Roper Jr., for example, was twelve in 1676 when the Rowlandson house burned down and he was the only male to escape. His father, Ephraim Roper Sr., lost his first wife at that time, but he, too, his second wife, and their new daughter were killed in 1697, leaving only the one surviving son.

Fear of Indian capture loomed larger than death for English settlers convinced of the rectitude of their Protestant faith and the absolute errors of the papist French or heathen Indians. Many were captured from Lancaster, however, Mary Rowlandson being only the first and most famous. Later captives ended up further north than Rowlandson, in French hands in Canada. In King William's War, Elizabeth Howe and her son Peter were taken from her sister's house to Canada. Redeemed four years later for a ransom, Howe returned to Marlborough. The 1697 raid spirited away eight

Plate 1. Henry Willard house, Lancaster, Massachusetts, built in 1680s, photographed about 1893. Henry Willard returned to the destroyed town of Lancaster and built this two-story, double-pile house on his eastern second division lands. Willard's house grew as the town was rebuilt; its unusual six-bay front suggests an original three-bay core. A lean-to was added to the rear of the structure. (Reprinted from Henry S. Nourse, *History of the Town of Harvard, Massachusetts* [Harvard, Mass., 1894], p. 83. Courtesy of the Library of Congress.)

Plate 2. Caleb Sawyer house, Westminster, Massachusetts, drawn about 1893. In the 1690s Caleb Sawyer, the grandson of Nashaway pioneer John Prescott, built a moderately sized one-story house with an off-center chimney and an entry that led directly into the front room. These more open and asymmetrical three-room vernacular houses became increasingly common in the eighteenth century. (Reprinted from Henry S. Nourse, *History of the Town of Harvard, Massachusetts* [Harvard, Mass., 1894], p. 35. Courtesy of the Library of Congress.)

more people. Three of the eight returned to Lancaster by 1699. The other five vanished and were never heard from again.

Captives were part of the three-way contest of cultures in the Northeast among Indians, French, and English. The capture of New Englanders added to French and Indian numbers and struck a symbolic blow against the New England errand into the wilderness. The French and Indian populations were not only smaller in size but also at a demographic disadvantage compared with the rapidly rising numbers of English settlers. The French, therefore, intended to keep their English captives, and with Indian aid, they abducted large numbers of English settlers, hoping to convert them to Catholicism, naturalize them as French citizens, and increase the ranks of the habitants of New France. The English responded by seizing French soldiers in battle and then exchanging them for English civilians.[22] Indians with a developed taste for trade goods captured English settlers for the hefty ransoms available from the French authorities, rather than the traditional purpose of adoption into their own communities as replacements for those warriors lost in battle.

Other types of exchanges were also effected to obtain the return of the settlers. In 1705 Samuel Sewall recorded more "bad news" from Lancaster: "Three men carried away from Mr. Sawyers Sawmill." Thomas Sawyer, his son Elias, and John Bigelow, a carpenter from Marlborough, were captured by Indians and taken off to Canada. Upon reaching Montreal Sawyer shrewdly "observed to the French Governor, that on the River Chamblee was a fine site for mills; and that he would build a sawmill for him, provided he would procure a ransom for himself, his son and Bigelow." Governor Vaudreuil readily agreed to the bargain for sawmills were scarce in Canada. The Indians, anxious for European goods, sold Elias Sawyer and John Bigelow to the French, but they wanted to retain the miller to punish him for fatally shooting several Indians during the Lancaster raid. Tied to a stake and surrounded by kindling, Thomas Sawyer was rescued by a French friar who, according to an eighteenth-century local historian, "held forth what he declared to be the key to the gates of Purgatory." He told the Indians that "unless they immediately released their prisoner, he would instantly unlock those gates, and send them headlong thereinto." This successful intervention released Sawyer to build the mill. He completed it within a year; Elias remained another year to provide instructions on operating it. Over the next twenty years, five more captured millers built sawmills along the St. Lawrence River to obtain their release. Canada possessed nineteen mills in 1719. An English visitor counted twelve mills built between Trois Rivieres and Quebec alone that were constructed on English models.[23]

Craftsmen were scarce in Canada and could command good wages for their services. Many captives stayed on after the cessation of hostilities to pursue these opportunities; as one English blacksmith was advised, "you can get a rich living there." But few were as valuable as millers, who could purchase their freedom with their skills. Between 1675 and 1769, at least 1,641 New Englanders were captured, about 300 in each of the first three wars and 500 in the French and Indian War. Many never returned to New England; only 46 percent definitely came back. Of the substantial numbers held in French Canada, almost one-half chose to remain. Young women were the most susceptible to conversion. Captives—most of them young men and women—who became Canadians, according to ethnohistorian James Axtell, very often did so out of love. Elias Sawyer returned from his ordeal bearing a colorful plate that, according to old stories, was the gift of a young Indian woman whom he had promised to return to and marry (although once he was surrounded by his kinsmen and neighbors, it is explained, he retracted his promise). Even if this particular tale is apocryphal, Indian captors did succeed in luring many New Englanders into remaining and choosing their way of life after hostilities ended, as exemplified by Eunice Williams, the most famous captive of Queen Anne's War, whose story was popularized by her father's narrative, *The Redeemed Captive,* which held all New England transfixed.[24]

By 1707 the war began to pass by the people of the Wachusett. Lancaster's militia responded quickly that year to a surprise attack on Marlborough and encountered the raiders at Weshakim. For these citizen-soldiers, Showanon's long-empty village would become known as the site of the "Indian Fight." The early settlers had known the Nashaways at Weshakim as neighboring villagers. Ironically, Lancaster's last Indian attack in 1711 killed an Indian servant working in the fields while the settlers escaped to the garrison.[25]

Eighteenth-century residents of the region, who had had no sustained contact with Indians for two decades, began to perceive all Indians as barbarous foes. Twenty-one soldiers were stationed in Lancaster's twenty-seven garrisons while the local militia undertook patrols around the Wachusett in search of Indian raiders in 1711. Three years later they located a small band of Indians living at Weshakim who were stealing settlers' corn and were a "Terror to the women and children." Local military leaders were "directed to find out and Spake with the said Indians," to determine their identity, and "to treat them civilly and to forbid their committing any further Disorder."

Joint colonial and British military expeditions in 1709 and 1711 to seize Quebec ended in frustrating failure, and the New England soldiers crept back to their towns. The failed Canadian invasions and protracted border warfare extracted a heavy price. The exhausted belligerents in both Europe and North America came to peace in April 1713. The Treaty of Utrecht marked a turning point in the struggle for European domination of the continent. British territorial gains in the West Indies, along Hudson Bay, and in Acadia represented possibilities for the expansion of New England settlement.[26]

Colonizing Nipmuc Country

Peace launched colonists into the borderlands. In the Wachusett, settlers had returned to Lancaster during a quarter-century of external threats, continuing the process of serial town settlement. Colonists had dramatically increased their population and devised a garrison mode of town settlement. But their simultaneous defensive posture and expansive mode brought further conflicts—both imperial and internal—that engulfed the townspeople of Lancaster. Conflicts and contradictions in the institutions governing town founding required creative but conservative adaptation of customary strategies to changed conditions.

Members of the colonial elite turned their attention from prosecuting hostilities against the Nashaways, Nipmucs, Narragansetts, and other Indian peoples to acquiring large tracts of their land along the inland Massachusetts frontier for the purpose of founding towns. Joseph Dudley led the effort: as president of the Dominion of New England, he organized towns and confirmed Indian land transfers in the outer reaches of Massachusetts Bay in 1686; as governor of Massachusetts, he built forts that advanced settlement in northern New England in the 1700s; and as town proprietor, he helped to found numerous inland communities in central Massachusetts just south of the Wachusett. The General Court appointed Dudley and William Stoughton to study Indian titles in Nipmuc country after several Nipmucs contested English land takeovers in central Massachusetts in May 1681. Dudley and Stoughton, with John Eliot as their interpreter, met some remaining Indians in Cambridge. They persuaded these former occupants to transfer to the colony title to a vast region of Nipmuc country, a tract of about a one thousand square miles, for fifty pounds, a coat, and a twenty-five-mile tract for their new home. The committee found "the best land, most meadowed and capable of settlement" in north central Massachusetts, but no action was taken to promote its colonization. Initiative for settlement passed to those settlers located in the Wachusett.[27]

Several Lancaster notables purchased a twelve-mile-square area from John and James Wiser of Natick, from Indians who had served as English spies during Metacom's War, and from three other Christian Indians. George Tahanto, the Nashaways' remaining representative and a nephew of Showanon, conveyed the land between the western end of Lancaster and the "Wachusett Hills" to English settlers in 1701. Showanon's station at Weshakim, the original Nashaway village in the Wachusett, became English property. Tahanto displayed his familiarity with English legal conventions and the history of English-Nashaway land transactions. He recounted the twelve pounds paid initially to Showanon for the purchase of Nashaway and the forty-six shillings given to James Wiser. John Houghton and Nathaniel Wilder would pay him eighteen pounds "to have and to hold [the lands] forever." Tahanto undertook to secure a General Court survey of the grant's bounds and fill out the necessary deeds and conveyances.[28]

At the close of Queen Anne's War in 1711 numerous townspeople organized to develop the forty-square-mile tract called "the Additional Grant." They covenanted together to share equally in the considerable costs of development. They petitioned the court to confirm the grant since "considerable money" had "been paid to George Tahanto and other Indians." The court approved in 1713, making Lancaster's total area almost one hundred and fifty square miles. This new land company, a separate society to hold and dispose of town land, did not depart sharply from earlier modes of town formation in the seventeenth century. All the various types of town foundings—individuals receiving a grant, land companies carving out single townships, towns budding off—all required New Englanders to form an organization of individuals who owned the land, issued shares, distributed land, engaged in the other necessary details of settlement, and shared in the costs of developing the plantation. A committee of the Lancaster subscribers allotted forty acres of the best ground to each share.[29]

But this new largesse created conflict within a town just beginning to enjoy peace. The Additional Grant's proprietary ranks were exclusive: ninety-nine individuals had bound themselves to contribute to the costs of the purchase and in turn to receive shares in the land grant. The owners of the original grant rights numbered far more, while other Lancaster landowners did not share in subsequent land divisions. But this new land promised to open opportunities for families to settle their kin nearby and so attracted claimants other than the Additional Grant investors, highlighting the overlapping corporate bodies within Lancaster. Twelve nonresidents holding original grants in the Nashaway Plantation demanded their "Just Rights" in the Additional Grant in 1716 based on the passage of those grants down to them. But they made their appeal to the proprietorship, the institution responsible for land divisions in eighteenth-century Lancaster, itself a new corporate body that had emerged to meet the challenge posed by the new imperial scrutiny of the New England town and its land policy.[30]

In Lancaster, as with other towns, the original undertakers (grantees) in the plantation had been shareholders, able to receive home lots and initial divisions from the common land based on their shares. Those undertakers passed their rights down to heirs or transferred them by sale to purchasers. Other land was sold to sojourners (residents of the town), who held no shares in the common fund of land.

Historians of New England have shown that several distinct but overlapping communities constituted the towns of New England. In his historical study of the proprietorship, John Martin has envisioned three concentric circles. The largest circle includes all town residents. The middle one includes inhabitants with the franchise and perhaps some stake in land divisions. The smallest circle, representing the most exclusive group, comprises the proprietors, resident and nonresident, who owned the majority of the town's lands and controlled the political sphere as well.[31]

The mixed public and private nature of the seventeenth-century town corporation confused the issue for people at the time (as it has for later historians). Lancaster and its selectmen conducted the land corporation's business—the private matters of allocating land rights and adjudicating property claims—alongside the public work of education, defense, and taxation. Townspeople disputed matters of land, taxes, and the franchise because the town's role as an exclusive private institution clashed with its more open, public function. Lancaster resolved the Additional Grant land conflict by creating *two* proprietorships, clearly restricting entry to those with recognizable claims to membership in the respective bodies. Lancaster's proprietors met to consider the nonresidents' petition; they resolved that the original proprietary group "had no right nor interest in said Land purchased of ye Indians." Instead, "the Inhabitants of Lancaster" who purchased the Nipmuc land were "set off as a proprietary," a separate group, with their "proper Right to order. Divide, Improve, and dispose" of their land as they saw fit.

Lancaster's town records show that residents and proprietors had begun meeting as distinct bodies in the previous year, 1716. Throughout New England, the institution of the proprietorship legally separated from the town government during the period from 1685 to 1720 because of new imperial challenges to the New England town, a challenge that emerged during the 1680s. Edmund Andros, governor-general of the new Dominion of New England, threatened the land system, which was the material basis of town life, and so the New England town itself. Andros declared invalid those land titles not based on the king's own grant, placing most New England land grants in jeopardy. Further, he held that towns had assumed unwarranted powers by granting land, conducting land divisions, and holding common land. Towns were not legal corporations under English law and had no authority to hold town meetings. As Andros informed Lynn residents: "There was no such thing as a *Town* in the Country."[32]

New England townspeople responded to this challenge by transferring title from the town as a shareholders' community to particular residents known as proprietors, the owners of a town's undivided land. The General Court in 1692 charged that "the proprietors of the undivided or common lands within each town and precinct in this province . . . shall and hereby are impowered to order, improve or divide in such way and manner as shall be concluded and agreed upon by the major part of the interested, the voices to be collected and accounted according to the interests." Colonial legislators specified the proprietors' powers for managing lands, taxation, and meetings. In Lancaster, Joseph Wilder acted as the proprietor's clerk to consider land divisions and roads as well as church and school operations. At town meetings where John Houghton served as town clerk, town officials were selected. Since proprietors were distinct from townspeople, the Wachusett's venturesome conservatives had ingeniously met challenges to the town system by incorporating institutional innovation into the proprietary—the core institution of serial town settlement—when faced with the new imperial conditions in Massachusetts and the increased heterogeneity of local interests. These conservative adjustments were intended by the New Englanders to preserve their familiar town institutions and allow the land system to continue.[33]

Lancaster's successful defensive reorganization against Indian and imperial foes altered the institutional balance in town and caused conflicts to break out among the residents. When the Reverend Andrew Gardner arrived, the resumption of ministerial rates revealed the presence of a new settlement pattern and a division among different parts of town. Residents of Lancaster, even under the threat of attack, no longer huddled in a single place. The original cluster at George Hill had proved too difficult to defend, and those who resettled the town, both returning refugees and new arrivals, moved east to gather in the more secure end of town around the growing number of garrisons. Of the eleven garrisons in 1704, at least six lay east of the old town center at the confluence of the two branches of the Nashua. Josiah White's garrison was situated just over the waters on the east side of the Neck, while the others were far to the southeast of the enormous township, and Simon Willard's garrison was located close to the border with Groton in the Still River village. The two other garrisons were sited substantial distances north and south of the original center.[34]

Twenty-one petitioners, those remaining on Lancaster's original home lots at George Hill, the town center, united together. The original 1653 covenant levied a tax on home lots for the minister's maintenance because all early settlers held such lots. Half a century later, the petitioners claimed, "several of the sd [said] Inhabitants are removed" from those more exposed western lots, "which are left destitute and unimproved," and they relocated on eastern second-division lots, on which no rates were levied. The tax burden, the western petitioners argued, fell solely on their shoulders. The divided townspeople asked the House of Representatives in 1703 to readjust the rates, but the house instructed the inhabitants to follow the provincial tax.[35]

No sooner had this discord begun to subside than a more contentious and extended dispute broke out. The residents' successful appeal for General Court assistance in building a new meetinghouse revived the conflict along spatial lines in 1704. The town meeting agreed upon the structure's dimensions but disagreed on its location. The first two houses of worship had stood on George Hill, southeast of the cemetery, the site of the town center. But this site was inconvenient for the new settlers and younger sons who had moved east for safety and fresh supplies of land. A majority voted for an eastern site in 1706, but a vocal western minority supported rebuilding the meetinghouse "in its usual place." Subsequent meetings continued the debate but failed to reach any agreement. In a society that valued consensual politics, all the parties to the dispute, including the selectmen, petitioned the colonial authorities in Boston for assistance in resolving the controversy "to endeavor that peace with truth and equitie may be promoted amongst us."[36]

Both houses of the legislature heard the competing parties. The westerners claimed that the colony's security interests would be served by a western site for the church, parsonage, and burial ground, anchoring the remaining settlers "on the west and exposed side" as "a Guard to the others on this side as well as to themselves." The more numerous easterners pointed to the town's future in their June 1706 petition. History taught the perils of a western location, "having lost two [meetinghouses] already burnt by the enemy on that side." The majority had spoken in the town meeting; with two-thirds of the residents and lands on the east, "that side [not] only is, but forever is likely to be the biggest by far." The new settlement pattern demanded change.[37]

Both sides looked to Boston "to put a final end to the affair" and restore comity to the community, but Council and House of Representatives deadlocked. The Council held for the original site because the members recognized the value of frontier residents as a defensive barrier for the colony, which might overrule majority interests. The House of Representatives disagreed, given "the disasters that hath fallen" the west side, with "most of the first planters' children being removed to the eastside," and given the majority's vote at town meeting. The court ordered construction halted. These disputes in Lancaster and Boston held up completion of the new meetinghouse and restoration of the town's harmony for two long years. With the new structure's construction halted and the old one a burnt ruin, residents had to huddle together in the parsonage to hear the new minister, John Prentice. Only half of the congregation could crowd inside; the rest were "forced to stand abroad" in all sorts of weather.

Only the accession of a new generation to local leadership broke the deadlock. John Houghton, town clerk and community leader, wrote to the colonial authorities to resolve the matter. Houghton's father, an early subscriber to the 1653 covenant, had brought his family to a home lot on the west side of the Nashua. The elder Houghton had left Lancaster during Metacom's War; his sons resettled east of the town center. John, the eldest, served as schoolmaster, clerk, selectmen, assessor, and representative to the legislature. His tenure as town clerk lasted almost four decades, while he traveled to Boston as representative for fourteen years. He rose to the County Court of Common Pleas in 1718. His ascent to town leadership was representative of the significant shifts—both spatial and generational—within the town.[38]

Houghton resolved the crisis in 1708 when he offered land for the new meetinghouse. His brother Robert served as chief architect and builder, while Thomas Wilder donated the land opposite for the burial ground. Prentice, the new minister, was at the start of a four-decade-long ministry, and his parishioners renewed the Church covenant binding them "to walk in love one towards another."[39]

Thomas Wilder Jr., the son of the west-side pioneer Thomas Wilder Sr., had moved east with his brother. The Wilders' and Houghtons' attainment of leadership status signified the transmission of authority to a new generation. Resettlement under wartime conditions had shaped the community. Expansion splintered unity; more people, more garrisons, and more interests fractured the town's internal quiet and raised the call for the General Court to arbitrate. But the center held as a new generation devised new solutions. War became a distant threat; peace returned in town by 1710 and in New England as a whole by 1713. The people of the Wachusett had reorganized into garrison life to fend off French and Indian attacks, reconfigured their settlement's institutions to prevent imperial interference, and restored the town's consensual politics.

Indian Fighters

War and discord had not checked town settlement, as colonists learned to innovate and expand their local institutions in the decades after Metacom's War. During the French and Indian wars they had filled in the frontier towns, incorporated Nipmuc country into English hands, and were poised to move into the borderlands. After the Treaty of Utrecht in 1713 English settlers advanced into new areas. Settlement proceeded along several fronts: from the Wachusett migrants moved southeast to Worcester and northwest to new agricultural areas; in the Connecticut River valley, settlement activity extended beyond the Massachusetts border into New Hampshire and Vermont; towns were founded to the northeast of the Wachusett, in the Merrimack River valley; and finally, speculators attracted pioneers to towns in the lower Kennebec and Androscoggin River region.

Indians had been vanquished in southern New England, but in the outer, remote areas of northern New England, the peace of 1713 only meant a cold war for the French and their Abenaki allies, whom New Englanders called the Eastern Indians. When Governor Dummer's War broke out in 1722, the residents of the Wachusett no longer huddled in their garrisons. Instead, settlers joined scalping sorties in the far-off Maine woods, and Indian fighters became the town founders of the 1720s when the General Court granted new towns beyond Lancaster during wartime.[40]

When hostilities began in 1722 near Brunswick, a familiar pattern of sudden raids and constant terror again spread across the northern frontier. Indians boldly entered Lancaster fields in August to question settlers about the whereabouts of several of their comrades who had been apprehended near town and imprisoned in Boston. They approached a woman working alone, according to the account in the *New England Courant,* and "examined her," "cut off the Hair on one side of her Head," and carried her off. They eventually freed their captive, who, traumatized by her ordeal, fainted at the garrison upon her return. Once again threatened in their homes and fields, Lancaster's residents returned to their defensive posture, a stance familiar to many of the veterans of the previous frontier conflicts. But there were some significant differences in the leaders' response and settlers' attitudes during Dummer's War.[41]

Lancaster's leaders commanded the colonial military forces in central Massachusetts. They had ample experience in town defense and deep roots in serial town settlement in the Wachusett, and they drew upon this experience in their joint roles as Indian fighters and town founders in the 1720s. Sergeant Hartwell, like many of his neighbors, was a soldier-farmer; he tilled fields in Lancaster, he became the second settler in the new Wachusett plantation of Turkey Hills, and he served the colony in Groton. Lieutenant Jabez Fairbank, a grandson of John Prescott, had seen his father and two brothers slain in the earlier Indian wars. Captains Josiah Willard and Samuel Willard were grandsons of Simon Willard. Samuel built up his estate in the center of Lancaster. He bought the "night pasture," his grandfather's garrison house, and Edward Breck's lot where he lived. Josiah moved to Turkey Hills in 1724, the third settler in town. Finally, Captain John White was the grandson of John White, Lancaster's richest pioneer, whose daughter, Mary, had married Joseph Rowlandson. White's estate was the largest on Lancaster's tax assessments list in 1721.[42]

Local leaders and town residents manned Lancaster's defense forces. Josiah Willard commanded a local company, which guarded the settlers and searched for Indians in the Wachusett. Samuel Willard mustered fifty-two men at his house in Lancaster in July 1725 and led them toward Mount Wachusett. They tracked Indians to the west of the mountain and then turned north when they heard gunfire. However, they encountered only bad weather and several moose thereafter and returned to Lancaster at the end of the month. White, the village blacksmith, led several scouting sorties in search of Indians, and he also encountered few foes. Fairbank watched the settlers return to garrison living, their lives afflicted again by the burdens of part-time soldiering and full-time farming: "the poor people are many of them obliged to keep their own Garrisons." Some were "Imployed as Guards" while others labored part time, which left them little time for "Getting Bread for their Family." Fairbank found his supply of men rather thin for the defense of the town, much less for mounting scouts or patrols to detect the approach of Indian foes. The locals were ready to "guard the people about their fields" or range about to the next town and "home by Wachusett hill," but they balked when the call came to leave their imperiled homes and families for long stretches of time.[43] Long-distance expeditions against the Indians, which were part of the colony's new offensive strategy, proved popular for military leaders but held little appeal for Lancaster's soldier-farmers. When the residents refused to join a distant expedition, suspicion fell on Hartwell, who had become local commander. He reported to the colonial authorities that when Colonel Eleazer Tyng called for "all the Scouts & Standing Soldiers" to report to Dunstable with provisions for fifty days, "most of our inhabitants refuse to go." John Houghton, town patriarch, explained the locals' perspective and the soldiers' refusal to obey orders to the lieutenant governor. Since "the men were heads of families," he related, and the enemy was expected at any moment, "great danger" might befall the settlement during their absence. Houghton felt Tyng's expedition would serve little point since, as far as Lancaster's inhabitants could see, the patrol's purpose was their protection, and "we cant Imagine that we shall be much guarded by him." Dummer subsequently found Hartwell "not in the least to blame" since he had done little more than faithfully report his fellow settlers' reluctance to leave their frontier stations, a familiar response by settlers to calls for extended stays far from home.[44]

Captain Josiah Willard led the men from Groton, Lancaster, and Turkey Hills who had been ordered to serve with Colonial Tyng at Dunstable. He recognized that this fifty-day excursion would be a burden for his men since "they will be much exposed."[45] His relative Samuel Willard assumed a critical role in scouting expeditions for Indians in the regions of northern New England on the borders of the Wachusett that became fertile territory for town foundings in the next generation. He led troops through extensive expeditions along the Merrimack and Ashuelot River valleys in New Hampshire and on into Maine. September found Willard on the march again, as a "young mohawk" scout led them up the Merrimack as far as Saco Falls. The Indian assured them "that he can Lead us to the Indians Head Quarters" where the Abenaki foe resided. What Willard and his troops encountered was five hundred miles of terrain, including fertile intervales between steep mountains, which they later described in vivid detail to their children and neighbors. Migrants from the Wachusett proceeded to settle those areas of southeastern New Hampshire in the next several decades of the eighteenth century.[46]

This third generation of town founders in the Wachusett, after the pioneer and resettlement eras, perpetuated many family traditions regarding the mediation of English-Indian relations and the founding of new towns. Gone, however, were the first generation's firsthand relationships with the Indians. John Prescott and Simon Willard had sought out the Nashaways along the inland waterways to exchange beaver pelts and set up trading posts. John Eliot and Daniel Gookin had pursued missionary labors in the villages of central Massachusetts. Indian hating, a more abstract and absolute activity, replaced the earlier complex relationship between neighboring English and Indian villagers. Josiah and Samuel Willard's vision of the frontier, recounted in their scouting journals, was as a region free of "Indian savages." Relations with Indians still were critical to frontier residents and to colonial officials, but an aggressive, militaristic tone dominated the exchange. Lieutenant Governor Dummer gave the following instructions to Captains Willard, White, and Blanchard: "You must Kill, Take and Destroy to the utmost of your power all the Enemy Indians you can meet with in your March, and Search for their Corn, destroying all you can." As Indian fighters became the new town founders, war in the Wachusett—originally a purely defensive measure to accompany town settlement and maintain the English presence—became an opportunity for early eighteenth-century town founders to accumulate bounties for scalping Indians or land grants for military service.[47]

The colonial authorities offered a sizable bounty for every scalp to encourage frontier fighters to track down hostile Indians. Those handy with a gun or in need of money, "volunteers without pay or substance," organized private companies to exploit these opportunities. One hundred pounds was offered "for the scalp of any male Indian of the age of twelve years or upward." Women and children, scalped and unscalped, went for half-price.[48] The career of the most famous Indian fighter of Dummer's War, John Lovewell, highlighted the opportunities available on the borders of New England. Lovewell was a second-generation Indian fighter; his father had fought with Benjamin Church in Metacom's War.[49]

Lovewell and other "Volunteers" offered to fight Indians for the colony— for a price. They offered to "Imploy themselves in Indian hunting one whole year" for a daily wage of five shillings "in case they kill any enemy Indians." If they killed none they would receive nothing "for their wages, time and trouble." These bounty hunters, different from Fairbank's local scouting parties or the Willards' Maine expeditions, ranged through unknown areas for long periods, intending to destroy the remaining New England Indians. Lovewell had little trouble raising two expeditions at the end of 1724 and the beginning of 1725. The first party of thirty men returned triumphantly to Boston with their single trophy, the "scalp of an Indian man and a captive, a lad of about 17 years of age," and they were rewarded with a bonus of fifty pounds over their regular bounty.

Lancaster's John White joined Lovewell's second company of eighty-seven volunteers as second in command, a position that took him far into the unknown areas of New England. White raised his own company of volunteers in April as Lovewell prepared for his boldest sortie. While Indian fighters like White kept to paths along the rivers, Lovewell set off north toward Lake Winipesaukee, where his third and final expedition tested the limits of his boldness or folly. Lovewell's Fight in May 1725 was the most famous encounter of Dummer's War, leaving an enduring legacy in New England folk memory as the press, clergy, and plain people variously recalled the "Fight at Pigwacket."[50]

Lovewell and his inexperienced company discovered a lone Indian shooting ducks. They advanced but were fired on by another Indian. They promptly took the life and scalp of the attacking Indian: the company's chaplain, "a twenty-one year old student of theology, proceeded to peel it off." Suddenly, a band of Indians burst into the clearing and, as the *Boston Gazette* told its readers, "Captain Lovewell and Ensign Robins were mortally wounded by the Indians first shot from their Ambushments, who (notwithstanding supporting themselves by such Trees as they could lay hold on) kept firing on the Enemy, and Encouraging their Companions, they both had their Guns in hand, Lovewell's being cock'd and presented when he was past speaking."

The scalp hunters withdrew to make a last stand, and later in the morning the Indians resumed the fray. Both sides sustained heavy casualties as Indians and Indian fighters fought to exhaustion. Francis Parkman wrote a century later that little distinguished these two bands of warriors skirmishing in this clearing on the edges of the British cononial world: "Indians had the greater agility and skill in hiding. . . and the whites greater steadiness . . . in using their guns. . . . The Indians howled like wolves . . . while the whites replied with shouts and cheers." Two-thirds of the English lay dead or wounded; the rest struggled back south.[51]

White went north to bury Lovewell and eleven others. Lieutenant Governor Dummer feared "that if the enemy are such strength as to defeat Lovewell they will thereupon be upon our frontiers in great numbers." White returned to muster another group at Lancaster. He and Willard were busy that summer and fall as the frontier towns remained in a state of fear. White's last company of volunteers, exhausted and "taken very ill with a Bloody Flux," returned to Lancaster to learn from the governor that the colony had "lately concluded a cessation of armes with the Penobscott Indians" and their services were no longer required. The Indians were spent by heavy losses and disappointed by the meager aid they had received from the French. Four leaders of the Eastern Indians signed a treaty in Boston in December that submitted their people to English rule. Within the year all the tribes of the eastern frontier put down their arms. The latest crisis on the expanding frontier of New England was over.[52]

Scouts from the Wachusett had been instrumental in the defense of the frontier towns and in clearing the way for settlement to follow onto new lands, many of which had been explored during the hostilities. White and his fellow volunteers from Lancaster had opened a vast area of northern New England through their wartime service. Indian fighting, a new venture, engaged the energies of frontier residents. The process of town formation in the Wachusett entered a new stage with the close of the war in 1725. Fifty years after Mary Rowlandson was carried away from her home in Lancaster, settlers resided in numerous communities throughout an expanding area of the Wachusett. They had learned to defend their homes and pursue their foes while continuing to plant towns and clear fields until there were few areas of New England where a frontier station did not exist. Indian fighters pushed the remaining Indians to the edges of northern New England, opening large areas of the region for immediate occupancy and by their military service providing their offspring with claims against the colony that could be readily translated into farms on that very frontier. Those volunteers and veterans would be commemorated in popular song and General Court decree, providing institutional and ideological legitimacy for them to continue town settlement.

Remembering Lovewell's Fight

> Of worthy Captain LOVEWELL I purpose now to sing,
> How valiantly he served his country and his king;
> He and his valiant soldiers, did range the woods full wide,
> And Hardships they endured to quell the Indian's pride.
>
> *The Voluntier's March* (1725)

Owing to the battles fought to defend the frontier, new heroes—Indian fighters—entered the collective memory of New England. The singular figure of Benjamin Church was joined by Lovewell and "his valiant" volunteers. The long process of serial town settlement was punctuated periodically by ritual statements to legitimate the changes in the material and mental world of the townspeople of the Wachusett. New voices and genres appeared to celebrate this new mythic and militant image of New England town formation; balladeers joined ministers and magistrates as keepers of the errand in the wilderness.[53]

The first voice in praise of the Indian fighters came from a traditional figure and from a familiar place but offered a new version of the New England heroes. The Reverend Thomas Symmes mounted the pulpit to reassure his flock as soon as news of Lovewell's Fight reached Bradford. His sermon included "agreeable Lamentations" to comfort the bereaved, but he also had the more direct purpose of offering "a Spur to Virtue."[54] If defending church and town were not enough, Symmes bolstered providential authority with public opinion to boost Massachusetts Bay's citizen-soldiers in their battles:

> When Surviving Soldiers (and particularly such as have been Eye-Witnesses of the Fall of their Brethren, and fought with uncommon Bravery) . . . take Notice that the Death of their Officers or Fellow-Soldiers is deeply resented by the People of GOD, that they still speak of them with great Honour in their Lamentations, this will Animate them, we hope, to do Worthily, and rather Die with Honour, if call'd to Battle, than live with Disgace; and for their Cow-

ardice, have the offer of a *Wooden Sword,* and be Branded with the Infamous Character of a *Coward,* even by the Weaker Sex.[55]

Symmes appended a historical preface to his sermon that summer when it was published bearing the title, *Lovewell Lamented, or a Sermon Occasioned by the Fall of the Brave Capt. Lovewell and Several of his Valiant Company, in the Late Heroic Action at Pigwacket.* Symmes memorialized all Lovewell's soldiers, since "the Remarkable Preservation and Success of Soldiers," he envisioned, would be important "in future Expeditions and Military Actions." His writings incorporated the distant borderlands, the "Howling Wilderness . . . very far in the Enemies Country," where soldiers practiced an "Indianized" mode of warfare. "This Action Merits a Room in the History of our *New-English* Wars." Actions on the margins of New England society became celebrated at the center.[56]

The very next year Samuel Penhallow wrote *The History of the Wars of New-England with the Eastern Indians.* Penhallow, an English missionary sent to follow John Eliot's work as "apostle to the Indians," became discouraged with Massachusetts politics. He removed to Portsmouth, New Hampshire, and by an advantageous marriage became a substantial merchant and political figure. Penhallow's plain style contained a broader account of the Indian attacks on New England towns and English expeditions to the northern borders beginning in 1702. His was a provincial perspective, bringing the "shattered company" into the imperial errand. The Indian fighters appeared in a patriotic light. Captain Lovewell "was endowed with a generous spirit and resolution of serving his country." Although his men's "actions in this war can bear no comparison with those of our British forces," it would be wrong "not to mention the bravery of these worthies," who died "for the interest of their country." He closed with the recent peace conference and hopes for the "happy fruits of peace unto these provinces."[57]

Benjamin Colman, eighteenth-century Boston cultural leader, clarified Penhallow's cosmopolitan themes in the preface to the posthumous publication. The Indian wars were part of "the many difficulties and troubles" that attended the growth of the English settlements. Colman's religious and global perspective, "tracing the footsteps and windings of Divine Providence, in the planting of colonies and churches, here and there, through the earth," was similar to Edward Johnson's. But this would be no mere "planting" of a few churches in a wilderness, according to Colman, but rather the founding of a province in a global empire. Readers' attention was focused on the rise and growth of colonies as the world-historical event. Penhallow and Colman incorporated the Indian Wars and provincial politics into the long-term story of New England town formation.

The most popular, immediate, and enduring narrative of Lovewell's Fight appeared as a broadside in Boston streets only a few days after the first reports of the engagement reached officials. On May 31, 1725, an advertisement appeared in James Franklin's *New England Courant* for "an excellent new song" for sale at Franklin's shop: "The Voluntier's March; being a full and true Account [of] the bloody Fight which happen'd between Capt. Lovewell's Company, and the Indians at Pigwoket." Ambushes and captivities of frontier residents were familiar fare in Boston papers, but this ballad glorified the new mode of aggressive Indian fighting and acclaimed the arrival of a new hero into the colonial canon: "Of worthy Captain LOVEWELL / He and his valiant soldier did range the woods full wide."[58]

The Song of Lovewell's Fight acclaimed these Indian fighters for their Indianizing behavior and for their new corporate identity as a "company of volunteers." Lovewell and his soldier-farmers fought under the imperial banner, but also collected a bounty for their native scalps. These part-time warriors drew attention not for their virtue but for their valor. His men were eager for a fight as they marched through the woods. Lured forward by a single Indian, who wounded Lovewell, they "scalp'd the Indian" but fell into an ambush. Lovewell commanded his heavily outnumbered troops: "Fight on, my valiant heroes!" and they fought "till the setting of the sun." The balladeer listed the heavy losses on both sides, almost half the English killed and wounded "for which we all must mourn." The song also commemorated the bold deeds and names of the fallen:

Our worthy Captain LOVEWELL among them there did die;
They killed Lieutenant ROBBINS, and wounded good young FRYE
Who was our English Chaplain; he many Indians slew,
And some of them he scalp'd when bullets round him flew.

In this ballad the "valiant English" behaved almost indistinguishably from the "rebel Indians," all yelling hideously. But the patriotic rhyme glossed over the spectacle of Sabbath breaking and scalping sorties, led by "our English Chaplain," taking place on the margins of British North America. New Englanders recognized the changes in their behavior toward the Indians and in their attitudes toward the land by their popularization of this most famous encounter of the Indian wars.[59] *The Voluntier's March*— "a rude song," according to John Farmer and Jacob Moore's *Collections, Historical and Miscellaneous* of 1823—engaged the popular memory of New England. Farmer and Moore remembered that the ballad "was written about one hundred years since to commemorate one of the most fierce and obstinate battles which had been fought with the Indians." Their ethnographic account stated that the ballad was sung throughout a considerable portion of Massachusetts and New Hampshire and served "more than almost anything else to keep in remembrance" this critical engagement in the expansion of New England.[60]

Indian fighters returned home to become town founders in the next decade. John White and the Willard brothers were leaders in both enterprises, as the pantheon of heroes extended in the popular press and imagination to include ordinary townspeople. New heroes were created, and these were shorn of providential design and exemplary status that had so characterized their predecessors. Indian fighters joined the Reverend Symmes' "Ministers and Magistrates" in the popular memory of the anonymous balladeer, along with the imperial perspective of Samuel Penhallow. All these accounts incorporated the Indian wars and the actions of the eighteenth-century soldier-citizens into the history of town formation. Volunteers and veterans were commemorated either before the General Court or around the hearths of the Wachusett.

Lancaster's volunteers had defended their garrison houses, pursued the remaining Indians in the region to the borders of Canada, and founded new towns throughout New England. A cluster of military claims for the vacant lands of the Wachusett provided the basis for a new era of town foundings in the region. John White's widow Eunice petitioned for unappropriated lands from the court in 1725. She recounted his missions "against those barbarous savages": he had marched under Lovewell, been sent to bury Lovewell, and volunteered for a final sortie "beyond Pigwacket." The court granted her one hundred pounds, but her offspring would have little trouble securing shares in the numerous towns being carved out of the northern borderlands in the Wachusett in the second quarter of the eighteenth century.[61]

II TOWN SETTLEMENT IN THE EIGHTEENTH CENTURY

As town settlement was renewed and expanded in the eighteenth century, it became a more bureaucratic and democratic process. Colonization accelerated and extended to the west and to the north of Lancaster after the Peace of Utrecht in 1713. New villages on the outskirts of older, more populous towns clamored for independence. A growing number of peripatetic town founders pushed deep into the contested borderlands between Indians, French, and the English in northeastern North America. The Massachusetts General Court, concerned about building frontier townships as a means of defense and expansion, carved out whole series of townships in the land that had been expropriated from the Indians after Metacom's War. Patriarchs in long-settled towns, where land reserves had been parceled out and filled up, began worrying about providing for the next generation, so they became proprietors of new towns. Those willing or forced to move their families in order to secure land settled early in several northern or western plantations as an investment. The dramatic growth of New England's population combined with patriarchs' concerns about providing sufficient land for their sons increased both the number of town proprietors and the number of new towns in the early eighteenth century. Two significant conditions—the greater distance between new inland settlements and older coastal ones and the competition among multiple sites for settlers—slowed the economic development of the new towns and their passage toward political autonomy. Conflicts arose over the pace of development and the speculative nature of many settlements. On balance, the business of town founding accelerated the process of colonization and swept the people of the Wachusett farther into the borderlands of northeastern North America.

Families and farms remained the ends and the means for serial town settlement in the eighteenth century. Prosperity and maturation brought social differentiation and conflict to established Wachusett towns, while more open proprietorships continued to serve as engines for the economic development of distant plantations. With a more active land market came a regional system of older eastern and newer western towns, a market shaped by the broader political and imperial context. New England continued to expand dynamically by modifying familiar institutions, such as the proprietorship and the town, rather than by degrading or replacing the process of serial town settlement in response to changing conditions created by its own success and the expansion of empire. War receded and Indian fighting became a military adventure on the faraway frontier, while the Wachusett landscape was transformed into a network of farms, roads, churches, and schools, demonstrating the establishment of stable social institutions. The first narratives of Lancaster's founding centered on this material transformation as the critical achievement of New England. Local histories aimed to bind together the generations and to construct a progressive interpretation of the settlement process. Stories about Indian fighters and first families, who were now sufficiently removed from the "wilderness work" of Edward Johnson or Mary Rowlandson, kept alive and reshaped the memories of settlement to instruct a new generation of townspeople and their town founders.

3 Lancaster and Its Offspring: Serial Town Formation Enters the New Century

> God of his abundant Goodness hath multiplied his People in our Land, &
> increased them in this Part of the Country, so that it hath been thought need-
> ful & convenient, to have an increase in our Counties.
> John Prentice, *King Jehoshaphat's Charges to the Judges* (1731)

Lancaster's minister, John Prentice, celebrated the establishment of the new county of Worcester in August 1731, an event made possible by the ever-growing population in the Wachusett. But even as the Wachusett's population increase brought optimism, it also raised concerns—voiced by elite and yeomen alike—about the continuation of familiar social forms. Prentice warned against worldly seductions. "Courts held in Country towns," he announced, lured persons to spend their "Time . . . run[ning] to a great deal of Extravagance of Speech . . . Excess and Intemperance." The increase in population and extension of colonization brought about social differentiation and conflict.[1]

The late seventeenth-century resettlement had brought new families and houses scattered throughout Lancaster's ample and augmented territories; clusters of villages had formed, and these soon demanded their independence as towns. Serial town settlement resumed after the Peace of Utrecht in 1713. The General Court renewed its granting of towns in the northeastern borderlands between the French and British settlements, beyond Lancaster into Lunenburg and other parts of the northwest Wachusett. The business of town founding—building roads and taverns and collecting proprietorships—provided opportunities for people with substantial capital and connections, as well as for peripatetic settlers with plenty of kin, to occupy distant plantations. Despite renewed warfare in the 1740s, a new generation of town founders kept moving west, past Lancaster to found such towns as Lunenburg and Fitchburg by the mid-eighteenth century.

Lancaster in 1725: Country Town

Lancaster's increased population and enlarged borders required continued institutional innovations. Local roads radiated out from the town center to the mounting numbers of farmsteads; as garrisons grew into villages,
roads extended east and west to the Still River, Chocksett, and North
Nashua regions. The new eastern meetinghouse required new roadways.
North and south "ways" connected the town's four millers and four taverns. Major colonial routes ran east and west through Lancaster, linking the
Connecticut River settlements with the eastern towns of Groton and Concord and the bay. Finally, the transportation system bent around to accommodate the new shire town of Worcester.[2]

Schools, a powerful local means of cultural transmission in New
England, faced the challenge of decentralized settlement. By 1647 the General Court had required every town of fifty families to "appoint one within
their own town to teach all such children as shall resort to him to write and
read" and those towns reaching one hundred families to "set up a grammar
school, the master thereof being able to instruct youth, so far, as they may
be fitted, for the university." The devastation and privation of war had
played havoc with expectations of maintaining an educational hierarchy on
the frontiers of Massachusetts. John Houghton had acted as schoolmaster
in the first years of resettlement; in 1703, "frontier Towns" had been
excused from grammar school support as "it is unsafe for the children to
Passe to and from the Schools." When the region had regained its prewar
population, the County Court had cited Lancaster "for want of a Gramer
School" in 1715. The town had answered that they had commissioned a
"young Mr Pierpoint" as a teacher, but that an "Indisposition of Body" prevented his arrival; without a teacher qualified in the classics, they had got-
ten by with a writing school. The scarcity of schoolteachers in the seventeenth century had led to a 1699 effort to centralize education by operating
a grammar school in the shire town (or county seat) which was supported
by a countywide levy. Lancaster and other "Country towns" had feared the
cultural consequences of a single grammar school, for it would disadvantage "the middle sort of men," who supplied the "genarallyty of the Pulpits," and advantage rich men's sons, who were able to board at distant
new schools and were often reluctant to serve as ministers in remote areas,
leaving "Country people" with few men fit for public business.[3]

Instead, Lancaster and other growing country towns had opted for
decentralized schooling. Free schools replaced the system of mixed-tuition
and town support. Lancaster's residents allocated twelve shillings to "Mr
Osgood for going after a school-master" in the competition for recent college graduates; in 1718 they secured Samuel Stow, the first in a long line of
Harvard students who kept school in town. Moving the schools answered
the needs of rural communities with inhabitants scattered throughout town.

The town schoolmaster, Edward Broughton, conducted classes one hundred and fifty days on the Neck and another seventy-five days at Still River in 1723. The next year he added another site, Wataquadock, to the east. Terms lengthened and the town employed several schoolmasters spread among the clusters of settlement by 1732.[4]

Conflict over the location of the meetinghouse revealed the contradiction between the forces of communal dispersion and the cultural imperatives for centralization. After several ministers had been lost to the hazards of wartime, John Prentice had taken over in 1704, married the minister's widow, and begun a forty-year tenure. During his early years, the parsonage served as a garrison and several parishioners were killed or captured in the Indian wars. Prentice's neighbor, the Reverend Ebenezer Parkman of Westborough, recorded in his diary in 1723: "I walked to the Meeting House with a Pistol in my Hand by reason of Danger of the Indians." Townspeople crowded uncomfortably into one meetinghouse to hear Prentice preach, but they defeated proposals to build two meetinghouses and divide Lancaster's ecclesiastical order. The modest enlargement of the existing structure required a committee of town notables to "dignfie the seats in the meeting house" in 1727. Seating the meetinghouse signified the hierarchical social order of the community and allowed the committee to make adjustments in family status.[5]

Housing, also, indicated the increasing differentiation in town. The expanding settlement provided opportunities for a new provincial elite. While the people of the Wachusett had rebuilt their homes during decades of wartime raids, some townspeople began to construct grander structures than those previously found in the seventeenth-century landscape. The average early eighteenth-century structure was a one-story, single- or double-room structure with an asymmetrical facade and chimney placement. These dwellings frequently faced south to maximize natural exposure and heating, without regard for visual display. But larger, two-story, double-pile houses had begun to appear in emerging eighteenth-century country towns such as Lancaster. Captain John Bennet's House, circa 1717, also served as a tavern, proudly facing road traffic from the east, securely sited on the eastern side of the Nashua River and on Northfield Road. Built by one of the town's wealthiest men, this house's facade featured symmetrical windows, door, and chimney. Oriented away from the southern sun, the house emphasized the power of visual spectacle and symbolized its owner's status. The town's wealthiest citizens added to the stock of two-story dwellings in the second quarter of the eighteenth century. While simple, single-story dwellings still dominated in Lancaster, several two-story, double-pile houses, three of which still survive, were built on the neck. Captain Samuel Willard, Worcester County notable and the town's wealthiest resident, built a large and imposing structure around 1727 (see plate 3). Whether restrained by his provincial status or his local roots, he did not commission a rigidly sym-

Plate 3. Samuel Willard house, Lancaster, Massachusetts, built about 1727. Worcester County notable Samuel Willard built himself a large and striking residence in early eighteenth-century Lancaster. This double-pile, two-story house stood alongside several other large homes in Lancaster's Neck district. Yet Willard sought to minimize the gap with his fellow, less wealthy, townspeople; his house continued in the local vernacular housing tradition with its asymmetrical front facade and side elevations. (Author's photograph.)

metrical front facade or chimney placements. Still, this dwelling represented the pinnacle of presentation in Wachusett housing, a form reserved for only the wealthiest and most cosmopolitan residents.[6]

The region's growing gentry gathered in the new county courts formed in 1731. The spreading settlements of Central Massachusetts and the surge of town founding prompted a move to secure needed governmental services closer than the neighboring Middlesex and Hampshire Counties. The successful petitioners expected Marlborough to receive the Superior Court and Lancaster, the inferior courts. Lancaster's Joseph Wilder feared the carnivalesque atmosphere of court days and Worcester received the prize instead. Wilder did become a judge on the Court of Common Pleas, helping to consolidate a regional elite of Wilders and Williards. These men mediated between the towns and the colonial authorities, as well as between the towns and the wider Atlantic commercial world. Enmeshed in a maturing commercial economic and social structure, the courts served as arbiters of economic relationships and a platform for the gentry to display political and cultural distinction before their peers and the populace.[7]

After Metacom's War, Lancaster's expanded boundaries and population increase produced flocks of infant communities. The process of serial town settlement accommodated them. Four claimants for independence came forward in the 1730s with different sources of authority and degrees of success. First, the residents of the northeastern villages of Bare Hill and Still River petitioned at a special town meeting in May 1730. These villages traced their roots back to Simon Willard's original land grants and contained influential residents. The town opposed their request for a strip of land three miles wide along the entire eastern boundary of Lancaster and delegated a committee to determine how far the petitioners were located from the meetinghouse. After two years of meetings, the General Court granted the new town of Harvard in a region southeast of Lancaster, its western border marked by the river, and its southern border extending five miles south of the northern Lancaster township line, thereby incorporating sections of Lancaster, Groton, and Stowe (see map 11).[8]

This successful effort from the northeastern quadrant brought forward two other groups, both from the south in May 1733. Twelve dozen southwestern householders claimed significant hardships because they resided "at such a remote distance from the place of public worship" that their travels to worship required "more labor than is proper for a day of holy rest." They claimed that their sizable core of families, with additional ones expected, would sustain a separate meetinghouse. Gamaliel Beaman had led this southwestern movement of young families to the hills of Chocksett about 1720. At the same time Beaman brought his petition, a southeastern group asked for the incorporation of all the remaining eastern territory not taken by Harvard; they echoed the southwesterners' arguments about difficulty of travel to worship and the presence of the requisite numbers. Town meetings were roiled for several years with petitions and arguments. New Englanders' expectations of convenient access to religious and social events along with the realities of Lancaster's spacious boundaries clashed with townspeople's reluctance to build new meetinghouses and split up the town's religious community. Finally, although the southwesterners led by Beaman failed in their petitions because of their relative youth and contentious manner, the southeastern group prevailed in 1738; they received the town of Bolton from the General Court, with a western border shared with Lancaster and an eastern one located about four miles east.[9]

The smallest village within Lancaster, in the northeastern Nashua Valley, petitioned the town in 1737 with similar arguments, but they used a different strategy from Beaman's group. Originally more isolated because of their great distance from Lancaster's center, they had grown in numbers more rapidly than Chocksett and had attracted many of the grandsons of the Additional Grant's proprietors—Houghtons, Wilders, Carters, and members of other prominent families. Shrewdly, they stressed comity rather than conflict. They allied with the old town's residents to defeat the Chocksett group and so were able to win consent more easily for their own town of Leominster in 1740. Aside from its residents' strategic political maneuvers,

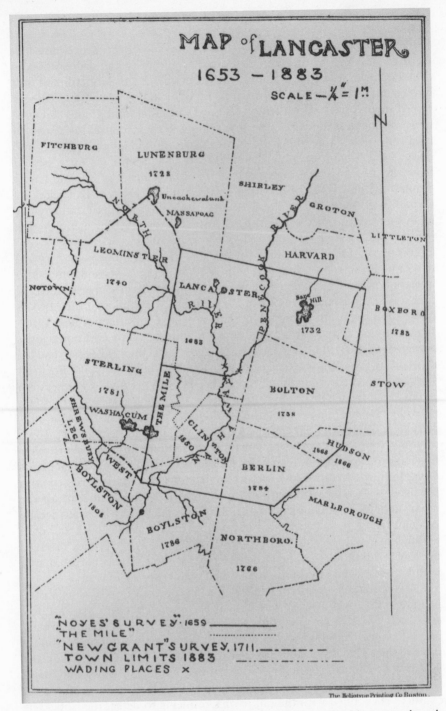

Map 11. Lancaster and its contiguous communities. Lancaster's original large 1659 boundaries had been increased with the 1711 Additional Grant on its eastern borders; new villages within Lancaster began clamoring for independence in the ensuing decades of eighteenth century. (Reprinted from Henry Stedman Nourse, *The Early Records of Lancaster, Massachusetts, 1643–1725* [Lancaster, 1884], p. 8. Courtesy of the American Antiquarian Society.)

the petitioners possessed several crucial advantages. Leominster's town center lay seven miles from Lancaster, with a long high hill and few settlers on the road between the two towns. The petitioners included several influential older men, who remained in Lancaster but had children and land holdings in the north Nashua valley.[10]

When Beaman's Chocksett petitioners renewed their requests, demanding even more territory than the Leominster group, they focused their efforts on relocating Lancaster's meetinghouse. Edward Hartwell, Worcester County's new Justice of the Peace, issued a warrant for a town meeting at which it was decided to create two precincts within the town of Lancaster and build two meetinghouses. The second precinct (Chocksett, later to become Bolton) received a smaller allocation than the older one, which received the new First Church building. The old meetinghouse was pulled down and its "clabord and nails" used to construct three new schoolhouses at dispersed sites.

The division of Lancaster was over by 1743; three new towns and two precincts had been carved out of the original town's immense territory. The budding process provided for the eventual founding of separate communities to accommodate outlying residents, isolated from a distant town center, who sought local control as their communities matured. The varying speed and success of the four groups demonstrated the benefits of adopting an orderly approach that was supported by the town patriarchs, but also proved that a contentious effort of latecomers drawn by cheaper, distant land could succeed. The process of town settlement was sometimes messy and could accommodate both sorts of groups. Increase meant innovation. The maturing of Lancaster as a country town had brought spatial and social differentiation to the cultural landscape of colonization. New, elaborate houses and courthouses appeared to signify the consolidation of a county elite. At the same time, more farm families clamored for access to local religious, political, and education institutions.[11]

Beyond Lancaster

The General Court renewed town founding in the Wachusett after the Peace of Utrecht in 1713 as a defensive measure for colonial security and as a necessary means of maintaining New England society and culture. Residents had filled in the town borders and incorporated the neighboring Nashaway lands during the resettlement after Metacom's War; both processes had led to the budding of new towns. In the post-1713 boom, however, colonists moved out from the older core areas of central Massachusetts into colonial reserves appropriated from the Nipmucs and other Algonquian people in the contested northeastern borderlands between New England and New France. The General Court, eastern townspeople, and

Wachusett entrepreneurs developed a sure-footed and standardized model of town formation by establishing a series of bureaucratic procedures: the court's appointment of a supervisory committee, the control of a proprietary group, the one-time admission of grantees, and the fulfillment of formal conditions by settlers. Through this process, new towns arose at an ever-quickening pace characteristic of eighteenth-century colonization.[12]

Locals referred to the Nashua Valley northwest of Lancaster as Turkey Hills because of its abundant supply of wild turkeys and other plentiful game. Wachusett scouts ranged through those woods during the war years, while eastern leaders passed out grants in these unappropriated western lands to resolve community and individual claims on the colony. Dorchester and Woburn received land grants as reserves for their crowded towns. Samuel Page, another claimant, was looking for an attractive homestead, not a bankable resource. He took immediate occupancy. Born in Groton in 1672, he had traveled to South Carolina, returning later in life penniless, widowed, and with seven children. In 1718 he moved west with his new wife, Martha, and his children, cleared some land, and built a log cabin in Turkey Hills, where the family remained as solitary squatters for several years. But this piecemeal appropriation of the wild turkeys' home did not last long.[13]

With the coming of peace in 1713, the Massachusetts General Court considered the creation of tiers of townships along the colony's borders to defend against French and Indian foes as well as to advance claims against its northern English neighbors. Numerous petitions flooded the Court claiming straitened circumstances, similar to the claims of Sudbury's sons three quarters of a century before. In 1719 the General Court granted "two new Towns" west of Groton, with a "Quantity of Land" not to exceed six miles squared, the recognized limits of a township, to be "laid out" in "a defensible manner." Eighteenth-century authorities renewed the settlement process armed with a clear blueprint for ordering settlement and hastening development of the numerous townships opening in the 1720s. A court-appointed committee of five men, responsible for allocating land and organizing local institutions, supervised settlement of the two new plantations, South Town (also called Turkey Hills) and North Town. Eighty grantees were admitted into a proprietorship (the parcels of land limited to two hundred and fifty acres) for which the grantees were to pay the province five pounds. Grantees were obliged to "build a good dwelling House," "to break up and sufficiently fence in three acres of land at least" within three years, and to contribute "towards the building and finishing of a Convenient House for the Publick Worship of God." Two weeks later three colonial notables, a surveyor, and four chainmen walked the boundary lines, encountering only the squatting Page household, a welcome haven in the wintry Wachusett.[14]

Plans were quickly made to create a proprietary group, which would have more authority and responsibility for the plantation's progress than its seventeenth-century counterparts. The court's committee assembled at the Jonathan Hubbard Inn in Concord in May 1720 to admit the eighty grantees to Turkey Hills. The grantees were admitted all at once, forming and completing a new corporate body. This event departed from the previous pattern of settlement. Opportunities were ample to be an eighteenth-century proprietor. The grantees came in with substantial initial numbers, they were organized for development purposes, and they had no previous ties to the settlement—almost half coming from Concord and Groton and the rest from other eastern towns. Fathers subscribing for sons accounted for one-quarter of the subscriptions. By contrast, seventeenth-century grantees, with their limited numbers, had only slowly added to their ranks, and they had often closed entry quickly to the municipal corporation. Furthermore, Turkey Hills's grantees only made a small down payment, part of their five-pound fee, with later payments coming at the drawing of lots and laying out of landholdings. The sole representatives native to the region were "Mr. Samuel Page of Turkey Hills" and his son Joseph, who reserved two places in the new plantation.

That fall the committeemen gathered in Cambridge to allocate lots. The first division of home lots—"No Lott to be Less than forty & five Acres," being of "the best land"—was laid out in half-mile ranges. These standardized allotments were far larger than Lancaster's had been and often ignored the irregularities of the town's topography and variations in its soil quality. Directives had been issued from the very start of settlement for building roads, schools, and a meetinghouse (to be located at the center of the survey). The colony's plan for settlement called for a standard-sized township with a central common, and the General Court's committee had followed almost verbatim that directive in the process of shaping the settlement, admitting grantees, and providing for village institutions.[15]

Settlers besides the Pages remained scarce during these years as the colony became embroiled in Governor Dummer's War in 1722. Settlers had to reside in garrisons while building their new homes in the recently granted, vulnerable borderland community, following lessons learned through decades of living in a defensive posture in the Wachusett. Lancaster's military leaders took charge of protecting the infant settlement. Captain Josiah Willard left Lancaster for Turkey Hills while commanding frontier patrols in the Wachusett. Willard reported that "we have made no discovery of the enemy yet among us, but live in daily expectations of them." He elaborated on how Turkey Hills's settlers had turned into farmer-soldiers: "we have here . . . 9 families posted in 5 garrisons which are all willing to stand their ground if they can." But farmers had to leave the wooden palisades to clear the forest and till the fields. "When our men go out to work they must have a guard to expose themselves," Willard wrote. And the women had to turn back attackers; one Turkey Hills woman drove off the Indians by throwing boiling soap in their faces, and on other occasions the women repelled Indians with gunfire. Willard concluded his report by seeking additional military support.[16]

Distinguished alumni of the frontier school, Indian fighters such as Josiah Willard and Edward Hartwell had left Lancaster to head the new frontier town, joined by other migrants attracted by the prospect of establishing their families on farms of their own. Lieutenant Hartwell, for example, took time off from his military expeditions to clear his land and build a home in Turkey Hills. He finally moved to the new town in August 1725, writing to Governor Dummer to obtain leave. His new location, he promised, would allow him to be in good capacity "to serve both my King and Country."[17]

At the end of the war, the settlement quickly became established. By 1726, only one year after Willard reported the existence of nine families in Turkey Hills, town residents reported twenty-six houses raised with "ten of them Settled and Inhabited." The settlers journeyed to Groton to report on their compliance with the court's mandates, since time was running out on fulfilling the conditions for their grant. More migrants arrived and houses constructed. When the General Court's committee visited Turkey Hills in August 1727 to review the settlement's progress, the town's taxpayers resented the committee's intrusive supervision as well as their burdensome reimbursements. Nonresident grantees created another problem. These people never set foot in Turkey Hills but speculatively traded their shares, slowing the town's development. The committee found that:

> Several of the Lotts in Sd Town Are Not Settled as injoyned by the General Court. And their Committee and Several that to this Day have Never Done Any Labour at all on them, but yet the Persons who Drew them Have hitherto kept the Lotts from Others Likely to Settle them, And have Only Traded them from One Man to Another for excessive Gaine & Prices, Which Practice is Directly Contrary to the Written Conditions & Provisos Upon Which Each Person had his Lott of the Committee Which Practice Tends Greatly to Retard the Settling Sd Town, and Oppression of those Who must finally Do it.

The court desired expeditious settlement. The delinquents were called to account, but only four lots were declared forfeited, to be sold promptly for no more than fifty pounds: ten times the original subscriber's price for a right to a lot in an undeveloped wilderness, but a bargain for a full share in a growing community. As the pioneers cleared their lots and local inspection of the settlement became necessary, more attention focused on the site. Residents assisted in these efforts; they in turn desired full control of their affairs.[18]

In August 1728, the plantation of Turkey Hills was incorporated as Lunenburg, the name suggested by one of the titles of the newly crowned King George II. The first town meeting was held on August 2; the inhabitants chose officers, with Josiah Willard and Samuel Page among the select-men and Edward Hartwell treasurer. The town's proprietors continued to meet separately to consider matters involving land. When they collected information on the ownership of proprietary shares, they found that nearly all the nonresidents had sold or transferred their rights to town residents.[19]

Turkey Hills had become Lunenburg through the coordinated efforts of interlocking levels of the colony: the General Court and its committee, proprietors and settlers, fathers and sons, military leaders and migrants. There were substantial continuities between the seventeenth-century settlements and the first frontier towns of the eighteenth century. The General Court carved out two towns from its wilderness stock, appointed a committee of its members, and gave definite directions for the shape and progress of the settlement. The villages bore a strong resemblance to their seventeenth-century predecessors. Fathers, such as Samuel Page, often provided the means for their sons to start a new farm family on the frontier. But on the eighteenth-century frontier, new relationships connected the older towns and the newer plantations. Absentee investors aided the resident inhabitants in developing the Wachusett for family farming. The eighty resident and nonresident proprietors gathered with the General Court's committee to report on their accomplishments in the Wachusett, with shares in the venture passing quickly to those on the site. The speed of Lunenburg's settlement and its successful entry into the ranks of New England towns demonstrates that town settlement had developed into a bold and expansive enterprise. Indian fighters had led the way from Lancaster to Lunenburg. Leaders in the parent community, such as Edward Hartwell and Josiah Willard, moved to Turkey Hills and provided the residents with experienced town officials and military officers.

Beyond Lunenburg

War and migration energized colonization during the extended "cold war" between the end of Queen Anne's War and the onset of King George's War; serial town settlement continued to accelerate in pace and expand in scope. Eighteenth-century colonists jumped well beyond their predecessors' cautious movements. The number of peripatetic settlers mounted, taking advantages of new opportunities outside established town borders. The people of the Wachusett looked north of Lancaster into the borderlands of the colony and up to the Connecticut River, the spearhead of English expansion, to match French military efforts and attract Indian trading partners. Town founders built a series of trading posts, military garrisons, and farming communities on both banks of the upper Connecticut. Enterprising townspeople created a commerce of colonization: they moved beyond forming proprietorships and obtaining land to scouting, building roads, tavern keeping, and surveying. Entrepreneurship reinforced the colony's military activities and also incorporated an increasing number of ordinary citizens as town founders.

The Reverend Andrew Gardner became the minister of Lunenburg before its incorporation. He was the son and namesake of the Reverend Andrew Gardner, the minister of Lancaster who had been killed during an Indian raid. He served as Worcester's minister in 1719 and then preached in Rutland and other Wachusett towns before the call came from Lunenburg. He did not last long before he asked for his release in 1730, claiming the indifference of his parishioners. This situation may have been exacerbated by his own lack of a "grave and sober demeanor," since he was reported to be apt to "indulge in a levity of manner on the Sabbath" and had a "predilection for hunting," practicing his marksmanship on wild turkeys and other game even on the holy day. Gardner remained in town as the first grammar school teacher and acquired many acres in Lunenburg. He also extended his interests northward, serving as the chaplain of Fort Dummer, and becoming one of the first grantees of Charlestown, New Hampshire, as well as several other northern plantations. He moved frequently and was buried at Bath, New Hampshire, where residents named a permanent monument, Gardner Mountain, after this roving spirit.[20]

The close of Governor Dummer's War initiated almost two decades of cold war. The French strengthened their position by building a fort at Crown Point and counted the Abenakis as allies in the Champlain River valley (see figure 2). The English, too, were busy in the northeastern borderlands. They constructed Fort Dummer on the upper Connecticut in 1728, garrisoned the post, and sent a minister to woo the Indians away from the French. English colonists looked to the region for new stocks of land in the 1730s. Soldiers, traders, and farmers jostled together in these new frontier communities with their Indian neighbors; many settlers came from the Wachusett. No. 4 (later Charlestown, New Hampshire) was established in 1740. When France and England quarreled over the succession to the Austrian throne, the old battle lines formed again in North America. These northern outposts, populated by residents of the Wachusett, became the defensive perimeter for English colonization. The Abenakis withdrew to Canada and the familiar guerrilla warfare resumed in the mid-1740s.[21]

The frontiers of New England settlement surged along a variety of fronts up the Connecticut River and in the Wachusett itself during the second quarter of the eighteenth century (see map 12). Whole series of settlements were planned, platted, organized, and populated according to the standardized pattern represented by Lunenburg's founding. Border townships to the north of Lunenburg, created in the two decades after 1713, protected the older settlements to the south. Fortified settlements guarded the new townships from the French and Indian raiders. Town founders in the Wachusett

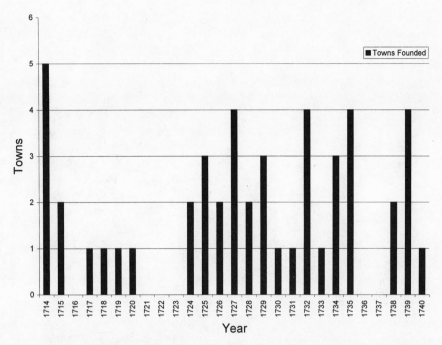

Figure 2. Town foundings in New England, 1714–1740.
Data from William Francis Galvin, *Historical Data Relating to Counties, Cities, and Towns in Massachusetts*, 5th ed. (Boston, 1997).

availed themselves of the opportunities for land grants and proprietary shares by participating in these new plantings. Many inhabitants of Lunenburg were active in the northwest Wachusett; they surveyed tracts of wilderness, built roads to connect old and new towns, served as proprietors of new plantations, manned the forts running up the Connecticut River, and protected their families at home during the ensuing warfare.[22]

The business of town founding was served by the synergistic link of war and colonization. To secure land and connect old and new townships in the vulnerable northeastern borderlands required building roads, undertaking scouting sorties, and surveying land. Colonel Josiah Willard and several others of Lunenburg were granted a township (Arlington, New Hampshire) in 1735 on the condition that they build what became known as the Northfield Road. In the words of the grant:

clear and make a convenient travelling Road, twelve feet wide, from Lunenburg to Northfield, and build a house for receiving & Entertaining travellers on said Road, about midway between Northfield and Lunenburg aforesaid and for the Encouragement of a Suitable Family to settle in said House, it is resolved that here shall be granted to him that shall Dwell in said House for the space of seven years from the Grant one hundred and fifty acres of land.[23]

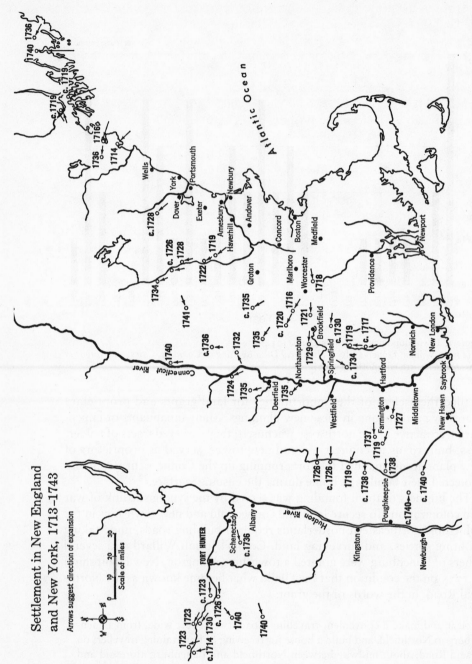

Settlement in New England and New York, 1713–1743

Arrows suggest direction of expansion

Scale of miles
0   10   20   30

Map 12. Settlement of New England and New York, 1713–1743. After 1713 extensive migration burst north well beyond the late-seventeenth-century resettlement. Colonists flowed north into New Hampshire and the Merrimack Valley and along the upper Connecticut River and the eastern coast of Maine; they went west to the Berkshires and into northwest Connecticut as well as filling in the northwestern

Roads opened for military purposes later served as highways for migrating families. Many residents of the Wachusett helped build and later traveled the forty-two-mile stretch of road that connected the newest frontier with the older "lower towns." After their success, the grantees returned the next year to propose a second "house of entertainment" for "the great ease and comfort of persons travelling that road." They received another parcel of four-hundred-and-fifty acres of northwestern Wachusett land. Willard and his half-brother Benjamin Bellows, a surveyor and settler in Lancaster and Lunenburg, also secured land north of Northfield for their scouting services along the western frontier. Willard commanded Fort Dummer for a season and was a grantee of Northfield, moving to the upper Connecticut River valley in the 1730s. Another early settler of Lunenburg, Nathan Heywood, laid out many of the townships springing up in the second quarter of the eighteenth century on the Wachusett's borders. He received a farm in a new Wachusett township granted to veterans of the Canada Expedition of 1690. Roads and surveys were the physical traces of the patterns of migration and kinship by which the people of the Wachusett constructed new communities such as Lunenburg in the image of the older villages. Grantees of the newest frontier settlements in the undivided lands of Massachusetts Bay built roads linking the old towns to the new ones for the migrants making the trek north and west. Those migrants were often their very own family members and neighbors.[24]

Lunenburg was no longer Lancaster's outpost after those newer settlements opened in northwestern Wachusett and the upper Connecticut River valley in the 1730s. At the beginning of this decade of expansion, most of Lunenburg's settlers located in the southwestern section of the original grant. John Fitch, the sixth of eight children, left Billerica for Lunenburg at the age of twenty-four in 1732; his family resided in the most thickly settled part of town. But the cycle of pioneering resumed with the rise of a new generation. When David Page of Lunenburg's first family came of age in 1729, he received a western lot of land in the uninhabited third division range of Lunenburg's lands. He married Priscilla Boynton, daughter of a Northfield Road petitioner, and moved west to build their log cabin on a steep hillside. He worked all winter on the cabin with his father and brothers, traveling between the family homestead and the western clearing. The young Page expected other settlers as neighbors; but he also anticipated hostile Indian visitors and built a wooden stockade to surround his cabin. Others soon came from Groton, Lancaster, Woburn, and Rowley; they also built garrison houses. Samuel Poole left Stoneham about 1740 and built a garrison in the southwestern corner of Lunenburg (later Fitchburg) (see map 13). There his brother James soon joined him. The two brothers shared Samuel's garrison, one of the five in town. The western section of Lunenburg took on a settled appearance despite the hazardous conditions. David Page's path through the woods became the road to another new Wachusett

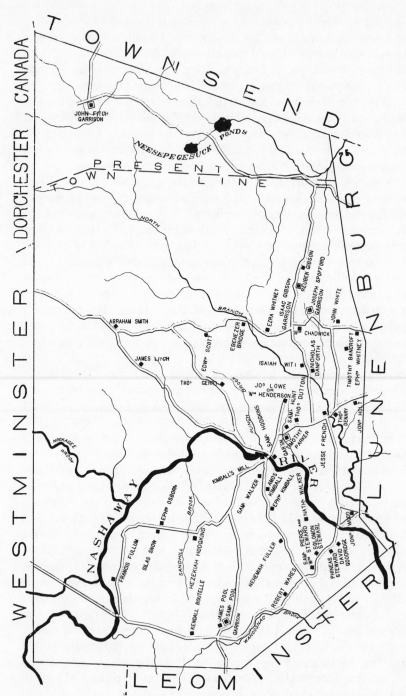

Map 13. Fitchburg and its early settlers, 1764. The map shows what became the town of Fitchburg, west of the original Lunenburg grant, west of the earliest Lunenburg settlement. John Fitch arrived in the area in the 1730s; his garrison (upper right on the map) stood at the northwest corner of Lunenburg's borders. (Reprinted from Henry A. Willis, "The Birth of Fitchburg," *Proceedings of the Fitchburg Historical Society* [Fitchburg, 1894–97], vol. 2, p. 36. Courtesy of Cornell University Libraries.)

plantation (later Ashburnham). Settlers and scouts making that journey stopped at the Page household where David was a licensed innkeeper. He also pursued trade with some distant Indians, often complaining to his neighbors that he was forced to travel great distances to find the scattered hunters. Others wondered whether these haphazard movements resulted from his questionable trading practices, for according to one set of reminiscences, "it was his custom to argue that his foot weighed four pounds and his hand one pound and that such measures for goods were entirely fair!"

Settlers followed David Page and spread out from the original eastern section of the town to the western bounds of the township.[25] John Fitch sold his southeastern homestead after seven years and bought 120 acres on the northern town border in 1739. He built his new house seven-and-a-half miles from the town center at a point on the Northfield Road called "the rendezvous," where travelers and scouts split off north to New Hampshire or west to Ashburnham and the newest plantations. The number of families moving to these northern border towns increased rapidly. Fitch realized the site's commercial potential and promptly set up an inn.[26] Village entrepreneurs located their enterprises far from the original town center, paralleling John Prescott's move to his southern mills in seventeenth-century Lancaster.

War enveloped New England again and raids fell on these exposed, younger communities. King George's War broke out in 1744 as England and France quarreled over the succession to the Austrian throne, and inland New England once again became the site of a conflict with European roots. Raids fell especially hard on tiny, fortified Connecticut River outposts in the valley; there were thirty-six separate raids in the spring of 1746, and the northern border towns were deserted. Wachusett farmers manned the parapets of the fort at No. 4 along the Connecticut. Colonel Samuel Willard commanded a local regiment for the 1746 attack on the French fortress at Louisbourg. Blockhouses or garrisons were constructed on the colony's northern borders to protect residents of exposed Wachusett townships such as Lunenburg. The court assigned soldiers to and appropriated funds for these remaining settled towns "to put the inland frontiers in this province in a better posture of defence" and resumed the payment of scalping bounties. Edward Hartwell raised a company of forty-seven men in 1748; each week the company assembled at John Fitch's garrison and received their assignments for scouting or garrison duty. Lunenburg's residents resumed their familiar Wachusett mentality, of a beleaguered border town under siege. Twenty years after Dummer's War, however, Hartwell commanded a much larger defensive force.[27]

Four soldiers were stationed at Fitch's home when the Indians finally attacked in 1748. As a result of that attack, Fitch was captured. He later wrote an account of his ordeal, producing a captivity narrative in the fashion of Mary Rowlandson's. He began similarly:

On the fifth day of July . . . the Indian Enemy appeared and shot down one soldier upon being Discovered & Immediately drove him & the other soldiers into the Garrison and after besieging the same about one Hour & half they killed the other soldier through the port Hole in the Flanker and your petitioner was Left alone with his wife and five children soon after which he surrendered and became a prisoner with his said family & the Enemy took and Carried away such things as they pleased & Burnt the House and Garrison with the Rest and then we Entered into a melancholly Captivity with one small Child on the mothers breast and two more became suckling Children.[28]

After the attack, alarm spread through the colony. The *Boston Weekly News Letter* reported the death of the soldiers and speculated on the fate of the Fitches: "The Master of the House Mr. John Fitch 'tis thought was seized by them in the Field, as he was spreading Hay and his Wife as she was bringing Water from the Spring about 20 Rods distance, a Pail and her Bonnet being found near the Path."[29]

Three days later, numerous Wachusett townspeople—old and new—pleaded their case to the court: "the Indian Enemy have very lately been among us in considerable numbers & with unusual boldness." While Elizabeth Poole worked in the isolated fields of western Lunenburg binding flax, Indians suddenly appeared between her and the house. James Poole had left the fields for his team; he decided to remain with the children in the garrison when the Indians attacked. Elizabeth left on her own and took to her heels with the Indians in pursuit. Racing toward Leominster, she evaded her pursuers and reached the blockhouse in town, where she sounded the alarm and secured assistance for her beleaguered family.[30] One Lunenburg resident was surprised while searching for a stray cow; another new settler was attacked while hoeing corn in his fields. "One of our Garrisons" was "destroyed," and "we Caint many of us, labour on our Farms or abide in our towns." Lunenburg's selectmen and military officers added their concern about the panic spreading in the Wachusett: settlers were "quitting their Habitations," and "Garrisons built by order and Direction of the General Court are already deserted." With most northerly and new settlements abandoned, Wachusett residents began to fear a complete rollback of the frontier like that which had occurred during Metacom's War. The governor could only advise settlers to carry "their Arms and Ammunition with them." The war was over by fall, terminated by the Peace of Aix-la-Chapelle, followed by a prisoner exchange. Townspeople had displayed great fortitude during the four long years of King George's War. Northern outposts had been temporarily abandoned and frontier settlers' terror had resumed, but local military forces, reinforced by colonial soldiers defended the region. No destruction comparable to the 1676 raid on Lancaster occurred. The prolonged anxiety of the resettlement period had been avoided.[31]

When John Fitch returned from his captivity in Canada, he built a new house on the site of his ruined garrison in Lunenburg and immediately asked the colony for compensation for wartime losses. The autobiographical account of Fitch's captivity included for the court a recounting of his community service. This account is revealing, especially when compared to John Prescott's account of his own service almost one hundred years earlier, because it shows the greater geographical dispersion of eighteenth-century village life. Fitch told the court about moving to a location seven-and-a-half miles from Lunenburg's meetinghouse and three miles away from any other inhabitants. He had built himself a house, "Improved so much Land as to raise provisions for his growing Family," and "Entertained & refreshed Travelers" on the Northfield Road. Fitch was without any neighbors to share a garrison. But when war returned, his remote location strategically served the colony as a fortified site for the exposed settlers and colonial military forces in the borderlands. Soldiers were soon stationed there, while local and out-of-town scouting parties retired there as a "place of Resort & Refreshment." Fitch closed his captivity narrative, not with a tale of providence but with a request for provisions. His "removes," in contrast with Mary Rowlandson's, found him at the crossroads of activity in the Wachusett, all roads connected with town settlement. The court granted him eighty pounds in compensation for his losses.[32]

Samuel Hunt and several of Lunenburg's other newest western settlers petitioned for a separation at a March 1757 town meeting. Hunt had arrived in Lunenburg from Tewksbury in 1749 at age thirty-eight, with his wife Hannah and five children. The next year he opened a tavern on the road to the town center. His fellow petitioners, Amos and Ephraim Kimball, started up saw- and gristmills there, and the site quickly became the center of a growing artisan community. The westerners' petition launched a debate and prompted a committee report but no action. They renewed their drive for recognition four years later, complaining about the great distance from the town's meetinghouse, but their request for a new town was "passed in the Negative." With subsequent efforts blocked by the selectmen, the forty-three inhabitants who wished to establish their own community approached the General Court. While the court could not agree immediately, Lunenburg's town officials acknowledged the inevitable and agreed to the petition. The settlers "on the westerly part of Lunenburg" appeared six days later in Boston to secure their charter of incorporation on February 3, 1764, quickly filling in the blank space for the new town's name with Fitchburg, for John Fitch.[33]

A new set of village entrepreneurs had taken charge of town settlement in the middle years of the eighteenth century. The Reverend Andrew Gardner, Colonel Samuel Willard, John Fitch, and David Page all represented different levels of rural society in the Wachusett, but the renewal of colonization—appropriating colonial land reserves and founding new towns—gave all four men the opportunity to provide for their families' maintenance and more. Town settlement revived and expanded in the eighteenth century for several reasons: the continued demographic success of the colony's residents, the large amounts of unappropriated land recently cleared of their Indian occupants, several generations' experience of successful frontier living, the maintenance of familiar family and village ties, and the expansive entrepreneurship of the colonists. The broader geographic scope and growing numbers pushed the settlement process toward a new configuration. The colony turned to men such as Colonel Willard and Benjamin Bellows for valuable experience and for the capital resources that were needed for economic development or provincial defense, a situation similar to that of years past when Willard's grandfather, Simon, and Daniel Gookin played leading roles. These notables in return secured shares in a series of townships opening up one after another in frontier areas. As town founders, they maintained and expanded their roles as regional figures, members of an interlocking elite group reaching out to the borderlands of the Bay Colony, where they encountered other mobile Massachusetts men.

David Page had not been interested in settling down; he had begun squatting in Turkey Hills because he lacked the required capital to stake his claim in founding towns. He was willing to move, and his wanderlust pushed him out to the margins of New England. In 1748 he led his family westward to Petersham, a Wachusett settlement founded by veterans of White and Lovewell's expedition. He uprooted his family several times over the next fifteen years, travelling further north up the Connecticut River valley to areas where he became either a grantee or landholder (see table 3). In 1763 he obtained a charter from Governor Benning Wentworth of New Hampshire for lands along the upper Coos River. First, he sent his son David to clear the wilderness grant. Then, he and three other settlers joined the young man, soon bringing their families and livestock. The pioneers named their new towns Lancaster and Lunenburg. Three generations of the Page family had been pioneers, taking them from Groton to South Carolina to Turkey Hills to the upper Coos River.[34] Lunenburg's founding, the creation of fortified communities beyond Lancaster and Lunenburg, and the business of colonization that connected them all accelerated the process of town settlement in the Wachusett and spun its people off deeper into the borderlands of the northeast.

Enterprise was not limited to the elite or the peripatetic. John Fitch, a carpenter, innkeeper, land trader, and farmer, had a town named after him, an honor denied colonial notable John Prescott in the seventeenth century. Fitch represented a new kind of town founder. He had been willing to move to an isolated site and exploit the opportunities opened by eighteenth-century colonization. Although the money that came with his father-in-law's death gave him a more ample stake in society—his new house surpassed most of his neighbor's dwellings in size and elegance—he continued

Table 3. David Page's land holdings, 1748–1763

Year	Location
1748	Petersham, Mass.
1749	Dublin, N.H. (grantee)
1751	Walpole, N.H.
1752	Rockingham, Vt.
1761	Woodstock, Vt. (principal grantee)
1762	Wallingford, Vt.
1763	Windsor, Vt.
1763	Haverhill, N.H.
1763	Lancaster, N.H. (principle grantee)
1763	Lunenburg, Vt.
1763	Jefferson, N.H. (grantee)

Source: Page genealogy in Doris Kirkpatrick, *The City and the River* (Fitchburg, Mass., 1971), p. 411.

to ply his trades, till his fields, and traffic in lands in the 1750s. He also pursued opportunities as a grantee in new townships and purchase uncultivated lands in new settlements in central Massachusetts and New Hampshire. Towns were no longer settled on an agricultural base with expansion resulting from the budding of new settlements. Instead, commercial possibilities existed from the start, and the vast geographic area involved meant that the enterprise of town founding itself could provide opportunities for many early settlers. In this manner the process previewed some nineteenth-century town foundings in the Midwest.

The First Centennial Celebration

> Man is formed for Society. The social principle within him doth not confine itself to the narrow bounds of a family, friends, relations, or a neighborhood; but extends itself further, to districts, towns, provinces, and kingdoms.
> Timothy Harrington, *A Peaceable Temper and Conduct Divinely Enjoined*
> (1759)

In 1759, at the birth of Princeton (one of the numerous Wachusett towns created north of Lancaster during the eighteenth century), Lancaster's fifth pastor, Timothy Harrington, preached a message that spoke of the social body as expanding far beyond the "bounds of a family, friends, relations, or a neighborhood," but extending outward to embrace New England society as a whole. Harrington traveled through central Massachusetts occupying several pulpits after taking his degrees at Harvard College. He settled in the far frontier at Lower Ashuelot (Swanzey, New Hampshire) in 1741, the settlement's first pastor. His tenure there was brief, for King William's War

halted colonization along the upper Connecticut River valley; the plantation was abandoned and its few buildings burned by Indians in 1747. Harrington returned to his wife's family in Lexington, where he kept school
until called by the First Parish in Lancaster in 1748. His installation
brought many of the colony's clerics to Lancaster. John Hancock of Lexington urged Harrington to read history. The Harringtons took their settlement in land rather than cash and beautified their homestead with an
avenue of elms.[35]

Five years later Harrington reflected on his frontier experience and on
Lancaster's past in the town's first local history, on the occasion of the
town's centennial. Harrington discussed the process and progress of town
settlement over the first hundred years of English colonization in the
Wachusett. He listened to the stories of the aging pioneers and wrote from
the frontier perspective, which Samuel Penhallow lacked and the Mathers
disdained. When Harrington spoke to his parishioners on May 28, 1753, he
admitted Showanon into the ranks of town founders, and he chronicled
raids, ordeals of captives, and ministerial deaths, but he focused on the
transformation of the wilderness outpost into a flourishing country town.

Harrington began with the classical typological narrative of "wilderness
work" made available by Edward Johnson. His epigraph—"Many a time
have they afflicted me from my youth, yet they have not prevailed against
me"—illustrated the theme of Lancaster's endurance under adversity. He
drew analogies between his audience's experiences and those of their predecessors; he recounted the first generation's "afflictions of Israel," the
"preservation of the Christian Church," and "the remove . . . into this
then howling wilderness" by the Israelites and the Puritans. Then Harrington halted his Christian chronicle, to begin the "particular consideration of
the affairs of this town." "In the year 1645, Showanon, alias Shaumauw,
proprietor of Nashawogg, and Sachem of the Nashaways, who lived at
Waushacum, informed Mr. Thomas King, of Watertown (with whom he
traded and for whom he had a considerable friendship) of the said tract of
land as well accommodated for a plantation, desiring that the English
would come and set down by him." This amicable tableau of Showanon's
visit to Watertown characterized the early period of "peace and prosperity,"
when the Indians were "very serviceable" to the settlers, supplying them
with corn and game "on very moderate terms." Metacom's War swept
away all these peaceable beginnings, through Harrington reminded his listeners that Metacom and others had lured the friendly Nashaways into the
hostilities. Harrington filled the remainder of his history with a series of
"sorrowful occasions." Inhabitants were carried away from their houses
and ministers were slain in the fields. Harrington detailed the names and
dates of every ambush and attack, only pausing for a brief ecclesiastical history of Lancaster, an account mostly of the ministers' short tenures and
their abrupt departures, some killed by Indians and others driven out by

controversy. Lancaster, Harrington recalled, had long been a frontier station, often suffering "the fury of the enemy."[36] Looking back from 1753, Harrington did not castigate the barbarous foe or extol the piety of Puritan pilgrims; colonists became Indian fighters and the settlers of Lancaster he praised for their endurance through adversity and their progress in the wilderness. Mid-eighteenth-century Lancaster was no longer a frontier station.

Lancaster, Harrington announced, had become "fair and flourishing." He focused on the transition from wilderness to garden.

> Surely, it was God that brought a vine from far, cast out the heathen before it, planted it, and caused it to take root and fill the land; so that the hills are covered with the shadow and the boughs thereof are like the goodly cedars. God grant that the hedges may not be broken down, that it may never be plucked by those that pass by, that the boar out of the wilderness may never water it, nor the wild beasts devour it; but may the glory of the Lord be upon it from generation to generation.[37]

Harrington's ministerial forbears had seen material and spiritual dangers lurking on the frontier, but Lancaster's parson had only praise for his flock's achievement under the severest afflictions. He emphasized their endurance under attack and their transformation of the wilderness; he said little about the strange occurrences that had so concerned the Mathers or the dangers of the heathen and the forest that Mary Rowlandson had found so frightening.

Harrington brought the efforts of Lancaster's pioneers within the holy circle. He used rich Biblical imagery: "The solitary places rejoice, the wilderness blossometh as the rose." Their venturesome parents had come to this inland region so that "they might leave you in the enjoyment of the gospel in its purity." He spoke of "their fair temporal inheritance." He offered no jeremiad, in which the present generations' shortcomings were measured against their ancestors' virtues; rather, they were told "ye are risen up in your fathers stead; and prosperity shines in full orb upon you." At their centennial, Lancaster's residents offered their children their own expansive example for emulation as a "growing people." Harrington charged the children to continue their fathers' work in town settlement whereby "the habitations of cruelty" become "a valley of vision." Lancaster had reached maturity, but colonization continued within the Wachusett. Memories of their fathers' "wilderness work" would bind the generations: "Be ambitious of imitating whatever was excellent in your ancestors." Harrington's explicit concern in history-writing was to connect the generations.[38]

This history centered on a sequence of events—relations with the Indians—and on a physical transformation—the creation of a New England townscape. Indians were integral to the story, not preparatory or antagonistic to it; they were constitutive of colonization. The settlers of Lancaster fashioned their history out of local materials—Indian attacks and town settlement—to make the creation of New England their own story. Their experience on the frontiers of the colony was brought into the mainstream of the Puritan mission, although not as a chronicle of exemplary figures or of great deeds. The everyday activities of town-building had continued through decades of warfare and provided the basis for the renewal and extension of serial town settlement.

Six years after this address, Harrington spoke to the plantation of Princeton, an "infant plantation" in the Wachusett. This village had achieved the requisite size and population to be incorporated as a district. The minister instructed them on the more difficult achievement of becoming a society. He offered the residents of Princeton a divine, moral, and historical foundation as a community in his sermon, which he titled *A Peaceable Temper and Conduct Divinely Enjoined*. The primary dangers facing new plantings was now internal, so he delivered a latitudinarian message of sociability: "Peace and friendship are the soul and cement of society." Peace and harmony, "in a natural and in a moral way, lay a foundation for the prosperity of the district." The production and transmission of local history only strengthened the process of uniting a multitude of individuals. Harrington was well aware of how the "private interests" in eighteenth-century plantations could diverge from the "public system." Town settlement had demonstrated that it contained the means to foster increase and still maintain peace. Lancaster's story of a wilderness becoming "a valley of vision" was a powerful example of material success for the newer foundings of the Wachusett. To achieve those results had required both the emergence of peripatetic individuals such as Timothy Harrington and the post-1713 renewal of town settlement. Lancaster and Lunenburg had become surrounded by flocks of newer foundings by the mid-eighteenth century. But maintaining the chain from "generation to generation" was equally important to New England town founders and local historians. The commemorative narrative of the Wachusett's founding both bound the new settlers to their ancestors and incorporated new figures and new relationships not present in earlier histories—the Indians were seen as founders and townspeople chronicled as Indian fighters.[39]

The new bureaucratic method of town settlement would expand. Critics raised fears of decline, but the memories of previous generations facilitated the filling up of the Wachusett with proper New England towns.

4 *Narragansett No. 2:*
Reproducing Families and Farms

> We may go on with great Encouragement, Boldness, and Dispatch to fill up
> such Vacancies as will still remain, between the Old and New Settlements. . . .
> For, that many of our Old Towns are too full of Inhabitants for Husbandry;
> many of them living upon small Shares of Land, and generally all are Hus-
> bandmen. . . . And also many of our People are slow in Marrying for want
> of Settlements.
>
> John Wise, *A Word of Comfort to a Melancholy Country* (1721)

After the Peace of Utrecht in 1713, colonial authorities turned
from the defense of frontier settlements to the expansion of New England.
Ipswich's minister, John Wise, articulated the commonly held view that colonization should "with great . . . Dispatch . . . fill up such Vacancies as
will still remain, between the Old and New Settlements"; tellingly, Wise
focused on the hunger for land felt by residents of older towns rather than
on the imperative of securing the colonial frontier. Conflicts about the dis-
posal of unappropriated lands arose among competing parties in different
branches of government. After lengthy legislative battles, eastern patriarchs
and western settlers succeeded in extending the process of serial town settlement, both accelerating its pace and expanding its scope. Numerous large
land grants were made simultaneously to whole categories of petitioners,
who carved the territory up into towns and divided themselves into proprietary bodies; towns were to distribute their land and organize local institutions more rapidly than before. Settlers, however, were slow to arrive, and
incorporation took longer to achieve than people hoped with so many competing sites. The General Court initiated changes in the process of town settlement after 1713; Lunenburg and its sister township Fitchburg were of a
standard size and were developed under a set procedure. When the flood-
gates opened in the 1720s and 1730s with the block grants, things changed.
Huge tracts of land in Worcester County, New Hampshire, Vermont, and
the District of Maine passed out of the public domain into the hands of var-

ious proprietary groups. The General Court entered the land office business, sponsoring the settlement of the seven Narragansett townships, the fifteen Canada townships (Canada was the name of one of the Wachusett grants), and the twenty-six Frontier townships, transforming the process of serial town settlement into an unprecedented experiment in rapid territorial expansion and popular proprietorship. Contemporaries worried that the scale and pace of this process opened the way for land speculation and would give rise to social disorder, a view that has been debated by historians of these eighteenth-century speculative townships.[1]

Indeed, the controversy over whether the rapid expansion created social disorder entered quickly into historical writing by contemporary participants such as Thomas Hutchinson, who charged the "land-jobbing" represented a decline from the seventeenth-century practice of compact settlement. Later students of eighteenth-century town settlement also saw social declension in the "speculative townships." Frederick Jackson Turner and his students, such as Roy Akagi and Lois Mathews, vilified eastern land speculators who exploited western frontiersmen. Mathews highlighted the well-documented case of Narragansett No. 2, the future Westminster, Massachusetts, as an example of a new "carelessness concerning some institutions which were traditionally very dear to the descendant of the Puritans."[2]

The court was under pressure from two directions to quicken the pace of settlement: imperial officials were still anxious to defend the empire's borders from French and Indian foes, and masses of petitioners in the older towns were seeking new lands on which to establish their children. Veterans of military campaigns in the Narragansett and elsewhere claimed proprietary rights in the territory from which Indians had been evicted; the General Court recognized the link between conquest and colonization, and this recognition became the basis of a regional system tying together eastern and western towns.

In the third generation of New England settlement, fathers in older towns sold their proprietary shares in the new towns to actual settlers in order to accumulate property where they were; in the fourth generation, sons and daughters turned proprietorships into family farms. In Narragansett No. 2 that transfer of property was well under way by 1751, but the development of family farms was still in its infancy. Kin groups facilitated both migration from old towns to new ones and the reconstruction of community life in western settlements. In comparison to previous experiences Narragansett No. 2 was farther from migrants' places of origin and the plantation's land market was more active than in earlier townships, conditions that posed challenges to the orderly process of settlement. People and property were transferred to the new town more rapidly than was political power; delays in achieving autonomy and self-government posed the greatest problems to the Wachusett towns founded in the eighteenth century.

Narragansett No. 2 was not alone as a new settlement in the region. Central Massachusetts filled up with towns between 1730 and 1750. Lancaster and Brookfield were no longer isolated outposts. These mature towns in southern Worcester County divided or budded, but the greatest activity took place in the more remote, northwest sector of the county (see map 14). Nine towns were opened for settlement in the 1730s, ranging from the northwest quadrant of the enormous Rutland grant, which eventually became Hutchinson, then Barre, to the western reaches of Lunenburg, soon to become Fitchburg. The General Court made several grants simultaneously. Veterans and their descendants utilized their claims in five Wachusett towns: two Narragansett townships (Templeton and Westminster), two Canada townships (Ashburnham and Winchendon), and Petersham, a town granted specifically to claimants from the Lovewell and White expedition. These plantations proved slow in attracting settlers and fulfilling the Court's stringent conditions. Those towns such as Fitchburg or Westminster that were closest to older, incorporated towns were most successful in the 1730s and 1740s. Those on the margins of the Wachusett, such as Dorchester and Ipswich Canada (later Winchendon and Ashburnham), were either abandoned during the imperial wars of the 1740s or waited until midcentury for settlers. Although the development was uneven, New England expanded dramatically in the eighteenth century.[3]

The Narragansett Grants

The town of Westminster traces its origins as far back as December 10, 1675, when Massachusetts Bay soldiers faced their Indian opponents during Metacom's War. The governor's proclamation promised the soldiers that "if they played the man, took the fort, and drove the enemy out of Narragansett country, which is their great seat, they should have a gratuity of land, besides their wages." A decade later "soldiers . . . in the Nipmug Country, and at the Narragansett Fort" appealed for their land. The successful petitioners never took up their grant "in Nipmug Country." In 1727 those "present at the Fort and Fight at Narragansett, or descendants of those who were there" again petitioned the General Court for a grant "of such vacant lands as may serve for settlements." The two houses of the legislature, the House of Representatives and the Council, were unable to find common ground, however, thus forestalling any action for five years. The House approved the petition and appointed a committee to lay out a grant similar to that planned in 1685, but the Council balked. At the next session the Council followed the advice of the assembly, but its restrictive deadlines for organizing the petitioners and proprietors led the House to withhold its consent. Finally, in 1728 the three parties agreed to granting "two townships of the contents of Six square miles each in some of the unappropriated Lands of this Province." Public advertisements invited veterans or "their lawful Representatives" to come forward with their claims. The flood of

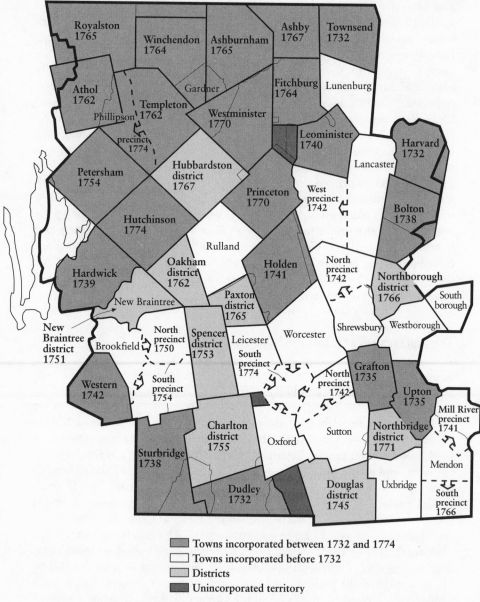

Towns incorporated between 1732 and 1774
Towns incorporated before 1732
Districts
Unincorporated territory

Map 14. Worcester County towns, circa 1774. The map displays the political boundaries of the towns with their dates of incorporation. (Reprinted from Michael Steinitz et al., *Historical and Archaeological Resources of Central Massachusetts* [Boston, 1985], p. 83. By permission of the Massachusetts Historical Commission. Courtesy of Cornell University Libraries.)

petitions and a smallpox epidemic made compiling lists of grantees and the actual claimants a difficult task. The claimants now petitioned in 1729 for additional townships as well as more time, since because of their great numbers, "the granted land would make so small a Portion to each Family, as will be of little or no Benefit to them." The House of Representatives agreed to the principle of 120 grantees per town, but the Council opposed handing out any more town grants. This stalemate continued for two years. Finally, the petitioners' standing committee composed a joint statement with the House committee which they submitted to the Council in January 1732.[4]

The petition address opened by reminding colonial officials of the promises made to the soldiers upon the battlefield during a harsh winter when the "whole Country was filled with Distress & Fear." Valiant soldiers had traditionally, beginning with the ancient republics, received gratuities in addition to wages. Furthermore, the petitioners announced, their army was composed not of outcasts but of men from good New England families. The original 1685 grant, land long since distributed in the "Heart of the Country," was far more valuable than their request of remote borderlands. Finally, they turned to the problem of eight hundred claimants receiving only two townships.

> Beyond what has been offered, it should be Considered that to grant the present Petition, and [to] give [out] such a quantity of Land as may be worth Settling, and [to do so] upon Conditions of bringing forward Townships is more agreeable . . . for the publick Good than to Give away Tracts of Land [as currently planned] and suffer and even tempt men to let [the tracts] ly waste and unimproved[;] for in the way that has been proposed, and in which some Progress has been made, the Land will be divided into such Scraps that they will not be worth receiving.

Such a restrictive policy would lead to morselization, the petitioners argued, altering the land system of family farms and disrupting serial town settlement as the means of continuing New England society. They charged that an opposing plan would offer lands to idle speculators and political favorites; such schemes for settlement would come to naught, leaving the valuable lands "to ly waste and unimproved." They feared the recreation on the frontier of conditions in the old towns. The petitioners' rhetoric referred to the "bringing forward of Townships," the traditions of New England settlement that had achieved the public good of the Commonwealth as well as the private needs of its farm families. Eighteenth-century Bay Colony residents feared mounting demographic pressures in the older towns; such innovations as large-scale granting of series of townships could be justified as these venturesome conservatives' response to the New Englanders' demographic success.[5]

The Council bent before the strongly articulated petition, but Governor Belcher balked. The veterans enlisted several powerful colonial figures to use their interest with the governor. With the petitioners' numbers rising to over 840, the House of Representatives and Council authorized five more townships in June of 1732. Governor Belcher signed the grant eight months later. The grantees met that very same day to instruct their clerk to divide up the entire body into seven equal blocs and advertise a general public meeting. The 848 individuals came from twenty towns, with the largest number from Boston, Cambridge, Concord, and Charlestown. They gathered on the Boston Common on June 6, 1733, for a two-day meeting that sorted the general body of Narragansett grantees into seven distinct bodies. The various proprietary committees met that fall to choose their sites by lot. James Lowden and a company of those living in Cambridge, Charlestown, Watertown, Weston, Sudbury, Newton, Medford, Malden, and Reading were assigned "Number Two at Wachusett." Initiative passed to the respective proprietary committees. The legislative battles that had given rise to the grants had preserved the outlines of town founding. Families had turned back any competing vision of large-scale development in favor of serial town settlement.[6]

The grantees had waited a long time; they traveled greater distances than did settlers in the seventeenth-century, but they carried familiar expectations. The General Court's grant had made the proprietors responsible for establishing sixty families with a minister within six years, with lots assigned for minister, ministry, and school. Because they had far more participants in the process, the proprietors turned to the committee system. Westminster, or Narragansett Township No. 2, one of the two original 1729 grants, was located in northern Worcester County above the original Lancaster towns on a range of elevated lands that separates the waters of the Connecticut River from those of the Merrimack, about fifty miles west-northwest of Boston and twenty miles north of Worcester. The committee members called a meeting of the grantees in 1733 by posting advertisements in Watertown, Sudbury, Cambridge, and other proprietary towns. The one hundred and nineteen grantees, residing in nine towns west of Cambridge, met there to establish a standing committee to direct their affairs and a dividing committee to survey and divide the lands. After meeting several times that winter, the proprietors turned matters over to the committees. The dividing committee labored that winter and spring, laying out first-division lots of sixty acres.[7]

When spring arrived, the next general meeting was held in Watertown to draw the home lots. The first-division lands were set up in nine rows of rectangular plots, sixty acres in size (see map 15) with a central path, Main Street, located between lots eight to twelve on one side and one to seven on the other. The small common extended before the intended meetinghouse lot at the center of the plan. Unlike in earlier settlements, further divisions

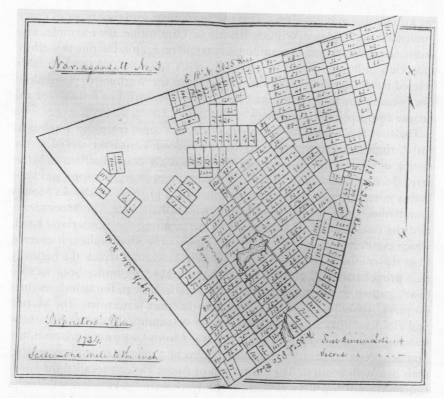

Map 15. Narragansett No. 2 lots, first and second division lands, drawn from the Proprietors' Plan of 1734. (Reprinted from William Sweetzer Heywood, *History of Westminster, Massachusetts* [Lowell, Mass., 1893], pp. 58–59. Reproduction of an original survey of the dividing committee of proprietors, 1734, for second division lots. Courtesy of the American Antiquarian Society.)

of land quickly followed, enriching those holding proprietary rights. Second-division lots, also sixty acres in size, were laid out in 1741 to the north of the first division plots, with the remaining allotments on the outskirts of the town center. The familiar rectangular shapes were supplemented by meadowlands assigned to individual owners. The 1755 third division completed Narragansett No. 2's land division, all within a single generation. The spatial pattern of settlement was a familiar one, the linear township with dispersed farmsteads.[8]

Although land was generously distributed, settlers remained scarce in the new plantation, and this posed a difficulty. Sixty families needed to be settled by 1741, the General Court had stipulated, or the grant would be forfeited. Strenuous efforts were required to people new plantations in the second quarter of the eighteenth century since so many competing sites were opened up at the same time. Proprietors offered bounties to those who would "Erect and build a house" and "Clear and fence three acres of land fitt for mowing and Plowing." There were rewards for other types of development as well: Major William Brattle of Cambridge, for example, also received a grant of land for building a sawmill on his lot. Despite this effort, only two buildings stood in 1737, Brattle's sawmill and the log cabin erected by the dividing committee. Progress in the Wachusett proved slow, not because the proprietors had speculative designs, but because of the intense competition for settlers.[9]

The first few settlers in Narragansett No. 2 came from the Wachusett rather than from the proprietary towns. Indeed, Lancaster served as the source of settlers and supplies during these early years. Fairbanks Moor arrived from Lancaster in March 1737 with his wife and six sons and later built a home on his lot, which he had purchased in 1736. Fairbanks Moor's grandfather, John, had been an early settler of Lancaster. The Moors traveled the twelve miles to Narragansett No. 2 along the Sunderland road, which connected Lancaster with the Connecticut River Valley; it entered from the southeast, passed along Wachusett Lake, and struck the highway that proprietors had cleared to reach "the Meeting-house Spot in said town," at which point the migrants cut a path through the woods to their property. Abner Holden and his family came from Watertown. The Moors' and Holdens' first winter in Westminster was unusually severe, the snow standing four feet deep for months. Cut off from Lancaster's gristmill, the families prepared bread by pounding grain in a mortar and supplemented their diet with venison. The young son of Abner Holden recalled the isolation on the northwestern borders of the Wachusett: "A Howling wilderness it was, where no men dwelt; the hideous yell of wolves, the shriek of wolves, the gobbling of the turkeys, and the barking of foxes was all the music we enjoyed; no friend to visit, no soul in the surrounding towns, all a dreary waste exposed to a thousand difficulties." Eventually, others joined these two families in this howling wilderness, and the town contained about 30 inhabitants by the close of 1740 and 125 a decade later.[10]

Crowded eastern towns supplied most of Westminster's first settlers, those who arrived from 1737 to 1750. Almost one third came from Watertown, Cambridge, and Sudbury, and nearly half from the nine proprietary towns since proprietors supplied most of the information about the new settlement. Seventeenth-century settlers had secured ample reserves of land for themselves and their children, but those reserves were gone by the early eighteenth century as the third generation came of age. In the village of Chebacco, part of coastal Ipswich, the population doubled between 1695 and 1718, and the price of land rose more than 40 percent over the next three decades. In Concord, the average landholding in 1663 had been 259 acres, but it had dropped to only 56 acres by 1759. Seventeenth-century towns such as Watertown and Sudbury had always sent off migrants looking for fresh land and social opportunity; witness Marlborough's and Lancaster's foundings. But the pace of outmigration picked up noticeably in the early eighteenth century. In Andover the proportion of men moving nearly doubled from almost 22 to 39 percent between the second and third generations; more than half of the men in the fourth generation left that inland town, which had been founded in 1646. And they dispersed in many more directions than the earlier migrants had; Andover's fourth generation migrants moved to fifty-two different communities, including Connecticut and New Hampshire.[11]

Moving to new towns had always been a familiar strategy to settle the next generation on farms of their own. As older towns founded in the seventeenth century grew crowded and the price of land rose, patriarchs resorted to more complex strategies to accommodate their large families. One eighteenth-century father, Nathan Birdsey of Stratford, Connecticut, described his plight in a letter inquiring about new plantations in western Massachusetts. "As God has blest me with a numerous off-Spring, and it Suiting my Affairs much better to bring my Boys up to Husbandry than to put em out to Trades; but not having Land Sufficient for Farms for em all; I purpose if God shall please to Spare mine & their lives, to Sell Some out-Pieces of Land, & purchase Some of em Settlements in Some new Towns where Land is good & cheap, & ye Title uncontroverted, & Shall be glad of your advice where it wou'd be best to purchase." Seventeenth-century families, arriving early in towns with large land reserves, had often been able to locate children on continuous farms or consolidate their strips of land into larger farms. During the war years, farms and towns filled in behind the exposed borders. In the post-1713 boom, as town granting soared, some families looked to western lands as Birdsey did. Others utilized veterans' claims, purchased one of the many new proprietorships, or entered the land market to secure land for their heirs. In some towns with maturing economies, some sons could take up trades or go off to sea rather than pursue farming, but these paths often required bits of land, too. Many fathers without land enough, who preferred agriculture to trade, were able to sell expensive pieces of land in older towns and settle their sons in the "new Towns where Land is good & cheap."

New England colonists' goal, historians James Henretta and David Vickers have shown, was to achieve a competency—a "comfortable independence"—for their families and to provide the same for their progeny. Families and fathers often freely entered the land market, not with an animus toward commercial transactions, but to secure land for their heirs. Serial town settlement was the broader means of maintaining desired material way of life and set of cultural norms, a series of familial decisions writ large, the means by which families reproduced and secured farms. Expectations of settling their sons did not change only the means of securing these familiar cultural goals.[12]

Eastern and western towns were linked together in the process of town settlement in the eighteenth century, the east sending off migrants to found the west's new towns. These demographic movements within a large, flexible social system resulted from a series of strategic decisions made locally as to which families provided migrants, whether sons and daughters moved on or stayed put on the farm or nearby family lands. The press of petitions flooding the General Court after 1713 and the heated rhetoric of the Narragansett veterans came from concerned heads of families who found it increasingly difficult to maintain family competencies and saw these new townships as an answer. Third-generation fathers, faced with diminished prospects of settling the next generation on family land, sought land on the frontier. Many in Concord looked west to the new townships opening up in Nipmuc country and other, more distant areas where the Indian inhabitants had fled or been dispossessed after Metacom's War. The patriarch of the Barrett family of Concord had held a commanding estate and rights to future divisions when Concord was an infant plantation. By the 1720s, however, Humphrey Barrett's grandchildren, Benjamin and Joseph, began several ventures to secure rights in townships in the Wachusett and New Hampshire. They joined with their neighbors to obtain permission from the General Court to purchase land (in what would later become Grafton) in central Massachusetts. One Barrett eventually moved there. Another group of petitioners who lamented that they were "without land for their posterity" received the township of Peterborough, New Hampshire. None of the petitioners moved there but instead sold their rights to Scots-Irish immigrants. In such situations, the sale of those rights, if not the settling of the land itself, helped solve the problem of supplying lands for the rising generation. The Barretts' speculations were successful. When Benjamin Barrett died in 1728 only two sons, James and Thomas, could be settled on his Concord estate, but the income from the sale of frontier lands provided for two younger sons in Paxton, another Wachusett township. James Barrett continued these ventures by buying lands in Concord for two sons, in part from sales of land in these western townships.[13]

Westminster's proprietors were often fathers and other kin responsible for providing land for the young generation. Joshua Bigelow of Watertown had fought in the famous swamp fight of Metacom's War and received a lot in the first division. He moved to Worcester, where he set about improving a special grant alongside other members of his family. Eliezer, the youngest of his twelve children, looking for better opportunities for his own expanding family, moved from Watertown to Narragansett No. 2 in 1742, accompanied by his elderly father. Eliezer was able to settle three of his four sons around him on Westminster's ample lands. Although Joshua Bigelow was the only original proprietor to ever live in Westminster, over one-quarter of the settlers were sons whose fathers purchased farms for them or conveyed land to them by other means. Almost half of the settlers were related to a proprietor. So fathers either secured land rights as grantees of Narragansett No. 2 or purchased rights through the land market. Families did not necessarily move west immediately; their Wachusett shares served as a land reserve similar to the large unimproved parcels that seventeenth-century settlers had accrued from proprietary shares.[14]

Proprietors and settlers were bound together by patriarchal ties, while migrants used kinship groups to facilitate migration and community formation. The Miles family included two brothers and a cousin, who had been established by their fathers in a similar manner to the Bigelows. John Miles occupied lot number fifty-seven in 1751, then owned by his father, John, of Concord. Three years later he came into full possession, and by 1759 he was the third-largest property owner in Narragansett No. 2. He became active in proprietary and town affairs. His brother, Noah, came to Narragansett No. 2 at about the same time and located on an adjoining lot that his father deeded him in 1754. Their cousin Reuben, also from Concord, came to town about as early as John and Noah; he purchased lot number fourteen in 1749 and eventually acquired extensive landholdings, money at interest, and a slave. Almost all the settlers (89 percent) had some other kin among them; almost half were part of an extended kin network comprising fifteen families. Family ties often determined which settlement was chosen among the numerous possibilities. The web of kinship provided the means by which shares passed to settlers and the bonds of community solidarity were constructed.[15]

The Bellows-Willard-Stearns families formed one kin network of special importance in the Wachusett. In 1635, John Bellows, the emigrant founder, left London for Plymouth at the age of twelve; he soon removed to the new town of Marlborough. His youngest son, Benjamin, became a town founder when he moved to Lancaster in 1704, marrying the widow Dorcas (Cutter) Willard, and then went off to Lunenburg as one of its first settlers in the 1720s. Benjamin Bellows's daughter Judith, who was married to Fairbanks Moor, arrived in Westminster when settlement began in 1737. In 1735, Bellows's son Benjamin Jr. had married Abigail Stearns, the daughter of Lunenburg's first minister. Abigail's two brothers, John and Thomas, had moved to Westminster in 1737. Benjamin and Abigail Bellows followed in 1745, surrounded by the earlier arrivals: Benjamin's sister Judith with her husband, Fairbanks Moor, and Abigail's two brothers, John and Thomas. This group of interrelated families removed to Narragansett No. 2 in the space of a few short years.

Benjamin Bellows Jr.—Colonel Bellows, as he became known—left behind his house and farm in Westminster in 1753 to venture north to Walpole, New Hampshire. Over three generations the Bellows clan took part in founding four frontier settlements, moving from the coast to the Wachusett and then into New Hampshire.[16] Family ties drew the settlers away from the older established communities of the east. Kinship networks provided the connective filaments of a pattern of community formation that sustained countless numbers of families who ventured across New England, moving away from familiar places accompanied by kin and arriving at their destination to find old acquaintances.

The Bellows clan also provides clues about the process by which proprietary shares of Narragansett No. 2, drawn up by committees in Cambridge, became the working family farms of Westminster. Benjamin Bellows Sr. married the widow of Henry Willard. Her nephew, Jonathan, picked lot number eight in 1734, based on his father Jacob's right, and he then passed it on to her son Benjamin in 1737. Resident settlers owned almost half the proprietary shares (45 percent) in 1741, 85 percent in 1751, and almost all shares (89 percent) had been transferred to those living in the new plantation by 1755. Frederick Jackson Turner's depiction of eastern capitalists exploiting western settlers must be revised: rather than exploitation, we find that the individuals who reached the Wachusett, accompanied by their families, actively engaged in the enterprise of town founding.[17]

Residents became proprietors, accumulating land either when they decided to move to the new settlement or after their arrival. The transfer of property was facilitated by their geographical proximity or familial relationship to an original proprietor of the town. The General Court visitation in 1751 found that resident proprietors had been busy in the land market; several had acquired two proprietary shares, and the average holding already amounted to 268 acres. Nonresident proprietors, owners of the remaining 15 percent of the shares, had been content passively to collect the 100 acres of land in the three divisions that were granted to each proprietary share.[18]

Settlers had been stocking up on land, the most readily available resource, but living and working conditions varied in Narragansett No. 2 at midcentury. In 1751 thirty-two residents had fulfilled the conditions of settlement that had been set in 1735: to build a house no less than eighteen by sixteen feet and to clear and fence three acres. Twenty-two other settlers had arrived only very recently, since winter. Most had cleared and fenced three or four acres; many had begun building a house; a few had brought their families there. The authorities made special note of those settlers whose sons, an important source of labor in the preindustrial family-farm economy, were on the site or were coming. A few left substantial evidence of cleared acreage but were no longer present in town: "duty once done now deserted." Finally, seventeen grantees had done no work on their lots and were subject to forfeiture of their shares in the advancing settlement. Some of the homes of the early settlers were substantial dwellings, similar to houses going up all over central Massachusetts.[19]

The committee reported eighty-two property owners, only seventeen of whom never became settlers. Many of the sixty-five resident proprietors were not yet permanent residents of the community; they cleared their land in the summer and returned to their home towns in the winter. John Adams of West Cambridge described the seasonal character of town founding in a letter to Governor Isaac Hull of New Hampshire. Adams owned a farm in Ashburnham, a new Wachusett settlement that bordered on Westminster.

Early in the spring I took my axe on my back and set out for my new country . . . began to chop down the timber on two or three acres . . . went
back . . . worked at Medford in the summer making bricks or shoes. In the
fall I again went to my land . . . cleared off my wood . . . sowed two acres
of rye . . . returned to West Cambridge . . . worked through the winter
making shoes with Mr. John Russell; in the spring went and disposed of my
bricks . . . went again to my land; my rye looked well; but had no barn, built
one that summer . . . sowed a little more . . . returned to Mr. Russell's in
the winter. In the spring went to my land . . . made some provisions for a
house, and in the year 1770 . . . my partner being as ready as I was, we were
married. Having provided a team to carry her furniture and a horse for her,
and another for myself, we set off for the woods.[20]

The process of breaking up the soil and building a family dwelling took
time and backbreaking toil. A working farm that could support a family of
five or six was no sudden creation, but the product of years of labor.

Eighteenth-century town settlement, with its flood of petitions and flock
of new towns required significant revisions in the method of serial town settlement. Eastern towns and western plantations, patriarchs and sons, proprietors and settlers, were linked together. Family relations and the land
market facilitated the movement of settlers to distant locales.

Growing Pains

Narragansett No. 2 developed slowly as a political unit and as a religious
community. The lack of local governmental autonomy, which had plagued
the early days of Nashaway, also hindered the new town. The direction of
town affairs remained firmly in the hands of the proprietary committee,
specifically the nonresident proprietors. The proprietorships were engines
for development, but they also became centers for disputes over development. The conflicts arose, not between capitalists and farmers, but between
fathers and sons over the pace of development and the payment of taxes.
The relatively younger settlers sought to wrest control from the older nonresident proprietors, often their fathers, in order to direct the new plantation's affairs. Disputes could grow bitter. The arrival of the new minister, an
eastern representative who assumed authority and demanded deference
from his frontier flock, paralleled the contemporaneous conflicts between
nonresident and resident proprietors. The town church was always
an arena of possible contention. Theological battles between Narragansett
No. 2's minister and his congregation spilled over into economic disputes
over the payment of ministerial salaries in the cash-starved plantation.
Accusations of ministerial overbearing intersected with those about
improper doctrine. In the 1740s and 1750s, during the enthusiastic religious revival known as the Great Awakening, settlers' battles for authority

in the religious and political spheres became overheated in the harsh environment of the northwest Wachusett.[21]

Money was often at the root of battles between settlers (some with proprietary shares and others without) and nonresident proprietors (who were charged with ordering the new settlement). Proprietors organized township grants, secured settlers, and built community institutions. Upon receiving their grant, the proprietors quickly set up governing committees and land divisions; then they waited for settlers to arrive. After Fairbanks Moor and others made their way to the new plantation, matters of infrastructure became significant: laying out roads to Lancaster, building a meetinghouse, and establishing saw- and gristmills. The proprietors trekked to Westminster in 1739 to attend their first and last on-site meeting for many years to celebrate the dedication of the meetinghouse, a rough, framed building without pews or furnishings that sat amidst a few houses and barns. They had their meeting in Cambridge the next fall. The settlers sought greater control over their lives, but their efforts were continually defeated. They were not able to relocate the proprietors' meetings to the town, to finish the meetinghouse, or to force the proprietors to bear equal taxes with the settlers for ten years after "the time of settling is ended." These divisive issues exposed the fault lines of diverging interests in the settlement's development.

Grantees had obtained their grants intending to eventually sell or possibly convey them to a family member. Their returns on these small investments were not expected to be immediate. In fact, the longer the proprietors could wait as more and more migrants arrived and cleared their lands, the greater would be their return, especially if their expenditure could be limited, and accelerating the pace of development required greater infusions of money in a capital-scarce colony. Furthermore, many proprietors held interests in several plantations, making them less committed to the development of any one. The settlers, by contrast, had different interests; their comfort, safety, and prosperity depended on the rapid progress of the rude township into a mature town. They had made their commitment to transforming the "howling wilderness" in the Wachusett into a "garden." But this required roads, mills, meetinghouses, schools, and a minister, all of which cost money. These disbursements required the proprietary body's approval at distant meetings that the settlers could not attend. Despite these contentious developments, proprietary shares slowly but surely passed from nonresidents to residents throughout the 1740s and 1750s.[22]

Narragansett No. 2 secured its first minister in 1742, when Elisha Marsh accepted the settlers' call. He had been born in Hadley in 1713 and graduated from Harvard College in 1738; he then preached at various frontier plantations in need of a permanent minister. Marsh chose William Cooke to preach his ordination sermon, a minister who shared his distrust of the enthusiasm of the current religious revival. Residents and nonresidents all stood together in October at the community ceremony to install the first permanent minister in the struggling settlement. Cooke warned his young charge against embracing the dangerous notion that conversion consisted of "great Terrors and Convulsions, succeeded by sudden and rapturous Joys, which the Gospel knows nothing of."[23]

The Great Awakening had come to Worcester County when George Whitefield traveled west in October 1740. In the mid-1730s Jonathan Edwards of Northampton had become concerned about a growing belief that salvation could be achieved through reliance upon human ability, a view bordering on heretical Arminianism. Convinced that this belief threatened the doctrine of justification by faith alone, he had begun preaching against it, and his sermons had initiated a revival that had swept through the Connecticut Valley. Whitefield contributed to this revival through his radical, innovative methods of itinerant evangelizing, emotional extravagance, and merchandizing. The revival left an enormous social and cultural upheaval in its wake. Many established ministers, such as Ebenezer Parkman, had lauded the infusion of religious enthusiasm at first. But Whitefield and the itinerant revivalists who followed him threatened to shatter the fixed and organic relationship between the established minister and his people that lay at the center of the orthodox system. New Lights challenged a ministry disposed toward reason and routine instead of inspiration and enthusiasm. A clerical counteroffensive soon followed. Ministers throughout New England embraced Charles Chauncey's *Seasonable Thoughts on the State of Religion* (1743), which attacked untrained itinerants. Lancaster's John Prentice told the Marlborough Association, which included most of the Wachusett ministers, that itinerancy threatened to "destroy the Peace and Order of these Churches, and to throw them off the good Foundation upon which they were settled by our wise and Pious *Ancestors*." Elisha Marsh, with his liberal and rational leanings, had accepted the call to Narragansett No. 2 in the midst of this exciting but turbulent time.[24]

Marsh settled into his new position. In 1745 he married Deborah Loring, the widow of Thomas Lothrop; she brought great wealth and fine possessions to her new husband's frontier station. Marsh complained of delays in the payment of his small salary, while the townspeople criticized his practice of hiring farm laborers at church services. When matters came to a head, Marsh exercised veto power at church meetings, a controversial increase of clerical authority assumed by ministers in the eighteenth century. Marsh joined his ministerial colleagues in affirming the arguments in Chauncey's *Seasonable Thoughts* and the Marlborough Association's criticism of Whitefield.[25] Conflicts such as Westminster's had been contained in the past: evangelically inclined congregations, given to emotional expressions of inner salvation, stood for a spirited ministry, while a liberal minister, inclined to skepticism and coolness toward emotional excess, was reliant instead on good works, good learning, and good order. But residents' resentment of eastern authority and the heat of the Great Awakening pushed this dispute toward the boiling point.

William Baldwin led an attack on Marsh for personal and theological reasons, but a majority of the church still supported Marsh in 1746. A year later the situation had deteriorated; several of the leading settlers submitted charges to a church council alleging his poor performance in the ministry and his propagation of such unorthodox doctrines as "every one under the light of the Gospel might be saved if they would do what they could and he would assure them that there was Salvation purchased for every one that was present." Matters grew so heated that Marsh turned Noah Pratt out of the minister's house, snatching Pratt's gun and grabbing him by the throat while swearing that "I have a good mind to split your brains with it." Pratt stormed over to Fairbanks Moor's farm to borrow a gun and returned to Marsh's farm, where the minister reiterated his threat to "split his brains out" if he ever came within sight of his walls again.[26]

The Marlborough Association convened a church council in 1747, where all the charges were dismissed except the one about expressing faulty doctrines. This mild rebuff did not satisfy Baldwin, who went to Boston to confront Nathan Stone, one of the members of the ecclesiastical council. Stone told Baldwin that he was an "impudent fellow" to have come. Baldwin, rendered speechless at this snub, returned to Narragansett No. 2 and wrote an angry letter to Stone, since personal contact could only "provoke me to speake unwisely." Even after he moved to Newton, Baldwin continued his campaign to have Marsh disciplined for his highhanded manner and dangerous beliefs. In town the minister's remaining critics kept a close watch on his sermons. Joseph Holden, an early settler and church deacon, recorded Marsh's frequent absences from the meetinghouse and his delivery of "old sermons," along with annotated accounts of his deviations from accepted orthodox doctrines. Marsh, for his part, complained about the size of his salary and its belated payment. Twice the minister summoned the proprietors into the Court of General Sessions; he lost both cases. In turn Marsh was called before the court for spreading malicious reports about one of his parishioners. While opposition to his preaching and performance remained covert during this period, the proprietors refused to increase his relatively meager salary, even by five pounds, despite his annual appeals throughout the 1750s.[27]

With the hiring of Marsh, the resident proprietors Fairbanks Moor, Joseph Holden, Philip Bemis, and Benjamin Bellows had succeeded in securing a minister, but other issues remained unresolved. They continued their efforts to shift proprietary meetings to Narragansett No. 2 but lacked the necessary number of votes. The inhabitants petitioned the General Court in 1744, complaining about the lengthy travel required to attend the meetings and about being outvoted by nonresidents who had little first-hand knowledge of frontier conditions and needs. They charged that, although the proprietors had been "prevailed upon to vote for raising Money" to support a minister and lay out roads, they were "free and generous" only in incurring tavern expenses, leaving little left in the treasury towards "Speedy Settlement." The settlers asked the General Court to incorporate the plantation into a town, making town meetings the forum for much of the community business now conducted in Cambridge or Charlestown, and to require nonresidents to pay an equal share of taxes until sixty families were settled. The court promised to appoint a committee to consider the proposal, but no record exists of further action.[28]

The balance of power shifted conclusively in the 1750s. The nonresident proprietors had laid out more roads, adding a pulpit and seats to the meetinghouse. But when the proprietary committee was enlarged, no resident proprietors were added. The residents approached the General Court again in 1750. They complained of the nonresidents' delay in settling or sending others. They requested future meetings to be held in the town. When no response came from the nonresidents, the court appointed a visitation committee, ordered proprietary shares forfeited if delinquent in duties, and moved proprietary meetings to the Wachusett. Next fall the Narragansett No. 2 proprietary meeting elected only residents as officers, consolidating this momentous shift in power. The meetinghouse was finished and a bounty offered to attract more families. The General Court committee came to Narragansett No. 2 in 1751, when it inspected all the settlements established during the previous twenty years in the colony, and it found almost 90 percent of the proprietary shares owned by residents. The gradual transfer of property—the proprietary shares—to residents eased the crisis.[29]

As town residents raised taxes, the nonresidents raised the cry of injustice and proposed incorporation to the General Court in 1755. The new plantation was "completely filled with Inhabitants," they charged, who existed in "a flourishing condition." With all lands taxed equally, those "who have got good improvements pay nothing for them," while those who do not live in the place and "have made no improvements on their lots" carried an equal tax burden to those "whose lots have greatly increased in value." If the town were incorporated, they argued, only improved acreage would be taxed; unimproved land would be exempted. Joseph Holden and thirty-nine other settlers demurred. The residents were unwilling to see their tax base reduced. The settlement was not in a flourishing condition as represented by the nonresidents: two-thirds of the inhabitants were still unable "to raise their own provisions" on their farms. The township's health was endangered without the absentee proprietors' continued contribution. These matters sat for several years during the late 1750s.[30]

Meanwhile, Marsh's opponents moved ahead. They succeeded in calling another church council in 1757, presided over by Ebenezer Gay, a well-known advocate of liberal theology. Many of the leading citizens of the township subscribed to a petition charging the minister with preaching against original sin, doubting the accuracy of Biblical texts, ignoring the vote of the Church concerning the "Relation to the Baptism of Children," and "Saying that mankind are more naturally inclined to Good than Evil." Despite the supposed sympathetic hearing that Gay would give Marsh, the council found that the Wachusett minister had moved so far from accepted orthodoxy that he was advised to "recant his Errors and amend his misconduct." The local church could dismiss him if he refused this admonition. Marsh refused to mend his ways, and the church voted to dismiss him in April 1758. The proprietors concurred and matters seemed settled. Marsh, however, refused to admit the legality of the church's dismissal because it lacked council direction, and he attempted to continue to perform his duties. When an appeal to the colonial attorney supported the church's action, Marsh stopped his efforts but continued to protest. A year later he claimed his annual salary and sued the proprietors. The case worked its way up to the Massachusetts Bay Superior Court.[31]

Parties in Westminster became polarized. In 1759 the Superior Court recommended arbitration, the proprietors refused. Joseph Miller, town notable, solicited the sage advice of one of the remaining nonresident proprietors, John Hunt of Watertown. Instead of advice, Miller received a stinging rebuke for chasing the case through the courts along with a paternalistic dressing-down for involving the eastern worthy. "I cannot conceive," Hunt wrote, "who were your advisers" in these affairs, but "I beg of you not to be so headstrong as to Burthen us with such unnecessary Charges as must attend such foolish proceeding." To distant parties, the resident proprietors' decision to pursue matters against the minister appeared foolhardy. Miller and other townspeople relented; arbitration determined that the minister was owed sixty pounds and his court costs.[32]

After years of turmoil the settlers requested their autonomy: "we Labour under many Difficulties and Disadvantages by reason of our Lying under a proprietary without Having the power and privileges of a Town." Governor Thomas Pownall signed the bill of incorporation on October 20, 1759, "erecting the new Plantation called Narragansett no. 2" into a "District by the name of Westminster," giving the inhabitants all the privileges of a New England town except that of sending a representative to the House of Representatives. But the taxation conflict did not disappear. The residents had requested nonresidents' support for ministerial tax and road construction costs for seven additional years. The nonresidents countered with a long list of improvements they had paid for, including the gristmill, meetinghouse, and settlers' bounty, all borne to develop the plantation. They claimed that incorporation could have come as early as 1751, but as generous nonresidents, they had been willing to wait until the settlers "could *stand upon their own Leggs*." Indeed, by moving the meetings to town, the residents obtained a majority and laid excessive charges on proprietary rights. Recent sales of land by absentees had not brought their owners back the "fees" paid upon them. Such hardships, they claimed, certainly had not been intended by the court when it granted the plantation in honor of the service of their forefathers in Metacom's War.[33]

The residents countered each charge. Families and roads had come slowly to the new settlement in the Wachusett. Progress had not come from the proprietors' fiscal contributions, but rather from the frontier inhabitants whose labors had increased tenfold the value of nonresidents' landholdings. All that was asked was a small tax to be "cheerfully paid a little longer." The General Court accepted its committee's recommendation of a half-penny per acre tax on the nonresidents for four years to support the minister. But the proprietorship ended its reign as Narragansett No. 2's central governing body. Initiative passed to the townspeople gathered in their district meetings. The occasional proprietary meeting, held after the important district meetings, concerned minor readjustments to the third-division lands. The last recorded gathering was held in 1779, nine years after Westminster had been raised to the full status of a town.[34]

Marsh remained in town for a time and became the proprietary clerk, putting to use the liberal education that had got him into such difficulties in the meetinghouse. His relationships with his neighbors continued to be contentious as he refused to pay taxes and became involved in a violent assault upon a neighbor. Eventually, Marsh joined many of his Wachusett neighbors in following Benjamin Bellows to Walpole, the outpost on the banks of the upper Connecticut River in New Hampshire. There, in Cheshire County, he assumed the uncontested prominence that had been denied him in the overheated days of the Great Awakening. He took up the law, a profession to which he was temperamentally better suited. He was appointed Judge of the Court of Common Pleas, awarded an honorary degree from Dartmouth College, elected selectmen and town moderator, and sat in the House of Representatives in 1780–81. Marsh also raised cattle and drove them to the Boston market. In 1784, while on one of these marketing expeditions, he suffered a severe fall and was carried to the Lancaster house of his brother-in-law, where he died. As minister, he had been caught in the crossfire of the Great Awakening, a casualty of the breakdown of ministerial authority. That ecclesiastical battle between pastor and parishioners had been aggravated by the economic disputes over the costs of developing Westminster and the political struggle between the eastern figures of authority and western settlers demanding their autonomy.[35]

Founding, developing, and establishing the new township in the Wachusett had been a long and difficult process. Tensions had mounted when access to land had been threatened since the larger structures of imperial and political power increasingly determined land policy in the Bay Colony during the eighteenth century. Conflicts flared between and within families over issues of developing new towns. The establishment of family farms to meet the goals of the older generation and the needs of the younger one brought discord. Often the townspeople had to take their grievances to the General Court. With court assistance, the proprietary transferred property and power to Westminster. The reallocation of authority followed realities on the site, allowing the town to develop more coherently and resolve its conflicts. Those unable to succeed in Narrangansett No. 2 would find niches when the Wachusett extended farther north.

Creating Family Farms

Westminster's families and farms grew spectacularly during the first four decades of its history (see table 4). After a slow start, the settlement attracted young and growing families. Westminster counted 466 residents at the first colonywide census in 1764; Lancaster, the oldest town and core Wachusett settlement, had 1,999 inhabitants. Harvard, Bolton, and Leominster, Lancaster's eighteenth-century offspring, had 1,126, 933, and 743 residents respectively.[36] Households throughout the region held an average of five-and-half members, while household size in Worcester County and the colony as a whole averaged six. Westminster's inhabitants were balanced evenly between males and females; they were young, male, and unmarried or young and newly married. Relatively few families had completed their childbearing when the census was taken. More mature settlements such as Lancaster and its sister villages held more women than men. With few families and lots of land, the town had ample room for families to accumulate reserves for future generations. Each family occupied its own dwelling. In 1760 there were about seven persons per square mile; population density increased to fifteen persons per square mile by 1770 and to thirty-eight by 1790, when Westminster's third-division lots were trans-

Table 4. Population of Westminster, 1737–1800

Year	Population	Annual rate of increase
1737	15	—
1740	30	26
1750	125	15.3
1760	325	10.0
1770	671	7.5
1780	975	3.8
1790	1176	1.9

Sources: Population figures 1737–1750 are estimates based on William Sweetzer Heywood, *History of Westminster, Massachusetts* (Lowell, Mass., 1893), p. 479. The estimates for the period 1759–1780 are based on the number of polls appearing on the town tax lists, using a multiplier of 3.9 derived from the 1764 provincial census (Valuations and Taxes, Town Clerk, Westminster). 1790 Federal census data reprinted in Heywood, *History of Westminster*, p. 479.

Plate 4. Fairbanks Moor house, Westminster, Massachusetts, built in 1737. Moor was Westminster's first settler and built a single-story, single-room home. It grew as he made additions to the dwelling. (Author's photograph.)

ferred to Gardner. Older eastern towns, such as Andover, contained forty-one persons per square mile in 1764; Concord, a more specialized market center, already had forty-four inhabitants per square mile by 1754. In coastal Essex County over a quarter of all families shared a house with another family.[37]

Greater variety and differentiation in housing and social status occurred in the midcentury Wachusett; the rebuilding that took place in the second quarter of the century continued in the older towns such as Lancaster, while newer northwestern towns such as Westminster had a flurry of house building. Still, like their seventeenth-century predecessors, most settlers lived in single-room and single-floor dwellings in Westminster or Fitchburg. The General Court's records from the 1751 visitation describe many residents' lodging as a "hut." Fairbanks Moor, Westminster's first settler, built a single-room dwelling in 1737, and later added to it (see plate 4). Benjamin Garfield occupied a more substantial single-story double-pile dwelling. Another early settler, William Bemis, constructed a two-story saltbox in 1747. Unlike the older settlements where substantial housing took generations to appear, Nathan Wood built a substantial double-story, double-pile home in 1764, within twenty-five years of the town's settlement; the house, one of a cluster of larger dwellings along Westminster's main east-west highway, was more similar to Samuel Willard's 1727 home than most of Wood's more modestly housed neighbors (see plate 5). Prosperous settlers

Plate 5. Nathan Wood house, Westminster, Massachusetts, built in 1756. Nathan Wood's substantial double-pile, two-and-a-half story house, built in the town's first decades, marked a break from the single-story homes that early settlers such as Moor had built. Wood left over-crowded Concord in 1756 and built this vernacular Georgian-style home on his proprietary lot southeast of the town center, located on the main road leading west to Lancaster and south to Worcester. The house had a pedimented doorway that opened onto a small lobby flanked by two parlors; the interior had striking paneling. (Author's photograph.)

in the newer towns built more substantial homes than their seventeenth-century ancestors had, but homes still located within the vernacular order.

The other major development—a new landscape of power—added to this visible demarcation of social differentiation and came from outside the region and local tradition. The Worcester County gentry, such as the Chandlers, Wilders, and Willards, began building central-hall mansions that followed Georgian house designs in both their exterior decoration and their interior layout. At mid-century Worcester County notable Colonel Levi Willard, a great grandson of Major Simon Willard and allied by marriage with Worcester's Chandler family, occupied a grand two-story house, known locally as "the Mansion House," just down Lancaster's Neck Road from the Samuel Willard house. The third story was added later in the century (see plate 6). In 1771 Lancaster lawyer John Sprague built another central-hall house in that same Neck District, an area already dominated by large two-story central-chimney houses. The house's classical trim and ped-imented doorway presented a new Georgian form to the town. In the new Wachusett plantation of Princeton, one of New England's new mansion

Plate 6. The Levi Willard House, Lancaster, Massachusetts, built about 1750. Known locally as "the Mansion House," this imposing structure was built at mid-century for Worcester County notable Colonel Levi Willard by his cousin Aaron Willard. Located just down Neck Road from the Samuel Willard house constructed a quarter century earlier, its size and height distinguish it from the many impressive houses built in eighteenth-century Lancaster. (Author's photograph.)

houses, Moses Gill's house was erected on a dramatic height of land on a three-thousand-acre tract just south of Mount Wachusett; the house, with its hipped-roof and four chimneys, one rising up from each corner, stood in sharp contrast to Gill's neighbors' simple one-story structures (see plate 7). The new regional elite turned to Georgian-style architecture, the growing number of prosperous yeomen from the older towns built larger homes, and the residents of the newer settlements quickly erected houses, some that emulated their neighbors'.[38]

Families quickly accumulated proprietary shares and landholdings as the proprietors dispensed three 60-acre allotments in twenty years, a far cry from the cautious meting out of small home lots and strips in outlying common fields by the restricted proprietorships of the early seventeenth century. In 1751 the average land holding was 250 acres. Resident proprietors averaged 268 acres (nonresidents held 180 acres), yet many residents had only cleared 3 or 4 acres (see table 5). By the time Westminster was incorporated in 1759, almost all the land had passed to the resident farmers and all the township's land had been divided and distributed. The eighty property owners on the town's first tax list owned an average of 360 acres per person. The town's livestock included 53 oxen, 170 cows, and 52 horses,

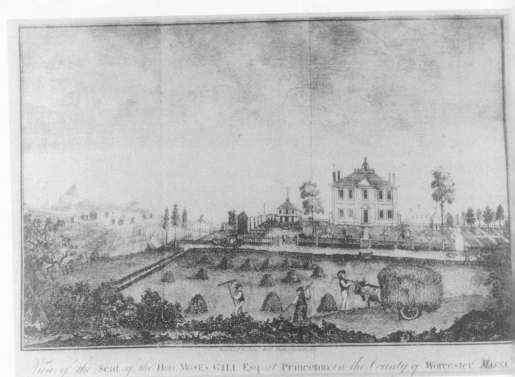

View of the Seat of the Hon MOSES GILL *Esq at* Princeton *in the County of* Worcester MASSA

Plate 7. Moses Gill house, Princeton, Massachusetts, built about 1767, in a late eighteenth-century engraving. One of New England's new mansion houses, Moses Gill's Georgian home, with its four chimneys paired at each end, its central hall, hipped roof, gardens, and fences, stood on a three-thousand-acre tract just south of Mount Wachusett with a magnificent view of Boston to the east. Gill intended to see and be seen. (Reprinted from Francis Blake, *History of Princeton, Massachusetts* [Boston, 1915], vol. 1, p. 270.)

which compared favorably with more established agrarian communities; the holdings of sheep and swine were lower. Four individuals in town held money at interest.[39] Daniel Hoar of Concord, the largest landowner in town, had located on a lot owned by his father and conveyed to him in 1744. He quickly became a town leader, serving as assessor and selectman for many years. His real and personal property accounted for over 6 percent of the town's total assessed value in 1759. John, his brother, located nearby and was reported to the General Court as a permanent resident in 1751.[40]

Westminster's leading property owners in 1759 were members of kin groups established by a paternal proprietor who settled several sons on ample lands; these families persisted for a generation or two before beginning the cycle of town founding all over again. These early settlers were active in the town's affairs and busy accumulating and developing their lands. Eliezer Bigelow and his son Elisha occupied adjacent farms in 1759. Eliezer's early

Table 5. Landholdings in Westminster, 1751–1865

Year	No. of farmers	Total land holdings (acres)	Average no. of acres/farmer	Total no. of improved acres	Average no. of improved acres/farmer	Improved acreage/total acreage
1751	82	20,520	250	n.a.	3–10	
1759	56	28,800	514	n.a.	n.a.	
1771	128	28,800	225	2,706	21.1	9.4%
1781	178	28,800	162	4,126	23.2	14.3
1801	197	19,783	104	4,517	22.9	22.8
1825	240	19,704	82	10,860	42.3	55.1
1865	220	21,273	97	11,690	53.1	55.0

Sources: For 1751 the General Court report listed 82 owners of 114 proprietary rights, which at this time included three divsions of land totaling 180 acres. The estimate of improved farmland comes from the committee's description of the condition of each lot, General Court Visitation, 1751, Mass. Archives, vol. 116, p. 113, Boston. The town's 1759 tax list was the source for landholdings, Misc. Bound Mss., 1756–60, Massachusetts Historical Society, Boston. The number of farmers was defined as all those on the tax list who owned real estate or livestock. Data for 1771–1865 comes from the colony and state property assessments, reprinted in William Sweetzer Heywood, *History of Westminster, Massachusetts* (Lowell, Mass., 1893), pp. 479–81.

arrival with his father, a veteran and a proprietor, enabled him to accumulate enough land to provide Elisha with land when he came of age. Elisha's Dartmouth-educated son, Abijah, later recalled that "at the age of 21, my father had no other property, but a lot of land, wild as the God of nature made it, in a town then almost a wilderness." The third leading taxpayer in 1759 was John Miles, who had arrived by 1750 with his brother Noah, occupying land deeded by their Concord father; their cousin Reuben was second on the list.[41]

Westminster's farmers like most northern agriculturists, practiced mixed husbandry, cultivating crops and raising livestock. Farmers in this agricultural system, Robert Gross reminds us, "saved on labor by exploiting land." When the colony surveyed all its towns and farmers in 1771, only a few acres of tillage or cropland yielded Indian corn and small grains such as wheat and rye, providing residents with food. Meadow and pasture for grazing constituted the bulk of improved lands. New England farmers had long sought haylands and pasturage, and the rich meadows along the Nashua River were no exception to the rule that riverine lands drew settlers. In Westminster, half the land was in pasture, 10 percent in tillage, and the rest in meadows; the older Wachusett towns of Lancaster and Harvard had more land in crops and less for pasture (see table 6). The 20 improved acres on an average farm were dwarfed by the areas of woodland and uncleared acreage that provided farmers with fuel and served as a reserve for expansion.[42]

Westminster's farmers slowly built up their farms, clearing land and accumulating livestock. Livestock was the focus of the agrarian economy. The vast majority of improved lands were devoted to pasturage for grazing and meadows for hay; farm animals were the most valuable of farmer's personal property. Cattle occupied center stage, as many farmers owned a pair of

Table 6. Land usage in towns of Massachusetts, 1771 (percentage of improved acreage)

Town	Tillage	Upland meadow	Fresh meadow	Pasturage
Lancaster	20.6%	22.7%	20.0%	36.7%
Harvard	21.7	16.8	31.1	30.4
Fitchburg	25.9	30.2		43.9
Westminster	10.9	30.7	8.5	49.9
Concord	20.2	40.3[a]		39.4
Connecticut River Towns	49.5	37.5[a]		13.0
Ipswich[b]	8.9	14.9[a]		53.4

Sources: 1771 Tax Valuations—Westminster: Mass. Archives, vol. 134, p. 301, Boston. Fitchburg, Harvard, and Lancaster: Bettye Hobbs Pruitt, ed., *The Massachusetts Tax Valuation List of 1771* (Boston, 1978), pp. 306–72. Concord, Connecticut River Towns, and Ipswich: Robert Gross, "The Problem of Agricultural Crisis in Eighteenth-Century New England: Concord as a Test Case" (paper presented at the annual meeting of the American Historical Association, Atlanta, Ga., 1975).
[a] Total meadow.
[b] Ipswich salt marsh contained 22.7 percent of improved acreage (not included in Ipswich numbers).

oxen and two or three cows. Sheep and swine ownership varied more widely, with an average of over five sheep and one pig per farm, comparable to the older Wachusett towns: Lancaster and Harvard had much larger total herds but many more farmers and farms in town (see table 7). The Wachusett cattle trade was competitive with the better-known centers in the Connecticut River valley. Fresh lands supported cattle and cultivation comfortably. Tillage and pasturage yields were high, compared with the declining yields in such older towns as Concord. With only 10 percent of its improved acreage devoted to grain cultivation, Westminster probably produced small surpluses on the 2 or 3 acres that each farmer devoted to grain. The older Wachusett towns, which had twice the acreage planted in corn and wheat, were sited in an eastern Worcester–western Middlesex county "breadbasket" with high yields, similar to the Connecticut River valley towns whose grain surpluses came from their greater number of acres in cultivation rather than higher crop yields. Westminster's farmers needed these small surpluses. Farmers in the Wachusett, like most New England farmers, did not aim at self-sufficiency. The mythic image of the hardy subsistence-oriented yeoman who produced all the food and goods necessary for his family has been replaced by an understanding of the complex network of exchange of goods and services that made up the local exchange economy, which was embedded in a complex web of social relationships. The cultural values of interdependence and the goal of family competency drove farmers to look to the market, trading their small surpluses to obtain things that were not available from their holdings. Account books of farmers and artisans show that coopers would trade barrels for grain, while farmers without oxen could obtain a team for plowing by promising to lend their labor at harvest time. The economic realities revealed by these stark tax inventories recount how many farmers did not own all the items they needed to be fully self-sufficient—the necessary improved acreage, livestock, tools, or labor supply.[43]

When the town assessors counted residents on September 1, 1783, Westminster had come of age. This rare town census and the 1784 town valuation allow a detailed glimpse into the way in which the process of serial town

Table 7. Average farm holdings of livestock in towns of Massachusetts, 1771 (number of animals/farm)

Town	No. of Farms	Horses	Oxen	Cows	Sheep	Swine
Lancaster	305	1.3	1.5	3.3	7.6	2.1
Harvard	159	.9	1.6	3.6	5.2	1.7
Fitchburg	59	.7	1.1	2.6	5.9	1.7
Westminster	128	.6	1.4	2.9	5.6	1.1
Concord	218	1.2	2.9	4.3	6.1	2.0

Sources: See table 6.

settlement worked on the family level. The population had shot above 1,150, and some second-generation Westminster residents were doubled up in their farmhouses. Average landholdings declined as new family farms were carved out of vast reserves created by the early land divisions. Serial town settlement shifted its focus; families with ample holdings continued to provide young sons with land in town, while others began to send their offspring to found and populate new towns in northern New England. Average household size had climbed slightly to 5.6, but few households contained 5 or 6 persons; most had either 4 or 7 members, indicating the emergence of young, second-generation families as well as large, completed ones.[44]

James Cowee headed a household with eight members and owned 266 acres, two houses, and two other buildings. His son James had a wife and child but no real property. The elder James Cowee, born in England about 1726, had come to New England as an indentured servant; after completing his indenture, he came west to the Wachusett. He bought Elisha Marsh's lot in 1750 and married Mary Pearson in 1757; she had eleven children over the next eighteen years. The older Cowee sons and daughters had left their father's household in 1783 to start their own families. John and David, the oldest sons, owned farms. Their younger brother James had only a cow and pig; he and his bride, Susannah Baldwin, lived with their baby daughter, Persis, in a house built on his father's large estate. Susannah would follow the example of her mother-in-law and bear fifteen children.[45]

Landholdings varied greatly by the 1780s. While the average was 114 acres, only one-third of the resident owners actually held more than 100 acres, with many owning only between 40 and 60. Cleared land amounted to 18 percent of the town's land, a substantial increase since 1771. The typical 1784 farm contained about 21 improved acres; the remaining 80 acres was unimproved (compare to table 5). New farms were hiving off from the vast family holdings, just as new towns had hived off from the colony's unappropriated land. Edward Bacon had come from Cambridge in 1772 at age twenty-eight to purchase a second-division lot and build his family farm; he planted 2 acres of crops, had 7 acres in mowing, and cleared 12 acres for pasture, close to the average. The bulk of his estate remained in his 66 acres of unimproved land, a reserve for future generations. Such a moderate-sized farm could not support large numbers of offspring; the homestead would pass down to his son Edward, his grandson Edward, and his great-grandson Charles, a single male in each of the next four generations.[46]

Those who were able to settle all their children in town, the goal for farm families in preindustrial society, were kin groups that secured proprietary shares and accumulated land through all three divisions. The Bigelow clan had provided for three generations in the new settlements of the eighteenth-century Wachusett. Eliezer had moved to Westminster with his father Joshua (the only original proprietor ever to live in town) as the settlement first began to attract residents in 1742. The father and son had left Watertown, Joshua going first to Worcester (another central Massachusetts town resettled after Metacom's War), eventually both moving to their lot in Narragansett No. 2. Eliezer collected his share of successive land divisions. Although his oldest son left for Portsmouth, New Hampshire, he was able to settle the rest of his sons on substantial farms of their own in Westminster before his own death in 1762. Elisha, the second son, occupied a home lot southwest of his father and added to his property in the ensuing years. In 1783 he was operating a tavern on the major road leading through town. He also had one of the largest working farms, comprising 62 acres, as well as over 440 unimproved acres, the largest holding in town. Joshua, his younger brother, took over their father's 100-acre farm, over a third of which was improved, a substantial proportion for Westminster's new farms. Joshua, Eliezer's youngest son, had married in 1760 and occupied a lot purchased the previous spring. In 1783 he owned a farm of 120 acres, close to the town average, but with very little of it cleared or cultivated. The second generation of Westminster farmers had come of age by 1783; all three Bigelows owned moderate working farms as well as ample land for their offspring. The Bigelows' achievement in Westminster had been made possible when their grandfather took up his proprietary rights in central Massachusetts and their father moved there, at that time only a small outpost in the Wachusett. Joshua Bigelow became the patriarch of a well-established lineage in town, similar in significance to that established by John Prescott a century before. In 1790 Joshua would sell his farm to his brother Jabez and relocate to Worcester in Otsego County, New York, where his eldest son had moved, repeating the pattern of his grandfather Joshua. Other fourth-generation Bigelows would move to towns in New Hampshire, Vermont, and New York, continuing the process of serial town settlement into the postrevolutionary frontier.[47]

The story of two Concord families illustrates the advantages of anticipating land grants and migrating early. John Baker had arrived from England in the 1720s and moved from Charlestown to Concord in the process that Virginia DeJohn Anderson has called the "Great Reshuffling." Two brothers in a family of twelve looked to the Wachusett, a region familiar to Concord residents. Richard, the younger brother, moved to Lancaster, married Mary Sawyer, and bought a home lot in Westminster at the age of twenty-six. As his children came of age, they went north to the New Hampshire frontier, and he passed his 100 acres on to his youngest son, Joel, who continued his father's pursuit of brick making and farming. Robert Baker lingered longer in Concord than his younger brother before trying his luck in Marlborough. When the fifty-five-year-old came to Westminster in 1775, his sons were already looking for their own settlements. In 1783 he and his three sons shared 120 acres; the four families had one house, no barn, no horses, and no oxen, illustrating the dangers of arriving too late in a maturing town.[48]

The Hoar family took advantage of the proprietary shares becoming available in new eighteenth-century communities and had more success than the Bakers in placing the next generation. The father's decisive actions allowed his sons to secure a niche in the new social order; each son was established on a farm of over 100 acres, the size of Richard Baker's farm. When Daniel Hoar began looking for a farm, he became one of the earliest settlers in Narragansett No. 2. First he settled on a marginally located lot in the community. After his marriage he moved to a more centrally sited farm owned by his father, who remained in Concord. Daniel became a prominent figure in town and accumulated sufficient lands to provide for his two sons upon his death in 1782. The elder son, Stephen Hoar, occupied a 200-acre farm with 57 improved acres in 1784, one of the largest working farms in the area. Samuel, his younger brother, owned 140 acres, but had only 1 acre under cultivation and 7 devoted to pasturage at that time. Stephen and Samuel's Uncle John, Daniel Hoar's older brother, also held an early proprietary share; he had cleared some farmland on his home lot by 1751, but he remained in Lexington and passed his Wachusett lands on to his son, John, when he came of age in 1763. John owned an average holding; 24 of his 122 acres were under improvement. Timothy Hoar, Daniel's younger brother, purchased a lot of 60 acres in 1761, right after his son Timothy's birth in Concord. In 1783 he was no doubt using his lot to raise livestock, as the bulk of the holding was in meadow and pasturage, a not unusual practice at this time, as Concord farmers (their own lands unable to support more cattle) looked west for additional grazing lands. Son Timothy eventually relocated to Westminster in 1790 after he started his own family.[49]

About 10 percent of the family heads did not own land in 1783. Many of Westminster's landless men were young sons waiting for their land; James Cowee Jr., for example, was just eighteen and recently married when the census was conducted. Others were poor, and had come to the Wachusett in search of opportunity. Ephraim Wetherbee, for example, migrated from Marlborough to locate next to his more successful brother Nathan but was forced to sell his land; and his untimely death left his family destitute, to be supported at public expense. Artisans also made Westminster their home. Jonathan Phillips, a cooper, owned a half-acre of tillage for his garden crops and three cows but no farm. The number of artisans rose steadily in older, commercializing towns such as Concord or Lancaster, where residents increasingly followed artisanal pursuits, which required only a small garden plot. Westminster had few mills or merchants; six mills and one merchant were listed on the 1784 valuation. Relatively few residents had money lent out at interest. The town had almost eighty nonresident landowners, but they held an average of only about 64 acres per person, the size of a single lot from one of the land divisions. Many were similar to Timothy Hoar of Concord, who had purchased land to pass on to a son. Others from neighboring towns utilized their lands for grazing livestock before eventually disposing of or conveying their lands to others. These holdings were not farms; only about 12 percent of their total acreage was improved, and that almost exclusively in pasturage.[50] These patriarchs were guided by goals of family settlement and personal independence. They operated within a demanding agrarian world where intense activity was necessary to obtain a living from the soil and constant attention had to be paid to securing the means to settle the next generation on farms of their own.

The older towns looked to Westminster and other eighteenth-century town foundings to continue serial town settlement in New England. Charles Grant's analysis of a Connecticut auction township in the 1730s, reveals a similar extension of serial town settlement in the western lands. While Grant worked within the Turnerian paradigm of democratic settlers struggling for economic and political autonomy on the frontier, his findings fit Westminster's story. Connecticut's fourth-generation residents facing population pressure and government inaction, looked to the northwest corner of the colony, where Indian removal had opened up the last available parcels of land. Family groups migrated together to Kent, Connecticut, providing social cohesiveness to the new settlement. Absentees sold to residents, incorporation as a Connecticut town soon followed, and residents received political authority.[51]

As post-1713 British North America expanded, new bureaucratic structures were established and innovations developed to meet the increased numbers of people and places involved in colonization. Hundreds had gathered on the Boston Common to organize their proprietorships. Serial town settlement had been transformed into a regional system of town founding connecting eastern and western towns, woven together by a web of kin—often proprietors and settlers, fathers and sons. Family migration was composed of kin groups; obtaining and developing a family farm guided economic activity. Greater distances were traveled, and more choices were possible. Eighteenth-century town founders, bound by the aim of competency and armed with familial strategies, were nevertheless dependent upon extensive engagement with the market. The "Massachusetts Colonial System," as Charles Clark has labeled it, was poised to launch into northern New England. Colonization of those borderlands would coincide with the dissolution of the region's colonial relationship with Great Britain.[52]

The First Families

> It is impossible for us to enter into the feelings, which must have actuated the first settlers. The prospect of converting a wilderness into a fruitful field, and making the desert rejoice and bloom as the rose, must have cheered, and gladdened their hearts. But on the other hand, dangers were to be encountered, and hardships endured. Exiled from the abodes of civilized men, they found themselves joint-tenants of the forest with savages and wild beasts.
>
> Charles Hudson, *A History of the Town of Westminster* (1832)

When Charles Hudson, the pastor of Westminster's First Universalist Parish, wrote the town's first history in 1832, he created a family narrative of pioneer days. Hudson did not connect these town founders with a providential design or Indian fighting; he made clear in his preface that "Westminster is not associated with scenes of Indian butchery, nor has it been the birthplace or residence of men whom the country delighteth to honor." His history would be a "particular history," of interest primarily to those connected with the events recorded. The early settlers tracking their way through the forest became the heroes of Hudson's story. The history of the town became the history of its "first families"; serial town settlement in Westminster featured grantees, proprietors, and migrants. Hudson showed little need to connect this story with larger narratives of New England or the nation.[53]

Four decades earlier the Reverend Peter Whitney had written the first regional history of the region; his *History of Worcester County* (1791) chronicled the settlement and progress the Wachusett—town by town. Whitney wrote at a moment of state- and nation-building, and he saw his work as paralleling that process. He envisioned his history as contributing to a larger Massachusetts history, which would be compiled when "various gentlemen" wrote "a history of their particular counties." His model included accounts of "the civil and ecclesiastical state of the counties, their population, and their improvements in arts and manufactures." Tables and statistics of political leaders and town tax valuations framed Whitney's fifty town histories. "Authentic facts" about civil society contributed to the construction of the new polity, as well as the demonstrating the achievement of rising republican people.[54] The first wave of early national historical institutions that were concentrated in New England, such as the Massachusetts Historical Society, which was founded in 1791, were reluctant to adopt a local focus. But, beginning in the 1820s, town and county historical societies were established; grand projects sprang up for publishing colonial records; sixty town histories were produced before the Civil War; and the events and themes of New England history caught the imagination of orators, poets, dramatists, and especially writers of fiction. The women and men who accounted for this surge in local history production, historian David Hall reminds us, had a paradoxical relationship to the past, a sense of simultaneous distance and closeness. They felt increasingly cut off from the receding village culture of their towns, yet desired to be connected by a shared ancestry and unbroken cultural transmission—themes to which the nineteenth-century historians of the Wachusett would return again and again.[55]

Charles Hudson sensed he was living in a new generation, cut off by "progress" from the region's rich colonial past. He was pastor of the Universalist parish from 1824 to 1842 and contributed numerous sermons and publications on theological issues. He was also active serving as state assemblyman, state senator, and U.S. representative. Following his short history of Westminster, he wrote lengthy histories of Hudson, Lexington, and Marlborough, Massachusetts. The local historian, he explained, aimed to establish connections between early settlers and present-day residents: poring over local records and family papers in archives, communicating near and far with "elderly inhabitants" who had information about mostly forgotten events, and reviewing the new official state and federal censuses and valuations. This generation of historians was a "statistical people," as historian Patricia Cline Cohen has put it, and we see this characteristic clearly in Hudson. Hudson opened by discussing the town's natural resources and concluded by giving population and economic statistics, including a discussion of local products as well as a new emphasis on the commercial and industrial prospects with information collected from the town's manufacturers. Significantly, he separated the ecclesiastical history of Westminster from the town's social history, that latter section being the centerpiece of his work.[56]

"The early history of Westminster is but little known," Hudson began; it had been settled so recently that it was not the site of an Indian massacre, yet long enough ago that record-keeping was not up to current standards. Many actors in those scenes had passed off the stage. Hudson's history, unlike the earlier one by Edward Johnson or later ones by mid-nineteenth century local historians, had no lengthy English prolegomena or seventeenth-century prelude. The routine business of organizing settlement took on paramount importance. The story began with the Narragansett grants, the legacy of the seventeenth-century Indian wars. Hudson described the growing numbers of claimants, the devolution of authority to proprietors, and the work of their committees in organizing settlement. Careful attention was paid to the proprietors' efforts at dividing lands, laying out lots, and securing mills; Brattle's mill was emphasized, a foreshadowing of contemporary interest in industrial sites. Hudson then announced the problem that beset these founders: still, despite the proprietors' efforts, Narragansett No. 2 awaited its first settlers. "The proprietors were not very desirous of leaving the comforts of civilized life near the metropolis, and settling themselves in a wilderness, made vocal by the howling of wild beasts."[57]

Hudson wrote a narrative focused on those families who were willing to remove to the wilderness. He noted the importance of chronicling the "dates at which the different families came into the place," validating the claims of present-day residents to be representatives of the pioneer families of the past. His goal was to evoke "the feelings" of the pioneers, "the prospect of converting a wilderness into a fruitful field" (a familiar trope in both spiritual and material histories), but also the dangers and hardships to be endured. "Exiled from the abodes of civilized men, they found themselves joint-tenants of the forest with savages and wild beasts." Civilized society was so much a part of nineteenth-century values, that voluntary exile from it became a heroic act. Fairbanks Moor, he tells, moved his family from Lancaster, building the first framed house and first public house. An "active and enterprising Citizen," he later moved off to the upper Connecticut River valley, drawn by his interest in land speculation, only to be slain by Indians. Next in Hudson's narrative, we read of Deacon Joseph Holden, who arrived the same month in 1737 as Moor to clear land. He went back to Watertown for his family. Returning, he left his daughters in Lancaster while he and his sons took off for "the wilds of Naraganset," to build their house. Both families—the Moors and the Holdens—raised their houses the very same day, marking a day of communal celebration. The first families wound their way from Lancaster through the "trackless desert" to "Naraganset No. 2." The Holdens persisted, Abner Holden, the father, becoming the first deacon, and his son Abner taking up both town offices and national ones, having "the fortune . . . to Witness all the difficulties and dangers through which the infant settlement had to pass."[58]

In Hudson's narrative, the heroic moment came that first winter, which was among the most severe of the century. This hardy group of pioneers was living in "the howling wilderness," as Hudson quoted Abner Holden, without roads to the distant settlements, cut off from mills to grind their grain, and surrounded by "the hideous yells of wolves." After surviving the winter, the pioneers were joined by more families; the first children were born in the settlement; and more houses, a meetinghouse, and mills were built. Hudson chronicled thirteen "first families"; those families who left town he dispatched with a few sentences, while those who remained received more complete family histories. War interrupted the slow progress of settlement in 1742; Hudson searched to uncover the pioneers' feelings, with "death by torture or protracted captivity" perhaps "haunting their imagination." However, no attack ever fell on Narragansett No. 2, and Hudson was able to locate only one "authenticated incident," when William Bowman was surprised in the fields by the "insidious enemy" before eluding his pursuers and fleeing for "Graves' Fort" in 1748. Later, Hudson pointed to Westminster's participation in the Revolution, as one of the "little republics" that resisted British encroachments and resolved on nationhood.[59]

Hudson wrote for a new generation, intent on improvement and civilization. As he closed his chronicle of eighteenth-century families and farms, he entered the modern world of Westminster, leaving behind the congregational monopoly of religion, the neglect of correct schooling, and the "low revels" and litigation that had accompanied pioneer days. His nineteenth-century account hailed the town's increasing religious diversity, its improved public schools and private academies, and its growing manufacturing industries. Hudson was concerned about stagnant agricultural production, and concluded that "nothing but improving her water power, or establishing other manufacturing business will enable this town to maintain her standing among her sister towns." If the manufacture of textiles, combs, shoes, could be introduced, Hudson believed, agriculture would rebound and the wealth and population of the place might increase.[60]

The agrarian world of the seventeenth and eighteenth centuries was fading before the new industrial order. The town's population, rising for two generations, halted as its sons and daughters moved to Fitchburg or Lowell. Local history changed with the work of town founding in the Wachusett completed. Hudson incorporated the early settlers into the secular narrative of New England; the founding fathers of the eighteenth-century town became the roots of the nineteenth-century society. Thus, Hudson's work provided the cultural foundation for a genealogical establishment. Material deprivation moved to the fore, replacing the dual dangers—material and spiritual—of Indian attack, which were the staple of earlier histories. People who remembered the early settlers were passing away. Old ways also passed; the narrative of town founding came to be seen as material for local history, rather than as an ongoing blueprint for town formation as before. This history of town founding owes its form and meaning to both the eighteenth-century farm families that settled the town and the nineteenth-century local historians who wrote it. Full blown nostalgia and a myth of settlement would await the midcentury centennials of Westminster and the other eighteenth-century foundations. Town settlement and local history relied on a network of families and farms.

III THE CREATION OF GREATER NEW ENGLAND

Colonization burst northward from southern New England with the removal of the French threat at the close of the French and Indian War. The New England frontier pushed from coastal areas into the backcountry of Maine and up the Kennebec; in New Hampshire, migrants streamed northward up the Merrimack and Connecticut Rivers; and into New York, they moved north along the Hudson and Mohawk Rivers. A total of 283 towns were founded between 1760 and 1776 in New England as the annual average rose from six settlements per year before 1760 to eighteen per year after 1760. The northeasterly thrust into Nova Scotia, one historical geographer reminds us, "was but one edge of a broader northward surge that had followed on the elimination of the French threat from North America." Over seven thousand New Englanders would venture to Nova Scotia in a few short years, part of the expansion of settlement that took place in British North America after 1760 that historian Bernard Bailyn referred to as "an expanded world" with the new settlements curving from Nova Scotia to Florida in a vast inland arc. But this Greater New England was not simply an extension of the original New England. The transplantation would bring about dramatically different results in the rapidly changing political and cultural climate of late eighteenth-century North America.[1]

For Massachusetts migrants in the 1760s moving to the backcountry meant moving north. As war waned in the 1750s different and equally attractive paths opened for the continuation of serial town settlement. Colonel Benjamin Bellows took advantage of the patronage of New Hampshire's Governor Benning Wentworth and, with his own dynastic ambitions, created a sole proprietorship along the upper Connecticut River in the 1750s; settlers poured up the river valley in the next decade to an area northwest of the Wachusett familiar to soldiers and settlers. Timothy Houghton and John Seccombe led boatloads of people to the rocky Atlantic

South Shore of Nova Scotia to plant cherished New England traditions in the British military colony's rocky soil. Nova Scotia also brought New Englanders into contact with the rich Acadian farmlands and the fishing banks. Colonists were lured there by imperial subsidies and official assurances of town settlement. At these margins of British North America there was great difficult in planting New England town institutions, especially the Congregational Church.

Quite different political and economic structures awaited migrants and accounted for their differential experience in New Hampshire and Nova Scotia. The social democratization unleashed by the War for Independence only accelerated that process. The tumultuous events of the revolutionary era brought severe challenges to northern town founders; challenges came from humble town founders as well as British imperial officials. The means and successes of integrating northern settlers into either the new nation or the reduced British empire varied in the immediate postrevolutionary period. In Nova Scotia, British mercantilist plans did not reach deep into the soil of the Planter townships. The isolated outsettlements lacked the infrastructure or autonomy for extensive economic development. The sundering of Greater New England required Nova Scotians to assume a new identity, even if it was one constructed out of New England cloth. In New England, serial town settlement speeded up. Walpole quickly replicated Lancaster's progress, rapidly becoming a country village, but commercialization came to the countryside and fostered changes that were not always welcome. Walpole's print entrepreneurs promoted their version of New England history throughout the new nation. In both regions, new fruits of serial town settlement emerged—the outsettlement and the commercial village. The people of the Wachusett traveled far from their core region as serial town settlement moved into the late eighteenth century, led by people with high hopes and powerful cultural traditions.

5 New England Moves North: The South Shore of Nova Scotia

> The proclamation of Governor Lawrence [that he] sent to New
> England . . . and the reports of the returned militia, painted the country in
> most glowing colours. They represented it as the spies sent by the Israelites to
> report on the Valley of the Jordan, as a land flowing with milk and honey. The
> old folks have told us that a favorite way of putting it in Connecticut at this
> time, was that down in Nova Scotia the pigs ran about with knives and forks
> sticking in their backs saying 'Eat me! Eat me.'
>
> *Cornwallis Township Records*

After the expulsion of the Acadians in 1755, the British encouraged Planters—migrants from New England—to pursue farming on the
recently vacated marshlands on the Bay of Fundy and fishing along the
rocky South Shore of the peninsular colony (see map 16). New Englanders
received the reports of returned militia, Governor Charles Lawrence's
proclamations, and their own agents' accounts that "painted the country in
the most glowing colours." Thousands of settlers, mostly from Rhode
Island and Massachusetts, answered Lawrence's invitations, which assured
the prospective migrants that the political and religious shape of their life
would be a familiar one. But this new "Great Migration," a similarly well-
organized corporate venture, had very different results from the simultaneous dispersal up the Connecticut River into northern New England.[1]

Wachusett town founders had critical roles in the formation of two
Planter Nova Scotia townships on the South Shore: Chester and Yarmouth.
The Reverend John Seccombe and Major Timothy Houghton, town nota-
bles from Harvard, Massachusetts, joined with others from Rhode Island
and Massachusetts, leading a boatload of settlers to the foot of Mahone
Basin, located sixty miles from Halifax, where they founded the town of
Chester in 1760. Unlike New Hampshire's Benjamin Bellows, these patri-
archs could not replicate familiar political and social institutions of New
England life in the British military colony. The more humble town founder,

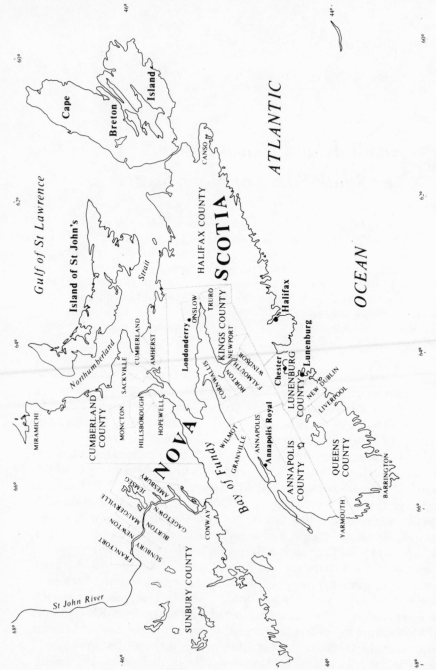

Map 16. Planter Nova Scotia, 1767. New England Planters moved to fishing townships along the rocky Atlantic Coast or agricultural ones on the dyked lands of the Bay of Fundy. (Reprinted from Margaret Conrad, ed., *They Planted Well* [Fredericton, N.B., 1988], p. 8. By permission of Acadiensis Press. Courtesy of Cornell University Libraries.)

Jonathan Scott of Lunenburg, Massachusetts, joined his brother in Yarmouth, Nova Scotia, on the western edge of the South Shore in 1764 to try his hand as a fisherman. Scott, lay preacher turned minister in the weakly planted religious establishment, was caught up in the religious debates and ousted from his parish in the social turmoil of the Allinite New Birth revival that consumed the colony during revolutionary years. It was during those years that Nova Scotians transformed their New England heritage into a new Nova Scotian identity.

Towns into Townships

The British had received Nova Scotia from the French in 1713 as part of the Treaty of Utrecht but its population remained largely French and Indian until midcentury, when the British decided to establish a counterbalance to the French fortress at Louisbourg. Halifax was founded in 1749. Ethnic diversity and imperial control marked the settlement process. British soldiers and Newfoundland Irish indentured servants were unsuitable recruits for the new colony. New England traders, attracted by the prodigious amounts of public monies being expended on the new colonial venture, were successfully established in Halifax. Over two thousand "foreign Protestants" joined them in 1751 and 1752; these Swiss and German immigrants settled in Lunenburg on the South Shore within easy range of Halifax's military protection. With the coming of the Seven Years War, the new governor focused his suspicions on the colony's entire Acadian population, who were forcibly removed. In 1755, Captain Abijah Willard led a company of soldiers drawn mostly from Lancaster, Harvard, and Lunenburg to dislodge the French from their fortified positions in the Bay of Fundy. Willard reluctantly carried out the unhappy task of destroying the Acadian villages and pushing out their inhabitants: "I ordered the whole to be Drawed up in a Body and bid the french men march off and set fire to their Buildings and Left the women and children to Take Care of themselves with great Lamentation which I must Confess it seemed to be something shocking." These military activities cleared the way for the recolonization of the Acadian sites on the Bay of Fundy as well as the formation of new settlements on the South Shore, where the Wachusett colonists headed.[2]

British officials looked south to New England for colonists to replace the Acadians and expand the settlement of Nova Scotia; New England had a long history of commercial ties to Nova Scotia—its fishermen were aware of the bountiful offshore fishing banks, and its soldiers had vivid memories of the rich marshlands cultivated by Acadians. Governor Lawrence proclaimed in October 1758: "I shall be ready to receive any Proposals that may be hereafter made to me, for effectually settling the said vacated or any other Lands within the Province aforesaid," promising a bounty that included rich marshland, "interval Plow-Lands, producing Wheat, Rye, Barley, Oats, Hemp, Flax . . . cultivated for more than a Hundred Years past" as well as similar quantities of rich "Upland, clear'd and stock'd with English Grass, planted with Orchards, Gardens." In his second Proclamation on January 11, 1759, Lawrence answered the land-hungry New Englanders' questions about land amounts, quit rents, the constitution of government and "free exercise of their religion" (see plate 8).[3] The terms for access to farmland seemed familiar to the New England settlers. Townships were to consist of 100,000 acres of land with "Quantities of Land granted . . . in Proportion to the Abilities of the Settlers to plant, cultivate or inclose the same." Quit rents would be collected only ten years after the grant was made. No one person could possess more than 1,000 acres. In a critical provision Lawrence assured the prospective migrants that their political and religious life would take a familiar shape: "That the Government of Nova Scotia is constituted like those of the Neighboring Colonies; the Legislature consisting of Governor, Council, and Assembly; and every Township, so soon as it shall consist of Fifty Families, will be entitled to send Two Representatives to the General Assembly. The Courts of Justice are also constituted in like manner with those of the Massachusetts, Connecticut, and other Northern Colonies." Full liberty of conscience was promised, and "Dissenters" were to be "excused from any rates or taxes . . . for the support of the Established Church of England." The very word "Township," however, created disagreement and disharmony between the Halifax government and the residents of the outsettlements. New Englanders assumed that it indicated a familiar mode of community formation, where town proprietors were entrusted with all details of settlement and freemen governed local matters.[4]

New Englanders prepared to migrate with these promises of generous allotments of land before them. Agents were dispatched to meet with Halifax officials and view possible sites. Free associations of New Englanders were the primary organizers of colonization; townspeople met in Connecticut, Rhode Island, and Massachusetts to form grantees' organizations. Farmers located sites on the Bay of Fundy and along the Annapolis and St. John Rivers—sites remembered from the wars to be filled with trees, rivers, and Acadian dykes. All summer of 1759 the Nova Scotia Council met with New England agents. Removal was delayed by uncertainty about the siege of Quebec, sporadic guerrilla warfare, and the flooding of dyked marshlands. Migration began in June 1760; a flotilla of twenty-two ships hired by Halifax brought Connecticut settlers to Horton and Cornwallis. Kinship ties were strong; perhaps two-thirds of Horton's settlers hailed from five or six towns within twenty miles of New London. This was an older family-oriented group; less than one-third were single. Settlers turned to exploiting the land. The provincial surveyor, Charles Morris, laid out Horton's home lots around a parade square. The divisions of farmland—dyke land, marsh upland, and

PROVINCE of NOVA-SCOTIA,

By His EXCELLENCY,

CHARLES LAWRENCE, Esq;

Captain-General and Governor in Chief, in and over His Majesty's Province of *Nova-Scotia* or *Accadie* in *America*, Vice-Admiral of the same, &c. &c. &c.

A PROCLAMATION.

HEREAS since the issuing of the Proclamation dated the Twelfth Day of October 1758, relative to Settling the vacated Lands in this Province, I have been informed by Thomas Hancock, Esq; Agent for the Affairs of Nova-Scotia, at Boston, That sundry Applications have been made to him in Consequence thereof, by Persons who are desirous of settling the said Lands, and of knowing what particular Encouragement the Government will give them ; Whether any Allowance of Provisions will be given at their first Settlement ; What Quantity of Land will be given to each Person ; What Quit Rent they are to pay ; What the Constitution of the Government is ; Whether any and what Taxes are to be paid ; And, Whether they will be allowed the free Exercise of their Religion ?

I HAVE therefore thought fit, with the Advice of His Majesty's Council, to issue this Proclamation, hereby declaring in Answer to the said Enquiries, That by His Majesty's Royal Instructions to me, I am impowered to make Grants in the following Proportions, Viz.

THAT Townships are to consist of One Hundred Thousand Acres of Land, or about Twelve Miles square : That they do include the best and most profitable Land ; and also, That they do comprehend such Rivers as may be at or near such Settlement ; and do extend as far up into the Country as conveniently may be, taking in a necessary Part of the Sea Coast.

THAT the Quantities of Land granted will be in Proportion to the Abilities of the Settlers to plant, cultivate or inclose the same, viz. That One Hundred Acres of wild Wood-Lands, will be allowed to every Person, being Master or Mistress of a Family, for himself or her self ; and Fifty Acres for every White or Black Man, Woman or Child, of which such Person's Family shall consist, at the actual Time of making the Grant, subject to the Payment of a Quit-Rent of One Shilling Sterling *per Annum* for every Fifty Acres ; such Quit Rent to commence at the Expiration of Ten Years from the Date of each Grant ; and to be paid for His Majesty's Use, to His Receiver-General at *Halifax*, or to His Deputy upon the Spot.

THAT the Grantees will be obliged by their Grants to Plant, Cultivate, improve, or inclose, one third Part of their Lands within the Space of Ten Years ; another third Part within the Space of Twenty Years ; and the remaining Third within the Space of Thirty Years, from the Date of their Grants.

THAT no one Person can possess more than One Thousand Acres (by Grant) in his or her own Name.

THAT every Grantee, upon giving Proof that he or she has fulfilled the Terms and Conditions of his or her Grant, shall be intitled to another Grant, in the Proportion and upon the Conditions above-mentioned.

THAT the Lands proposed to be settled situated on the Bay of *Fundy*, as expressed in the former Proclamation, will be distributed with such Proportions of interval Plow-Land, Mowing-Land, and Pasture, as will be sufficient to maintain the respective Families that shall be established thereon : Which Plow-Lands, &c. produce Wheat, Rye, Barley, Oats, Hemp, Flax, &c. and have been cultivated for more than one Hundred Years past, never failing of Crops, nor needing to be manured.

THAT the Government of *Nova-Scotia* is constituted like those of the Neighbouring Colonies ; the Legislature consisting of Governor, Council, and Assembly ; and every Township, so soon as it shall consist of Fifty Families, will be intitled to send Two Representatives to the General Assembly. The Courts of Justice are also constituted in like manner with those of the *Massachusetts, Connecticut*, and the other Northern Colonies.

THAT as to the Article of Religion, full Liberty of Conscience, both by His Majesty's Royal Instructions, and a late Act of the General Assembly of this Province, is secured to Persons of all Persuasions, Papists excepted, as may more fully appear by the following Abstract of the said Act, viz.

" PROTESTANTS dissenting from the Church of *England*, whether they be Calvinists, Lutherans, Quakers, or under what " Denomination soever, shall have free Liberty of Conscience ; and may erect and build Meeting-Houses for Publick " Worship, and may choose and elect Ministers for the carrying on Divine Service, and Administration of the Sacraments, " according to their several Opinions ; and all Contracts made between their Ministers and their Congregations, for " the Support of the Ministry, are hereby declared Valid, and shall have their full Force and Effect, according " to the Tenor and Conditions thereof : And all such Dissenters shall be excused from any Rates or Taxes to be made and " levied for the Support of the Established Church of *England*. "

THAT no Taxes have hitherto been laid upon His Majesty's Subjects within this Province ; nor are there any Fees of Office taken upon issuing the Grants of Land.

THAT I am not Authorized to offer any Bounty of Provisions.

AND I do hereby declare, That I am ready to lay out the Lands, and to make Grants immediately, under the Conditions above described ; or to receive and transmit to the Lords Commissioners for Trade and Plantations, in order that the same may be laid before His Majesty for His Approbation, such further Proposals as may be offered by any Body of People for setling an entire Township, under other Conditions that they may conceive more advantageous to the Undertakers.

THAT Forts are established in the Neighbourhood of the Lands proposed to be settled, and are garrisoned by His Majesty's Troops, with a view of their giving all manner of Aid and Protection to the Settlers, if hereafter there should be any need.

GIVEN *in the Council-Chamber at* Halifax, *this* Eleventh Day *of* January 1759, *in the* Thirty-second Year *of His Majesty's Reign.*

By His Excellency's Command,
with the Advice of His Majesty's Council,
Jno Duport, Secr Conc

Cha: Lawrence.

GOD Save the KING.

BOSTON in NEW-ENGLAND: Printed by John Draper, 1759.

Plate 8. The broadside by Nova Scotia governor Charles Lawrence. ("A proclamation: Whereas since the issuing of the proclamation dated the twelfth day of October 1758, relative to settling the vacated lands in this province . . . I am impowered to make grants in the following proportions . . ." [Boston, 1759]). Lawrence sets out the conditions for New England migration to Nova Scotia in the 1760s. (Courtesy of the Massachusetts Historical Society, Boston.)

woodland—went around that central plot. Grants ranged from two shares to half a share; two-share grants went to well-connected migrants, most older household heads received one-and-a-half share grants of 750 acres, and young and single or newly married men were given 250-acre half-shares, while the rest received 500-acre grants. The entire township was distributed in the first four years of settlement. By dividing the entire township into individual holdings with little land left in reserve, Horton's settlers revealed their deep-seated desire to own their own land as well as their economic motives for emigrating. Providing land for future generations, once a communal responsibility, became the private duty of landowners.[5]

New England fishermen headed for the South Shore of Nova Scotia; after becoming familiar with its rocky coasts by making short stays there to cure their catch of cod, they looked forward to permanent homes that were four hundred miles closer to the fishing banks than their New England residences. In the late spring of 1760, six vessels brought fifty to seventy families to Liverpool, the largest and best established of the South Shore communities. Most came from Cape Cod fishing communities; many had personal experience from military expeditions. One hundred and seventy grantees received the township. In July the first proprietary meeting chose a moderator, clerk, and committee to lay out town lots and build a mill. The proprietary meeting made all the important township decisions including land allotments, fishing privileges, mill sites, local offices, and the hiring of the minister. One of Liverpool's greatest gains was the emigration of the Reverend Israel Cheever, who preached in private homes and the schoolhouse until the first permanent meetinghouse was built in 1774. Here, migrants looked to the sea rather than the land for their livelihood, busily building sheds and flakes to pursue fishing. Liverpool prospered. By 1762 ninety families, a total of 504 settlers, made the township the second largest in Nova Scotia. Liverpool supplied fish and timber for the West Indies and merchant shipbuilding for Halifax merchants. It was a cohesive, homogeneous society of New Englanders with some rough frontier edges, but transplanted Planters held out hopes of developing into more than a marginal outsettlement.[6]

Two town notables from the Wachusett founded another South Shore community, the township of Chester in Lunenburg County. Chester's first two decades differed considerably from the New Englanders' experience in the farming communities on Minas Basin and the fishing colonies on the South Shore. Their township enjoyed neither Horton's abundant agricultural opportunities or Liverpool's demographic success. However, Chester became linked to its neighbor, the Swiss-German settlement of Lunenburg, and embarked upon a more ethnically diverse course than the other marginal outsettlements along the bleak and rocky Atlantic shoreline. The Reverend John Seccombe and Justice Timothy Houghton provided the community with greater religious and political stability than the other Planter townships in the difficult early years of Nova Scotia's recolonization after the Acadian expulsion, and these town founders became two of the more visible Patriot figures, standing out during the War for Independence in this military colony where most colonists ultimately sided with the British or stood uneasily on the sidelines as their cousins to the south took up arms.[7]

Chester's lands jutted out into Mahone Bay along the rugged, indented southern shore of the colony. The thin and rocky soils were derived from the granite spine of Nova Scotia's geological base; however, the site looked seaward. At the extreme end of the point is a peninsula; at either side of the peninsula, the long arms of the sea reached inland and formed two harbors along with several coves where three rivers emptied into the bay. The thirty-five islands in the bay made the area a blending of land and water. The scouts for the colonists reported ample water power and the possibilities of a good living from lumbering and fishing. The prospects for coastal trade were also considerable; the front harbor could accommodate large ships, while the islands afforded protection from the ocean. The location was ideal: forty-two miles east to Halifax and twenty-three west to Lunenburg.[8] The area was not unknown to colonists. Several New Englanders from the pre-Planter migration were already on the site before Chester's granting in 1759. Charles Morris and Jonathan Prescott worked for the settlement from their station in Halifax. Morris had come to Nova Scotia as an officer in the New England militia in 1745 and remained to live in the provincial capital. Prescott was born in Littleton, Massachusetts, in 1725 and was a surgeon and captain of the engineers at Louisbourg in 1745. After the war he stayed in Nova Scotia as a merchant and accepted grants in Halifax and Lunenburg. He settled in Chester where Joseph, his eldest son, later became a farmer. Prescott had deep roots in the settlement of the Wachusett in the seventeenth century. His great-great-grandfather, John Prescott, had been a town founder of Lancaster. John's son Jonathan had moved to Concord, and other Prescotts had moved north; Peterborough, New Hampshire, was named after Jonathan's uncle Peter.[9]

Governor Lawrence issued a grant in October 1759 to Timothy Houghton and William Keyes, on behalf of seventy-three applicants, for "Erecting" the township of Shoreham "at the Bottom of Mahone Bay." Chester's grant was conditional upon the settlement of eighteen grantees and their families within one year with the grantees to improve one third of their land within ten years or the entire grant would be void. Sixty-five individuals from Massachusetts Bay received one share each, and the eight Nova Scotians only half-shares, a share to consist of five hundred acres. The grant that Houghton and the other Massachusetts men received from the authorities in Halifax seemed to contain the standard language of New England township grants. The primary organizers were recognized on behalf of themselves and other named grantees; the township's location was specified in detail; and stipulations were given about the number of families to be settled and the amount of land to be cleared within a specified time. But important differences existed from Massachusetts grants, which revealed British intent to create a centralized form of government in Nova Scotia and avoid planting a second New England. A township was a unit of land and defined by survey whether peopled or not, while a town was the incorporated political entity within the territorial definition of a township. The township was "given, Granted and confirmed . . . unto the Several Persons hereafter Named" in severalty, not to the grantees as "tenants in common," as Massachusetts grants stated. If the majority could not agree upon a division of the lands in five-hundred-acre shares, the Government would appoint a committee to do so. No land could be alienated in the first ten years without permission from Halifax.[10]

Timothy Houghton had been involved with Nova Scotian affairs for some time. His mother, Mary, was a great-granddaughter of Simon Willard, the Wachusett Indian trader. Born in Bolton, Massachusetts, in 1727, he had served in the Crown Point expedition in 1755 as an adjutant in his uncle Colonel Samuel Willard's regiment. The following year he led a company of soldiers to Nova Scotia. His grandfather, John, had left Watertown for Lancaster in 1652, four generations earlier, and his father, John, had become Justice Houghton and a member of the General Court from Lancaster. Jonas Houghton, Timothy's great-uncle, a resident of Bolton and surveyor of the new town of Harvard, also surveyed many new towns in Massachusetts and New Hampshire and received proprietorships or parcels of land in those plantations. Now Timothy, related to these seventeenth- and eighteenth-century Wachusett town founders, led the extension of serial town settlement to the northern outpost of Chester.[11]

Provincial officials and prospective migrants recognized Timothy Houghton's hand in organizing the transfer of families and materials. The governor authorized Houghton and William Keyes as the representatives for the township's grantees. Houghton arranged for the grant with the Governor's Council because of his prior military service in the colony. Houghton also applied to the Council for subsidies to transport the colonists to the site. Those in New England also acknowledged his authority as town founder; but Houghton did not move to Chester immediately, instead, he directed Chester's early affairs from the Wachusett. The loose pages in the back of the township records contain many handwritten instruments signed in Bolton that authorized him to act as the signatory's representative in township affairs. Most of those Harvard and Bolton residents would never relocate to Nova Scotia. The peopling of Chester was a slow process.[12]

In Halifax the new governor, Jonathan Belcher, watched the colony compete with other British North American destinations for "persons of substance" in the early 1760s. He answered the Board of Trade's complaints about continuing to subsidize new migrants in 1760 with the retort that disbanded soldiers, the cheaper alternative, "are the least qualified from their occupation as soldiers of any men living to establish new countrys." He was sure that every soldier that came into the province since the establishment of Halifax had left or "become 'a Dram Seller.'" That December he could point to boatloads of migrants arriving at Horton and Liverpool; several proprietors had come to build houses in Chester and other communities "chiefly by the sea." Chester's colonists had not contracted early enough that year to make the trip, he wrote; "however persons of considerable substance are engaged in them . . . who are making preparation to come to their lands as early . . . next year as the season will permit." Belcher blamed the great proprietors of New England for misrepresenting the opportunities in Nova Scotia; they took "great pains . . . to retard the progress of these settlements," he charged. By spring 1761, with peace coming, the competition for settlers in the hinterlands of British North America picked up. Many proprietors declined the trek to the northernmost province, Belcher reported, with "the other provinces being very Solicitious to detain them to settle their own Frontiers." Part of his government's problem came from its focus on finding only "people of Ability" (that is, wealth or status) to colonize the region. Other officials in Halifax more realistically assessed the likely candidates for emigration in 1762: "That people of Ability and in easy Circumstances only should be encouraged to come and settle Here, will be found a very impracticable Scheme. . . . The labouring people, who work and live frugal, are in general not the people of Ability, but they are the real riches of all Countries, the foundation of all Husbandry and Manufactures."[13]

Chester did have men of stature as town founders; Major Timothy Houghton and the Reverend John Seccombe left Boston in the summer of 1761 with their families and several other Wachusett migrants. Five days later they sailed into Chester—"a most beautifull Harbour," as Seccombe recorded in his journal—to the sound of guns marking their arrival. Seccombe viewed the new sawmill, the country lots laid out, and the bounties of nature in those first few days. He noted "two indian squaws brought in a birch canoe 5 salmon & 80 salmon trout" as well as "seal skins and eels to sell." Seccombe then traveled to Lunenburg, which had been established to reinforce British presence in North America in territory contested by the Micmac peoples. A defense-minded military had laid out Lunenburg as a fortress community with closely packed houses connected to each other by a stout palisade, the short outer walls of Cape Cod houses replaced by massive fireplaces and chimneys. Their windows served for little more than gun ports. The houses were all sited around a spacious parade square.[14] Seccombe enjoyed German mutton, fowl, and beer; his initial visit blossomed into extensive contacts between Chester and Lunenburg. Philip Knaut, the minister's host on this trip to Lunenburg, was included in the "List of the names of the first Class of Settlers" that closed Seccombe's journal and would soon join Chester's residents.[15]

Seccombe's cosmopolitan tastes could not be satisfied long in the isolated coastal station of Chester. After supervising the laborers clearing his Chester lots, he went to meet Halifax's notables during a month-long visit; he called on Governor Belcher and then moved on to the home of provincial merchant Jonathan Prescott. When he was in the capital, Seccombe's diet improved noticeably with "fine Tarts," cheese, "*Frontenac* & other Wines," "a fine sallad," and a "very good Hasty pudding made of new England meal[,] a great Rarity in these parts," a far cry from the "Moose Stakes" and beaver he had at Chester. After a short visit back home, he returned to the capital ten days later where he received provincial news and dispatched letters to New England. Nova Scotia's paucity of regular Congregational ministers meant that Seccombe would split his ministerial duties between Halifax and Chester for the next two decades.[16]

John Seccombe was born in 1708, the son of a merchant in Medford, Massachusetts. He waited tables upon entry to Harvard College and was made keenly aware of his family's relative lack of social status. He received numerous punishments for disciplinary breaches of the college rules but left his enduring mark upon the college community by writing a humorous poem, "Father Abbey's Will," that celebrated the college sweeper and went through numerous reprintings. In 1732 Seccombe became the minister of the wealthy Wachusett community of Harvard where he received a substantial settlement. Born outside the educated elite of Massachusetts, Seccombe entered its inner circle by his marriage in 1736 to Mercy Williams, the granddaughter of the Reverend Solomon Stoddard. Legend held that Mercy's father, William Williams, had promised to furnish as large a home as Seccombe's father, now better established, could finance. John Seccombe built a mansion house that dominated Harvard's town center with a gambrel roof, several chimneys, imposing wooden interior decorations, and fine landscaping. A row of elms trees, described as the longest in New England, were planted from the parsonage to the meetinghouse. He also constructed a summer cottage on an island in the town's Bare Hill Pond, where he entertained the ministerial association and other dignitaries.[17]

Seccombe's ministry became controversial when rumors arose that his wife charged him in 1738 with an improper relationship with a family servant. He "offered Christian satisfaction for his Offence," but his colleague, Ebenezer Parkman, noted that Seccombe's "ill Conduct" upset the local ministers and brought several of his distressed parishioners to Parkman's door. Seccombe was sympathetic to the religious revivals of the Great Awakening, and this only exacerbated his rocky relationship with the Marlborough Association, especially after he sponsored a visit by George Whitefield in 1745. Repercussions continued from his parishioners about the marital discord and from other ministers about his New Light leanings. Seccombe asked to be dismissed from his congregation in 1757. He

departed from the affluent town and embarked for the harsh rocky coast of
Nova Scotia, where he hoped to achieve the uncontested social status that
had eluded him in the Wachusett.[18]

John Seccombe and Timothy Houghton led the committee appointed to
admit settlers to the township of Chester. Farmers with a family of more
than seven and with livestock were to receive a share and a half; farmers
with families of six or fewer, one share; and single men above the age of
twenty-one, one-half share. Chester's original ranges of grants hugged the
harbor; substantial individual allotments behind the ranges were made to
prominent provincial leaders (see map 17). The New Englanders, armed
with Governor Lawrence's use of the word "township," had arrived in
Nova Scotia with the intent of replicating their familiar, localistic mode of
governance. "The Liverpool grant played upon the very strong corporate
traditions in New England resettlement," historian Elizabeth Mancke
states, but it did not give the settlers vested corporate rights as a proprietorship to complement their heavy responsibilities for organizing the settlement. These contradictions probably did not draw the notice of the busy
arrivals, but later posed a grave problem and elicited strong protests. Governor Lawrence in his two proclamations and his interviews with prospective settlers had seemed to give full assent to their customary election of
town officers. A legislative act was passed in 1760 "to enable proprietors to
divide their lands held in common and undivided." Proprietors in the first
townships appointed committees to apportion the town plot and divide
farm lots. Lawrence soon died, however, and the king disallowed that 1760
enabling act. Proprietary committees then had to be appointed by the governor and Council. The settlers found themselves on a collision course with
a colonial administration intent on creating a Virginia-style centralized government where appointed, not elected, county magistrates and officials held
power in the localities. The legislative session of 1761 extended the judicial
system of Halifax and its General Quarter Sessions of the Peace and Inferior
Courts of Common Pleas to the newly established jurisdictions of Lunenburg, Annapolis, and Kings Counties. Timothy Houghton was appointed
justice of the peace for Lunenburg County in 1762. Another act provided
that surveyors of highways should be chosen by the Grand Jury at the General Sessions of the Peace.[19]

The grantees in Nova Scotia found the government set to intrude in the
appointment of proprietary committees as well as town officers. Furthermore, many grantees had not arrived and others had arrived in their place,
requiring new grants to be made. Reallocating shares in the settlements was
a familiar prerogative of town proprietors in New England, so the threat
that this job would be taken over by colonial administrators drew an angry
protest. In 1762, eight Liverpool settlers petitioned against the government
intrusion:

Map 17. Chester Township, circa 1766, redrawn in 1834 by William Mackay. ("Plan of the Townships of New Dublin, Lunenburg, and Chester." Courtesy of the Nova Scotia Archives and Records Management.)

> We your memorialists proprietors of the Township of Liverpool look upon ourselves to be freemen and under the same constitution as the rest of His Majestys King George's other subjects not only by His Majesty's Proclamation but because we were born in a Country of Liberty in a land that belongs to the Crown of England, therefore we conceive we have right and authority invested in ourselves (or at least we pray we may) to nominate and appoint men among us to be our Committee and to do other Offices that the Town may want. His present Excellency, your Honour and the Council of Halifax have thought proper to desrobe and deprive us of the above privileges which we first enjoyed. This we imagine is encroaching on our Freedom and Liberty and depriving us of a privilege that belongs to no body of people but our-selves.

Despite the petitioners' claims that the disallowance of self-government would cause departures by a significant number of colonists, their arguments fell on deaf ears in the Council.[20]

The Kings County inhabitants next addressed the Board of Trade directly in London, stating that one of the major inducements for migration had been the promise of their own town government. Charles Morris, chief surveyor and a critical figure in early negotiations with the colonists, and Richard Bulkeley, provincial secretary, substantiated this position in their report on the state of the settlements in 1763: "Among other promises to induce them to come this was not the least prevalent that they should be intitled to the same privileges they enjoyed in the other Colonies—and in particular that of being constructed in Townships—and having officers chosen by the respective Towns—and regulate their own affairs—this would be very essential to establish peace and good order." They suggested a legislative act incorporating the townships and allowing them to choose a president and six assistants as a corporate body.[21]

In 1765 what emerged from several years of legislative activity in the Assembly and Council was "An Act for the Choice of Town Officers and Regulating of Townships," which gave the provincial authorities victory over the settlers who wanted direct town government. The county grand jury could nominate two or more persons for each town office, but the Court of Quarter Sessions had the power to choose and appoint. In practice the New Englanders in the remoter outsettlements were left to govern themselves, but Halifax could always intrude and overrule local procedures, as Timothy Houghton and other Planters would learn.[22] From the tone of the Liverpool and Kings County memorials, the defeat of New England traditions must have been a bitter loss.

In January 1762 Governor Belcher reported the successful transplantation of thirty families at the bottom of Mahone Bay, comprising about 120 persons with livestock, with no improvements "but what the present inhabitants made." He expected that, with the convenient location, its "good boat harbours," "well elevated lands with spruce and fir," and streams for sawmills, "the inhabitants will soon be in a good way of supporting themselves by lumber trade and fishery." But rosy expectations of growth were not to be realized as quickly in Chester as in Liverpool or Horton. When Charles Morris reported on provincial conditions to London in 1763, he counted almost 1,800 families in Nova Scotia; almost half the total lived in Halifax and Lunenburg, the pre-Planter British foundings. The capital's population stagnated while the outsettlements were growing. The entire colony contained between 8,200 and 9,000 inhabitants in 1763. Among the New England settlements, Horton, with 154 families (689 individuals), and Liverpool, with 100 families (634 individuals), claimed pride of place within the farming and fishing townships, respectively. The Minas townships of Kings County contained the core of New England settlement.[23]

Chester and other South Shore communities were a different story. The previous winter had found them in great distress. Morris expressed little hope that the upcoming winter would be any better, with "few persons of ability among them," little livestock, and "want of craft for fishing." Chester had about thirty families who subsisted "chiefly by Fishing and getting Lumber." They had cleared only thirty acres of land between them, one-hundredth of Horton's improved acreage. Almost all the townships and counties reported indigent settlers, discord about lack of security in land grants, and confusion in local governance.[24] The "Great Migration" from New England would soon be over. Halifax had challenged the townspeople's claims of local autonomy. The new Nova Scotians would be forced to improvise politically, economically, and socially.

A Province Too Much Dependent on New England

As hostilities ended and settlers streamed into the northern borderlands after 1763, Chester's economic and social development was blocked. Planter settlements remained isolated and scattered throughout the peninsula; religious leaders and institutions had been weakly transplanted; the province continued its economic and social dependency on New England; and local sources of political authority were weak. After only five years, new migration from New England halted. The Royal Proclamation of 1763 had hastened the population flow northward by forbidding settlement west of the Appalachians; however, the treaty of Fort Stanwix opened up the southern Ohio country in 1768. That same year the removal of the British military establishment from Nova Scotia to Boston dried up the greatest source of money in the province. An economic downturn quickly followed these two events and further discouraged prospective migrants. After establishing hegemony over North America in 1763, the British government had few effective plans for its new territories. Pressing events to the south over the next two decades would relegate the Atlantic region to a marginal role in the imperial system.[25]

Events in the province also reoriented New England migration. Whole-sale land speculation began. Imperial subsidized settlement ended; private settlement would rely on the European model of landlords with large hold-ings and tenant farmers. Halifax merchants and officials began the boom. These men and their British business partners, as well as colonial land-jobbers and former military officers, all became caught up in "a veritable carnival of land-grabbing." The provincial elite, feathering their own nests, cared little about fostering indigenous sources of economic growth in the outsettlements. Over five million acres of land were given away by 1773, but few settlers came to these newly granted lands. Indeed, many of the New England planters became discouraged and left the region, which became known as "Nova Scarcity" during the decade. When migration resumed in the mid-1770s, colonists came from the Scottish Highlands and Yorkshire, diluting the New England influence.[26]

The provincial government recorded 13,374 inhabitants by 1767; this was a young population with high fertility. Nova Scotia's population was scattered across the peninsula within ethnic enclaves. Halifax had been founded in 1749 as the new capital, a capital that was "imposed on the cap-tive portion of an old French colony," as the geographer Graeme Wynn has written. A decade later, it had become an English and Anglican outpost in an American colony composed of Acadian returnees and New England migrants, two of the oldest European peoples in North America. Farming towns clustered on former Acadian lands on the Minas Basin and along the Bay of Fundy; fishing villages dotted the jagged Atlantic coast southwest from Lunenburg. Chester had grown to 231 residents by 1767. Like most fishing outposts, it contained an oversupply of single men: it had 50 percent more men than women—high, but not as severe an imbalance as south-western townships such as Yarmouth. These latter towns exhibited a tran-sient character, composed of but few year-round resident families with a seasonal influx of single men who arrived to fish in the summer. The reli-gious demographics are equally unbalanced: Chester, for instance, con-tained 227 Protestants and only 4 Catholics.[27]

This part of Greater New England became integrated into the New England economy by the "aggressive commercialism" of its merchants. The paucity of roads in the hinterlands inhibited the development of a domestic market and even made outsettlements turn to Boston suppliers rather than local ones. Skilled labor and financial institutions were sorely lacking. British military and commercial spending was confined to Halifax. Without an integrated commercial system, Nova Scotia's economy was captured by the "imperial" ambitions of New England's merchants. The majority of trade was in New England hands by every measure: total tonnage, value of imports, and value of exports. Imports continually exceeded exports, as the colony struggled to produce enough food to feed its population and to find a major export staple.[28]

Most Nova Scotians remained agriculturists. The Bay of Fundy's reclaimed marshland supplied good yields of grain crops, such as wheat, barley, and oats, and its upland clearings provided for pasture land, Indian corn, gardens, and orchards. Livestock holdings and grain production increased in the first two decades of recolonization; still, total amounts remained below the bountiful Acadian years. These goods went to Boston markets, not Nova Scotian ones. "If this should continue which must be the case until the roads are made good," Michael Francklin wrote to the Lords of Trade in 1766, "we shall be a Province too much dependent on New England and remain in a feeble languid state." The agricultural townships' high population turnover allowed for the consolidation of landholdings; the top 20 percent of Horton landowners controlled half the town's improvable acreage by 1770, closing off opportunities for new entrants within one generation.[29]

Lying closer to the capital, Chester and Lunenburg looked to the Halifax market. Lunenburg's more developed fields produced quantities of rye, barley, and oats, with yields comparable to those on the other side of the peninsula. Chester's newly cleared and rocky lots produced low yields of coarse grains. Small numbers of cattle and sheep could be pastured on the meadows; its residents owned in total but one horse, fourteen oxen, and forty-two cows. In the main, it produced lumber and fish. Chester's two sawmills produced wood products, mostly consumed locally, with limited quantities entering the export market. Eight fishing boats and five schooners reported modest quantities of dried and pickled fish from the resident and offshore fisheries. A rude and harsh sufficiency hung over the town. As a whole, Nova Scotia competed unfavorably with Newfoundland in the valuable West Indies market for fish, which was its major export staple. While the fishery provided much employment, the returns from the trade did not go to provincial merchants; the colonial relationship with New England continued in the fisheries. Not until the British closed the port of Boston in 1774 did Halifax-owned vessels carry more than one-fifth of the cod shipped from that port.[30]

Such a rustic situation must have been galling to John Seccombe, who had migrated from the rich Massachusetts town of Harvard. Ties of dependency continued in the outsettlements' social and religious affairs. A solicitation of charity for Nova Scotia's dissenting clergy sent to the Reverend Andrew Eliot in Boston contained this sobering appraisal of Seccombe's lot in 1770: "He has never had any Establish'd Salary, but receives about £20, per annum from his Parish, which contains a few Industrious, but poor People, He has expended all the Money he brought with him into this Country (and which we are inform'd was considerable) in Buildings & other improvements, on a new Farm, which has reduced him to very necessitious Circumstances: He has had some small relief from this Town." Seccombe often returned to Massachusetts to visit old friends in Harvard and stock up on supplies. After one such visit in 1770, he wrote:

I have enjoy'd a good measure of health ever since I came into Nova Scotia, but have had it in a higher manner since I was last at New England. I took a great deal of pleasure and satisfaction in visiting my friends there, & very particularly at Harvard. I sensibly grew fatter and stronger than before, & continue so to this day. . . . The grain, butter and other things, which were given me by my friends at Harvard were very acceptable, & will be very beneficial to us. . . . You live in a country where there is a plenty of all the necessaries & comforts of life. It is far otherwise with us at Chester, for sometimes it may be said (of some at least) that they are in want of all things.[31]

Most Chester grantees had either never arrived or not stayed long. Only two of the seventy-three 1759 grantees' names appeared in 1764 when a new grant was issued to those who actually settled the site, a percentage far less than Horton's one-third or Liverpool's one-fifth. But Chester's empty lots provided opportunities for Lunenburg's crowded colonists. Seccombe was successful in attracting industrious settlers from the very start of settlement. Philip Knaut, John Seccombe's host on his first visit to Lunenburg, had come as a furrier from Saxony in 1749 and had prospered in Lunenburg by his milling for his neighbors and trading for furs with the Indians. Knaut moved to Chester with a private land grant of 750 acres that he shared with Timothy Houghton; the two migrants also went into the sawmilling business together. Adolph Wiederholt, another Lunenburg host of Seccombe's, had arrived in 1751 from Marburg, Hesse-Cassel, at the age of thirty-five. He appeared on John Seccombe's list of the "first Class of Settlers," along with two other Lunenburg families.[32]

Chester's ethnic diversity made it a far different place from Harvard, Massachusetts; social improvisation was both possible and necessary along the isolated South Shore. Bruin Comingo, John Seccombe's Lunenburg German ministerial protégé, had arrived from the province of Groningen, the capital of Friesland, in 1751; he signed his name and occupation "Bruin Romkes, woolcomber." Comingo (as he became called) moved to Chester upon its founding, to prepare himself for the ministry under Seccombe's tutelage. Comingo was ordained in Halifax in 1770 as Lunenburg's Dutch Reformed minister. John Seccombe delivered the ordination sermon at the elaborate ceremony attended by the governor and Council in Halifax; he appended a justification for the unorthodox ordination, which recounted the efforts of Lunenburg's families to obtain a minister. "We do not mean that our procedure in this affair should be made a precedent," the clergymen stated, but they defended their action upon the principle of local choice. Lunenburgers "have fixed their eyes upon one among themselves Mr. Bruin Romcas Comingoe known by the name of Brown."[33] The transplanted New Englanders, few in number and limited in power, struggled to establish the church in the isolated outsettlements as the one local force to counter British efforts to centralize political power in Halifax.

Housing was one successful transplant; New England vernacular architectural forms became dominant in Nova Scotia. Migrants' first houses were often mere shacks. Then regional variations occurred. The simple frame house or hall-and-parlor folk houses—single-story rectangular asymmetrical structures with a large kitchen or hall space—were located all over the peninsula, especially in Acadian areas. The exterior appearance of these houses became indistinguishable over time from that of homes built by the New Englanders even as their interior layouts revealed a French heritage (see plate 9). But Cape Cod houses dominated along the South Shore; this style was more formal and rigidly symmetrical than the hall-and-parlor. These structures had one and a half stories, low walls, a central chimney, and a pitched gable roof, with two large parlors flanking the entrance and three or more smaller rooms in the rear. Massachusetts settlers who came to that rocky shoreline brought the Cape Cod house; then it was adopted by Lunenburgers and the post-revolutionary British arrivals. Settlers constructed some houses with pre-cut lumber they transported from New England. By 1800 another New England form—vernacular versions of the Georgian house that appeared throughout the pre-revolutionary colonies—a symmetrical structure with two stories and central hall, was built in Loyalist communities. Maritime architecture emerged out of the transfer of New England materials. But the borrowing was selective, with Nova Scotian forms evincing an economy of materials and plainness of decoration compared with their southern counterparts. Several Cape Code houses still stand in the Chester Basin area—the Ernst-Emms and the Borgard houses—along with the Block House built about 1759 for garrison living by Jonathan Prescott.[34]

As conflict escalated in British North America between rebellious colonists and imperial authorities, Halifax officials feared the New England migrants' republican sympathies and disloyal tendencies. They worked to prevent the Planter townships from developing into autonomous centers of power, always the official policy, and to increase their scrutiny of local leaders. In September 1774 Governor Francis Legge declared: "Meetings and Assemblies of the People at different times in several of the townships have been called and held for various purposes contrary to the Publick good." Halifax attempted to extend its authority into the outsettlements after the April 1775 outbreak of hostilities at Lexington and Concord; local magistrates such as Chester's Timothy Houghton were instructed to report disloyal behavior and have male adults over the age of sixteen subscribe to the governor's loyalty oath in the fall. Still, Patriot activity was limited and numerous vessels from the South Shore and Bay of Fundy settlements sailed to supply besieged British forces in Boston.[35] But the governor and Assembly's blundering invigorated the Patriot cause by passing militia acts that would remove some local militia to the capital and levy taxes to cover these costs. Dissent rose in the militia and protests poured into Halifax from the hinterlands as townspeople complained about the loss of needed farm labor in the fields and the scarcity of cash. Still, most protestors professed their

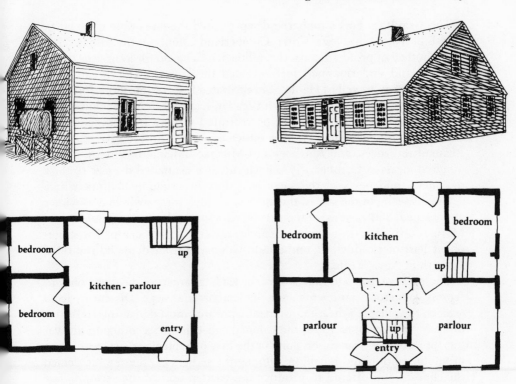

Plate 9. Simple frame and Cape Cod houses, late eighteenth century. The simple frame or hall-and-parlor house (*left*) was a single-story asymmetrical form with a large kitchen space. The Cape Cod house (*right*), a story-and-a-half form with two front parlors and three rooms in the back, was transplanted all along Nova Scotia's South Shore, even reaching the German township of Lunenburg. Some settlers even built their houses with precut lumber brought from New England. (Reprinted from P. Ennals and D. Holdsworth, "Vernacular Architecture and the Cultural Landscape of the Maritime Provinces: A Reconnaissance," *Acadiensis* 10 [1981] : 90. Courtesy of Acadiensis Press.)

loyalty to the British side. Even the Yarmouth petitioners emphasized their poverty and vulnerability: American vessels had carried off several militia officers two weeks earlier, and now the settlers asked "to be Neuter," their only motivation being "self-preservation."

> We do all of us profess to be true Friends & Loyal Subjects of George our King. We were almost all of us born in New England, we have Fathers, Brothers & Sisters in that Country, divided betwixt natural affection to our nearest relations, and good Faith and Friendship to our King and Country, we want to know, if we may be permitted to live in a peaceable State, as we look on that to be the only situation in which we with our Wives and Children, can be in any tolerable degree safe.

The unsympathetic Council considered the request "utterly Absurd."[36]

The assault on Fort Cumberland represented the most potent threat to British hegemony in Nova Scotia. Cumberland County in the Minas Basin was a hotbed of protest against the militia acts. The month-long siege of the decrepit and undermanned fort revealed the lack of widespread local Patriot support as well as Halifax's exaggerated fears of rebellion. Jonathan Eddy, a Massachusetts-born Patriot leader, traveled to Massachusetts to garner support for an invasion; he recruited settlers from Machias (in Maine) and Maugerville (a Yankee settlement on the St. John River), some Acadian returnees, and Maliseet and Micmac Indians to join about one hundred locals in October 1776. Each side overestimated the size of their opponent, and news of the siege was slow in reaching Halifax where rumors flew about the size of the invasion. Eddy's force dwindled as winter approached, and various stratagems failed. Finally, the long-awaited Royal Marines arrived at the isolated site and routed the Patriot camp. The subsequent Patriot exodus in Cumberland County further depleted the rebel strength in Nova Scotia.[37]

Chester's two town founders were the leading targets of the new policy to repress dangerous sentiments after the Cumberland siege. Dissent by local leaders, the pillars of the establishment, appeared most dangerous to British officials. In December 1776, the Council called John Seccombe to answer for "preaching a sermon, on Sunday the first of September last, tending to promote sedition and rebellion" among the settlers of Chester. He denied the charges and offered to produce the written text of the sermon. The Council's next meeting brought further charges that "he had pray'd for the Success of the Rebels," at which point the Council forced the venerated minister to give £500 security for his future good behavior and to refrain from preaching until he signed a formal recantation. Several other prominent individuals with strong ties to New England were able to clear themselves of similar suspicions.[38]

Timothy Houghton, Chester's founder and chief magistrate, became the only official tried in the province for "high misdemeanors." His successful prosecution and subsequent imprisonment reasserted royal authority in the Planter townships in the aftermath of the Cumberland raid; the establishment of autonomous centers of power in the New England townships always worried imperial officials. Houghton's case staked out a policy of legal repression and dismissal from government office that proved to be a potent example to wavering settlers. Officials took advantage of Chester's factionalized polity: an "old" New England led by Anglican Jonathan Prescott that looked east to Halifax, and a "new" New England headed by the Congregationalist Houghton that looked west to Lunenburg, where the Anglo-German elite ruled the county.

William Harrison, a non-Planter resident of Chester, was taken to the safer venue of the Halifax justice of the peace on December 19, 1776. There he testified about his knowledge of Houghton's beliefs:

Timothy Houghton Esq of Chester said that the King had broke his Coronation Oath by establishing the Roman Catholic Religion at Quebec and that he could not in Conscience serve his Majesty, and further declares that the said Houghton has frequently declared to him the deponent that he would not on any account or for any consideration supply the King's troops then at Boston with any kind of relief or necessaries and further that the conduct of sd Houghton has always been in opposition to Government.[39]

Houghton, it was claimed, had echoed New Englanders' familiar charges about a corrupt British government, but his purported remarks were unique among Nova Scotians in making constitutional claims against the oaths of allegiance. Three other depositions followed, all drafted by the attorney general or Council secretary. Among these depositions, it was claimed that Houghton had said he could no longer serve the king as a justice of the peace because the "the King was a Papist" and Lord Bute (the king's adviser) was a "Stewart" (that is, a Catholic Stuart) and that Houghton had brought out "a Law book to shew & prove that no Protestant was bound in Allegiance to the King any longer than he continued protestant." One deponent even alleged that Houghton stated at the Lunenburg court house that "there was but four well affected men to his Majesty at Chester and left himself out." Martial law allowed the government to remove the case from Lunenburg to the Halifax Supreme Court and treat the sedition trial as if it were a treason trial.[40]

Houghton pleaded not guilty, but was convicted and sentenced to six months in jail and a fine of £50. The senior magistrate, now stripped of his commission as justice of the peace and militia captain, petitioned within two months for remission of his sentence. The new governor freed Houghton from his Halifax prison to rejoin his family and busy sawmill business in Chester on the condition that Houghton subscribe to the oaths of allegiance. Houghton retook the very oaths that he had publicly scorned and gave security for a year's "peaceable behavior towards his Majesty." Family accounts maintained that he was forced to sell substantial amounts of land in order to pay the fines and post security. Through the selective but effective use of the legally mandated repression of sedition, Halifax authorities had made an example of disloyal magistrates after witnessing the perils of Cumberland's unsupervised sedition. Chester residents had informed on both Seccombe and Houghton; the War for Independence was after all, a civil war. Persecution and prosecution of prominent Planters such as Seccombe and Houghton, aside from silencing their dissent, demonstrated the continued power of the state and the isolated character of Patriot sentiment.[41]

Privateers and economic deprivation constituted the greatest wartime threat to Chester's residents. Liverpool's Simeon Perkins chronicled the litany of hostages, lost ships ("they have taken near 20 sail"), ransom, and looting, all "by my countrymen." "The privateers were a totally disruptive influence," historians Gordon Stewart and George Rawlyk write, "in a region where almost the entire population lived in or near communities on the sea, where both communications and economic transactions depended entirely upon coastal shipping." The 1782 raid on Chester revealed the isolated shoreline community's vulnerability as well as the resourcefulness of Jonathan Prescott, the town's new military leader after Houghton's removal. Several armed privateers captured a Chester fishing boat, had its owner pilot them through the island-dotted Chester harbor, and opened fire. Prescott returned the fire and struck one ship. When the armed privateers landed and asked permission to bury their dead, Prescott devised a strategy to spare the town and outwit the invaders. Inviting them to lay down their arms and enjoy his hospitality, they were interrupted by the announcement of one hundred men from Lunenburg. The privateers quickly returned to their ships and the next morning Prescott presented them with an impressive military display to warn off any invasion of town. Although most men in the township were away or at sea, Chester's women carrying broomsticks for rifles and wearing their scarlet-lined gray cloaks inside out, tricked the privateers by creating the illusion of numerous regular troops guarding the town; the enemy picked up anchor and sailed off to attack Lunenburg instead.[42]

Such threats and the continued anxiety and economic suffering pushed many residents into the loyalist camp. Rural residents fled to the cities and emptied already sparsely settled townships. Timothy Houghton did not live out the war; he died in Halifax during the smallpox epidemic in 1780 at the age of fifty-three. Many revolutionary-era Planters, alarmed at the "distress" caused by New England, joined the New Birth Allinite movement, reconfiguring their New England identity by refashioning their New England religious heritage into a particular Nova Scotian one. After the War for Independence, high hopes rose again for prosperity in Nova Scotia.

Who Ever Knew a Fisherman Thrive?

The loss of the American colonies promoted a renewed focus on Nova Scotia. Another "Great Migration," this time a Loyalist one, renewed the province's American population; these new colonists expected to recreate their familiar agrarian and commercializing world in a more hospitable political climate. Halifax's royal officials also hoped that an aggressive British mercantilist policy would spur the colony's economic development by curtailing New England's aggressive merchants from trading within the newly constricted British American colonial world, providing a protected market for their fisheries and carrying trade. Nova Scotia's New England planters, fearful of the dramatic influx of loyalists, hoped to profit from the resumption of British capital investment and military presence. While some well-placed colonists would do well from the imperial largesse, Chester and other outsettlements would not.[43]

The Loyalist migration resumed the subsidized British colonization of Nova Scotia. Some 35,000 Loyalists left the American colonies bound for the Atlantic region, about 15,000 going to Nova Scotia and about 11,000 to New Brunswick, a mainland region hived off from the peninsula as a separate colony in 1784. The major migration left New York City and landed at two sites, one at the mouth of the St. John River in New Brunswick, and another, Shelburne on the South Shore. The tent town of Shelburne had an instant population of 7,600; "the inhabitants vie[d] with each other in making fine appearances." Officials resumed a land policy of small freehold plots of land reversing the prerevolutionary trend toward large estates. Still, the strenuous efforts required to extract slow and grudging returns from the rocky Nova Scotian soil discouraged many. "Even the most industrious farmers," Jacob Bailey wrote, faced years of struggle before they could "raise provisions sufficient for their families." A few Loyalists located in Chester in 1784. With some property, but unacquainted with farming, "they expended their money on buildings and unprofitable pursuits." These Chester families soon returned to the United States, as did many of the migrants once they realized the limits of the Atlantic region's economy and society.[44]

American independence and British imposition of mercantilist restrictions created opportunities (or so it appeared for a while) for Nova Scotia to become a "new" New England. The Atlantic Provinces, once located at the margins of the empire, would replace the United States as the agricultural supplier and provincial entrepôt for the lucrative West Indies trade. British pamphleteers lauded the region as "commanding [an] inexhaustible mine of wealth to the empire at large." S. Hollingsworth, author of *An Account of the Present State of Nova Scotia*, wrote of the rich pine forest with "enough lumber to supply all the English islands for some ages to come," "fisheries upon every part of the coast" where "an infinite number of cod is taken every year," along with a fur trade and "lands well adapted" for producing ample grain supplies. Acts permitting the importation of goods from the United States into Nova Scotia were passed for specified periods of time, their provisions to lapse as soon as the colonists could stand on their own. But that day never came. British policymakers did not consider development of the northern colonies a high priority. Imperial neglect, structural limitations of the provincial economy, and the aggressive efforts of New England merchants conspired to continue the Atlantic region's underdevelopment.[45]

The postwar economy did boom. High prices for land benefited previous arrivals. Governor Parr set bounties for shipbuilding and mill construction. Two sawmills opened in Chester. But sawmills built in coastal settlements soon stripped local lumber, and the cost of transporting distant wood supplies limited expansion. "The want of Inland Navigation and of Roads of Communication with the Interior Parts of this New Country . . . so great enhances the price of this article to the Shippers," one South Shore merchant lamented, "as to put it out of their power to continue that trade without considerable Loss." Ship construction rose, but vessels built in Chester and other ports were small in size and tonnage and not capable of entering the ocean traffic. Nova Scotians, forced to import American food and lumber to ease their own local shortages, could not supply surpluses for export; fine flour and grains continued to flow from the south even as the agricultural townships flourished with high prices, because domestic grains were coarser in quality. When British orders in council allowed American wood, livestock, and provisions to enter the West Indies, Nova Scotia merchants concentrated on the dried fish and salted meat trade. But their participation in the carrying trade was crippled by an inability to put together balanced cargoes of goods.[46] (See map 18.)

Americans competed vigorously in the fishery, both legally and illegally. Nova Scotia barely surpassed the American catch from local waters in the 1780s. The peace treaty allowed American fishing rights as well as gave permission to process their catch on the uninhabited stretches of the Atlantic shore. Newfoundland's dried cod exports were almost nine times greater than exports of the four Atlantic provinces combined, as the British colony had trouble securing export trade. Smuggling boomed. Goods smuggled from Passamaquoddy Bay into New Brunswick and then to Halifax became British goods according to colonial trade restrictions. When Jay's treaty in 1794 admitted American ships to British West Indies ports, Shelburne and other South Shore merchants suffered a fatal blow to their aspirations of dominating the Caribbean trade.[47]

British government payments did flow into Nova Scotia; remittances to local Loyalists added up to almost half a million pounds between 1763 and 1790. Britain also supported the civil and military establishments in the Atlantic region, paying the salaries of judges, minister, and soldiers. But this imperial bounty was unevenly distributed: Halifax grew, while outsettlements benefited little. Chester merchants such as John Prescott profited handsomely from provincial bounties and supply contracts, but the majority of the populace that lived on the periphery was left to depend on scanty local resources.[48]

Chester's residents continued to struggle, limited by the town's poor soil, slow population growth, and lack of resources for economic development. Fifty-eight percent of the town's taxpayers called themselves farmers in 1793. Most of the grantees had not even claimed a portion of the lands to which they were entitled. Residents occupied farmlands that ranged from 40 to over 200 acres, with an average of 144 acres. Less than 10 percent of

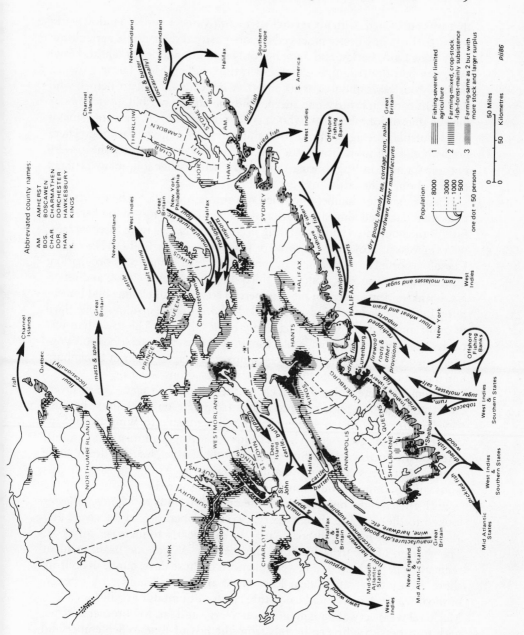

Map 18. Settlement patterns and economic activity in northeastern America, circa 1800. (Reprinted from Graeme Wynn, "A Region of Scattered Settlements and Bounded Possibilities: Northeastern America, 1775–1800," *Canadian Geographer* 31 [1987]: 330. Courtesy of *The Canadian Geographer*.)

that was cultivated, with an average of 13 cultivated acres per landowner in 1783. Farmers in Chester practiced a more pastoral than arable agriculture. They grew corn, barley, and oats, but only small quantities of wheat. However, few had flourishing livestock operations either. Most farmers owned three or four cows and five or six sheep. Army Captain Robert Bethel, who had eight cattle and forty-one sheep, paid the largest tax bill, four times as high as that of John Prescott, who was next on the list. On the other side of the peninsula, the agricultural townships practiced mixed farming. There herds of eight or more neat cattle and flocks of twenty or thirty sheep were not uncommon; in neighboring Lunenburg, with richer soil, many farmers owned about eight cattle but kept no sheep.[49]

Chester exported lumber and dried fish through Halifax. The town's two mills manufactured almost a quarter of a million board feet of lumber. One-fifth of the adult men had a seafaring occupation; twelve were listed as master of a vessel. However, there were few other opportunities. No one in Chester reported a profession, government office, or commercial occupation; Lunenburg, by contrast, contained thirty-four merchants, clerks, and retailers. Local residents relied on the commercial resources of Halifax and Lunenburg. In towns such as Windsor, unskilled laborers made up almost one-third of adult males, while Chester had only eight laborers. The town had just twelve craftsmen—including a blacksmith and five carpenters, possibly connected with the maritime industry—compared to eighty-eight in Lunenburg and almost forty in less populous but more prosperous Windsor.[50]

Settlements were isolated from each other along the rugged coast. Overland transportation remained precarious from Chester to Halifax, because travelers first had to cross the uninhabited peninsula to Windsor. In September 1794 the Reverend Thomas Lloyd, an Anglican missionary sponsored by the Society for the Propagation of the Gospel, froze to death while attempting to cross the peninsula in a snowstorm. As late as 1864 discussions still continued about completing the Windsor road.[51]

With thirty-eight miles of shoreline and thousands of islands, Chester looked to the sea. The shore fishery, two men operating in the rivers and along the coast in a small boat, "may be said yearly to increase" in 1795. The rhythm of the fishery ran by the seasons. A Mahone Basin resident remembered: "Fish used to be very plentiful in those days, a mile or so from shore. Many were caught near Rose Head and Grass Island . . . oftenest in shoal water. A man could catch three or four quintals of codfish in a day. Mackerel were very abundant, good ones large and fat. My brother and me, with four nets caught 110 barrels from the last of June to September and attended farming besides. The herring fishing was also good."[52] Few fishermen prospered in the South Shore's isolated outsettlements; livelihoods were even more precarious than those of their New England counterparts. All along the Atlantic shore fishermen were engaged in a relentless battle with the elements, their catches variable and cure unreliable, and loss of profit always possible. "Who ever knew a Fisherman thrive?" lamented Loyalist William Paine in 1788; "I am persuaded that a coast calculated for fishing; is so far from being a benefit, that it really is a *curse* to the Inhabitants . . . [they] will ever be *poor* and *miserable* . . . At Salem, Marblehead, and Cape Ann . . . [fishermen] are the most wretched of the community." Loyalist migrants had come and gone along the South Shore. Imperial efforts to secure Nova Scotia's place as a shipping entrepôt, shipbuilding center, and breadbasket, to replace the newly independent New England and middle colonies, were intermittent and unrealistic. While domestic merchants came to dominate the resident fishery, profits concentrated in Halifax. Little sign of economic benefits were visible in the sheds and shacks of the fishing villages. Neither the migratory nor resident fishery proved an effective motor of growth for the province, offering up only a meager subsistence for its practitioners. But a colony-wide New Birth revival did offer the possibility of a new sense of mission for Nova Scotians.[53]

A People Highly Favoured of God Indeed

> Many if not the greatest Part of the Towns and Settlements in this Land have no Ministers to teach or instruct them, and a Number of small Settlements and Villages never had any settled Gospel minister, or constant Teaching in the Things of Religion, since this Land was inhabited by the English. . . . And many Places are much wanting in Schools for the Instruction of Youth, either in the Principles of Religion or human Literature: and this Want of Instruction has been of more than twenty years standing; so the Youth in many Places, for want of proper and needful Instruction are much exposed, and are ready to take in and become exceeding fond of, and established in the Belief of the Sentiments which we have taken a brief View of in the foregoing Essay.
>
> Jonathan Scott, *A Brief View of the Religious Tenets and Sentiments Lately Published and Spread in the Province of Nova Scotia* (Halifax, 1784)

As Jonathan Scott, preacher and town founder from the Wachusett, battled against Henry Alline and his spreading New Birth revival, he provided a social historical explanation for this movement: the critical failure of colonists to transplant New England's ministers and schools to Nova Scotia. Scott, a fisherman-preacher, left Lunenburg, Massachusetts, for Yarmouth, Nova Scotia. He espoused a religious orthodoxy that harked back to his New England Congregational roots. His intellectualism contrasted markedly with the emotional revivalism of Alline, who was a tanner turned itinerant minister and, like Scott, a transplant from New England. While the lay preacher Scott became more orthodox, Alline turned "Anti Traditionalist." He transformed his own Congregational heritage in order to propel the outsettlements' residents away from New England toward a new, Nova Scotian identity. Scott and Alline's social and ideological battles spilled into print and gave rise to competing historical narratives about the success of serial town settlement in the province.[54]

Jonathan Scott's family had joined the northward extension of New England. His father John migrated from Ireland to Cambridge in 1729 before settling in Lunenburg, Massachusetts, where his eight children were born. Jonathan, his youngest son, was born in 1744 and was apprenticed as a shoemaker when his father died in 1756. Moses, his oldest brother, had settled along the Jebogue River in Nova Scotia by 1763. His apprenticeship finished and "having a mind to look [for] a Settlement for myself in life," Jonathan booked passage for Yarmouth. Moses was sick when he arrived, and so Jonathan nursed him back to health. He returned to his Massachusetts master's employ after finding few opportunities in the harsh outsettlement and without "so much as pitch on a Lot of Land to Settle on"; however, the two artisans quarreled and Scott had "neither Money nor Friends that could afford me much help," so Scott shipped out to Nova Scotia again in a fishing vessel for the summer season. In the fall, he took up farming, built himself "a log House," and returned to the sea each summer. He married Lucy Ring, the daughter of his captain, George Ring.[55]

Transplanting New England social and religious institutions to Yarmouth, the easternmost settlement on the South Shore, proved to be a difficult and contentious process. The first migrants arrived in 1761, and the first winter brought great distress; Yarmouth's Micmac neighbors eased the crisis by supplying eels and moose meats. While many returned home, new recruits brought the population up to about 320 in 1764; and by 1773 it stood at 673, with settlers coming from as many as twenty different towns in Connecticut and Massachusetts. Settlers scattered to sites throughout the township rather than huddle in Yarmouth harbor. The town of Jebogue (sometimes written as Chebogue) with extensive salt marshes as well as tillable marshes along the river, held the densest population, but Cape Forchu also attracted residents. The modest farmers in these areas averaged only five head of cattle and three cleared acres each.[56]

The Congregational church in Cape Forchu was organized in 1767 under the Reverend Nehemiah Porter. Porter's parishioners soon questioned whether their minister, who did not preach in the characteristic New Light emotional style, was "friendly to the revival of Religion," and they forced him to return to New England by 1771. This church went without a full-time pastor for the next twenty years. The Jebogue church leaders chose John Frost, a lay preacher from Argyle, Scotland, to be their minister. Divisions arose. Only a few settlers could covenant to form a church because many were unable to obtain letters of dismissal from their New England churches. Other settlers complained about Frost's formal preaching style. He refused to resign, and the "society," those not eligible for formal membership in the church, sought out the Reverend Ebenezer Moulton, an itinerant Baptist preacher who had been preaching in Yarmouth and several other townships. Even Frost's ordination failed to heal the divisions; "the irregular ordination of an unwanted, stubborn pastor, who had questionable talents for the ministry," historian Daniel Goodwin noted, "did little to unify the congregation." Finally, two ministers visiting from Massachusetts in May 1770 advised Frost and Moulton to "cease their Public ministerial Exercise," and suggested Jonathan Scott as interim minister.[57]

Scott had joined in Yarmouth's religious revival, leading private prayer meetings and preaching at John Frost's ordination in 1769. As the interim minister of Jebogue, Scott began his own personal passage from a self-taught lay preacher into a staunch advocate of the Congregational establishment. With the blessing (and the books) left by the two visiting Massachusetts ministers, Scott retreated "in Study and Preparation for Publick Service." Moulton returned to the meetinghouse in the fall of 1770, Scott led his followers into a private home, and the Jebogue church split again. Scott handled the religious schism better than his predecessor Frost had; by embracing a policy of prudence, most of the dissidents slowly returned to the fold. In January 1772 the Church and Society committees offered Scott the position of permanent minister. Scott took his new position seriously and, to buttress his own authority, he set off for Massachusetts at his own expense in March 1772. The Massachusetts ministers received Scott "in a most Christian manner" and admitted him to the ministerial association of southeastern Massachusetts. Peter Oliver, the chief justice of Massachusetts, and his wife gave Scott "a Present of Willard's Body of Divinity (a massive religious text)" and "three Bands and a large Cambrick Handkerchief." Scott returned to Nova Scotia with an allegiance to the Congregational establishment, having become a "regular Minister of the Gospel," according to Goodwin. "He adopted a much more impatient and superior attitude to unqualified preachers." His first calling became the Congregational order. He returned to New England for advice about church discipline and parish organization.[58]

Scott's effort to transplant orthodoxy to Nova Scotia floundered amid fading New England traditions and weak local institutions in the 1770s. Ministers and schools were scarce. Scott practiced a strict church discipline. He admonished townspeople for "Dancing and Frolicking with losse company," breach of Sabbath, cursing, and giving children too much freedom; he required transgressors to confess their sin publicly. Scott replied to critics with stern lectures about the special responsibilities of life in a young colony. Isolated from his ministerial peers and living in an outsettlement without roads, Scott wrote, "The Situation of the Church and People was about one hundred Miles from any Church or gospel minister." Two miles and a river separated Scott from the meetinghouse and most of his parishioners. He also squabbled with the congregation over his support. When they increased his salary and purchased land near the meetinghouse for a larger home, he unwisely replied, "what you have proposed to give, will half support my family," leaving those in Jebogue with the view that "Mr Scott was after Money."[59] Lucy died in 1777, leaving Jonathan with six children under the age of ten. These trying circumstances did not constitute the fatal blow to his ministry, however. According to his personal narrative, it was the Allinite New Birth revival, which swept through Nova Scotia between 1776 and 1783, that undermined his position.

As a precocious youth growing up in Rhode Island, Henry Alline had been fascinated with thoughts of personal salvation as well as the mysteries of God and eternity. He migrated with his parents to the Minas Basin township of Falmouth, but that settlement lacked a minister and regular religious instruction. The youth sank into a spiritual malaise, burdened by doubts about his salvation, until he had a dramatic experience of a New Birth in March 1775. "I enjoyed a heaven on earth, and it seemed as if I were wrapped up in God." Alline anticipated entering college as the first step toward the ministry. But the Revolution blocked his reintegration into New England society. Unlike Jonathan Scott who had become reconnected to New England, Alline looked inward toward Nova Scotia, and he transformed the religious heritage of the Planters during the tumultuous decade of the 1770s.[60]

His itinerant ministry was marked by doctrinal and organizational innovations. Alline started preaching in the Minas Basin townships, traveled to the Annapolis Valley and the St. John River region, and then swept through the South Shore communities by 1781. "Whole boat-loads" came to listen to him; many seemed "struck with awe" at his message of "the wonders of redeeming love." In Liverpool, the largest crowd "known in the Place since the Settlement of it" gathered to hear him. Alline traveled through forests thought impassable to reach isolated Yankee outsettlements. He and other itinerant preachers knit the colony together in an expanding social movement with an extensive evangelical communications network. New England planters, such as Liverpool merchant Simeon Perkins, clearly responded to Alline as representing New England revivalist traditions: "Mr. Alline made a long Speech, Very Sensible, Adding all sorts of People to a Religious Life, and gave many directions for their outward walk. This is a wonderful day and evening. Never did I behold such an appearance of the Spirit of God moving upon the people since the time of the Great Religious stir in New England many years ago."[61]

Alline, the self-proclaimed "Anti-Traditionalist," offered a militant anti-Calvinism, rejecting the idea that individuals were predestined to salvation or damnation and could do nothing to alter that course. "Men and Devils that are miserable are not only the Author of their own misery, but that against the Will of God, the Nature of God, and the most endearing Expression of his Love," Alline asserted. According to the historian of religion Nancy Christie, Alline's highly personal religion combined "a communitarian form of religious experience with William Law's emphasis on the individuality of the religious experience and Wesley's principles of freedom of will and universal salvation." He believed each person "capable of consenting to Redeeming Love." His conviction of the significance of the New Birth, "the ravishing of the soul by Christ," led him to assert that "that which is born of God cannot Sin." This radical emphasis on inward experience as the "one thing needful" for church membership made external forms relatively insignificant. His mystical reinterpretation of some of Christianity's chief tenets produced haphazard theology, but powerful rhetoric. Alline preached to the heart, aiming to "excit[e] high and boisterous Affections and Passions"—in Scott's critical words—and he "mightily succeeded therein." While Alline tempered "his perseverance of the true saints" with a fierce asceticism, many of his followers would not. Scott found such prospects of disorder of church and society appalling.[62]

These two humble New England migrants turned religious leaders battled for the hearts and minds of the Planters, telling competing histories about New England and its expansion to Nova Scotia. Scott reiterated the familiar declension narrative when writing his personal life history, making records for the Jebogue church, and drafting his own theological tracts. He mixed the personal, institutional, and polemical in these writings, which related his personal transformation, his troubles with church members, and then the arrival of the "wild, erroneous, disorderly, ignorant and separate Preachers" who destroyed his ministry and convulsed the colony. "The first of this Sort, who broke in upon both Church and Society, was Mr. Henry Alline, and soon after him a Number more, much of the same Description, rushed in, until Order, Union, and Peace were destroyed." Alline, "a young and unmarried Man, of no liberal Education, and but ordinary school Learning," arrived in Yarmouth in October 1781.[63] Scott knew nothing of Alline's arrival—"tho' others did"—until he saw the revivalist in the meetinghouse. His efforts to warn his parishioners of the great doctrinal danger that Alline represented met with no response. Scott attempted to engage and expose the itinerant in a theological debate. But Alline's only response to charges that he had betrayed Calvinist principles was, "I have nothing to say; you have settled the point, and have termed me an Impostor and have censured me very high," a reply that left Scott looking rather uncivil before Yarmouth's residents. Scott temporarily succeeded in driving him away. Yet soon he noted gloomily: "The sound of Mr. Alline's wonderful Reformation at Liverpool and Argyle, and other Places quickly reached Yarmouth, and excited warm Attention among Mr. Scott's People, and fully determined their Minds not to neglect a second opportunity for having the Benefit of Mr. Alline's preaching among them." When Alline returned to Yarmouth, he was met with great enthusiasm. "Such was the Rapidity of the Proceedings," Scott recorded, "that Mr. Scott did not know of his being in the Town until he observed the People hasting by his House to attend the second Meeting which was appointed after this, [Alline's] second Arrival in Yarmouth."[64]

Scott's authority in Yarmouth flagged as he directed his parishioners to stay away from the itinerant's meetings. When they ignored him, he chastised them further. Squire Crawley replied that Scott's "Doctrine was killing him." When Scott confronted a member of his Yarmouth congregation with evidence of Alline's heretical views, Amos Hilton found these criticisms irrelevant. Hilton told the apostle of New England Congregationalism: "It was no Matter of any great Consequence to him what a Man's Principles were, if he was but earnest in promoting a good Work." Without a context for theological debate or an institutional structure to support him, Scott held few weapons against his opponent. Alline's attraction came not from doctrinal clarity but from his persuasive rhetoric and the success of the revival, which Scott could not fathom.[65]

Scott assumed leadership in the opposition movement against Alline, receiving letters from other ministers and replying to Alline's Liverpool sermons and publications with his own: *A Brief View of the Religious Tenets and Sentiments Lately Published and Spread in the Province of Nova Scotia* (1784). In over three hundred pages, Scott combated Alline's mystical revolt against Calvinism, appealing directly to the authority of Scripture: "We may safely own ourselves Predestinarians if our Bibles teach us so." Discussions of their differences about sanctification and church order followed. Alline's erroneous teachings and practices of ordination and baptism mattered deeply to the Yarmouth pastor as he watched his own congregation depart from the fold to follow the itinerant: "Christ's Order is the Hedge which he has erected about his Church and Ordinances as a suitable Means of Safety and Preservation. . . . Look, wherever, you see the Hedge and Bulwark of divine Order broke down from about any Church or professing People, you may write Ichabod there, the Glory is departed." Scott borrowed the metaphor of a hedge surrounding the church, the powerful image used by Cotton Mather to denounce the expansion of settlement and the subsequent spiritual declension. Scott ended his analysis with a pessimistic lament about the disorganized state of Nova Scotia religion: "Absurdities, Inconsistencies, Mysteries, Blasphemies, Railleries, and Profound Nonsense and ridiculous Insinuations." He credited Alline's success to the failure of New England institutions—its "settled Gospel minister[s]," its "Schools," and its "Family Religion"—to take root "in this Land" and provide the necessary "Hedge and Bulwark of divine Order."[66] Scott had journeyed physically and theologically back to New England's religious orthodoxy. This voyage separated him from his fellow Planters and blinded him to the transformations that Alline and his followers had made.

Nova Scotians did not see the issues in Scott's theological terms. To many Planters, the New Birth revival was consistent both with New England Congregationalism and the New Light attitudes they brought with them from New England. Scott's carefully crafted appeal to reason and tradition fell on deaf ears; he wrote of enlightenment while his parishioners spoke of the spirit. Scott referred to "Information," "Light," and "rational Considerations," but they told him that his "Reasons . . . much disgusted the Brethren" and "that no one should hinder them of their Christian Liberty." Alline offered an ecstatic community, a new means of integrating isolated settlers and outsettlements along the barren coast. "The New Light–New Birth emphasis," according to Nancy Christie, "provided a new and powerful spiritual relationship between Christ and the enlightened and redeemed believer in a world in which all traditional relationships seemed to be falling apart." Finally, Scott's narrative of declension was not very appealing, especially in the face of Alline's more sympathetic rendering of the Planters' triumphant progress in taking over the New England heritage. Scott's crusade only furthered the process of disengagement from New England customs and consolidated his New Birth opponents. For the first time Nova Scotians had a common and distinctive religious identity.[67]

Henry Alline addressed the sense of personal confusion and institutional disorder that troubled the New England Planters of the migration and war years. The very times were disordered: "the Midnight Darkness . . . now overspreads the World," he announced, telling his followers that the war between Britain and America was a sign of a larger crisis of wickedness and corruption.

> The Great Men and Kings of the Earth grown proud and lofty; all Manners of Debauchery spreading like a Flood; Stage Plays, Balls and Masquerades received as an Indulgence from Heaven . . . while the Heralds of the Gospel, if any hold forth the Truth, are accounted as mad men and Enthusiasts; libraries glutted with Tragedies, Comedies, Romances, Novels and other profane histories . . . cursing, swearing and blaspheming, not only of Towns and Countries and received as expressions of Politeness; Drunkenness a common Amusement accounted neither Sin or Disgrace; the Rich exalted, the Poor trampled in the Dust; Signs and Wonders seen in the Earth, Air and Water; Wars and Rumours of War, yea, the most inhuman Wars spreading Desolation thro' the world like a Flood; and these most alarming Prodigies . . . as little regarded as the Shadows of Evening.

Unlike his ministerial counterparts in the rebellious colonies, Alline included New England in his portrait of a degenerate people. But God had singled out the migrants. The revival was a sign that Nova Scotians had become the chosen people. Alline assigned the revival supporters a key role in the formation of a new vanguard of visible saints to take over from a degenerate New England. While Scott defended the New England traditions, Alline claimed leadership of the Protestant cause for Nova Scotia. His critique of the war undermined the dominant New England culture and traditional society, while also providing new bonds of social unity.[68]

In a Thanksgiving Day sermon in 1782, Alline provided a historical meaning for Planters' experience of the disorders of migration and the confusions
of the revolutionary era. This commemorative oration recast the past, transplanting and transforming the available New England materials—"we have
a goodly heritage"—not into a political revolution but into a religious
revival and a new myth of settlement. He reviewed the history of New
England for his Yankee listeners and transformed the backwaters of Nova
Scotia into the center of Protestant cause, "this peaceable corner of the
earth," ordering a set of incoherent events into a providential narrative similar to Edward Johnson's history of the Great Migration in the *Wonder-
Working Providence of God* (1640). Migrants had been removed from the
corruption and backsliding of New England and Great Britain for a purpose:
"Your being called away from the approaching storm that was hanging over
our native land, and sheltered here from the calamities of the sweeping del-
uge." The migration had been ordered by God to remove the faithful from
the corrupt. Outsettlements, once thought to be marginal and forgotten,
were placed in this harsh location for a purpose: "O what Great things has
God done for this desert land! The wilderness is become a fruitful field, and
the desert blossoms as a rose." While the "scourge of war" enveloped New
England in darkness, Nova Scotians, a "people highly favoured of God
indeed," would assume the New England mantle of Christian leadership.
"Jesus has not only spread the mantle of his love over the lost world in general. But over you in particular: for your villages and Families happly enjoy
the droping of the sanctuary and effusions of his holy spirit." No longer inferior to New England or marginal to the Protestant cause, New England
planters were cast out of a world of lost traditions and insecure existence
into the beneficent light of recovered roots and divinely graced villages.
Alline's myth of founding took the familiar materials of the New England
past and fashioned them into a new identity for Nova Scotia.[69]

Social and cultural cohesion, which had not been achieved in the process
of settlement or by the development of a strong political and economic
establishment, had come about through the religious revival. The revival
freed the colonists from the constraints of an ever more distant New
England, and in its fierce climate served up a cultural identity for the
colonists to replace the one that no longer suited their situation. Still, Alline
worked with New England materials, even if to a traditionalist such as Scott
the results looked illegitimate. Tragically for Scott, his attack on Alline
forced a choice between the two preachers. Nova Scotians chose Alline and
welcomed a series of itinerant followers who laid the foundations for a
strong nineteenth-century Maritime Baptist presence. The former fisherman
was often left to preach in an empty meetinghouse. Yet the local church
members delayed for several years from the time of Scott's initial request for
dismissal in 1785 before letting him go in 1791. They clearly saw him as
one of their own that had stubbornly refused to go along with the revival.[70]

Ironically, Henry Alline and Jonathan Scott would both return to New England. Alline, suffering from tuberculosis, wanted to breathe his last in New England; he believed that his arrival, "to blow the gospel trumpet through the vast country," would persuade the Yankee homeland to follow the evangelical path. He proceeded through southern Maine and New Hampshire, dying on January 22, 1784, in the North Hampton, New Hampshire, home of the Reverend David McClure, in whose care he left "a number of hymns" to be published. His earlier writings profoundly affected the "New Light Stir" sweeping through the northern New England settlements. They provided Benjamin Randell and other Free Will Baptists with a much-needed theological system along with a New Light pietism and mysticism that looked back to a Whitefieldian past. Historian Stephen Marini has written that Alline's writings had "a nineteenth-century outlook that emphasized individualism, optimism, and sense of history." The publication of Alline's *Hymns and Spiritual Songs* two years later in Boston had powerful repercussions throughout all of the northern New England folk religion. Alline's works and travels accelerated the New Light Stir in the region, reversing in this case the colonial cultural relationship that had been forged between Nova Scotia and New England.[71]

Scott achieved success as a town founder—and, ironically, as a New Light minister—by emigrating to another recently founded outpost of New England, Bakers-Town, Maine. Having once preached in the vicinity, Bakers-Town residents called Scott as their minister in 1793. There he presided over the church for twenty-five years until his death as a town patriarch in 1819. Scott persevered over the community's separation into four towns, the church's splintering into different parishes, the founding of a ministerial consociation, and the creation of the Maine Missionary Society. The staunch anti-Allinite in Nova Scotia's religious upheaval was considered a New Light and evangelical minister in Maine's less heated climate. To compound the irony, back in Nova Scotia, as the Allinite New Birth movement matured and became institutionalized in the nineteenth-century Maritime Baptist church, the Baptist leadership excised their Allinite heterodoxy and appropriated the heritage of Calvinist Congregationalism, returning to what had been Scott's point of view.[72]

Timothy Houghton and Jonathan Scott had left the Wachusett in the 1760s expecting that serial town settlement of New England would continue with its proprietary prerogative and Congregational church discipline. Instead, they found themselves in a British military garrison colony where British officials' centralized authority and where Boston merchants' economic colonialism consigned South Shore colonists to a hardscrabble existence in fishing outposts along the rocky Atlantic coast. Under these stresses, the Planters had reconfigured their political institutions into a county-based government and imaginatively transformed their New England cultural inheritance into a powerful new identity as Nova Scotians.

6 Town Founding and
the Village Enlightenment:
Walpole, New Hampshire

> Were I to form a picture of happy society, it would be a town consisting of a
> due mixture of hills, valleys and streams of water: The land well fenced and
> cultivated; the roads and bridges in good repair. . . . The inhabitants mostly
> husbandmen; their wives and daughters domestic manufacturers; a suitable
> proportion of handicraft workmen, and two or three traders. . . . A school-
> master who should understand his business and teach his pupils to govern
> themselves. A social library. . . . A club of sensible men, seeking mutual
> improvement. . . . Such a situation may be considered as the most favorable
> to social happiness of any which this world can afford.
>
> Jeremy Belknap, *History of New-Hampshire* (1792)

In his 1792 history, Jeremy Belknap, a New Hampshire historian
and minister, painted an idealized representation of a New Hampshire community that took the familiar shape of a New England town, with its fields,
farms, and families. But the township had been transformed into a new
kind of settlement, the commercial village of the postrevolutionary era. The
cast of town characters expanded to include artisans and merchants, key
figures in the market society that slowly enveloped the region in the late
eighteenth century. Farmers' wives and daughters were identified as domestic manufacturers, while artisans achieved a new prominence. The schoolmaster instilled personal autonomy, and the elite circle of sensible citizens
promoted the enlightenment of the yeomanry. Commerce and culture had
come together in New England in the form of a village enlightenment at the
town center. Town founders migrated northward to New Hampshire, just
as they had to Nova Scotia, bringing with them the standard elements of
serial town settlement, but some new developments had intervened: a wider
dispersal of population, lengthy delays in incorporation, intracolonial
boundary disputes, and especially an accelerated pace of commercializa-

tion. These developments can be seen in striking detail in the story of how the people of the Wachusett moved up the Connecticut River valley to found new towns such as Walpole, New Hampshire, during the second half of the eighteenth century.[1]

As settlers clamored for new town grants in the Wachusett and other unappropriated areas of southern New England after 1713, migration surged into New Hampshire. While the settlement of the northern border-lands was checked by warfare among the English, French, and Indians during the second quarter of the eighteenth century, Massachusetts and New Hampshire clashed over their rival claims. A more diverse population moved into the disputed areas. The people of the Wachusett led the push up the Connecticut River valley in the 1740s and 1750s, forming one of the major streams of the movement of population up the river systems of northern New England. Massachusetts had attempted to impose its political and physical authority on the upper Connecticut River valley during the 1730s, but Indian wars and disputed boundaries hampered the Bay Colony; during the 1740s, settlers in those few outposts had retreated back to the Wachusett. Benning Wentworth, governor of New Hampshire, having enlarged his domain, took control of town settlement in this region during the late 1740s and 1750s.[2]

With the conclusion of the French and Indian War in 1763, a more populous migration left the Wachusett and other areas of western Massachusetts and Connecticut for the plentiful lands on the margins of British North America, New Hampshire and Nova Scotia, in particular. Largely owing to the efforts of one man—Colonel Benjamin Bellows, who had migrated north from Westminster to set himself up as a singular town patriarch—the town of Walpole had an unusual history. Walpole's settlers were able to plant a northern version of the New England town along the Connecticut River. Colonel Bellows, already a significant figure in town founding in the Wachusett, took an interest in the new lands being offered by New Hampshire's governor, Benning Wentworth. Bellows *was* Walpole in the early years; he occupied all the town offices and became the sole proprietor of its lands. He created a dynasty that dominated the development of the community and its institutions in the years before the War for Independence. Despite the autocratic form that this settlement took, the availability of cheap land attracted numerous settlers. The flood of migrants and the burgeoning market institutions eventually overwhelmed Bellows's plans for Walpole's future. The postrevolutionary transformation of Walpole and other upper Connecticut River valley towns into commercial villages occurred rapidly compared with the slow commercialization of previous town foundings. Walpole stood out for its commercial and cultural institutions, but pride of place went to the village print center. The local literati, that became known as the "Walpole Wits," contributed to a local newspaper, *The Farmer's Museum*, that attracted a readership throughout the new nation. The Walpole Wits devised a neoclassical version of vernacular village culture that signified and satirized New England. At the same time, other observers of towns throughout the region, such as Timothy Dwight and Jeremy Belknap, produced a regional portrait of town settlement that looked a lot like Walpole.

Looking North

With the pacification of the Eastern Indians after Dummer's War in 1725, English colonization resumed, so that during the second quarter of the eighteenth century as they filled up the land in central Massachusetts with towns, the people of the Wachusett looked to the contested northern borderlands to find new land for settlements. The colonies of Massachusetts, New Hampshire, and French Canada, as well as the Abenaki Indians, all made claims on these northern lands. The colony of New Hampshire, a coastal cluster of about a dozen towns with about forty-five hundred settlers in 1713, inched westward, growing five-fold in population by 1740. The Massachusetts Bay colonial system also grew rapidly, enveloping Maine and extending into the region between the Merrimack and Connecticut Rivers (see map 19). Massachusetts had built Fort Dummer on the west bank of the Connecticut to protect its northernmost settlement, Northfield, but the fortified log structure had also offered security to the increasing numbers of settlers requesting town grants along the upper Connecticut. The General Court granted over thirty townships between the Merrimack and Connecticut Rivers; a third were townships based on veterans' claims (Narragansett, Canada, and the frontier townships). Massachusetts also laid out four townships, No. 1 through No. 4, on the east bank of the Connecticut River.[3]

The proprietary form of town government facilitated northern migration from the Wachusett. Conceived initially as a solution to the problem of establishing provincial jurisdiction over sparsely settled territory, the proprietary system proved to be remarkably successful as an instrument for promoting geographical and economic expansion during the eighteenth century. There were various forms in which this migration took place. In many cases a group of young men from an older town purchased proprietary rights. They carefully planned their migration and maintained contact with the original settlement long after their removal. Londonderry's Scots-Irish population created several other towns. In another pattern, one individual, such as Josiah Willard or Colonel Benjamin Bellows, bought up a large portion of a single new township and took over responsibility for fulfilling the grant provisions and developing the settlement. A third alternative was that the proprietors in contiguous settlements could join together to stimulate regional growth. The proprietors in Lebanon, Hanover, Hartford, and Norwich, for example, arranged for the road from the pioneer

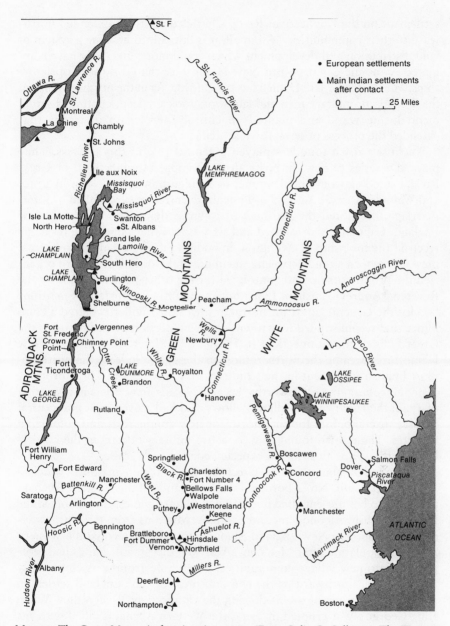

Map 19. The Green Mountain frontier, circa 1750. (From Colin G. Calloway, *The Western Abenakis of Vermont, 1600–1800,* Copyright © 1990 by the University of Oklahoma Press, Norman, Publishing Division of the University. All rights reserved. Reprinted by permission.)

settlement on the Connecticut River, Charlestown, to be extended northward to their communities. "All in all, it is difficult to imagine a system of land distribution and development which could more effectively have stimulated economic expansion in New Hampshire than did the proprietorships," the historian Jere Daniell has concluded.[4] As in the northern parts of the Wachusett, military men and surveyors took the lead, continued settlement during wars, and planted an entirely new chain of towns that extended the process of serial town settlement.

Wachusett town founders played a central role in this process. They planted a series of new outposts along the upper Connecticut, or Great River, extending from Fort Dummer to Arlington in 1733, No. 4 in 1740, and Walpole in 1752. A group of Lunenburg entrepreneurs, linked by intermarriage, promoted the business of town settlement in northern New England. Captain Josiah Willard and sixty-three other Lunenburg residents received the township of Arlington; in addition to the usual requirements, they had to open a road between Lunenburg and Northfield. Willard organized the proprietorship and contracted for the other items, assisted by the Reverend Andrew Gardner, Lunenburg's migratory minister. As petitions flooded the General Court for northern townships, Willard chaired a committee that recommended four townships lying north from Arlington to the Great Falls of the Connecticut in 1736; No. 4, later Charlestown, New Hampshire, became the northernmost of these, and indeed, the northernmost English settlement in the Connecticut Valley region. Three brothers from Lunenburg, the Farnsworths, became No. 4's first settlers in the spring of 1740; the Farnsworth-Willard-Bellows clan had moved west into central Massachusetts before looking north for new commercial and colonizing ventures. These town founders were active military officers in the borderlands in the 1740s awaiting an expected conflict with France.[5]

The Indian inhabitants of the Green Mountain region anxiously watched English expansion. No. 4 bordered the homelands of the Western Abenaki people, who became engulfed in the wider military contest that involved the French, English, Algonquian, and Iroquois. Migrants from the Nashaways and other southern New England Algonquians had augmented the Western Abenaki population after Metacom's War, and their family bands had reorganized into new village communities. The whole group was continually forced further northward by the constant press of New England settlers in the growing mosaic of towns dotting the Connecticut River valley. When King George's War erupted in 1744, the Western Abenakis allied with the French in an effort to check English settlement. French and Indian raiders attacked the fortified settlements along the Connecticut. No. 4's residents huddled behind their two-story stockade, endured captivity, and faced deadly skirmishes; discouraged settlers retreated to Lunenburg. When the war ended in 1748, the English and Indians remained on a collision course while the larger imperial conflict loomed.[6]

The war years saw the resolution of the boundary dispute between Massachusetts and New Hampshire, however. The Privy Council had drawn New Hampshire's southern border three miles north of the course of the Merrimack from its mouth at the Atlantic coast to its southernmost point and then due west until it reached New York, delineating a territory that exceeded even New Hampshire's own claims. The council had appointed Benning Wentworth as the new royal governor. Town founder and surveyor Benjamin Bellows of Lunenburg and Westminster, who was closely related to several upper Connecticut River valley colonists, surveyed Wentworth's dramatically expanded domain. Wentworth, anxious to occupy his colony's territory and increase his family's wealth, offered Colonel Bellows his choice of the unoccupied land along the upper valley. Bellows first chose an area with excellent waterpower, but its exposed position north of No. 4 caused him to reconsider, so he turned to a site just below the Great Falls, with fertile soil and a plentiful supply of salmon and shad. Located between No. 4 and Fort Dummer, the area was well known to Wachusett settlers and soldiers.[7]

In 1752 Wentworth issued a standard charter with few regulations to Bellows, his four sons, his brother-in-law Jonathan Blanchard, and sixty-one other grantees to settle a township called Walpole. Bellows and many others readily saw the advantages of colonization of northern New England; the region offered wide scope for the planning and planting of a new town. Such freedom was not available in the older areas, such as the Wachusett. Yet Bellows became the only original proprietor to settle in town, similar to John Prescott in Lancaster over a century earlier and Joshua Bigelow in Westminster more recently. Like Prescott, Bellows would be responsible for directing the town's development; like the Bigelow family, the Bellows family would be handsomely rewarded for their early arrival. Bellows was able to exert far more personal control over the town's land and institutions than his Wachusett counterparts, however, because of the dispersed mode of settlement in northern New England. Although in some New Hampshire towns 25 percent of the proprietors became settlers, the development of Walpole and other Connecticut River townships followed a different course. All grantees were required to cultivate five acres of land for each fifty acres of their share within five years.

Bellows quickly purchased the rights of some of the other grantees (as did Blanchard) and removed to Walpole, leaving his family behind on his eight-hundred-acre farm in Lunenburg. Bellows's sudden departure from Lunenburg, it is thought, was the result of an accumulation of debts. Unable to meet his creditors' demands, the colonel fled the Wachusett with sheriffs in pursuit. At the Massachusetts border, he paused, so the story goes, just long enough to assert that jail would be no place for him to meet his obligations. That Bellows later was able to move freely between New Hampshire and Massachusetts, however, suggests that he had been able to satisfy his creditors. Whatever the cause, Bellows's story reminds us that eighteenth-century town founding required risk taking in credit-poor colonial society.[8]

When Bellows arrived in Walpole in 1752, he found the site already occupied; John Kilburn and his four family members had settled there below the Great Falls in 1749 with their title from the Massachusetts grants of 1736. The proprietors of No. 3, as it had been called, one of Willard's four Connecticut River townships, had laid out lots, distributed them to sixty-odd grantees, raised revenue, and planned roads and mills. Yet no one came, and the proprietors had decided not to approach New Hampshire in 1742 after No. 3 fell under its jurisdiction. Meetings had grown fewer and the records closed in 1751.

Upon arrival, Bellows constructed an L-shaped palisaded garrison home overlooking his meadows. Only a few settlers followed him, all of whom built homes and made a start at cultivating the land. Bellow's family arrived in 1753 to occupy that garrison for nine long years. For war once again arose and stemmed the tide of settlement. Massachusetts' Governor Shirley warned: "the French seem to have advanced further towards making themselves Masters of this Continent within these last 5 or 6 years than they have done ever since the first Beginnings of their Settlements upon it."[9] Furthermore, the Iroquois and the Abenaki peoples were upset over English incursion onto their lands, and when they received word of a road and settlements planned deep in their homelands, the Abenakis delivered an ultimatum to No. 4, Bellows's northern neighbor. War parties descended upon it and the Merrimack River townships in 1754 because, according to the Indians, "the English had set down upon lands there which they had not purchased." That summer eight captives were taken from No. 4; alarm spread throughout northern New England. Bellows reported "people are in great distress" along both river valleys, unable to "Secure their grain nor hardly keep their garrison." Back in the Wachusett, settlers had already returned to garrison living before formal hostilities commenced. Bellows's sturdy structure became a regional storehouse for grain and other supplies for the neighboring, sparsely settled townships. It also became one of the chain of forts maintained by the Bay Colony along the exposed northern Connecticut Valley, stocked with cannon and staffed with militia. Violence struck Walpole as two men were picked off in the woods. Everywhere in New England, frontier folk feared the Indians' wrath. "Its now open War," Colonel Israel Williams declared in October 1754, "and a very dark & distressing scene opening."[10]

The climactic struggle for empire formally began in 1755 along the upper Ohio River between British regular troops and the French, while British offensives faltered in the Champlain Valley. French and Indian raids struck from Maine to the Virginia backcountry. "While Amherst, Wolfe, and Montcalm fought the epic clashes that helped decide the fate of the continent," historian Colin Calloway reminds us, "their less-famous counterparts—Benjamin Bellows at Walpole, Phineas Stevens at Fort Number Four, and their largely unidentified Abenaki adversaries—waged the Green Mountain phase of the struggle for continental supremacy." In August 1755 John Kilburn, his son, and two others in Walpole were returning from the fields when he spotted numerous Indians, "as thick as grasshoppers," according to one settler's narrative. They fled to his palisaded log house where they waited for the attack. Another party of Indians waylaid Bellows and his men returning from the town mill; Bellows made for the fort. Philip, a familiar Indian customer of Kilburn, appeared outside the house with the offer: "Old John, young John, I know you; come out here; we will give you quarter." Kilburn refused, and the ensuing battle went on until sundown when the Abenaki war parties withdrew. While Walpole was spared further raids, other outposts were struck in 1757 and 1758, and the conflict resembled a reprise of the defensive skirmishes of King George's War.[11]

The English carried the war to the Abenakis' homeland. Massachusetts and the British army provided more men for the garrisons; they organized scouting parties that struck far north at the Abenaki village of St. Francis. It was at that point that New Hampshire blazed the Crown Point military road (the plans for which had sparked the earlier Abenaki ultimatum) from opposite No. 4 through the Green Mountains to deep into the borderlands. The balance of power between colonists and Indians shifted; superior British resources began to overwhelm the French; and British and colonial armies uprooted French presence in the upper Ohio Valley and the Great Lakes. With the fall of Quebec in 1759, British colonists celebrated. As Jonathan Mayhew wrote, "Quebec, after repeated struggles and efforts is at length reduced: *Quebec,* I had almost called it that Pandora's box, from whence unnumber'd plagues have issued for more than an hundred years, to distress, to enfeeble, to lay waste, these northern colonies; and which might, perhaps in the end have proved fatal to them."

The frontiers of New Hampshire had been more effectively defended than in previous conflicts. Few settlements had been vacated; less than fifty settlers killed or taken captive. The Treaty of Paris, signed in 1763, made Canada an English possession, ending years of imperial warfare in the borderlands and securing the northern frontier of New Hampshire. Soldiers returned home with tales of rich lands. Soon, settlers would sweep up both sides of the Connecticut River.[12]

Those settlers flowing north found a unique proprietary township in Walpole. Almost immediately after Governor Wentworth had made the grant in 1752, Bellows had begun acquiring the grantees' proprietary rights. The New Hampshire land records list a lengthy stream of deeds, many from residents of Lancaster and Lunenburg, turning over their shares to Bellows for five pounds, none for more than ten, in the very first year of the township's history. His brother-in-law, Blanchard, and Theodore Atkinson, Secretary of the Province, joined Bellows in buying up Walpole's proprietorships (though they proved less savvy, often paying twenty-five pounds per right). In 1760 Blanchard's widow, Bellows's sister, sold her five shares to Bellows for sixty pounds. During the war Bellows and Atkinson increased their holdings until they held all the rights of the sixty-seven original grantees. Further, Bellows retained his interests in Lunenburg and acquired land in many of the new townships being granted by Wentworth during the third quarter of the eighteenth century.[13]

Bellows focused his attention on transforming these Walpole shares into a marketable land system. In 1756 he sold an undivided third of Walpole to Atkinson for five hundred pounds, which they divided ten years later. A map was drawn up in 1767 that displays the lots set off by that time. Atkinson received a strip of land (2,028 acres) from the east line of the town running west to the Connecticut River; Derry Hill (2,764 acres), which was in the southeastern section and not divided until 1781; and Boggy Meadow (1,000 acres), the richest land, adjacent to the river, which was not drained until the nineteenth century. Bellows owned the rest of the town, except for the governor's farm and church glebe at the northern border of the township. He kept the northern half for himself, especially the lands along the Cold River that meandered through that section. He laid out three ranges of one-hundred-acre lots, roughly parallel to the river. At a thirty-five-degree angle, four ranges of hill lots were laid out. Later studies have located Bellows's plans. Eventually, Atkinson decided that he had too many other provincial responsibilities and sold his land back to Bellows, who thereby gained control of all the land granted to the original proprietors.[14]

Colonel Benjamin Bellows, as joint and then sole proprietor, organized the town government and other necessary institutions during the war years. No record exists of any proprietary meeting. At the first town meeting, held in Walpole in March 1752, Bellows was appointed moderator, selectman, and town clerk, with his fellow landowners, Atkinson and Blanchard, as selectmen. The next year, he took over all of the offices. Then Colonel Josiah Willard became town clerk by 1754, with Bellows's name crossed out on the town records. The following year Benjamin Bellows III, took over as town clerk at the age of fifteen. With Atkinson and Blanchard living at great distances, and Willard quite busy with the affairs of Arlington, it seems unlikely that any of these men trudged through the snowy woods to Walpole in early March for the meetings. Rather, we must imagine Bellows all by himself in the privacy of his palisaded garrison home calling to order and writing up these unusual town meetings.[15]

Considerable friction existed between Bellows and Kilburn in the early years of the settlement, and Kilburn's name does not appear as a selectman until 1755. Kilburn, holding a worthless title, had lived in Walpole for several years—in considerable isolation from other colonists and with frequent apprehension about the possibility of Indian attack—until Bellows's arrival in 1752. He stubbornly clung to his title to the entire township and refused to accept any land from Bellows. At one point he actually left for Springfield, further north, rather than acknowledge Bellows's authority. Eventually, Bellows conferred 150 acres on Kilburn "in consideration of the duty being done on one right or share of land" in 1755. That same year Bellows built his own gristmill and began to supply grain to the few families in Walpole as well as neighboring townships. With the waning of the war, Bellows also made provisions for the religious life of the community. The town inhabitants' meeting "at the Fort in Walpole" in 1760 voted to call Jonathan Leavitt to become their minister, with a generous seventy-five pounds sterling settlement and an annual salary that began at thirty-seven pounds and rose annually. The residents voted to collect two pounds five shillings each from the approximately twelve families in town, with Bellows to provide the balance. The construction of a meetinghouse was facilitated by a similar taxing arrangement, with Bellows "to make up the rest."[16]

When hostilities ceased in northern New England, Bellows welcomed a flood of land-hungry migrants with generous terms and a developing town infrastructure. Purchasers could buy land for less than one-half pound per acre in the early 1760s; the very first arrival received a one-hundred-acre lot for thirteen pounds. Bellows attracted a blacksmith and other necessary mechanics. About forty-four families moved to Walpole during that decade. Many of these migrants came from Connecticut. The first provincial census of New Hampshire, taken in 1767, recorded a population of 308 beginning to cluster into a village pattern of settlement. By the early 1770s land prices rose to a little more than one pound per acre, and by the end of the decade some were paying Bellows's widow about two pounds per acre. Bellows controlled access to the land, which he sold by contract, reserving title until the terms of the contract had been fulfilled. In his 1777 will Colonel Bellows instructed his oldest son, who would become General Benjamin Bellows during the War for Independence, "to give deed to any and all persons that I have contracted with for lands; they fulfilling their contracts precisely and paying the same fully up, according to their bargains."[17]

English colonists jumped beyond the cluster of prewar outposts that had taken decades to move above Northfield. Instead, as an anonymous observer in *American Husbandry* wrote, "farms on the river Connecticut are every day extending beyond the old fort Dummer," no longer inching slowly along the river valleys but extending two hundred miles to the northern Cowass River intervales. The Fanning family left Stonington, Connecticut, for one of Benning Wentworth's New Hampshire grants, but they and many other migrants got no further than Walpole. So impressed with the fertile lands and agricultural improvements that were evident as they traveled up the east bank of the Connecticut River, that when they passed through the "small village" of Keene and entered Walpole, they decided to stop. There, they purchased a lot of land, "built a house of square timber, cut down the trees and cleared the land, so as to raise a good crop of corn the same year." The roof of the house was covered with bark, and the gable ends remained open for some time, "which enabled them to hear the barking of foxes, the howling of wolves, and the cries of panthers" as they sat before the hearth. The brooks teemed with trout and the river with salmon and shad. Wildlife abounded nearby. Other settlers regaled the Fannings with tales of wild bears and Indians, events still apparently fresh in their minds. About twelve or fifteen log houses clustered in town in 1762. The meetinghouse was unfinished, and roads were so primitive that there was no way to travel within the town except on foot or horseback.[18]

Bellows was a dominating presence in the town. He was a tall, stout man, weighing about three hundred and thirty pounds, and played an active role in managing his labor, supervising his workmen from the back of a favorite (and long-suffering) horse. He spared little expense in constructing an "exceedingly well-built and well-finished" mansion for his family. His granddaughter, who remembered his household as having "a patriarchal character," described how he provided for his family and his hired workers:

> A very large kitchen under the house, where a great oaken table lay always spread, was the eating-room of his workmen. He always maintained a separate table for his immediate family. . . . The Colonel raised his own stores, and killed an ox or a cow every week to supply the wants of his household. The winter stores were enormous in quantity. . . . The Colonel put down twenty barrels of pork yearly; eggs were brought in by the half-bushel; and his men stipulated that they should not have salmon oftener than three times a week.

He made four hundred barrels of cider annually from his orchards. With all this abundance, he entertained neighbors and travelers lavishly. To enhance the genteel character of his estate, he acquired a family chaplain, Elisha Harding from Brookfield, living in the Bellows homestead until the colonel died in 1777, after which time he moved to Bellows's son's residence. Bellows provided seven houses for his heirs, also of mansion proportions, built of solid masonry and heavy timbers, "with the idea of space and endurance," according to his granddaughter's reminiscences. Large windows and great fireplaces greeted visitors upon entering, and abundant wainscoting distinguished the interiors of these homes.[19]

Bellows never let his position in the town go unnoticed. Nor could he stand competition for leadership, which led to difficulties with the town minister, Jonathan Leavitt. The most vivid memories of one settler were of the town's pecking order as it was displayed during gatherings in the meetinghouse:

> Col. Benjamin Bellows was the most considerable man in town. . . . Mr. Leavitt, the minister, . . . wore a large wig, fully powdered, and when he entered the meetinghouse, the whole congregation rose to do obeisance to the man in black, who, in his turn, always responded with a formal bow. . . . Of

the ladies Mrs. Leavitt took the lead in dress; at church she wore a full suit of lutestring . . . holding a fan to shade the sun from her face, as were the fashion "down country." Next to her were the daughters of Col. Bellows, and their two half-sisters, Jennisons.

The two patricians did not get along. Leavitt's airs did not suit his parishioners or his patron, and Bellows saw to it that he was dismissed in 1764. One of the reasons for his removal was that Leavitt was detected leading home a runaway slave of his, a woman, by a rope around her neck that was attached to his saddle. Colonel Bellows, hearing of this barbarous behavior, exclaimed that he had "settled Parson Leavitt and would unsettle him."[20]

The Reverend Thomas Fessenden arrived to replace Leavitt in 1767 after a long series of frontier posts and pastoral stations in the Wachusett where his liberal views had made permanent settlement impossible. Bellows and Walpole, however, welcomed him. In 1767 Bellows paid one-third of Fessenden's generous financial settlement, as had become customary in Walpole, and provided one hundred acres of land to cover the costs of building a town grammar school in 1775.[21]

For a quarter of a century Benjamin Bellows presided over the formation of Walpole and the transfer of the system of serial town settlement from new areas of the Wachusett, such as Lunenburg and Westminster, to even newer ones in the upper Connecticut River valley. In the 1750s he monopolized the proprietorship and town government, establishing a personal and patriarchal system of governance. Bellows worked within the proprietary system of serial town settlement, rather than outside as had some of the great proprietors. Bellows achieved additional latitude from the military conflicts that enveloped the borderlands and made many investors and migrants steer clear of these new settlements during the 1750s.[22] Settlement activity halted with the war in the 1750s, a time during which Bellows and his well-placed partners acquired control of Walpole's lands. Peace in the 1760s brought new migrants to Walpole, who purchased land directly from Bellows; the outlines of a working town enticed northern-bound families such as the Fannings to remain. Transplantation under the auspices of Bellows's patriarchal and unchallenged rule had been successful; families had established farms, even though the planting of such institutions as local government and church had been weaker in northern New England.

Bellows died in 1777. He ended a life as a town founder by providing his children with a bounty of land—some six to eight thousand acres—in the new towns of the Wachusett and its offspring in the northern Connecticut Valley of New Hampshire and Vermont, along with over one thousand pounds in cash and other household and farm goods. He also bequeathed his position as a dominant presence in town and provincial affairs to his sons, particularly his three oldest sons. Benjamin Bellows III, the oldest son, took over his father's post as town moderator. He expanded the Bellows political interest into the new state of New Hampshire, marrying Phoebe Strong, sister of Massachusetts Governor Strong. He rose to the rank of Brigadier General during the War for Independence, and served in 1781 as State Senator and member of the General Court. His brother John took charge of raising troops and procuring supplies in the conflict. He, too, became a member of the State Congress in 1775–76, served in the Constitutional Convention in 1781, and became Senator of the State in 1786 and 1787. John pursued banking and farming. The younger brother Thomas Bellows, nicknamed the Squire, displayed less of the ambition of his older siblings but was content to occupy the family homestead and hold town and state office before beginning a thirty-year tenure as Cheshire County sheriff. During the turbulent revolutionary era the authority of town founders would become more difficult to transmit.[23]

Challenges

During the 1770s and 1780s, revolutionary-era northern New England became a vortex of competing forces. Three conflicts in particular served to break down established institutions. First, there was a conflict over authority between migrants drawn inland by generous New Hampshire land grants and New York landholders who claimed the same territory. Benning Wentworth's midcentury grants west of the Connecticut River in the Green Mountain region had attracted many settlers from New England whose experience of town government clashed with a more feudal form of land ownership and colonization practiced by New Yorkers. Led by Ethan Allen, these New Englanders in the Green Mountains (the Green Mountain boys, as they came to be called) took matters into their own hands, effectively stopping the intrusion of New York authorities. The second conflict arose on the heels of the first as a direct result of the independence movement among the Connecticut River townships. New Hampshire's authority, like that of New York's, was called into question and the situation eventually led to a break with New Hampshire and the establishment of a new Vermont authority. In this turmoil, the move toward democratization that was unleashed by the assault against the British and the Loyalist officials undermined the authority of patriarchal leaders such as Bellows and led to the fragmentation of political authority. The third conflict was religious in nature. Walpole's minister, Thomas Fessenden, held liberal views both in terms of theology and in terms of church governance, views that were informed by Enlightenment rationalism. He challenged from the pulpit the traditional interlocking authorities of church and state, further dissolved the familiar pillars of the Standing Order, and opened the door for a more pluralistic and contentious postrevolutionary cultural order in the 1790s.[24]

The first of these conflicts arose after the resolution of New Hampshire's southern boundary with Massachusetts, when Governor Wentworth began looking west towards New York to enrich his family and extend his authority. He granted 128 towns west of the Connecticut River before he left office in 1767. The border between New York and New Hampshire had remained undefined until the Royal Proclamation of 1764 recognized the Connecticut River as the division. Yet during the decade of the 1760s twenty-thousand New Englanders had flooded into the New Hampshire grants that Wentworth had given away or sold for a nominal share fee. One of these settlers was Ethan Allen, Revolutionary War hero and founder of Vermont, who fled the flush Connecticut land market and, displaying that familiar combination of entrepreneurial activity and family strategy, bought shares in Poultney and Castleton for a total of ten pounds in 1770. Difficulties in transplanting the New England town were compounded by New York's assertion of authority over the settlers. By 1774, Allen and his supporters, known as the Green Mountain boys, had united the people in the New Hampshire grants against the royal authority of New York by linking the local struggle against royal officials to the larger American movement against British imperial authority by using ideological and political confrontations.[25]

The next year violence broke out and enveloped local leaders, including General Bellows in Walpole. When New York's newly established loyalist Cumberland County supervisors pocketed correspondence from the New York City patriot Committee of Correspondence, aroused residents organized a provisional county government; local Whigs suspected that the New York courts would pursue debt collection and bring "the lower sort of the people into a state of bondage and slavery." The mobilized populace petitioned Colonel Thomas Chandler not to open New York's Cumberland County court in Westminster. Anti-Yorkers and the county sheriff's armed men converged on the courthouse, a battle ensued, and the anti-Yorkers fled to raise an armed response. General Bellows headed Walpole's company and joined four hundred men assembled in Westminster; the New York judges and their supporters were captured and put in jail, replacing the anti-Yorkers. Calls for revenge rang out. Bellows waded into the crowd and argued strongly for the legal resolution of the confrontation; he protected the prisoners from the angry gathering. The next day he succeeded in escorting the leaders of the "massacre" to Northampton, to be held safely "till they could have a fair trial." Bellows's moderation won the day, but Ethan Allen would successfully build upon the memory of the "Westminster Massacre" to form the new province of Vermont and challenge Walpole's notables.[26]

Bellows faced his next crisis of authority closer to home. The older Connecticut River towns along the east shore in New Hampshire, which included Walpole, had formed into Cheshire County in 1771 (see map 20),

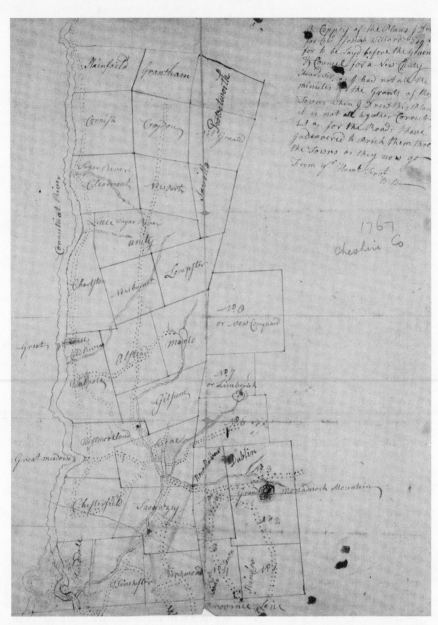

Map 20. Cheshire County, as surveyed by Benjamin Bellows Jr., 1767. Bellows's map provided the first view of the roads that ran along the Connecticut River and crisscrossed the new townships, bringing migrants north to southwestern New Hampshire from southern New England. The survey's purpose was to petition for a new county. It indicated a substantial presence of towns and townspeople. ("Plan for a New County." Courtesy of New Hampshire State Library, Concord, and David Allen, Old Maps, Inc.)

and they soon found themselves torn between allegiance to New Hampshire and allegiance to the new Vermont government that Allen had helped found in 1771. After the Declaration of Independence and the establishment of New Hampshire's statehood, the new constitution of New Hampshire created problems for the Connecticut River townships. The state constitution instituted a population-based system of representation, which contrasted starkly with the previous colonial government's town-based system. As a result of their weakened political position, these inland townships approached the state of Vermont in hopes of reuniting the entire Connecticut River valley region as a single political entity, which had been split by the breaking away of Vermont from the New Hampshire territory, but they were initially rebuffed. Insurgents in Grafton County (located just north of Cheshire County) and in ten towns west of the river held a convention in December and defended their right "to form themselves into an INDEPENDENT STATE." The Declaration of Independence had severed New Hampshire's royal authority, they announced, an act that allowed a return to the first legal stage of governance, namely, townships. Furthermore, they declared, the upper Connecticut River townships, east and west of the river, formed a distinct cultural region, tied to their original homes in Connecticut and Massachusetts by "manners, customs, and habits," and interwoven by "connections and commerce." The convention concluded by deciding to negotiate with New Hampshire.[27]

General Bellows attempted to broker a deal by enticing an indifferent New Hampshire Assembly in Exeter into annexing the entire valley, but when the assembly deferred to the Continental Congress in 1780, the valley townspeople organized a new jurisdiction. In Walpole in November 1780, Bellows chaired a meeting that called for a general convention. Forty-three towns on both sides of the river converged on Charlestown on January 16, 1781, where Bellows and other Cheshire County notables assured the delegates that New Hampshire would extend its authority across the river. Vermont's Ira Allen arrived at the last minute, however, with a dramatic offer from the state to admit the whole territory. Bellows's efforts were forgotten. Vermont admitted thirty-five New Hampshire representatives and established separate counties and courts for the eastern river towns. Separate jurisdictions claimed authority in Cheshire and Grafton Counties. Many local leaders received Vermont appointments, but General Bellows refused a militia commission.[28]

At that point, towns divided into Vermont or New Hampshire factions; townspeople split as to which official or court they would apply to for justice. "High words, party rage, and deep resentment were the effects of these clashing interests." Bellows pleaded with Exeter for action. Each side rounded up the other's officials, and "the horrors of civil war" appeared imminent. Colonel Enoch Hale, New Hampshire's Cheshire County sheriff, was captured by a rowdy band of Vermont sympathizers while conducting his duties and dispatched in a sleigh to Walpole. When released, he complained to the governor that, without orders and authority from the Exeter Committee of Safety, New Hampshire's authority was a dead letter. The conflict wound down when the New Hampshire Assembly lurched into action by calling out one thousand men and demanding an oath of allegiance from Tories and western rebels alike, and at the same time, General Washington warned Vermont's leaders that their entry into the confederation hinged upon the renunciation of their territorial additions. The eastern shore towns acknowledged New Hampshire's authority, and eventually General Bellows along with the established local and state Whig elite were able to turn back this political insurgency and retain their authority. Throughout the whole episode, Bellows's flexible political leadership had held the moderate Whig course, but he had never enjoyed the type of unquestioned patriarchal rule his father had.[29]

The third major conflict dividing the region at this time had to do with religious concerns. Greater New England nurtured a diversity of sects, a great many of which rejected Calvinist doctrines in "a mass movement of Dissent" that decisively broke the monopoly of New England orthodoxy. No region of North America during the revolutionary era witnessed a greater challenge to religious orthodoxy, the cornerstone of town settlement, than the newly settled towns of northern New England. The Congregational establishment had been weakly transplanted from Connecticut and Massachusetts; numerous towns had never secured a permanent minister. Many migrants moved up river to pursue greater religious freedom as part of the general questioning of authority unleashed by political independence and social upheaval, a demographic shift that further unraveled the bonds of traditional religious institutions. The dissolution of royal government and the writing of new constitutions intensified the call for religious freedom and the rejection of the authority of the state over religion. The result was the emergence of new churches, new doctrines, and new leaders. A diversity of sects proliferated along the northern frontier from Vermont to Nova Scotia. The challenge to Calvinism came in a bewildering variety of forms and voices—natural religion, Universalism, and deism were among the more popular beliefs.[30]

Walpole harbored religious innovation. Thomas Fessenden, the town's second minister, espoused an unorthodox theology that integrated a variant of the backwoods radical evangelicalism called New Light (which Stephen Marini and George Rawlyk have so ably located within the New Hampshire grants and Nova Scotia) with the more cosmopolitan liberal theology of Boston and Cambridge. Fessenden combined a life-long search for the sources of true religion with a pressing inquiry into the nature of authority in a revolutionary world. Fessenden, like many others in the post-1763 northward migration, could not find a place in the Wachusett social or religious order, so he answered the call to the frontier station of Walpole. There, his unusual personal demeanor and philosophical speculations found fertile ground.[31] Fessenden was raised and educated in the cosmopolitan atmosphere of Cambridge, Massachusetts. He held unorthodox views that upset many conservatives: Ebenezer Parkman, Northborough's long time minister, thought that Fessenden held "peculiar Notions about the Trinity" and that he claimed that "there is no Son of God before the New Testament." Parkman concluded that Fessenden had a bent to "make many Mysteries where there was none." Fessenden's views made it hard for him to secure a position as a minister. He spent a decade bouncing around frontier posts and military stations, landing at Lancaster, Princeton, and wherever his services were needed. Prospective ministers faced close scrutiny from regional ministerial associations and local congregations. In 1764, for example, the town of Dunstable divided sharply upon hearing Fessenden's probational sermons, in which he declared "that the Gospel had its Foundation laid in the Religion of Nature" and "we were not required to believe any Thing that our Reason could not comprehend." In the end, this natural religion proved too controversial for the people of Dunstable. Walpole, however, greeted the carpenter's son warmly with a call to its pulpit after the town had tired of the pompous Reverend Leavitt. Fessenden accepted the call, requesting that half his salary of fifty pounds be paid in cash—adding, with a taste of his usual wit, that a supply of too much produce would oblige minister "to turn *Marchant.*"[32]

Fessenden's writings revolved around the issue of authority in politics and religion. As obedience to the magistrate is "a duty enjoined by God," he wrote in 1776, we must have something more than "our own erroneous conceits" before we refuse to obey him. Nevertheless, when the ruler threatens the common good, his rights cease. Fessenden's ideas were defined and refined in the heated era of debates over the nature and extent of British authority; he discussed what was rightfully due to the rule and the subject, critical issues for a people reconsidering what constituted lawful power and how far the magistrate's authority extended in religion. Many people in the upper valley questioned state support of the Congregational establishment, and Fessenden agreed to the extent that the civil authorities held no just power in matters of conscience. All people had "the right of private Judgement in things both civil and religion." The magistrate could oblige all to practice some Christian religion but could not support an established church, a restriction that was the cornerstone of the standing order.[33]

Fessenden attacked other parts of the Calvinist edifice as well. He continued to develop his liberal, Arminian notions of personal responsibility and the benevolence of the Deity, moving away from the doctrines of innate depravity and predestination. He warned his parishioners in 1777 that they were the authors of their own miseries and errors. Personal responsibility was not an onerous burden, however, for reason and religion revealed the path "God hath directed them to walk" and "the ways of wisdom are pleasant." These optimistic formulations stood as a rebuke to the pessimism and harsh uncertainty offered by New Light Calvinists after the Great Awakening. The love of God was not an infusion of sudden enthusiasm, but a "steady sober calm rational affection of the mind and heart," he wrote in his treatise *The Science of Sanctity*, acquired by the study of both nature and of revelation, "to be explained by reason, common sense, and the analogy of things." "The Gospel had its Foundation laid in the Religion of Nature, and . . . we were not required to believe anything that our Reason could not comprehend."[34]

Fessenden advocated a sociable religiosity. "True religion . . . is no enemy to cheerfulness, pleasantry, and agreeableness in the young; nor to suitable diversions and recreations within the bounds of moderation: It makes a man the best companion, friend, and brother, in the world: It forbids the formal solemnity, and stiff ungracious airs, and awkward singularity of the Pharisees; and the unsociable affected gestures of the recluse and superstitious." Christians should display piety and virtue in "a public social nature." He practiced his own prescriptions: the short, stocky minister cut a highly visible and jovial figure around Walpole, wearing old-fashioned clothing and mounted on his horse with legs stuck out at odd angles. The minister recommended dancing to his daughters and attended frolics. To the denizens of Crafts Tavern, he became known as "Old Pam"—after the jack of clubs in the game of loo—for his skill in card playing.[35]

The doors to Fessenden's church swung open wide, welcoming all "to shine in the midst" of the town rather than "to live separate in a Corner." Walpole's First Congregational Church grew from twenty-five members in 1767, at the time of Fessenden's ordination to over two hundred members eight years later. Fessenden abandoned strict, Calvinist standards for church communion and adopted a form of Universalism, arguing that Christ atoned for all humanity. Universalist rational theology and advocacy of the rights of the common man appealed to the rural intelligentsia. Drawing on the European-led Enlightenment project and the local print revolution, Fessenden laid the foundations for Walpole's own Village Enlightenment; he also helped to bring about a new world of dissent and democratization that would profoundly unsettle him.[36]

The Village Enlightenment

Town settlement entered a new stage during the 1790s. Walpole coalesced at the town center, with stores and shops, merchants, artisans, and professionals. It became a commercial village, vividly described by Jeremiah Mason:

> This was a brisk, active village, with several traders, and many industrious mechanics, and two or three taverns. Walpole was, at that time, a place of more

business than any in that vicinity, and was much resorted to by the people of the neighboring towns. There was also a considerable travel from a distance, passing on what was called the great river road. . . . The inhabitants of that part of the Connecticut river valley were then just passing from the rude and boisterous manners of first settlers to a more civilized, orderly, and settled state. There was more motion, life, and bustle than in the older parts of the country.

Commerce and culture became intertwined in a process that I call the Village Enlightenment. What transformed Walpole and countless other communities was neither the efforts of an elite, nor the effects of the Industrial Revolution, but a sweeping commercial revolution, composed of the actions of thousands of ordinary men and women, who created a burgeoning market culture. The commercialization of rural life occurred unevenly in the rural northern United States and operated in tandem with the accelerating flow of information in the hinterlands that broke down the monopolistic position of traditional cultural mediators, people such as General Bellows or Reverend Fessenden.[37]

Walpole's most visible transformation occurred at the very center of town. The postrevolutionary era was distinguished by what geographer Joseph Wood has called "the rise of the New England village," a central place that was the product of the existing system of town settlement as well as of the new commercializing economy. Most seventeenth-century towns, such as Lancaster, had never been nucleated settlements with outlying common fields, the medieval English form; rather, the town center, with perhaps a meetinghouse and tavern, marked the physical and social center of a community with dispersed farmsteads scattered throughout the township, as depicted in a 1780 representation of Walpole. Population growth and the settlement of outlying areas led to the subdivision or "budding" process and eventual outmigration to new plantations, an extensive mode of town formation. But settlement intensified in the 1790s; gathered in the village were shops, stores, offices, and residences occupied by merchants, lawyers, doctors, tanners, printers, hatters, blacksmiths, and other artisans and professionals whose businesses required proximity to teamsters, stages, and travelers.[38]

The elder Bellows had planned the town center near his own house in the northern, inland part of Walpole, but the clustered settlement moved nearer to the Connecticut River and centered around Main Street with little reference to Bellows's plan (see map 21). In about 1793, Parson Fessenden's residence stood at the north end of Main Street; a bakery, hatter, tailor's shop, tannery, and several other stores and taverns lined the street. Where High Street intersected Main Street stood Crafts Tavern, which served as the town's preeminent place for the exchange of information, formal and informal meetings, and business contacts with the outside world. Across the street stood Isaiah Thomas's print shop and bookstore. General Benjamin

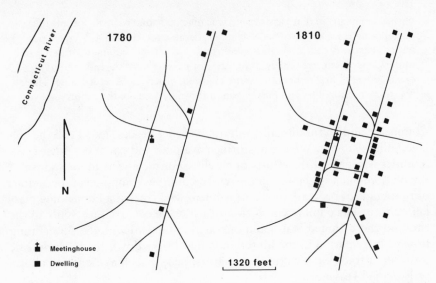

Map 21. Walpole town center, 1780 and 1810. The town was originally sited with farmlands along the Connecticut River and the town center in the north near Benjamin Bellows's lands. In the 1780s, the meetinghouse lot was bare. In the 1790s, however, commercial enterprises began to cluster around a new village commercial center farther south. (Reprinted from Joseph Wood, "The Origin of the New England Village" [Ph.D. diss., Pennsylvania State University, 1978], p. 228. Courtesy of Joseph S. Wood.)

Bellows subdivided his sixty-acre lots for commercial trade, and in 1792 and 1793 sold a series of fifty-foot lots to merchants and artisans. The following decade, Bellows developed the land to the west on Washington Street, paralleling Main, for residences and shops. At the foot of Main Street, a recently planted promenade of poplar trees led along Prospect Hill to the town's new meetinghouse, relocated from the northern part of town.[39]

Improvements in transportation promoted the passage of ideas as well as commodities to and from previously isolated communities. A post rider started visiting Walpole in 1784; by 1791 federal legislation established a weekly postal route from Concord; and a post office opened in town in 1795. Stagecoach lines proliferated in the hinterlands after 1800. A weekly stage traveled up and down the Connecticut River and to and from Boston in 1801. By 1803 the Boston stage ran through Walpole to Hanover three times a week. One English traveler to Walpole noted how hungry for news were residents of previously remote hamlets: "It was entertaining to see the eagerness of the people on our arrival to get a sight of the last newspaper from Boston. They flocked to the post-office and the inn, and formed a variety of groups around those who were fortunate to possess themselves of a paper. There they stood, with open mouth, swallowing 'the lies of the day,' which would be as readily contradicted on the morrow."[40] In 1799

General Bellows, his brother John, and several others received a charter to lay out and operate the Third New Hampshire Turnpike. The road was intended to channel the country produce of lower Vermont across the Connecticut River, through Walpole to Keene, and on to the state border, where it connected to the Massachusetts Turnpike that ended in Boston. The Cheshire Turnpike, chartered in 1804, crisscrossed the town. The boom in turnpike building, brief in its duration but momentous in its consequences, "visibly manifested the invisible economic network that was spreading across New England." Boston became the hub of a system with toll roads radiating outward towards Providence, Hartford, the Connecticut Valley, and New Hampshire and Vermont. Many of these chartered roads were linked together into longer channels for through traffic; these roads were built, wrote the Federalist Fisher Ames, "to facilitate country produce on its way to market." Turnpike corporations were issued legislative charters that gave them the privilege to collect tolls in exchange for building and maintaining more direct and better constructed roads than the town-built routes.[41]

Village entrepreneurs tackled other obstacles to long-distance trade. Enoch Hale, the Cheshire County sheriff, received a charter in 1783 for a span over the Connecticut River at the site first called the Great Falls—later, Bellows Falls—above Walpole. When completed two years later, the string bridge, the first across the Connecticut, spanned 365 feet and pushed the available bridge technology to the limit. The location of this bridge ensured that the Third New Hampshire Turnpike would pass through Walpole. The Bellows Falls Canal, the first navigation canal in the United States, bypassed the treacherous Great Falls that obstructed river traffic.[42]

Rural storekeepers were important middlemen between the rural web of local exchange and the urban and overseas long-distance trading networks. In the early years, Benjamin Bellows and other residents of prerevolutionary Walpole had to return south for their store purchases. The town's rural economy, like that throughout the rural North, remained a complex system centered on local exchange. Most of the goods before 1800, the historian Jack Larkin has written, "were consumed in the households producing them, or entered a thriving, complex, and predominantly cashless network of local exchange in which agricultural goods, farm labor services, and the work and products of generally part-time craftsmen were traded between households." But population growth and increasing affluence prompted enterprising rural residents to open stores in town. By acting as middlemen and bookkeepers for many local transactions, they accelerated the transition from a customary to a monetary economy and then to a full-scale market economy for labor and produce. Storekeepers looked to gather rural commodities for urban markets. John Andenoy advertised for human hair, while John Bellows Jr. sought hatting furs. Bellows offered to accept beef cattle in payment for store goods, and the grocer Moses Johnson was taking "good hard, sweet butter" for lemons. Walpole residents saw a vast assortment of goods for sale and services to hire. "Good wheat for sale," Alexander Watkins advised local residents, "brought from over the mountain where you all know they raise the best of wheat." Itinerant merchants also found Walpole an attractive market.[43]

Many merchants engaged in manufacturing, and they organized "putting-out" systems that depended on farm families. Colonel John Bellows's daughter-in-law, Aunt Colonel, grew enormous quantities of wool and flax to produce linens and garments during the wartime boycott of foreign goods. After the Revolution she organized an extensive wool and flax spinning business; those passing the Bellows house would notice several horses tied up as women came for their materials and returned with huge piles of spun yarn. The family also began a weaving business with a large number of workers, some of whom wove in the Bellows's basement. Rural women took advantage of opportunities for wage work in the early nineteenth century. After a brief boom in handloom weaving, straw braiding and palm-leaf hat making spread through the Wachusett and southwestern New Hampshire. Small cotton spinning factories opened after 1810.[44]

But rural artisans manufactured most of the growing numbers of commodities produced in town. The commercialization of rural life and the democratization of social life spurred rural artisans to rework their manufacturing and marketing methods to satisfy the expanding market as well as stimulate further demand. Many artisans moved gradually but steadily toward the status of artisan-entrepreneurs, market-oriented makers and purveyors of consumer items who both anticipated and participated in the backcountry's commercial revolution. Rural residents eagerly sought affordable objects that signified cultural authority—the books, clocks, and portraits that had once been the province of the aristocratic few—so as to fashion new social identities in bustling, nineteenth-century America. The shift towards a more elaborate consumerism, which had been restricted to urban centers in the eighteenth century, accelerated in the postrevolutionary countryside. According to one Vermont local historian: "As the condition of the people improved, then by degrees, [they] extended their desires beyond the mere necessaries of life; first to its conveniences, and then to its elegancies. This produced new wants, and to supply them, mechanics more numerous and more skilful were required, til at length, the cabinet maker, the tailor, the jeweller, the milliner, and a host of others came to be regarded as indispensable."[45]

Many enterprising craftsmen from southern New England moved to the upper Connecticut River valley's commercial villages. At least two clockmakers relocated from Connecticut, the center of the trade, to Walpole in the 1790s. Gurdon Huntington worked in Windham, Connecticut, during the 1780s before he removed to Walpole to sell his version of the traditional tall clock, an eight-day brass movement with a fashionable, eastern

Connecticut-style case. Another Connecticut migrant, Jedediah Baldwin, was trained by Thomas Harland, whose large shop and standardized production epitomized rural innovation; he moved to Hanover, New Hampshire, where he prospered. Half his seven-hundred-dollar income came from selling clocks and jewelry. Over an eighteen-year career he sold fifty-five clocks, for about fifty dollars apiece. In Walpole, Asa Sibley aimed at the households who could not afford to buy from Jedediah Baldwin; he sold a "wag on the wall," an uncased brass clock movement, that could be cased later by its owner, thereby making clocks available to rural customers previously unable to afford them (see plate 10). Other New Hampshire clockmakers innovated by devising what became known as the New Hampshire mirror clock; its redesigned movement reduced the amount of expensive brass needed, and its mirrored case was cheap to make. The New Hampshire clock was a low-cost, stylish timekeeper.[46]

Many cabinet- and chairmakers offered the latest in cosmopolitan tastes to upper Connecticut River valley customers during the 1790s. In neighboring Charlestown, Thomas Bliss and John Horswell advertised their arrival from Boston and displayed their familiarity with metropolitan furniture design and construction in a chest of drawers and a rare upholstered easy chair (see plate 11). Walpole and Charlestown attracted fourteen cabinet- and chairmakers before 1825, many moving from the Wachusett, where the furniture trade was rapidly expanding. The increased market allowed specialization; some chairmakers produced only Windsor chairs, a versatile form of furniture particularly well suited for the extensive division of labor, with its turned spindles and carved seat. Stephen Prentiss followed the practice of many newcomers and advertised in the *Farmer's Weekly Museum* when he opened his shop on Main Street in Walpole for "carrying on the chair making and painting business." Newspaper advertisements often boasted of the latest neoclassical forms, tea tables or sideboards, with urban-style decorative details. The rise of the neoclassical style in American furniture coincided with the proliferation of rural cabinetmaking shops throughout the northern United States. But village cabinetmakers did not just mimic urban shops; they combined London designs and sophisticated urban shop practices with traditional rural tastes and modest prices. Farther north up the Connecticut River, in about 1798, Allen Hayes and Sophia West, upon the occasion of their wedding, purchased a dramatic bow-front sideboard, derived from Boston-style cabinetwork, to decorate their new Windsor, Vermont home (see plate 12). The cherry used for secondary wood and the banding that wraps only two-thirds around the top edge are gestures toward frugality in this sophisticated piece. Such elements point to the innovative compromises that inland villagers sought when they purchased refined furniture.[47]

Walpole's rise as a print center, a special blend of commerce and culture, promoted new identities for rural residents. The conservative "Walpole

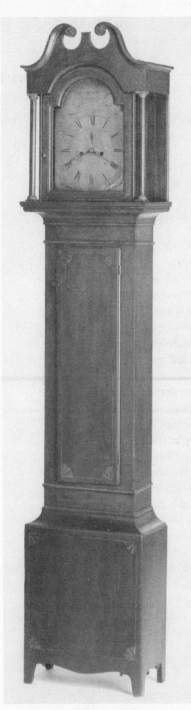

Plate 11. Easy chair, 1798, Bliss and Horswell, Charlestown, New Hampshire. Thomas Bliss and John Horswell, "cabinet maker from Boston" as their label announced, arrived in rural Charlestown in 1797; they made this upholstered easy chair that displayed their familiarity with metropolitan furniture construction and design. (From the New Hampshire Historical Society, Concord. Courtesy of the New Hampshire Historical Society, #F1876.)

Plate 10. Tall clock with an Asa Sibley eight-day movement, sold uncased, 1790. After the War for Independence enterprising artisans such as Walpole clockmaker Asa Sibley produced uncased clock movements for eager rural consumers who would purchase a case later when their finances permitted. (Visual Resource Collection, Old Sturbridge Village. Courtesy of Old Sturbridge Village.)

Plate 12. Bow-front sideboard, Windsor, Vermont, circa 1798. This sideboard was built of mahogany, cherry, and pine. Allen Hayes and Sophia West of the cosmopolitan Connecticut River town of Windsor commissioned this sideboard, a furniture form that signified urban sophistication with its bow-front shape derived from Boston designs. However, rural frugality remained, as the banding on the top only went two-thirds of the way around the sides and the expensive inlays did not all match. (Courtesy of the Bennington Museum, Bennington, Vermont.)

Wits," as they called themselves, held forth in the town's tavern and the local newspaper, the *Farmer's Museum*. The *Museum* carried their caustic commentaries on the democratization of society throughout the new nation. Along with several other upper Connecticut River valley commercial villages, Walpole developed into a major print center, which the historian William Gilmore has aptly defined as a "multiple-function cultural institution which included printing, publishing, bookselling and advertising." Isaiah Thomas, the major entrepreneur in the New England print trade during the revolutionary era, opened a printing office, bookstore, and newspaper (the *New-Hampshire Journal,* which later became the *Farmer's Weekly Museum*) in Walpole in 1793 with a former apprentice, David Carlisle. With printers setting up shops in Hanover and Windsor to the north and Keene and Brattleboro to the south, soon the region had six weekly newspapers in operation. They published a variety of print material in addition to local newspapers—books, pamphlets, broadsides, periodicals, almanacs, and reprints—as well as distributing print culture.[48]

Thomas's Walpole bookstore linked local book production with the long-distance market. The prerevolutionary countryside did not have bookstores, but their numbers increased rapidly after the War for Independence, vastly expanding the variety of book knowledge available to rural residents. The Walpole bookstore engaged in both wholesale and retail trade in books, almanacs, and pamphlets; in 1808 the shelves of the village bookstore contained 31,280 specified books along with several thousand other unspecified ones. Thomas promoted the circulation of information and distributed the mounting output of his presses by exchanging his stock with other printers; only one-sixth of the almost 1,500 titles that he produced, about a third of all of his books, had been printed in the region. The majority came from a long-distance trading network that stretched from Baltimore, Maryland, to Portland, Maine.[49]

Reading had always been an important activity in New England towns. But Joseph Buckingham, an apprentice in Carlisle's print shop, recalled that as late as the 1780s, "the houses of farmers, even those of the most affluent class, were not overstocked with books. . . . The Bible was the book for everyday reading, and with a very few others, chiefly of a religious character, supplied the rural population with the greater part of its intellectual entertainment." During the Village Enlightenment, however, traditional cultural mediators of received wisdom, such as ministers and lawyers, often were superseded by newly available printed sources of practical information and personal insight. A new, extensive mode of reading enhanced an individual's agency in directing his or her life and pushed rural folk beyond reliance upon devotional tracts and the sermons of a ministerial elite. Townspeople sifted through a variety of ideas and incorporated some of them into their everyday beliefs. Reading thus became less a conservator of convention and more a force for change.[50]

Newspapers were the single most important publications of the village press. The *New-Hampshire Journal* and other papers provided information about the growing variety of goods available from merchants and manufacturers. According to Gilmore, "the weekly newspaper, the fastest-expanding means of communication in the Early Republic, was crucial to the enlargement of commerce. It offered all businesses a brand new way of getting local feedback through direct appeal to consumers to reshape their personal consumption habits. The newspaper brought specific knowledge of goods and services to potential customers, and merchants learned quickly that advertising offered a potent alternative to neighborhood-based exchange relationships." Walpole's weekly newspaper also attracted aspiring literati, who were congregating in the commercial villages of the upper valley. The quotation on the masthead, "Where Liberty is, this is my country," by Benjamin Franklin, and the motto following it, "The Liberty of the Press is Essential to the Rights of Man," indicated how the newspapers achieved a community of readers. Villagers could imagine a new nation by reading about the contentious debates in the new Congress or even debate these issues themselves in the pages of the paper during the volatile 1790s.

Walpole's newspaper, with its coarse paper and large format, looked like many other weekly newspapers. Carlisle, the publisher, had an interest in literary matters, and the first year, a few of the town's writers sent in contributions. In all, it produced nothing exceptional, until in October 1795, Joseph Dennie moved to town "under the pretense of practising law" and began his "Lay Preacher" essays that brought Walpole's press to national attention.[51]

The Lay Preacher

> Musing on the fate of my paradoxes . . . I sat out one evening for this place [Walpole]. . . . On the road I formed that plan which I have since realized, and which has attached *some* success. There was a Press here, conducted by a young man [Carlisle], honest, industrious, and then a partner of Thomas. I determined, by the agency of my pen, to convince him that I could be useful, and then—my humble knowledge of human nature taught me—I was sure he would encourage me when his own *Interest* was the Prompter. Without saying a word respecting a stipend, I wrote and gave him an essay on "Wine and New Wine," and called it the "Lay Preacher." It had been objected to my earliest compositions that they had been sprightly rather than moral. Accordingly, I thought I would attempt to be useful, by exhibiting truths in a plain dress to the common people.
>
> Joseph Dennie, Letter to his mother, Mary Green Dennie (1797)

Dennie, "the American Addison," was chiefly responsible for the rise to national prominence of the *Farmers' Weekly Museum,* the emergence of Walpole as the central place in the New England Village Enlightenment, and the fashioning of the new satirical Yankee identity for New England. He was a leader of the new rising generation of Americans who took over from the revolutionary generation—Bellows and Fessenden in town, and the Connecticut Wits in literary circles—to champion an American literature that was neoclassical in its genres, but took the New England town as its subject. These enterprising literary craftsmen like other village entrepreneurs, decentralized production in an effort to attract the patronage of the commercializing countryside. Dennie, who affected the pose of a genteel amateur, in fact was a canny professional, who relied upon his editorial and authorial efforts to support himself. He created the persona of the Lay Preacher, putting on the mantle of traditional ministerial authority, but his role was as a new kind of cultural mediator, one who sold his goods—his literary products—"in a plain dress to the common people"—in the burgeoning marketplace for cultural commodities.[52]

A conservative critic of the democratizing effects of the Revolution, Dennie exhibited an enterprising spirit. He had been born in Boston in 1768, related to several generations of Boston merchants and New England printers. Dennie attended Harvard College, where his lively spirit caused considerable rebuke from college authorities, but his literary work appeared in the leading Boston periodical, the *Massachusetts Magazine*. His family's declining fortunes required that Dennie prepare for a career; he served as a law clerk in the Charlestown, New Hampshire, office of Benjamin West. Dennie began his literary career in 1792 with the *Farrago* series in the Windsor, Vermont, *Morning Ray*. There he offered a somewhat autobiographical portrait of a young lawyer who, instead of reading Blackstone, "studies Shakespeare in the Inns of Court." The town minister's death provided Dennie with the opportunity to serve as a lay reader for the local Episcopal society. He opened a law office in Charlestown and continued publishing essays in local papers. After a stint as editor of a failed Boston literary magazine, Dennie moved his literary and legal business to Walpole, where he made himself indispensable to Carlisle.[53]

Dennie's "Lay Preacher" essays, aimed at "plain husbandmen rather than the polished scholars," brought the paper and their author great acclaim, and the Walpole press brought out a slim volume, *The Lay Preacher, or Short Sermons for Idle Readers,* in August 1796. Dennie also provided summaries of "Foreign and Domestic Intelligence," "Literary Intelligence," and political satires for the paper, which now took a firm Federalist bent. Dennie had been running the literary and political departments for some time before he took over formal editorial control of the paper in April 1796, when Thomas dissolved his partnership with Carlisle. Dennie abandoned his fading legal practice and obtained an annual salary of 110 pounds as editor.[54]

Dennie aspired to be more than a country lawyer or amateur author, but living in New England in a postpatronage era, he had to confront the problem of becoming a professional man of letters. Genteel (rather than professional) authorship was the eighteenth-century standard, and that genteel status was affected in the familiar practices of publishing books anonymously or using pseudonyms in periodicals. Dennie's patrician pose is evident throughout his work. Yet the effort to establish a literary journal in Walpole, when even cosmopolitan Boston could not sustain one for long, required great effort and brought out the contradictory strains of literary entrepreneurship in Dennie and his circle.[55]

Dennie's greatest genius was in collecting the local literati, the Walpole Wits, whose poems and prose transformed what would otherwise have been a typical weekly newspaper into the leading periodical of its day. He reopened his column, "The Shop of Colon & Spondee," a collaboration in print with Royall Tyler, poet, playwright, novelist, and fellow lawyer. Dennie, Tyler, and other *Farmer's Weekly Museum* contributors had moved to the upper Connecticut River to advance their legal careers. "A set of young men, mostly of the legal profession, extending from Greenfield, in Massachusetts, to Windsor, in Vermont, a distance of fifty or sixty miles, were much in the habit of familiar intercourse for the sake of amusement and recreation," Jeremiah Mason recalled. "They occasionally met in a village tavern, but more commonly at the sessions of the courts." Lawyers were significant figures in newly settled towns in the postrevolutionary period because the commercialization of the countryside required legal and other services. What stood out about this circle of lawyers was their role as promoters of literary activity in the hinterlands, which the literary critic Robert Ferguson defined as a "remarkable symbiosis between law and literary aspiration."[56] The Walpole Wits naturally gravitated to the neoclassical forms of poetry and prose that distinguished early national literature. The social context of their professional lives in court and riding the circuit, unique among educated Americans of the time, promoted collaborative literary enterprises. Dennie enticed many rural lawyers throughout New England to contribute witty essays and satiric verses for the pages of the *Museum*. This paper reached its heyday in 1796 with volume four, when Dennie took over as editor. In 1797 the name was changed to *The Farmer's Museum and the New Hampshire and Vermont Journal,* and the last page was set off as a separate literary department called "The Dessert," with the remaining three pages devoted to "Politicks, Biography, Economicks, Morals and Daily Details." Dennie announced in July 1797 that the paper had subscribers in all the states of the republic except Georgia, Kentucky, and Tennessee, with over one thousand new readers added to the rolls in the last eighteen months. By December he had two thousand subscribers, a larger circulation than any other village newspaper in the United States (see plate 13).[57]

Joseph Dennie, the conservative representative of the postrevolutionary generation, made the local paper into an innovative forum for the articulation of New England's literary and cultural identity by incorporating the new commercial order while critiquing it. The Walpole Wits and other Federalist literati were Janus-faced with regard to the new commercial order and its attendant cultural changes. Neoclassical satire assumed that a community of values would be understood by a republic of like-minded readers, enabling it to ridicule those outside its clearly drawn boundaries. Humor was directed at those breaching the boundaries by "false elevation" of language. The American neoclassical poets preached correctness and regularity in expression and took social and political issues as their focus; their art was to be a public art. Ironically, their satirical portrait of postrevolutionary society was subverted for a series of aesthetic and social reasons.[58]

Dennie adopted the persona of the Lay Preacher, the title of his most famous literary work, to solve the problem of establishing and maintaining cultural authority. In an early column in the *Museum* Dennie mixed his inherited traditions, announcing that he was neither Universalist nor New Light, but "a *moral* preacher," not whining from the pulpit or demanding a salary, but "asking only for your reformation." From the secular side, this cultural arbiter advocated such standard Enlightenment values as the har-

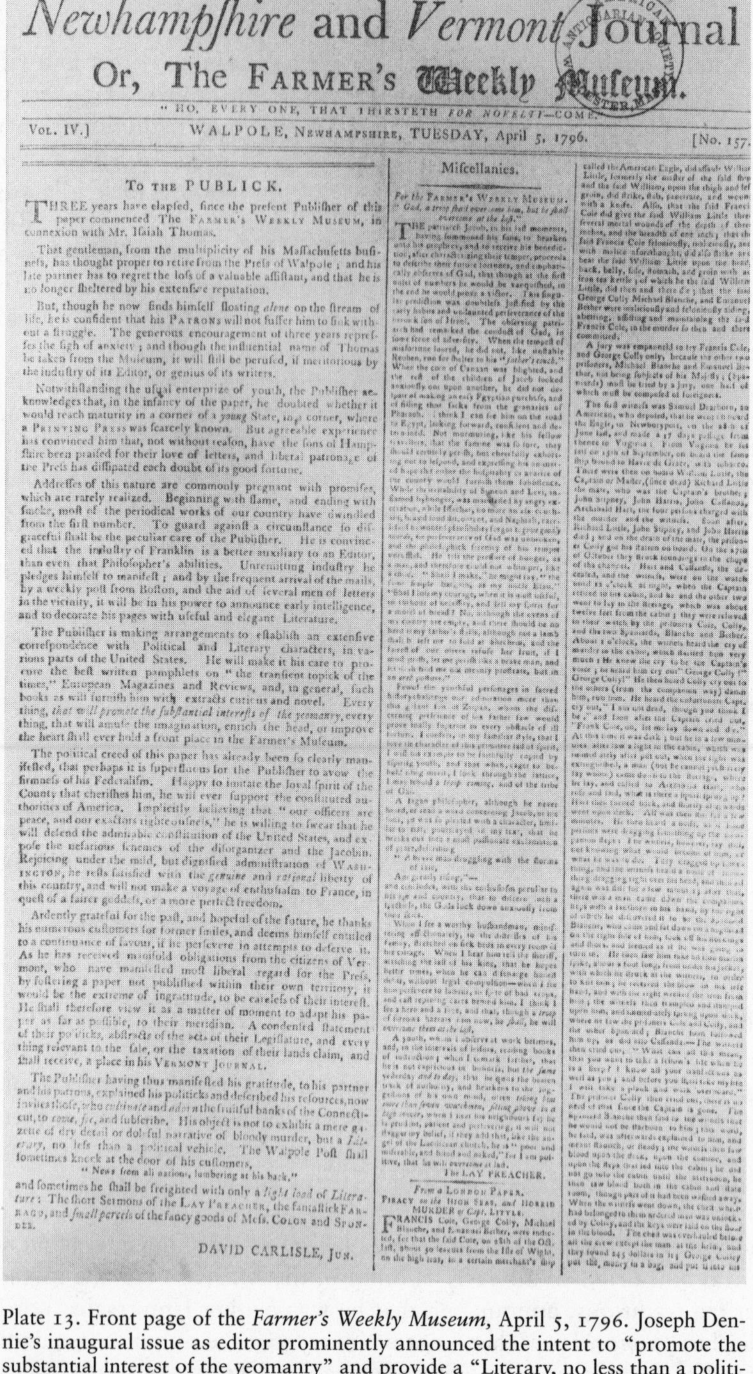

Plate 13. Front page of the *Farmer's Weekly Museum*, April 5, 1796. Joseph Dennie's inaugural issue as editor prominently announced the intent to "promote the substantial interest of the yeomanry" and provide a "Literary, no less than a political vehicle" in the rural New Hampshire newspaper. (Courtesy of the American Antiquarian Society, Worcester, Massachusetts.)

mony of nature, the efficacy of reason, and the importance of hierarchy and order, while opposing superstitions, old customs, and especially "French fashions." He usually began with a motto from the Bible, but satirized the doings of contemporary fops, dandies, and idlers. As moral monitor he preached on didactic themes, which drew upon New England's Puritan past, aiming "to instruct the villager." His own personal contribution was the periodical essay, the brief column or two of newsprint aimed at a far wider audience than traditional literary magazines. As Dennie defined his chosen genre:

> Some work must . . . be projected to fix volatility and rouse indolence, nei-ther too abstruse for the young, too prolix for the busy nor too grave for the fair. A performance, which should not resemble an austere monitor . . . but a pleasant friend, whose conversation at once beguiles and improves the hour. The design was at length accomplished. Certain geniuses of the first magnitude arose, who, in the narrow compass of a sheet of paper, conveyed more useful knowledge to mankind than all the ponderous tomes of Aristotle.

Public morals loomed large to Federalist authors, familiar with Mon-tesquieu's *The Spirit of the Laws,* who agreed that a virtuous citizenry was the basis for a stable republic. The emergence of popular politics and the democratization of social relations evoked fear and ridicule from Dennie and other conservatives, alarmed at the dangerous excesses of this "level-ling age." The fragile achievements of vulnerable republics, according to classical precedents, were at risk from the "democratic projectors" with their political speculations; "the Federal parson" oft turned political po-lemicist to point out the dangers of foreign influences and domestic factions that might corrupt and subvert the new government.[59]

The figure of the sturdy yeoman appeared frequently in Dennie's essays as an exemplary trope for his rural readers. This figure was drawn from a lit-erary and political pastoral, "the good shepherd of the old pastoral dressed in American homespun," to be held up as the republican exemplar of the virtuous citizen, close to nature, and seeking not the fashionable specula-tions of the city but the sufficiency and stability of field and farm. These cosmopolitan aesthetes evoked the Yankee yeoman as their voice, heighten-ing their reliance upon the village scene to perform their cultural work. With a defense of deference no longer possible amid the growing egalitari-anism unleashed by the Revolution, Dennie and others adopted the pose of the simple, independent farmer to critique any movement leading away from the hierarchical and stable local society of the past.[60]

Dennie and his contributors represented the tumultuous times with an apocalyptic tone in their public pronouncements. Royall Tyler's "Ode Com-posed for the Fourth of July," ostensibly a patriotic and familiar form of verse chosen for celebrating the new nation's birthday, published on July

19, 1796, descends into drunken disorder and gloomy political prognostications

> Squeak the fife, and beat the drum,
> Independence Day is come!!!
> Let the roasting pig be bled,
> Quickly twist off the cokerel's head,
> Quickly rub the pewter platter
> Heap the nutcakes, fried in batter

Tyler catalogues the tempting treats being prepared as the participants become boisterous and spirited.

> *Independent,* staggering Dick,
> A noggin mix of *swinging thick;*
> Sal, put on your russet skirt,
> Jotham, get your *broughten* shirt
> Today we dance to tiddle diddle.

The poem concludes with the end of the festivities and the specter of the French Revolution's guillotine linked to the homegrown Jacobin "Demos," or Democrats, so that the poem's invitation to take "one more swig" to celebrate "This glorious INDEPENDENT DAY" is less a cause for celebration than a call for alarm. New England's religious and republican institutions seemed precarious; for Dennie and Tyler, disorder, heightened by the mobbish uprisings in Massachusetts and Pennsylvania backcountry, always threatened to engulf the republic.[61]

The Walpole Wits often resorted to satirical representations of how American culture and knowledge itself had become debased in this "levelling age." Dennie and Tyler wrote literary "advertisements," their "Colon & Spondee" pieces, that parodied a country store's announcement of its stock, attacking the common people's overreaching of higher learning. In one such advertisement, "American Learning, 1798," they produced a comic squib about an arriviste speculator who, having amassed a fortune, has scholarly aspirations and sends a Boston bookseller the following letter:

> sur
> i wants to by sum Buks—as I am prodighouse fond of larnen—plese to send by
> the Bear here 5 hunder Dollars woth of the *hansumest* you have—Yoors &x.—

The republic of letters—with its hierarchy of talents that gave the Wits their status among the second generation of New England authors—was in danger of being toppled by a mobocracy of illiterate hoi polloi.[62]

In one of his "Colon & Spondee" essays, Tyler lambasted contemporary attempts to abridge texts to make the complexities of science understandable to small boys, a critique that Thoreau would later echo. In their satire, they suggested that the "same canning process" of knowledge now be extended to the level of infants by the sale of a new work, *The Pap of Science,* whereby geography, mathematics, history, biography, and politics could be made accessible to all through nursery rhymes. While Dennie and Tyler lampooned the reduction of literary works to mere commodities through their use of the mercantile metaphor—that is, the advertisements of Messrs. Colon and Spondee—the advancement of these rural satirists and the rise of the *Farmer's Weekly Museum* had been made possible by that very same mercantile culture, by the emergence of literary professionals and the extension of the reading public in the new nation. At the same time as Dennie was mastering the short periodical essay, Tyler was busy writing *The Algerine Captive,* a novel. Armed with their classical training and trying to combat the dangerous excesses of romanticism and sentimentality, the legal literati had tied their craft to the village world around them. They became the first American exponents of local color and vernacular language, paradoxically furthering the democratization of a culture they loathed so much.[63]

The sharpest attack on the democratic errors of the age came in the Federalist mock pastorals of country customs and characters that often appeared in the *Farmer's Weekly Museum.* There, Thomas Green Fessenden, the son of Walpole's minister, introduced New England village characters and vernacular speech through native verse, replacing classical allusions with American ones, and winning an immediate audience on both sides of the Atlantic. Fessenden worked his way through Dartmouth College by teaching school and publishing poems in the *Museum.* He studied law before becoming a newspaper publisher in Bellows Falls, across the river from Walpole. His first published poem, "The Country Lovers, or Jonathan Jolthead's Courtship with Miss Sally Snapper," written in 1795 while he was still at Dartmouth College, won Nathaniel Hawthorne's praise as an "original and truly Yankee effusion." It mounted a savage critique of the claims of political and cultural democratization by lampooning the low manners and language of Jonathan Jolthead, a rustic, naive, and ultimately pitiful figure, who became the model for a standard literary type. Prodded by his mother, Jonathan naively sets out to court Sally Snapper for her money. Sal quickly sees through the cloddish rustic and decides to make sport with him, taunting him for his ineptitude at courting, for his visit to the town where he put on "streaked *trowses*" (a reference to the sansculottes), and for his claim that he could not see the town because "there were so many houses." She rejects his father's offer of a bull calf as a wedding present, replying that he best "keep his bull calves at home." Slowly it dawns on Jonathan that he has become an object of ridicule, and he begins to quake from head to toe, until Sal douses him with a pail of water. Unlike later sentimental versions by James Russell Lowell, Fessenden's Jonathan character invites the reader's ridicule and casts doubt upon the abilities of the democratic man that Jonathan had come to represent. If the conservative implications of this comic grotesque depiction were not clear to his contemporary audience, then, Fessenden remarked, "the peasantry of New England as described in my poems, will be found to bear some resemblance to what they are in real life." "I will not assert," he maintained, "that I have not, in some instances, *caricatured* the manners of the New England rustic" so as to expose the political pretensions of the people, whom he saw as a foolish multitude easily led astray by democratic demagogues and the overabundance of print.[64]

In the *Farmer's Weekly Museum*, Fessenden depicted rural folk with condescension, laughing at the discrepancies between the intended meaning of the high-flown rhetoric used by the village character and the shared meaning understood by the more educated author and reader. In "Peter Periwinkle, to Tabitha Towzer," the country lover begins his description of his beloved with

> My Tabitha Towzer is fair
>   No Guinea pig ever was neater,
> Like a hackmatak slender and spare,
>   And sweet as a musk rat, or sweeter!

"Pining, poetical PETER" continues his incongruous comparisons of different parts of Tabitha's anatomy with barnyard animals. These earthy metaphors render her a grotesque object, quite the opposite of what the country lover intends by his passionate and romantic statements. Fessenden pokes fun at the efforts of the common folk to draw upon the conventions and vocabulary of romantic verse.[65]

Fessenden, under his nom de plume, Simon Spunkey, developed his satiric attacks on the democratization under way in American culture by pointing out, in "Simon Spunkey's Irregular Ode to Colonel Candidate of Fair Haven," the demagoguery in political elections and versifying about the false pretensions of rural learning in "'Love's Labour Lost' Peter Pumpkinhead defeated by Tabitha Towzer." This latter piece was an expansion of his earlier satire on rural courting rituals, where the suitor—showing off his education obtained through reading Morse's *Geography* and a few novels—tells his beloved of the promising future that awaits him after spending a mere month at an academy. In the notes to the poem, Fessenden writes that the new middling class of New England society are sending their sons off to get advanced education, "too many for the good of the community." Their smattering of English and Latin grammar makes them unfit to return to their "former laborious occupations," so instead they attempt "to *crowd themselves* into the learned professions."[66]

By the new century, the elder Thomas Fessenden also had faced the darker side of village history. The Walpole minister's Federalist beliefs and the town's commercial boom gave his 1795 Thanksgiving sermon an optimistic tone; he emphasized the new nation's history as New England's writ large. He celebrated the remarkable success of the Puritans' Great Migration and the progress of town settlement through the wilderness. Settlers had fled British persecution, struggled with famine and foe to establish their communities, only to face the rapacious British again: "they forced us into hostilities for the defence of all that is dear to man, the works of God for us were great in the war and peace which followed." A new day had arrived as the federal government grew, population increased, and the frontiers filled with settlers, "to make the wilderness like Eden."[67] By 1802, however, Fessenden sketched the same historical sequence in darker tones for the reign of reason was threatened. The parson remembered the Indian wars, the colonists' sacrifices, and the people's struggle for independence, placing them in sharp contrast to contemporary squabbles and selfish behavior. A minister who had once challenged the weight of tradition and celebrated personal sources of allegiance was moved to lament how far these democratizing trends had gone. "This idea of the sovereignty of the people too much prevails in towns and states." The eighteenth-century republican found himself operating in a "new system" of meaning where "every thing is to be understood directly contrary to its name." An age of reason "is no reason," when it came from Tom Paine's deistic tract. Fessenden had sought to open the minds of his countrymen, furthering the decentralization of cultural authority. But like many of his peers, the Old Revolutionary stood aghast and seemingly powerless as new ideas about equality emerged and a new rhetoric of liberty eroded the power of rulers and the church beyond anything he had ever envisioned. Now he looked for bulwarks to stem the rising tide of democracy. He turned from the orderly design of nature to the legacy of culture as he cherished the memory of New England's history of colonization alongside the great achievement of the revolutionary generation.[68]

The Walpole Wits authored a new postrevolutionary, village-centered history, satirically recreating the "happy society" that Jeremy Belknap, the New Hampshire historian, wrote about along with its disturbing mirror image of disorderly individuals cut loose from hierarchical structures. The New England town and its residents became the setting and subject for these authors. The town-centered cultural landscape allowed for the emergence of ambivalent attitudes, as the literary critic Lawrence Buell points out, extending from ideal models of perfect town societies to satirical exposés of actual villages with their bumpkinesque residents, a world turned upside down. This representation of village history drew upon the conventions of the New England past to critique present problems and warn about the future. The satire in their realistic contemporary sketches came from its nostalgic look back to the New England town as a self-contained "little community," to use the historian Darrett Rutman's phrase, where an organic interdependence and deferential pose had bound all the residents together. The neoclassical authors satirized the provincial in the name of cosmopolitan standards, creating a literature that, because of its detail, in the long run restored provincial culture to a central place. Longing for local society infused with face-to-face social relations, the postrevolutionary authors created an imagined community for both New England and the new nation through the commercialized marketplace for print, especially the *Farmer's Weekly Museum*. This literary reinvention of New England utilized a variety of traditional genres as well as innovative institutions in the service of conservative, even reactionary, social goals. Ironically, the Village Enlightenment in New England led to the democratization of knowledge that made possible the crafting of new identities for aspiring authors and rural readers alike, moving New England further away from that idealized golden age of homespun.[69]

The Walpole Wits' neoclassical world employed subversive satire, intentional as well as unintentional. If they intended to ridicule village provinciality from their cosmopolitan vantage point, nonetheless, their emphasis on the New England town—a "lococentric" emphasis, as Lawrence Buell has noted—had long-term effects. In their desire to advance a new American literature, they made New England culture the center. Their critique of excessive particularity and superstition came in the guise of the Jonathan character. The most famous of these Jonathans appeared in Royall Tyler's play *The Contrast,* where the provincial New Englander, hailed for his vernacular speech, homely wit, and independence, served as a foil for the manly Colonel, the republican paragon. The emergent folk hero Jonathan upstaged the stiff Colonel Manly. His compelling vivacity became a critical moment in the self-assertion of American culture, the basis of a native literature that Dennie had called for. While Thomas Green Fessenden's early verse drew upon his close knowledge of village customs and characters to make fun of his neighbors' follies as provincial bumpkins, the power and originality of the poetry brought critical acclaim as "a truly Yankee effusion" and also brought commercial success. And Joseph Dennie's Lay Preacher, ever vigilant about threats to the Republic of Letters, did his best to popularize periodical literature and break down the social exclusivity of art.[70]

This version of village history, often depicted as a cranky dead end in the passage to the American Renaissance of the mid-nineteenth century, offered several possibilities to its literary successors in its emphasis upon the local scene and use of comic grotesque. The Walpole Wits were venturesome conservatives, like the town founders who preceded them. This quality came from the contradictions in their relationship to the commercial society that they were dependent upon for their livelihood, the literary devices that they inherited, and the personal success that they sought. The Village Enlightenment moved on from commercial villages such as Walpole after a decade or two. The financial foundations of Thomas's press had never been secure. Printers and publishers relocated to growing regional centers where manufacturers clustered. Conversely, villages where cabinetmakers and clockmakers had once flourished saw their artisanal activity diminish. Aspiring and successful authors alike moved to more cosmopolitan centers such as Philadelphia, where Joseph Dennie became the editor of *The Portfolio* in 1801.[71]

Greater New England had been transformed into two distinct cultures. Transplantation proceeded quite differently in Nova Scotia and New Hampshire. Both colonies developed regional identities. In New Hampshire, rural settlers became increasingly integrated into a regional marketplace and culture through the successful migration of entrepreneurial town founders, such as General Bellows, and village historians, such as Joseph Dennie. Even Col. Benjamin Bellows, the powerful patriarch of Walpole, had been bound by localistic cultural institutions and settlers' expectations of competency, and had had to respect them in order to entice migrants to his new town. His son was buffeted by the republican ideology unleashed by the colonial struggle against Great Britain and the democratizing aftermath involved in the setting up of new governments in northern New Hampshire. In the indigenous postrevolutionary commercialization of the countryside, the mounting volume of print and other commodities these communities produced allowed many rural residents to create a society that dismayed many of the new nation's political leaders and literary gentry. But even the Walpole Wits, caustic critics of the new commercial order and the pretense to gentility, relied upon images and institutions that promoted economic and cultural change. Distant towns participated in the economic and political activities of the new nation. In this new nation, New Englanders constructed their regional identity around the story of a successful transmission of a unique village culture, the New England town.

In Nova Scotia the discontinuity in serial town settlement unleashed powerful forces for change of a different sort. A new Great Migration of New Englanders moved to a military colony run by a Halifax elite with little sympathy for cherished New England traditions of local autonomy. Plans to replicate the New England town were dashed by political, economic, and religious difficulties. Settlers did not achieve autonomy for their local institutions, imperial officials maintained their authority, even if they only exercised it intermittently. Economic underdevelopment occurred, rather than an extensive development of a vast hinterland, especially along the barren South Shore, as isolated settlers—who remained marginal to the aims of the British empire—became bound into a colonial relationship with Boston merchants. Later imperial initiatives intensified Halifax's access to capital, but little money trickled down to the coastal residents. The one particularly indigenous development that reached the outsettlements was the New Birth revival, an even more radical reformation than the New Light Stir of northern New England. Henry Alline and other charismatic itinerants mounted a powerful evangelical attack on traditional social relations.

"It overturned the culture of genteel dominance by challenging the very core of social deference" and breaking through "the passivity of the common people," according to one student of Canadian Protestantism. The Allinite movement completed Nova Scotians' disengagement from New England while providing a new identity created out of New England's historical sense of mission. While evangelical groups in the Maine and Vermont backcountry confronted the established social order, the religious revival in Nova Scotia continued its "religious outpourings" and came to constitute the established order. The consequence of the colonization of the New England town in Nova Scotia was the radicalism of Canadian evangelicalism.[72] The New England diaspora with its transmission of a common set of local institutions and collective memories had resulted in two very different forms of town settlement.

Epilogue:
The Myth of Town Settlement

Gentlemen:

Nothing could give me greater pleasure than to visit my native town on so momentous an occasion, but, owing to a press of business, I shall not be able. *Old Hubbardston*! The adopted home of my four grandparents . . . that home where they severally experienced all the hardships and privations of pioneer life, the birthplace of both my parents . . . the birth place and early home of myself and most of my brothers and sisters, that spot must ever remain dear to me.

Although an alien from my native country for more than 30 years, and a sojourner from the town of my birth more than 43 years, my mind often reverts back with pleasure to that place, and the scenes of my early childhood. . . . Although only nine years of age when I left the place, I can quite well remember the situation. Old Hubbardston surely must be a beautiful place now—it was so half a century ago.

Yours most respectfully . . .

> Asa C. Gates, *Commemoration of the One Hundredth Anniversary of the Incorporation of the Town of Hubbardston, Mass.* (1867)

The mid-nineteenth-century centennial celebrations of the Wachusett towns drew native sons and daughters back to their hometowns and directed public attention to the town foundings. In these rituals of village solidarity and collective memory, orators, letter writers, and ordinary citizens paused amid "the bustle and business of life" to reflect upon their "origins as individuals and as a community." The towns of the Wachusett had matured; most had reached their centennial, and Lancaster, the "grandmother of the Wachusett," celebrated its bicentennial. Commercialization had transformed the economy, the culture, and even the physical layout of these towns. Villages developed and connected farmers to the region and the nation. The people of the Wachusett had colonized northern New England and then surged across the continent. Centennial celebrations were designed to contain the implications of change by offering a discourse that

239

stressed the unbroken bonds between generations over time and the transmission of a town-centered cultural heritage across space. Speakers read letters from Nova Scotia or California in which migrants attributed their success to a village childhood and local institutions of town government. The "memory work" at these festivals celebrated the contributions of the early white settlers; orators lauded the transformation of the central Massachusetts landscape into a region of cultivated fields and village greens and told sentimental stories of times long past. In processions, townspeople came together to proclaim their common identity as a people, a region, and a nation, all rooted in their unique cultural creation, the New England town.[1]

Memories are things that we like to think with, historian John Gillis has written. These festivals centered on creating a New England historical identity; they were not merely reflections of past achievements but an integral part of the process of history making and identity formation. Orators and writers in the Wachusett sought to root their changing society in the local past. At midcentury that project was especially difficult: partisan and sectional conflicts tore older allegiances asunder; industrialization eclipsed the agrarian order; village improvement reshaped the colonial town. Orators pronounced the eighteenth century a "golden age" of stability and shared culture and placed it at the center of their historical myth. Their vision contained a contradictory view, one that regarded the past as morally superior yet materially inferior to the progressive yet problematic present. Local historians of the Wachusett sought to bind up the cultural contradictions and transcend divisions of region, religion, and class; in centennial celebrations, they hoped to achieve a united, homogeneous community for a day by commemorating a common past.[2]

These festivals are a neglected aspect of the local history movement in New England that flourished during the second quarter of the nineteenth century. Eighteenth-century literati had written a cosmopolitan form of history for the provincial gentry; postrevolutionary neoclassical authors had employed historical themes, if only to satirize their colonial ancestors. In contrast, the early nineteenth-century commemorations were local productions; local histories were usually commissioned and published by individual towns. And they venerated the past, which was now at a safe enough distance that no one need fear becoming caught in its constraints. A few of the orations delivered at centennial celebrations became famous, such as Horace Bushnell's address in Litchfield, Connecticut, and Ralph Waldo Emerson's speech in Concord, Massachusetts. But the occasions for these orations have been ignored. Centennials were major events: festivals sometimes lasted for two days, with several orations, processions, poems, tableaux, and toasts, and they drew hundreds of former residents from across the continent back to their hometown to commemorate the origins of the New England village.[3]

July 4, 1854, opened in Petersham with the first arrivals renewing old acquaintances while "the events of many years passed through the mind in rapid succession." Bells rang and cannons roared in the "quiet old town" to signal the start of a procession that made its way past buildings bedecked with banners to the improved village commons. Militia and fire companies, each with its own band, were followed by the organizing committee, the featured speakers, and then the "citizens at large." Significantly, no divisions by occupation or voluntary associations were visible, as had been the case in urban processions during the colonial and revolutionary periods. The massive assembly gathered at the town center to hear the morning's program. Place of honor was held by the centennial oration, a two-hour historical discourse, accompanied by introductions, hymns, and prayers. A picnic dinner followed. Numerous formal toasts were interspersed with shorter speeches and poems and the reading of letters from those "sons and daughters of Petersham" who were unable to attend. Then came spontaneous toasts. Images and metaphors of antiquity abounded: toasts to "the Old Homestead," "Our Native Town," and the "First Settlers of Petersham . . . May the principles which they inculcated be strictly followed by the present generation!" The "old" was exalted. The first to offer a toast was a volunteer company dressed as "Continental" soldiers; they were followed by "another remnant of the past," a couple dressed in antique costume, who were received with great acclaim. "An aged man, wearing the costume of the past generation," closed the toasts. "Relics of antiquity," including such artifacts as an Indian war club collected by the American Antiquarian Society, filled the stage. The evening festivities concluded with spectacular fireworks: "the last piece attracted particular attention by its appropriate design, representing an Indian equipped with bow and arrow, with the word 'Nichewaug' [the original name of the plantation] in letters of flame, and the date 1754."[4]

Centennial celebrations offered a narrative about the Puritan origins of New England and its continuities with the contemporary Yankee nation. Such popular events shaped collective memory by drawing selectively and creatively upon bountiful historical sources to present a commemorative narration about a particular past that served as a general narrative of a shared history. Narratives encode historical events in the familiar story elements of a common culture, producing social meaning by literary means. The commemorative orators in the Wachusett offered a grand historical epic of New England in three phases, from the Puritans' flight from persecution and their initial settlement of coastal towns through the War for Independence to the contemporary "age of inventions." In Lancaster, for example, Joseph Willard opened his address with "the ecclesiastical history of England, which tended to the growth of civil and religious liberty among ourselves." Indians had a more significant presence here than in previous histories but still stood outside the trajectory of time. The founding generation of each town took center stage, for it had planted the seeds of liberty and prosperity that had now come to fruition. White settlers had constructed "miniature republics"; the patriotic yeomanry assembled in town meetings, "these little democratic gatherings, where the pure and unsophisticated sentiments of freemen were faithfully expressed." The Revolution thus was imagined to have emerged from local institutions, as independence was achieved first in the town and then by the nation; the conflicts that had attended the revolutionary struggle disappeared from view. A progressive model of history replaced the providential framework of Puritan historians. Yet this was a Whiggish view of progress, in which innovations had conservative functions and continuity prevailed over discontinuity. Participants proclaimed a vital inheritance, a set of authentic and living traditions that were intended to guide natives of the Wachusett in a world of continental expansion and accelerating social change.[5]

Orators limned Puritan settlers as nascent Yankees, displacing the values of mid-nineteenth-century northern bourgeois culture onto the figures of colonial ancestors. The colonists were made of stern stuff: "under the congenial influences of labor, hardship, and frugality, that were the lot of our early predecessors, were nurtured sturdy and self-reliant traits of character." Their plain tastes and modest desires for a competency could also be contrasted with the contemporary dangers of "luxury and barbaric splendor." "The blood of these men and women flows in the veins of many now present," Willard reminded his Lancaster audience in 1853, hoping that his hearers had inherited their ancestors' restraint as well as their ambitions. In Willard's view, cultural continuity was based on racial solidarity. Imbued with a Romantic ethos, nationalists looked to customs and legends as the sinews of the nation-state; the founding generation of each town figured as the "folk."[6]

Local historians recounted stories about the travails of the early settlers, imaginatively recreating their journey through central Massachusetts. There were dramatizations of the settlers' encounters with the harsh terrain, terrifying animals, and hostile Indians—even "the howling of the wild beast" was made audible to the audience. The pioneers were lauded for enduring privations in order to establish the town's farms, roads, mills, and meetinghouse. These were family stories, not those of individual pioneers. In written accounts, lengthy sections on settler families became genealogies, recording vital statistics, land allotments, proprietary shares, and marriages. The ancestors of Lancaster had founded well-ordered societies, Willard concluded, "like one family in mutual dependence." He urged his listeners to emulate the organic community, "bound together by one invisible but enduring chain," in their own, far more contentious lives.[7]

"The Homespun Age of our people," as Horace Bushnell lovingly imagined it in his exemplary account at Litchfield County's centennial, rested between the unimproved wilderness and contemporary business civilization, when settlers occupied a cultivated landscape with established institutions: "the church, the school, the loom, the plough." Agriculture yielded "a comfortable support and a sure but small annual saving" as a reward for diligent labor. "Of Manufactories there were none," the Fitchburg orator remarked, "or rather I should say they were everywhere, for every farm house had its spinning wheel whose busy hum was a spell by which the careful housewife exorcised the fiend idleness." In Bushnell's rhetoric, homespun was a potent symbol, signifying a domestic economy and its "simple, godly" virtues. The wheel and the loom produced a "life centered in the family." Women were content to serve men as helpmeets. Children clad in homespun enjoyed a rough-hewn equality. Schools, "little primitive universities of homespun," awakened the scholars' intelligence but also kept them bound by a sense of "homely satisfaction." Young men and women were not tempted to leave for the city or to work in cotton mills. Instead of focusing on the vexing topics of urbanization and industrialization, Bushnell hailed migration as a way of propagating New England values: "the sons of Connecticut" who moved "to other States" succeeded because they had been brought up "in the wise economy of a simple, homespun training." The legacy of the homespun age was a surer basis for social order than "the romantic visions of our new seers," who sought to reorganize society on theoretical principles. For Bushnell, the history of homespun would spin its web of ancestral associations and offer its vision of agrarian stability to recenter society around the domestic hearth. This mythic time and place when the patriarchal core held fast counterbalanced a new century in which market exchange and geographical mobility threatened to destabilize the localistic culture of the New England town.[8]

The "hometown," another common rhetorical device of centennial orations, was intended to counteract the centrifugal forces of nineteenth-century life. Speakers celebrated an American pastoral, a culture of cultivation that lay between the sublime wilderness and the urban industrial scene. Even Mount Wachusett was domesticated. The festivities at Princeton, the hometown of Mount Wachusett, proclaimed that the mountain symbolized "nothing rugged" nor "anything of the wild or solitary," but rather a "grandeur that is refined." From its peak, one student of mountain scenery exclaimed, "the eye travels a complete panoramic circle of loveliness; an unbroken range of town and village, lawn, field, and forest, with silvery traces of streams; and, here and there dotting the surface, now expanding, and now hiding in some woody recess, many sweet lakes, in their placid waters mirroring all surrounding beauty; while everywhere are seen evident marks of the human industry, that has subdued and rules over all." This prospect from a distance blurred the differences that were emerging in the landscape of the Wachusett. Fitchburg had become a booming manufacturing center, with concentrations of great wealth and a foreign-born working class; as a result of great mechanical discoveries, "time and distance have been practically vanquished, and not only town and country made one, but the nations of the earth brought as it were face to face." Fitchburg's commodities circled the globe. Other towns founded in the eighteenth century had declined. Orators in such isolated hill towns as Hubbardston and Petersham bemoaned the centralization of wealth, population, and talent that left their residents bereft of heirs and stranded in a seeming backwater. The only consolation was that Hubbardston was a nursery of men, exporting its young people rather than its goods. Listeners were charged to "remember that men were the noblest products of any soil, that the lessons of thrift and industry and virtue which the young in these hilly quiet towns are getting will not be in vain." The image of the hometown became a refrain used to stimulate the emotions, to establish a filial attachment to the past, and to bind, tighten, and strengthen social relationships.[9]

Letters from migrants such as Nova Scotia's Asa Gates commemorated their birthplace. For Lancaster's bicentennial, leading literary lights Edward Everett, George B. Emerson, Jared Sparks, and William Prescott sent regrets while offering their thoughts about "the ancient town" and New England institutions, hoping to bring the past to the attention of "the coming generation." According to Emerson, "a New England town thus becomes itself a great school, the noblest conceivable in which a young man may learn to understand, to value, and to defend all his rights and privileges." Other letter writers dwelled on their memories of childhood in the Wachusett. The "dear old home" and "hometown" were described as concentric circles, moving out from the domestic hearth to the farmstead and then the bounded village. Orators and audience constructed the town as a place of memory, what Pierre Nora has termed *lieux de mémoire,* sites of memory, that are "at once immediately available in concrete sensual experience and susceptible to the most abstract elaboration." Concerned about the chaotic growth of cities and the breakdown of the agrarian order, speakers appealed to a pastoral past of family, household, and village embedded in the myth of New England settlement.[10]

"The cult of the New England village," according to Lawrence Buell, was a powerful ideal that took hold in the postrevolutionary generation; many writers at midcentury commemorated the vanishing countryside. Even orators who hailed change were alarmed enough about the instability of the "modern" that they appealed to "tradition" as well. Well-known and anonymous authors published autobiographical narratives of rural childhood, telescoping the personal and communal pasts. The village-centered landscape came to symbolize the values of the covenanted community, cultural enlightenment, and democratic self-government. This imagined past conflated the commercial village form of postrevolutionary New England with the orderly society of the colonial period; the geographical dispersion of the early settlements and the conflicts that attended and followed the Revolution were expunged from this image. Beyond these historical and geographical borrowings, "village became metaphor for inherited ideals of stable Puritan community and democratic society," according to historical geographer Joseph Wood, despite the actual incompatibility of a hierarchical community with a democratic republic.[11]

The conventional history told at town centennials, with its accounts of founders and farmers, differed from previous local histories. The Indians were no longer treated solely as the settlers' ruthless foe, as the Reverend Timothy Harrington had described them in his oration at Lancaster's centennial a century before. Joseph Willard expressed keen interest in stories about the native inhabitants of the Wachusett, the "gentle Showanon" and the Nashaways; he hoped to recover a more complete account of "the history of our tribe," its "power and decadency," and its relations with white settlers. Willard scoured the available sources, such as John Eliot's and Daniel Gookin's writings, John Winthrop's *Journal,* and local records, to trace the progress of Eliot's missionary work and document Showanon's invitation to the English to join his people in the Wachusett. "But, with the exception of a few glimmering, fitful lights, all is as dark as its fate." The mid-nineteenth-century local historian, safely located in a world without Indians, criticized his predecessor for his lack of interest in the Indians' customs and legends. "Very pleasant it would have been . . . to know something more of the history of Showanon's tribe, the Nashaway Indians; their numbers, traditions, habits, localities, the succession of their chiefs, anecdotes of their intercourse with the planters, the reason for their joining against their old friends the English, how many survived, and whether any of the poor creatures . . . ever ventured back in time of peace to visit the graves of their fathers."

Willard's lengthy account of "the poor wasted people" had a elegiac tone. "The Indian" had been ruined by proximity to the white settlers, who were "guilty of his debasement and moral ruin." Showanon's hopes for trade and protection from western tribes, tragically, were not served by the town's founding; instead, the Nashaways receded with the advance of English settlement. Of course, they returned to interrupt the narrative of peaceful colonization; with the outbreak of King Philip's War, Willard observed, the friendly Nashaways were forced to take up arms because of the pressures of pan-Indian solidarity and the English's failure to be a reliable ally. Lancaster's white residents temporarily fled the frontier, "but not so with the poor natives," lamented Willard; they were permanently scattered into slavery and exile. Willard issued a stunning denunciation of English persecution of the Christian Indians, based on Gookin's *Historical Account of the Doings and Sufferings of the Christian Indians.* Other orators focused on the tangle of moral and legal issues surrounding land titles. Westminster's historian conceded that no purchase of the town's lands had been made from the Indians but concluded that General Court title was sufficient, adding a contemporary, progressive interpretation that "a savage race was giving way to a civilized one." For these orators, romantic visions of the vanishing race made the injustices committed against the Nashaways deserving of atonement, since "an expiring nation, like expiring individuals should be regarded with sympathy." The once powerful enemy of Lancaster's English settlers was admitted and even welcomed—if only symbolically—on this day to join in the sacred return to the founders' burial ground.[12]

Examination of town histories illuminated other disturbing dimensions of the early settlers' character and actions; their zealous behavior, superstitious nature, and persecution of dissenters appeared as an unwelcome inheritance at these commemorative occasions. These flaws could be explained away by the necessities of their frontier station and by their overarching mission "to establish a pure and vital religion in this wilderness," according to Charles Hudson, Westminster's local historian. The spirit of toleration was unknown in that era, Hudson reminded his audience. And from their faults flowed all the bounties of the present age, for their greatest love, according to his Whiggish version of American history, was "civil and religious liberty." Hudson soared in his concluding rebuke to his contemporaries: "give me the stern integrity," "the manly, unconquerable perseverance," and "unfaltering faith" of the Puritan ancestors, instead of the present age's "easy virtue," "compromising policy," and "speculative doubting." What had begun as a labored apologia for the Puritans' deceptive dealings with the Indians and relentless persecution of dissenters ended up as a critique of present-day reformers and politicians.[13]

But the meanings of revolutionary liberty could not always be so easily contained. The inflammatory issues of sectional and racial politics intruded directly into the 1859 festivities. In Princeton, centennial speakers usually portrayed their revolutionary forbears as conservatives whose actions against the British were the inevitable result of their reliance upon the guiding principles and institutions established by the Puritan fathers. But that evening at Princeton, Ezra Heywood followed a toast to the "resistance of our ancestors to British tyranny" by inviting the assembly "to celebrate the deeds of revolutionists, of traitors, of insurrectionists." Disrupting the equanimity of the proceedings, in which past residents were blandly commemorated in short speeches, Heywood focused on a former minister who was erroneously dismissed for his suspected Tory sympathies and who subsequently voted against ratification of the federal Constitution because of its proslavery clauses. This towering exemplar, a "moral Wachusett," was part of a "sublime ancestry" that, Heywood thundered, was not being celebrated on this occasion. He delineated a less glorious lineage for the town and the commonwealth, pointing out the contradictions of both the revered past and the complacent present. In 1776 Princeton had unjustly hounded a moral minister from its pulpit; in 1859 the state legislature and town representatives were implementing the fugitive slave law. Heywood challenged his audience to commemorate and emulate a more radical ancestry. "Put your ear to the ground, and you will hear the echoing, earthquake tread of the impending second American Revolution. This very week its Bunker's Hill was fought at Harper's Ferry. The timid, faithless toryism of to-day, pales and trembles at the crack of insurgent rifles. . . . John Brown, braver than Warren, more self-sacrificing than Lafayette, with his Spartan score of followers, throws himself against a gigantic despotism, in defence of the principles of the fathers." No record remains of the response that evening to Heywood's radical interpretation of the Revolution, but when the printed text of the centennial appeared, a majority of the committee appended a note that Heywood's facts were in error and his remarks represented "an unwarranted . . . trespass upon the proprieties of the occasion."[14]

These commemorations gave the New England elite the opportunity to claim legitimacy as the region's natural leaders in an unbroken line of succession from the early settlers. Such assertions were necessary only because industrialization had increased social stratification and introduced ethnic diversity. Local historians were deferential toward Gardner's Levi Heywood, who owned the region's largest chair manufacturing firm. Industrial towns such as Fitchburg and Gardner were heterogeneous; Irish and French-Canadian immigrants had established Catholic churches, challenging the region's "peculiar, homogeneous, and unique" Protestant hegemony. But the centennial's processions, parades, and performances were orchestrated as if the town was a singular social entity, with unity and community celebrated by the thousands of participants. Few dissenting voices were raised, and discordant images were minimized.[15]

Yet the very success of serial town settlement undermined the historical narrative so carefully constructed at these centennials. The act of writing, performing, and publishing local history was an effort to restore a lost sense of community through story telling. Behind the much touted signs of success—railroads and factories in the Wachusett, native sons and daughters in such faraway places as California—lay barely controlled fears of social disorder and cultural fragmentation. Toasts celebrated those "attached to the soil" and ignored more peripatetic town founders, such as the Page family of Lunenburg and Benjamin Bellows. Anxieties about the distances traveled and the discontinuity experienced by participants lent an elegiac tone to the proceedings. "With all the hope of the new," Emerson told his audience at Concord's bicentennial, "I feel we are leaving the old." These celebrations betrayed participants' vain hope that pausing for a day, a temporary interlude in the busy-ness of contemporary society, could allow a symbolic return to revere the ancestors and that that would be enough to curb a restless people. Celebrants voiced doubts about the success of this restorative venture. A sense of mortality, signified by the passage of generations, shaped the stories of a century of life in the Wachusett. Orators and organizers emphasized the need to preserve records and memories before it was too late.[16]

A few speakers expressed fears about New England's waning influence in the expanding nation, as new territories and peoples overwhelmed the older region's legacy of liberty and toil. The centennial celebrations undertook the ambitious task of constructing a New England identity for the nation, as well as a Yankee ethnicity for residents. The best hope during an era of unprecedented expansion would be a transportable legacy in a form of town history and reverence for a place of memory. In a bid for cultural hegemony that was made even as the demographic and economic balance of the nation was shifting away from the region, centennial orators transformed the story of New England into the story of America. "National narrative," literary critic Jonathan Arac reminds us, "was part of the process by which the nation was forming itself."[17]

The centennial celebrations held in Wachusett towns were part of an early-nineteenth-century upsurge in history making: popular ceremonies commemorated Independence Day in Philadelphia, Evacuation Day in New York City, and Forefathers' Day (the anniversary of the Pilgrims' landing at Plymouth) throughout New England. All these observances involved the invention of traditions—"traditionalizing" in the vernacular form, as Susan Davis calls it—intended to establish rituals that sustained collective memories. The processions, parades, and orations dramatized to the participants the meaning of being a resident of a particular town, a New Englander, and an American. They relied upon a Whig vision of an organic society held together by precedents and historical continuities rather than the principles and contractual relationships that Democrats believed made up governments. Alexis de Tocqueville had deplored Americans' ahistorical penchant for moving on and disregarding the links between generations. Speakers at these commemorations hailed historical associations as "the golden chord" to bind one generation to the next and to forge emotional bonds between individuals and society. Finally, these festivals were part of the wider Euroamerican nationalist project of the nineteenth century, the invention of traditions attributed to the "folk," whereby new nation-states imagined themselves as communities united by shared roots and an unbroken transmission of culture. Such efforts placed a premium on locating national unity in the past, in cultural and ethnic purity, whether for a German or a Yankee nation.[18]

In the Wachusett, local history making relied centrally upon serial town settlement. As a historical process that was recreated over time and space by successive generations of families, serial town settlement simultaneously created continuity and legitimated change. Edward Johnson had framed the story of New England as the providential work of planting towns and churches in the wilderness of Massachusetts Bay. Daniel Gookin had attempted to incorporate the Indians into the narrative of the colony's founding. Timothy Harrington created the first history of town founding for Lancaster's centennial, peopling the region with Indians and Indian fighters, while Charles Hudson crafted a narrative of Westminster's eighteenth-century settlement around the stories of founding families.

Joseph Dennie originated the postrevolutionary village tableau peopled by homespun Yankee characters. The mid-nineteenth-century centennials worked with those materials, sentimentalizing Dennie's sarcastic tales and embedding Marsh's narrative into a larger history of English migration and settlement, American independence, and Yankee nation building. The rhetoric of loss and recovery pervaded centennial ceremonies, as the imagined countryside that orators invoked receded into the past. But the appeal to history did not involve a rejection of progress. Nor did commemorative speakers call upon their audience to create their communities anew; in contrast to utopian communitarians, they did not demand drastic alterations in economic arrangements and social relationships. These venturesome conservatives consecrated the process of historical change as well as memories of the past. After orators paused to pay respect to the ancestors' achievements, they welcomed the continuation of the capitalist transformation. After paying homage to the "hometown," they hailed the colonization of the continent. After evoking the imagined cohesion of the local community, they allowed the imagined community of the nation to grow. The process of nation building and history making would soon move beyond the Wachusett, and rural New England would serve as a quaint destination for tourists, writers, and artists in search of a vanished civilization. But for a moment in the mid-nineteenth century, the myth of serial town settlement would validate the mainsprings of national expansion. The invention of New England had deep roots in the Wachusett.[19]

Notes

Introduction

1. On the frontier as cultural zone, see Howard Lamar and Leonard Thompson, "Comparative Frontier History," in Lamar and Thompson, eds., *The Frontier in History: North America and Southern Africa Compared* (New Haven, 1981); William Cronon, George Miles, and Jay Gitlin, "Becoming West: Toward a New Meaning for Frontier History," in Cronon, Miles, and Gitlin, eds., *Under an Open Sky: Rethinking America's Western Past* (New York, 1992), pp. 3–27; Richard White, *The Middle Ground: Indians, Empires, and Republics in the Great Lakes Region, 1650–1815* (New York, 1991).

2. Sumner Chilton Powell, *Puritan Village: The Formation of a New England Town* (Middletown, Conn., 1963); Charles S. Grant, *Democracy in the Connecticut Frontier Town of Kent* (New York, 1961); John Frederick Martin, *Profits in the Wilderness: Entrepreneurship and the Founding of New England Towns in the Seventeenth Century* (Chapel Hill, 1991); Virginia DeJohn Anderson, *New England's Generation: The Great Migration and the Formation of Society and Culture in the Seventeenth Century* (New York, 1991); David Grayson Allen, *In English Ways: The Movement of Societies and the Transferal of English Local Law and Custom to Massachusetts Bay in the Seventeenth Century* (Chapel Hill, 1981).

3. David D. Hall and Alan Taylor, "Reassessing the Local History of New England," in Roger Parks, ed., *New England: A Bibliography of Its History* (Hanover, N.H., 1989), vol. 7, pp. xix–xlcii; Darrett Rutman, "Assessing the Little Communities of Early America," *William and Mary Quarterly* [henceforth, *WMQ*] 43 (1986): 163–78; Philip J. Greven Jr., *Four Generations: Population, Land, and Family in Colonial Andover, Massachusetts* (Ithaca, N.Y., 1970); Kenneth A. Lockridge, *A New England Town: The First Hundred Years, Dedham, Massachusetts, 1636–1736* (New York, 1970); John P. Demos, *A Little Commonwealth: Family Life in Plymouth Colony* (New York, 1970); Robert A. Gross, *The Minutemen and Their World* (New York, 1976).

4. Stephen A. Innes, *Labor in a New Land: Economy and Society in Seventeenth-Century Springfield* (Princeton, 1983); Richard I. Melvoin, *New England Outpost: War and Society in Colonial Deerfield* (New York, 1989).

5. Christopher Clark, *The Roots of Rural Capitalism: Western Massachusetts, 1780–1860* (Ithaca, N.Y., 1990); James A. Henretta, "Families and Farms: *Mentalité* in Pre-Industrial America," *WMQ* 35 (1978): 3–32; Winifred Rothenberg, *From Marketplaces to a Market Economy: The Transformation of Rural Massachusetts, 1750–1850* (Chicago, 1992).

6. On the reevaluation of Turner, see Patricia Limerick, *The Legacy of Conquest: The Unbroken Past of the American West* (New York, 1987); Cronon, Miles, and Gitlin, "Becoming West"; John Mack Farragher, "A Nation Thrown Back upon Itself: Turner and the Frontier," *Culturefront* 2 (1993): 5–9; Stephen A. Aron, "Lessons in Conquest: Towards a Greater

Western History," *Pacific Historical Review* 63 (1994): 125–47. On what has come to be called the "Puritan frontier," see Alan Heimert, "Puritanism, the Wilderness, and the Frontier," *New England Quarterly* 26 (1953): 361–82; Peter N. Carroll, *Puritanism and the Wilderness: The Intellectual Significance of the New England Frontier, 1629–1700* (New York, 1969); Alden Vaughan, *New England Frontier* (Boston, 1965); Douglas Edward Leach, *The Northern Colonial Frontier, 1607–1763* (New York, 1966).

7. Francis Jennings, *The Invasion of America: Indians, Colonialism, and the Cant of Conquest* (Chapel Hill, 1975); James Axtell, *The European and the Indian: Essays in the Ethnohistory of the Colonial North* (New York, 1981); Neal Salisbury, *Manitou and Providence: Indians, Europeans, and the Making of New England, 1500–1643* (New York, 1982); William Cronon, *Changes in the Land: Indians, Colonists, and the Ecology of New England* (New York, 1983); James H. Merrill, *The Indians' New World: Catawbas and Their Neighbors from European Contact through the Era of Removal* (Chapel Hill, 1989); James H. Merrill, "'The Customes of Our Country': Indians and Colonists in Early America," in Bernard Bailyn and Philip D. Morgan, eds., *Strangers within the Realm: Cultural Margins of the First British Empire* (Chapel Hill, 1991), pp. 117–56. For historiographical accounts, see James Axtell, "The Ethnohistory of Early America," *WMQ* 35 (1978): 110–44; James H. Merrell, "Some Thoughts on Colonial Historians and American Indians," *WMQ* 46 (1989): 94–119; Neal Salisbury, "The Indians' Old World: Native Americans and the Coming of Europeans," *WMQ* 53 (1996): 435–58.

8. Perry Miller, *The New England Mind: The Seventeenth Century* (New York, 1939), and *The New England Mind: From Colony to Province* (Cambridge, Mass., 1953); Sacvan Bercovitch, *The Puritan Origins of the American Self* (New Haven, 1975); Andrew Delbanco, *The Puritan Ordeal* (Cambridge, Mass., 1989); Philip Gura, *A Glimpse of Sion's Glory: Puritan Radicalism in New England, 1620–1660* (Middletown, Conn., 1984); David D. Hall, *Worlds of Wonder, Days of Judgment: Popular Religious Belief in Early New England* (New York, 1989); Janice Knight, *Orthodoxies in Massachusetts: Rereading American Puritanism* (Cambridge, Mass., 1991).

9. Frederick Jackson Turner, "The First Official Frontier of Massachusetts Bay," in *The Frontier in American History* (New York, 1920), p. 54; Roy Hidemichi Akagi, *The Town Proprietors of the New England Colonies* (Philadelphia, 1924); Lois K. Mathews [Rosenberry], *The Expansion of New England: The Spread of New England Settlement and Institutions to the Mississippi* (Boston, 1909).

10. Stephen Nissenbaum, "New England as Region and Nation," in Edward L. Ayers et al., eds., *All Over the Map: Rethinking American Regions* (Baltimore, 1966), p. 45.

11. John R. Gillis, "Memory and Identity: The History of a Relationship," in Gillis, ed., *Commemorations* (Princeton, 1994), pp. 3–24; also see the essays in that volume by Richard Handler, "Is 'Identity' a Useful Cross-Cultural Concept," pp. 27–40, and David Lowenthal, "Identity, Heritage, and History," pp. 41–57; Jonathan Arac, "Establishing National Narrative," in Sacvan Bercovitch, ed., *The Cambridge History of American Literature* (New York, 1994), p. 608. On collective memory, see Maurice Halbwachs, *The Collective Memory*, trans. F. J. Ditter (New York, 1980); Paul Connerton, *How Societies Remember* (New York, 1989); James Fentress and Chris Wickham, *Social Memory* (Cambridge, Mass., 1992); Patrick H. Hutton, *History as an Art of Memory* (Hanover, N.H., 1993); David Lowenthal, *The Past Is a Foreign Country* (Cambridge, U.K., 1985); Pierre Nora, "Between Memory and History: Les Lieux de Mémoire," *Representations* 26 (Spring 1989): 7–25. For specific case studies, see Yael Zerubavel, *Recovered Roots: Collective Memory and the Making of Israeli National Tradition* (Chicago, 1995); Michael Kammen, *Mystic Chords of Memory: The Transformation of Tradition in American Culture* (New York, 1991); Popular Memory Group, "Popular Memory: Theory, Politics, Method," in Richard Johnson et al., eds., *Making Histories: Studies in History Writing and Politics* (Minneapolis, 1982), pp. 205–52.

12. Innes, *Creating the Commonwealth*, p. 306; Edward Johnson, *Wonder-Working Providence*, ed. J. Franklin Jameson (New York, 1910), p. 195; Anderson, *New England's Generation*, pp. 91–92; T. H. Breen, "Persistent Localism: English Social Change and the Shaping of New England Institutions," in Breen, *Puritans and Adventurers: Change and Persistence in Early America* (New York, 1980), pp. 3–23; Stephen Foster, *Their Solitary Way: The Puritan Social Ethic in the First Century of Settlement in New England* (New Haven, 1971); Delbanco, *The Puritan Ordeal*, pp. 22–23; Allen, *In English Ways*.

13. Douglas R. McManis, *Colonial New England: A Historical Geography* (New York, 1975), pp. 36–39; Anderson, *New England's Generation*, p. 93; Douglas Leach, *The Northern*

Colonial Frontier, 1607–1763 (New York, 1966), chap. 3; D. W. Meinig, *The Shaping of America: A Geographical Perspective on 500 Years of History,* vol. 1, *Atlantic America, 1492–1800* (New Haven, 1986), p. 92.

14. Johnson, *Wonder-Working Providence,* p. 74; Henry Bond, *Genealogies of the Families and Descendants of the Early Settlers of Watertown* (Boston, 1855), vol. 2, p. 1038; John Winthrop, *The Journal of John Winthrop, 1630–1649,* ed. Richard S. Dunn, James Savage, and Laetitia Yeandle (Cambridge, Mass., 1996), pp. 60–61; Edmund S. Morgan, *The Puritan Dilemma: The Story of John Winthrop* (Boston, 1958), pp. 98–100.

15. Frederick Robinson and Ruth Robinson Wheeler, *Great Little Watertown* (Cambridge, Mass., 1930), p. 37; *The Records of the Court of Assistants of the Colony of Massachusetts Bay, 1630–1692* (Boston, 1904), vol. 1, p. 210; Powell, *Puritan Village,* pp. 76–79; Allen, *In English Ways.*

16. Powell, *Puritan Village,* pp. 75–77, 88; Nathaniel Bradstreet Shurtleff, *Records of the Governor and Company of Massachusetts Bay in New England* (Boston, 1853–54), vol. 1, p. 210.

17. Powell, *Puritan Village,* pp. 116–26.

18. Alfred Sereno Hudson, *The History of Sudbury, Massachusetts, 1638–1889* (Sudbury, 1889), pp. 160–61; Powell, *Puritan Village,* pp. 130–31.

19. Daniel Scott Smith, "'All in Some Degree Relations to Each Other': A Demographic and Comparative Resolution of the Anomaly of New England Kinship," *American Historical Review* 94 (1989): 44–79; Henretta, "Families and Farms," pp. 3–32; Grant, *Democracy in the Connecticut Frontier Town of Kent.*

20. Breen, "Persistent Localism," pp. 3–23; Anderson, *New England's Generation,* pp. 91–92; Innes, *Labor in a New Land;* Joseph S. Wood, "Village and Community in Early Colonial New England," *Journal of Historical Geography* 8 (1982): 333–46; Christine Leigh Heyrman, *Commerce and Culture: The Maritime Communities of Colonial Massachusetts, 1690–1750* (New York, 1984); Bruce C. Daniels, *The Connecticut Town, 1635–1790* (Middletown, Conn., 1979); Melvoin, *New England Outpost;* Edward M. Cook Jr., *The Fathers of the Town: Leadership and Community Structure in Eighteenth-Century New England* (Baltimore, 1976); Martin, *Profits in the Wilderness.*

21. Martin, *Profits in the Wilderness,* pp. 9–45; Akagi, *Town Proprietors;* Innes, *Creating the Commonwealth,* pp. 146–59.

22. Allyn B. Forbes, ed., *Winthrop Papers* (Boston, 1929–44), vol. 4, p. 164; Henretta, "Families and Farms," pp. 3–32.

23. Daniel Vickers, "Competency and Competition: Economic Culture in Early America," *WMQ* 47 (1990): 3–29; Anderson, *New England's Generation;* Martin, *Profits in the Wilderness;* Christopher M. Jedrey, *The World of John Cleaveland: Family and Community in Eighteenth-Century New England* (New York, 1979); Allen, *In English Ways.*

24. James Axtell, *The School upon a Hill: Education and Society in Colonial New England* (New Haven, 1974); Robert J. Dinkin, "Seating in the Meeting House in Early Massachusetts," *New England Quarterly* 43 (1970): 450–64; Innes, *Creating the Commonwealth.*

25. John J. Waters, "Patrimony, Succession, and Social Stability: Guilford, Connecticut in the Eighteenth Century," *Perspectives in American History* 10 (1976): 131–60; Waters, "The Traditional World of the New England Peasants: The View from Seventeenth-Century Barnstable," *New England Historical and Genealogical Register* 130 (1976): 3–21; Greven, *Four Generations;* Cook, *Fathers of the Towns;* Vickers, *Farmers and Fishermen,* pp. 73–74; Jedrey, *World of John Cleaveland,* p. 244.

26. Michael Zuckerman, "The Social Context of Democracy in Massachusetts," *WMQ* 25 (1968): 523–44; Zuckerman, *Peaceable Kingdoms: New England Towns in the Eighteenth Century* (New York, 1970); Anderson, *New England's Generation,* p. 123; Vickers, "Competency and Competition"; Breen, "Transfer of Culture: Chance and Design in Shaping Massachusetts Bay, 1630–1660," *New England Historical and Genealogical Register* 132 (1978): 3–17; Andrew Delbanco, "The Puritan Errand Re-Viewed," *Journal of American Studies* 18 (1984): 342–60; Leach, *Northern Colonial Frontier,* pp. 31–52.

27. Winthrop, *Journal of John Winthrop,* p. 615; Zuckerman, "Social Context of Democracy"; Wood, "Village and Community"; Anderson, *New England's Generation.*

28. Wood, "Village and Community"; Meinig, *Atlantic America.*

29. Johnson, *Wonder-Working Providence,* pp. 213–14. Subsequent page references are given parenthetically in the text. For reassessment of Johnson's work, see Sacvan Bercovitch, "Typology in Puritan New England: The Williams-Cotton Controversy Reassessed," *American*

Quarterly 19 (1987): 166–91, and "The Historiography of Johnson's Wonder-Working Providence," *Essex Institute Historical Collections* 21 (1968): 138–61; Ursula Brumm, "Edward Johnson's Wonder-Working Providence and the Puritan Conception of History," *Jarbuch für Amerikastudien* 14 (1969): 140–51; Edward J. Gallagher, "An Overview of Edward Johnson's *Wonder-Working Providence*," *Early American Literature* 5 (1971): 75–87, and "The Case for the *Wonder-Working Providence*," *Bulletin of the New York Public Library* 57 (Autumn 1983): 10–27; Cecilia Tichi, *New World, New Earth: Environmental Reform in American Literature from the Puritans through Whitman* (New Haven, 1979), chap. 2. See also Ormond Seavey, "Edward Johnson and the American Puritan Sense of History," *Prospects* 14 (1989): 1–29; Jasper Rosenmeier, "'They Shall No Longer Grieve': The Song of Songs and Edward Johnson's *Wonder-Working Providence*," *Early American Literature* 26 (1991): 1–20; Dennis Perry, "Autobiographical Role-Playing in Edward Johnson's *Wonder-Working Providence*," *Early American Literature* 22 (1987): 291–305; Andrew Delbanco, *The Puritan Dilemma* (Cambridge, Mass., 1989), pp. 189–93; Gura, *Glimpse of Sion's Glory*, pp. 229–32; Emory Elliott, "New England Puritan Literature," in Bercovitch, ed., *Cambridge History of American Literature*, vol. 1, pp. 205–25; Stephen Carl Arch, *Authorizing the Past: The Rhetoric of History in Seventeenth-Century New England* (DeKalb, Ill., 1994), pp. 51–87; Anthony Kemp, *The Estrangement of the Past: A Study in the Origins of Modern Historical Consciousness* (New York, 1994), pp. 105–36.

30. Alan Heimert and Andrew Delbanco, *The Puritans in America: A Narrative Anthology* (Cambridge, Mass., 1985), p. 113. See Gura, *Glimpse of Sion's Glory*; Seavey, "Edward Johnson," p. 25; Arch, *Authorizing the Past*, p. 86.

31. Tichi, *New World, New Earth*, pp. 39–42; William Frederick Poole, "Introduction," in Johnson, *Wonder-Working Providence* (Andover, Mass., 1867), pp. i–cxxxii; Elliott, "New England Puritan Literature," p. 219.

32. Theodore Dwight Bozeman, *To Live Ancient Lives: The Primitivist Dimension in Puritanism* (Chapel Hill, 1988), p. 116; Gura, *Glimpse of Sion's Glory*, pp. 230–32; Zerubavel, *Recovered Roots*; Arch, *Authorizing the Past*, pp. 60–63.

33. Arch, *Authorizing the Past*, pp. 64–65; Seavey, "Edward Johnson," p. 2.

34. Elliott, "New England Puritan Literature," p. 220; Perry, "Autobiographical Structures in Seventeenth-Century Puritan Histories" (Ph.D. diss., University of Wisconsin, Madison, 1986), p. 154; Gallagher, "Spiritual Biography," p. 80; Perry, "Role-Playing in Johnson," p. 293.

35. Seavey, "Johnson and the American Puritan Sense of History," p. 22; Jane Tompkins, *Sensational Designs: The Cultural Work of American Fiction, 1790–1860* (New York, 1985); Tichi, *New World, New Earth*, pp. 41–43; Elliott, "New England Puritan Literature," pp. 220–21; Gura, *Glimpse of Sion's Glory*, p. 230; Jesper Rosenmeier, "To Keep in Memory: The Poetry of Edward Johnson," in Peter White, ed., *Puritan Poets and Poetics: Seventeenth-Century American Poetry in Theory and Practice* (University Park, Penn., 1985), pp. 158–73; On the wilderness image, see Christopher Cernich, "'Salvage Land': The Puritan Wilderness and the Preservation of the World" (Ph.D. diss., University of Michigan, 1993), chap. 2.

36. Arch, *Authorizing the Past*, p. 70; Tichi, *New Worlds, New Earth*, pp. 43–44; Cernich, "Salvage Land," pp. 49–53; Seavey, "Johnson and the American Puritan Sense of History," p. 6.

37. Arch, *Authorizing the Past*, p. 73.

38. Cernich, "Salvage Land," pp. 44–56; Tichi, *New World, New Earth*, pp. 56–59.

39. Tichi, *New World, New Earth*, p. 52; Cernich, "Salvage Land," pp. 44–47; Arch, *Authorizing the Past*, pp. 83–85; Seavey, "Johnson and the American Puritan Sense of History," p. 4.

40. Arch, *Authorizing the Past*, pp. 51–56, 83–87; Seavey, "Johnson and the American Puritan Sense of History," pp. 24–25; Cernich, "Salvage Land," p. 43; Gallagher, "The Case for *Wonder-Working Providence*, pp. 10–27.

41. Rosenmeier, "To Keep in Memory," p. 173; Arch, *Authorizing the Past*, p. 82; Elliott, "New England Puritan Literature," p. 220; Gallagher, "The Case for the *Wonder-Working Providence*," p. 19.

Chapter 1. Indians, English, and Missionaries

1. Tales of Gluskap come from two collections, Charles G. Leland, *The Algonquin Legends of New England* (Boston, 1884), and Silas Tertius Rand, *Legends of the Micmacs* (New

York, 1894). Both use transcriptions taken from native speakers. I follow Rand's version, "Glooscap and his Four Visitors," pp. 253–57. See also Thomas Parkhill, "'Of Glooskap's Birth, and of His Brother Malsum, the Wolf': The Story of Charles Godfrey Leland's 'Purely American Creation,'" *American Indian Culture and Research Journal* 16 (1992): 45–69; Thomas S. Abler, "Protestant Missionaries and Native Culture: Parallel Careers of Asher Wright and Silas T. Rand," *American Indian Quarterly* 16 (1992): 25–37; Ruth Holmes Whitehead, *Stories from the Six Worlds: Micmac Legends* (Halifax, 1988); John Winthrop, *The Journal of John Winthrop, 1630–1649*, ed. Richard S. Dunn, James Savage, and Laetitia Yeandle (Cambridge, Mass., 1996), pp. 61–62.

2. Carolyn Merchant, *Ecological Revolutions: Nature, Gender, and Science in New England* (Chapel Hill, 1989), p. 44; Roger Williams, *The Complete Writings of Roger Williams* (New York, 1963), vol. 1, pp. 148–49; Henry Bowden, *American Indians and Christian Missions* (Chicago, 1981), pp. 109–11; Neal Salisbury, *Manitou and Providence: Indians, Europeans, and the Making of New England, 1500–1643* (New York, 1982), p. 37; William S. Simmons, *Spirit of the New England Tribes: Indian History and Folklore, 1620–1984* (Hanover, N.H., 1984), p. 41; Kenneth M. Morrison, *The Embattled Northeast: The Elusive Ideal of Alliance in Abenaki-Euramerican Relations* (Berkeley, 1984), pp. 60–71.

3. Simmons, *Spirit of the New England Tribes*, pp. 172, 234; Williams, *Complete Writings*, vol. 1, p. 24; Morrison, *Embattled Northeast*, pp. 64–67; Whitehead, *Stories from Six Worlds*, pp. 2–6; Gordon M. Day, "The Western Abenaki Transformer," *Journal of the Folklore Institute* 13 (1976): 77; William A. Haviland and Marjorie W. Powers, *The Original Vermonters: Native Inhabitants, Past and Present* (Hanover, N.H., 1981), pp. 191–96.

4. Rand, *Legends*, pp. 253–54; A. Irving Hallowell, "Ojibwa Ontology," in Stanley Diamond, ed., *Culture in History: Essays in Honor of Paul Radin* (New York, 1913), pp. 21, 28, quoted in Morrison, *Embattled Northeast*, p. 63.

5. Rand, *Legends*, pp. 255–57; Whitehead, *Stories from Six Worlds*, pp. 10–13.

6. Rand, *Legends*, p. 257.

7. Simmons, *Spirit of New England Tribes*, p. 234; Whitehead, *Stories from Six Worlds*, pp. 2–7; Morrison, *Embattled Northeast*, pp. 60–63; Peter Nabokov, "Native Views of History," in Bruce G. Trigger and Wilcomb E. Washburn, eds., *The Cambridge History of the Native Peoples of the Americas*, vol. 1, *North America* (New York, 1996), pp. 1–60.

8. John Winthrop to John Wheelwright, March 1639, in Allyn B. Forbes, ed., *Winthrop Papers* (Boston, 1929–44), vol. 4, pp. 422–23, vol. 3, pp. 101–2; Neal Salisbury, "Social Relationships on a Moving Frontier: Natives and Settlers in Southern New England, 1638–1675," *Man in the Northeast* 33 (1987): 89–99.

9. Simmons, *Spirit of New England Tribes*, pp. 6–7; Whitehead, *Stories from Six Worlds*, pp. 19–20; Morrison, *Embattled Northeast*, pp. 7, 65–70; Constance A. Crosby, "From Myth to History, or Why King Philip's Ghost Walks Abroad," in Mark P. Leone and Park B. Potter Jr., eds., *The Recovery of Meaning in Historical Geography* (Washington, D.C., 1988), pp. 200–201; Kenneth M. Morrison, "Towards a History of Intimate Encounters: Algonkian Folklore, Jesuit Missionaries, and Kiwakwe, the Cannibal Giant," *American Indian Culture and Research Journal* 3 (1979): 53–55.

10. See James Axtell, *The European and the Indian: Essays in the Ethnohistory of Colonial North America* (New York, 1981). For the sequence of contacts between the two cultures, see T. J. C. Brasser, *North American Indians in Historical Perspective*, ed. Eleanor B. Leacock and Nancy O. Lurie (New York, 1971); Salisbury, *Manitou and Providence*.

11. See John Donald Black and George William Westcott, *Rural Planning of One County: Worcester County, Massachusetts* (Cambridge, Mass., 1959), chaps. 2–3, for a discussion of the land, geology, soils, climate, agriculture, and vegetation of Worcester County; also see Doris Kirkpatrick, *The City and the River* (Fitchburg, Mass., 1971), chaps. 3–4; Massachusetts Historical Commission, *Historic and Archaeological Resources of Central Massachusetts* (Boston, 1985).

12. Kirkpatrick, *The City and the River*, p. 44.

13. Black and Westcott, *Rural Planning*, p. 19; Kirkpatrick, *The City and the River*, pp. 44–46.

14. Black and Westcott, *Rural Planning*, p. 17.

15. Thomas Dudley to Lady Bridget, Countess of Lincoln, in Everett Emerson, ed., *Letters from New England: The Massachusetts Bay Colony, 1629–38* (Amherst, Mass., 1976), p. 68; Josiah Temple, *History of Framingham, Massachusetts* (Framingham, 1887), p. 38.

16. Nathaniel Bradstreet Shurtleff, *Records of the Governor and Company of Massachusetts Bay in New England* [hereafter cited as *Mass. Recs.*] (Boston, 1853–54), vol. 1, p. 327; Margaret E. Newell, "Robert Child and the Entrepreneurial Vision: Economy and Ideology in Early New England," *New England Quarterly* 68 (1995): 223–56; Stephen Innes, *Creating the Commonwealth: The Economic Culture of Puritan New England* (New York, 1995); Richard Dunn, *Puritans and Yankees: The Winthrop Dynasty of New England, 1630–1717* (New York, 1971).

17. Winthrop Jr. to General Court, in Forbes, *Winthrop Papers*, vol. 4, pp. 422–23; Robert Child, "A large letter concerning the Defects and Remedies of English Husbandry Written to Mr. Samuel Hartlib" (1651), quoted in Dunn, *Puritans and Yankees*, p. 85; Newell, "Robert Child and the Entrepreneurial Vision," pp. 235–36; Samuel Eliot Morison, "The Plantation of Nashaway—An Industrial Experiment," *Publications of the Colonial Society of Massachusetts* 27 (1929): 212.

18. Samuel Eliot Morison, *Builders of the Bay Colony* (Boston, 1930), p. 245; this volume includes a biography of Child. See also Newell, "Robert Child and the Entrepreneurial Vision"; George Lyman Kittredge, "Dr. Robert Child the Remonstrant," *Publications of the Colonial Society of Massachusetts* 21 (1920): 1–146; Child to Winthrop Jr., in Forbes, *Winthrop Papers*, vol. 4, pp. 333–34. For Winthrop Jr., see Innes, *Creating the Commonwealth*, pp. 246–56; Morison, *Builders*; Dunn, *Puritans and Yankees*.

19. King to Winthrop Jr., in Forbes, *Winthrop Papers*, vol. 4, pp. 496–98. For Stephen Day's career, see Henry S. Nourse, "Lancaster," in D. Hamilton Hurd, ed., *History of Worcester County* (Philadelphia, 1889), vol. 1, p. 3; Morison, "Plantation of Nashaway," p. 212; Isaiah Thomas, *The History of Printing in America* (1810; New York, 1970), pp. 50–54; Bernard Bailyn, *The New England Merchants in the Seventeenth Century* (Cambridge, Mass., 1955), p. 62; George H. Haynes, "The Tale of Tantisques: An Early Mining Venture," *Proceedings of the American Antiquarian Society*, n.s., 14 (1901): 471–97.

20. John Winthrop Jr. to Henry Oldenburg, *Collections of the Massachusetts Historical Society*, 5th ser., 8 (1882): 133.

21. Child to Winthrop Jr., in Forbes, *Winthrop Papers*, vol. 4, pp. 333–34; Dunn, *Puritans and Yankees*, pp. 83–93; Innes, *Creating the Commonwealth*, pp. 237–70; Newell, "Child and the Entrepreneurial Vision," pp. 236–42.

22. Williams, *Complete Writings*, vol. 1, p. 179; Cronon, *Changes in the Land*, pp. 92–102; Salisbury, *Manitou and Providence*, p. 49.

23. Bert Salwen, "Indians of Southern New England and Long Island: Early Period," in Bruce Trigger, ed., *Handbook of North American Indians*, vol. 4, *Northeast* (Washington, D.C., 1978), p. 161; Laurence K. Gahan, "The Nipmucks and Their Territory," *Bulletin of the Massachusetts Archaeological Society* 2 (1941): 2; Frank G. Speck, "A Note on the Hasanamisco Band of Nipmuc," *Bulletin of the Massachusetts Archaeological Society* 4 (1943): 49–56; Dennis Connole, "Land Occupied by the Nipmuck Indians of Central New England," *Bulletin of the Massachusetts Archaeological Society* 38 (1976): 14–20; Temple, *History of Framingham*, pp. 38–39; Howard Russell, *Indian New England before the Mayflower* (Hanover, N.H., 1980); Neal Salisbury, "Introduction," in Mary Rowlandson, *The Sovereignty and Goodness of God, Together with the Faithfulness of His Promises Displayed: Being a Narrative of the Captivity and Restoration of Mrs. Mary Rowlandson and Related Documents* (Boston, 1997), pp. 10–14; Kathleen Bragdon, *Native People of Southern New England, 1500–1650* (Norman, Okla., 1996).

24. Francis E. Blake, *History of the Town of Princeton* (Princeton, 1915), p. 10; Abijah R. Marvin, *History of the Town of Lancaster, Massachusetts: From the First Settlement to the Present Time, 1643–1879* (Lancaster, Mass., 1879), p. 158; Sherburne Cook, *The Indian Population of New England in the Seventeenth Century* (Berkeley, 1976), pp. 53–56; Dean R. Snow and Kim M. Lanphear, "European Contact and Indian Depopulation in the Northeast: The Timing of the First Epidemics," *Ethnohistory* 35 (1988): 15–33; Dean R. Snow, *The Archaeology of New England* (New York, 1980), pp. 31–42.

25. William Wood, *New England's Prospect*, ed. Alden Vaughan (1634; Amherst, Mass., 1977), pp. 106–7; Salisbury, *Manitou and Providence*, pp. 30–33; William Cronon, *Changes in the Land: Indians, Colonists, and the Ecology of New England* (New York, 1983), pp. 37–47; Merchant, *Ecological Revolutions*, pp. 74–83; Bowden, *American Indians*, p. 99.

26. Bowden, *American Indians*, p. 99; Thomas Morton, *New English Canaan* (1632), quoted in Cronon, *Changes in the Land*, p. 61; Salwen, "Indians of Southern New England," p. 163.

27. Salwen, "Indians of Southern New England," p. 162; Kirkpatrick, *The City and the River*, p. 56; Marvin, *Lancaster*, p. 151; Merchant, *Ecological Revolutions*, pp. 74–81; Cronon, *Changes in the Land*, pp. 43–46; Salisbury, *Manitou and Providence*, pp. 39–41; James Axtell, *The Invasion Within: The Contest of Cultures in Colonial North America* (New York, 1985), pp. 137–39.

28. Gahan, "The Nipmucks," p. 3; R. A. Douglas-Lithgow, *Dictionary of American-Indian Place and Proper Names in New England* (Salem, Mass., 1901), pp. 131, 170, 177; Cronon, *Changes in the Land*, pp. 65–66; Crosby, "From Myth to History," p. 193.

29. William J. Eccles, "The Fur Trade in the Colonial Northeast," in Wilcomb E. Washburn, ed., *Handbook of North American Indians*, vol. 4, *History of Indian-White Relations* (Washington, D.C., 1988), pp. 324–34; Christopher L. Miller and George R. Hammell, "A New Perspective on Indian-White Contact: Cultural Symbols and Colonial Trade," *Journal of American History* 73 (1986): 311–28; Lynn Ceci, "Native Wampum as a Peripheral Resource in the Seventeenth-Century World-System," in Lawrence Hauptman and J. Wherry, eds., *The Pequots in Southern New England* (Norman, Okla., 1991), pp. 48–63; Salisbury, *Manitou and Providence*, pp. 147–52; Cronon, *Changes in the Land*, pp. 95–97; Peter A. Thomas, "Culture Change on the Southern New England Frontier, 1630–1665," in William W. Fitzhugh, ed., *Cultures in Contact: The Impact of European Contacts on Native American Cultural Institutions, A.D. 1000–1800* (Washington, D.C., 1985), pp. 131–61.

30. Henry Stedman Nourse, *The Early Records of Lancaster, Massachusetts, 1643–1725* (Lancaster, Mass., 1884), p. 10; Francis X. Moloney, *The Fur Trade in New England, 1620–1678* (Cambridge, Mass., 1931), p. 71. Nourse, a nineteenth-century local historian, reprinted many of the records of Lancaster, which he culled from various sources in several of his publications: *Early Records; The Military Annals of Lancaster, Massachusetts, 1740–1865* (Lancaster, Mass., 1889); and *Lancastriana: A Supplement to the Early Records and Military Annals* (Lancaster, Mass., 1900). Nourse also wrote the excellent town history of Lancaster that can be found in Hurd, *History of Worcester County*, vol. 1, pp. 1–45. Timothy Harrington, pastor of the First Church in Lancaster from 1748 to 1795, in his *Century Sermon Preached in Lancaster, May 28, 1753* (1753; Lancaster, 1853), pp. 60–61, is the source for these early tales. Also, see Marvin, *Lancaster*, p. 154.

31. Brasser, "Algonkians," p. 72; Cronon, *Changes in the Land*, pp. 54–68; Peacock, "Puritan Appropriation of Indian Land," *Ethnohistory* 31 (1984): 39–44; Francis Jennings, *The Invasion of America: Indians, Colonialism, and the Cant of Conquest* (Chapel Hill, 1975), pp. 80–82; Salisbury, *Manitou and Providence*, p. 43.

32. Henry Bond, *Genealogies of the Families and Descendants of the Early Settlers of Watertown* (Boston, 1855), vol. 1, p. 326; Morison, "The Plantation of Nashaway."

33. *Mass. Recs.*, vol. 2, pp. 54–56; Forbes, *Journal of John Winthrop*, p. 499; Axtell, *Invasion Within*, pp. 139, 143–44; Salwen, "Indians of Southern New England," p. 167; Salisbury, *Manitou and Providence*, pp. 39–47; Salisbury, "Introduction," p. 12.

34. Wood, *New England's Prospect*, p. 97; Gahan, "Nipmucks," p. 2; Axtell, *Invasion Within*, pp. 143–44.

35. Morison, "The Plantation of Nashaway"; Newell, "Robert Child and the Entrepreneurial Vision," p. 235; Bond, *Watertown Genealogies*, vol. 1, p. 376.

36. Nourse, *Early Records*, pp. 13–14, 15–16; Winthrop, *Journal of John Winthrop*, pp. 685–86; Harral Ayres, *The Great Trail of New England* (Boston, 1940).

37. Nourse, *Early Records*, p. 11; Winthrop, *Journal of John Winthrop*, p. 504; Nourse, "Lancaster," in Hurd, *Worcester County*, vol. 1, p. 3.

38. Nourse, *Early Records*, pp. 15–16.

39. Ibid.; Newell, "Child and Entrepreneurial Vision," p. 243.

40. For John Prescott, see Nourse, "John Prescott, The Founder of Lancaster, 1605–1681," in *Military Annals*, pp. 339–66; William Prescott, *The Prescott Memorial* (Boston, 1740), pp. 34–40; John Frederick Martin, *Profits in the Wilderness: Entrepreneurship and the Founding of New England Towns in the Seventeenth Century* (Chapel Hill, 1991), p. 19; Alden T. Vaughan, *New England Frontier: Puritans and Indians, 1620–1675* (Boston, 1965), pp. 215–16; Morison, "Plantation of Nashaway," pp. 207–10; Samuel A. Green, *Remarks on Nonacoicus, the Indian Name of Major Willard's Farm at Groton, Mass.* (Cambridge, Mass., 1893), p. 2.

41. Ola Elizabeth Winslow, *John Eliot: "Apostle to the Indians"* (Boston, 1968), p. 89; *Mass. Recs.*, vol. 1, p. 17; Salisbury, *Manitou and Providence*, pp. 176–81.

42. *Mass. Recs.*, vol. 2, pp. 55–56 (quot.); Winthrop, *Journal of John Winthrop*, p. 499; Axtell, *Invasion Within*, p. 139.

43. *Mass. Recs.*, vol. 2, pp. 84, 134, 176–77; Axtell, *Invasion Within*, pp. 139–40; Bowden, *American Indians*, p. 118; Winthrop, *Journal of John Winthrop*, pp. 682–83.

44. Harold W. Van Lonkhuyzen, "A Reappraisal of the Praying Indians: Acculturation, Conversion, and Identity at Natick, Massachusetts, 1646–1730," *New England Quarterly* 63 (1990): 401–2; Richard W. Cogley, "John Eliot in Recent Scholarship," *American Indian Culture and Research Journal* 14 (1990): 77–92; Thomas, "Cultural Change on the Southern New England Frontier," pp. 139–41.

45. Letter from John Eliot to Edward Winslow, *The Glorious Progress of the Gospel, amongst the Indians in New England* (1649), in *Collections of the Massachusetts Historical Society* [hereafter, cited as *Coll. Mass. Hist. Soc.*], 3d ser., 4 (1834): 81; Eliot to Henry Whitfield, *The Light appearing more and more towards the perfect Day, or, A farther Discovery of the present state of Indians in New-England* (1651), in *Coll. Mass. Hist. Soc.*, 3d ser., 4 (1834): 123; Von Lonkhuyzen, "Reappraisal of the Praying Indians," p. 402.

46. Daniel Gookin, *Historical Collections of the Indians in New England* (1792; Towtaid, N.J., 1970), p. 96; Winslow, *Glorious Progress*, quoted in Axtell, *Invasion Within*, p. 143; Elise M. Brenner, "To Pray or to Be Prey: That Is the Question: Strategies for Cultural Autonomy of Massachusetts Praying Town Indians," *Ethnohistory* 27 (1980): 146, 149; Whitfield, *Light appearing more and more*, p. 139; Axtell, *Invasion Within*, pp. 227–30; Salisbury, *Manitou and Providence*, pp. 43, 75; Bowden, *American Indians*, pp. 104–5.

47. *Mass. Recs.*, vol. 2, pp. 84, 134, 176–77; Whitfield, *Light appearing more and more*, pp. 138–39; Cogley, "John Eliot," pp. 85–86; *The Day-Breaking if not the Sun-Rising of the Gospel with the Indians in New-England* (1647), pp. 20–21; Thomas Shepard, *The Clear Sun-Shine of the Gospel Breaking Forth upon the Indians of New-England* (1647), in *Coll. Mass. Hist. Soc.*, 3d ser. (1834): 39–40; Neal Salisbury, "Red Puritans: The 'Praying Indians' of Massachusetts Bay and John Eliot," *William and Mary Quarterly* [hereafter, cited as *WMQ*] 21 (1974): 33; Axtell, *Invasion Within*, pp. 139, 230; Von Lonkhuyzen, "Reappraisal of 'Praying Indians,'" p. 406; William Kellaway, *The New England Company, 1649–1776* (London, 1961), p. 118. See also James Holstun, *A Rational Millennium: Puritan Utopias of Seventeenth-Century England and America* (New York, 1987); Theodore Dwight Bozeman, *To Live Ancient Lives: The Primitivist Dimension in Puritanism* (Chapel Hill, 1988), pp. 263–86.

48. *Mass. Recs.*, vol. 4, pt. 2, p. 22.

49. Nourse, *Early Records*, pp. 17–19; *Mass. Recs.*, vol. 2, p. 212, vol. 3, p. 203.

50. Nourse, *Early Records*, pp. 22–23.

51. Nourse, "Lancaster," in Hurd, *Worcester County*, vol. 1, p. 4.

52. Nourse, *Early Records*, p. 29; Bruce C. Daniels, *The Connecticut Town, 1635–1790* (Middletown, Conn., 1979), p. 120; Martin, *Profits in the Wilderness*, pp. 9–45.

53. Nourse, *Early Records*, pp. 33–37, 39–41; Nourse, "Lancaster," in Hurd, *History of Worcester County*, vol. 1, p. 7.

54. Nourse, *Early Records*, pp. 51–55; John Langdon Sibley, *Biographical Sketches of Graduates of Harvard University* (Cambridge, Mass., 1873–1919), vol. 1, pp. 311–17; Nourse, "Lancaster," in Hurd, *Worcester County*, vol. 1, pp. 8–9; Timothy Harrington, *Centennial Sermon*, p. 14.

55. Nourse, *Early Records*, p. 49.

56. Ibid., pp. 59, 74, 78.

57. *Mass. Recs.*, vol. 3, pp. 365–66; Samuel Gardner Drake, *The Book of the Indians; or, Biography and History of the Indians of North America*, 8th ed. (Boston, 1841), p. 269; William Simmons, "Southern New England Shamanism," in William Cowan, ed., *Papers of the Seventh Algonquian Conference, 1975* (Ottowa, 1976), pp. 249–50; Salisbury, "Introduction," p. 15.

58. Nourse, *Early Records*, pp. 28–31; Stephen A. Innes, *Labor in a New Land: Economy and Society in Seventeenth-Century Springfield* (Princeton, 1983), pp. 84–86.

59. Nourse, *Early Records*, pp. 28–31; Innes, *Labor in a New Land*, pp. 34–35; Martin, *Profits in the Wilderness*.

60. Bailyn, *New England Merchants*, pp. 53–57; Moloney, *Fur Trade in New England*, pp. 67–77; Innes, *Labor in a New Land*, pp. 9–33; Peter A. Thomas, "In the Maelstrom of Change: The Indian Trade and Cultural Process in the Middle Connecticut Valley, 1635–1665" (Ph.D. diss., University of Massachusetts, 1979); James Kimball, "The Exploration of the Merrimac River," *Essex Institute Historical Collections* 14 (1878): 159–60; Wilson Waters, *History of*

Chelmsford, Massachusetts (Lowell, Mass., 1917), p. 75; Merchant, *Ecological Revolutions,* p. 89; Cronon, *Changes in the Land,* p. 99; Vaughan, *New England Frontier,* pp. 215–16.

61. *Mass. Recs.,* vol. 1, pp. 81, 140, 174, 322; vol. 4, p. 354; Bailyn, *New England Merchants,* pp. 30–31, 55–56; Joseph Willard, *Willard Memoir, or the Life and Times of Major Simon Willard* (Boston, 1858), p. 157; Nourse, *Early Records,* p. 263; Moloney, *Fur Trade in New England,* pp. 67–75; Martin, *Profits in the Wilderness,* pp. 19–20.

62. Nourse, *Early Records,* p. 64; Nourse, "Lancaster," in Hurd, *History of Worcester County,* vol. 1, p. 11; Martin, *Profits in the Wilderness,* pp. 19–20; Green, *Remarks on Nonacoicus,* p. 2; Bailyn, *New England Merchants,* pp. 55–56; *Mass. Recs.,* vol. 4, p. 354; Moloney, *Fur Trade in New England,* pp. 74–75; Waters, *History of Chelmsford,* pp. 36–37. On monopolies, see Innes, *Creating the Commonwealth,* pp. 233–34.

63. Nourse, *Early Records,* pp. 33, 85; on Adams, see p. 10; *Records of the Court of Assistants,* comp. John Noble (Boston, 1870), pp. 39–40; Willard, *Willard Memoir,* pp. 325–33; Bailyn, *New England Merchants,* p. 56; Green, *Remarks on Nonacoicus,* p. 2.

64. Cronon, *Changes in the Land,* p. 103; Bailyn, *New England Merchants,* p. 56; Moloney, *Fur Trade in New England,* pp. 114–17; Willard, *Willard Memoir,* p. 327; Innes, *Labor in a New Land,* p. 33; Salisbury, "Social Relationships on a Moving Frontier," p. 93; Thomas, "In the Maelstrom of Change"; P. Nick Kardulias, "Fur Production as a Specialized Activity in a World System: Indians in the North American Fur Trade," *American Indian Culture and Research Journal* 14 (1990): 25–60.

65. Nourse, *Early Records,* pp. 82, 73, 91; *Mass. Recs.,* vol. 4, pt. 2, p. 341; Salisbury, "Introduction," p. 18.

66. Nourse, *Military Annals,* p. 361; Prescott, *Prescott Memorial,* pp. 39–40.

67. Richard I. Melvoin, *New England Outpost: War and Society in Colonial Deerfield* (New York, 1989), p. 41; Daniel K. Richter, *The Ordeal of the Longhouse: The Peoples of the Iroquois League in the Age of European Colonization* (Chapel Hill, 1992), p. 75; Salisbury, "Toward the Covenant Chain: Iroquois and Southern New England Algonkians, 1637–1684," in Daniel K. Richter and James H. Merrell, eds., *Beyond the Covenant Chain: The Iroquois and Their Neighbors in Indian North America, 1600–1800* (Syracuse, N.Y., 1987), pp. 61–73.

68. Nourse, *Lancastriana,* pp. 11–12; Gookin, *Historical Collections,* pp. 34, 38–43, 85; Richter, *Ordeal of the Longhouse,* p. 99; Melvoin, *New England Outpost,* p. 46; Colin Calloway, *The Western Abenakis of Vermont, 1600–1800* (Norman, Okla., 1990), pp. 70–75.

69. Nourse, *Early Records,* pp. 59, 74, 78, 90.

70. Gookin, *Historical Collections,* pp. 133–36; Frederick William Gookin, *Daniel Gookin, 1612–1687* (Chicago, 1912); Martin, *Profits in the Wilderness,* pp. 23–28; Guy Loran Lewis, "Daniel Gookin, Superintendent and Historian of the New England Indians: A Historiographical Study" (Ph.D. diss., University of Illinois, 1973).

71. Gookin, "An Historical Account of the Doings and Sufferings of the Christian Indians in New England in the Years 1675, 1676, 1677," *Archaeologia Americana, Transactions and Collections of the American Antiquarian Society* 2 (1836): 423–534; Dennis R. Perry, "Autobiographical Structures in Seventeenth-Century Puritan Histories" (Ph.D. diss., University of Wisconsin, Madison, 1986), pp. 77–85; Martin, *Profits in the Wilderness,* pp. 23–28; Axtell, *Invasion Within,* pp. 131–48.

72. Gookin, *Daniel Gookin,* pp. 62–89, 113–15; Martin, *Profits in the Wilderness,* pp. 23–28; Lewis, "Daniel Gookin," pp. 1–35; Neal Emerson Salisbury, "Conquest of the 'Savage': Puritans, Puritan Missionaries, and Indians, 1620–1680" (Ph.D. diss., University of California, Los Angeles, 1972), pp. 176–77; Frederick L. Weis, "The New England Company of 1649 and Its Missionary Enterprises," *Publications of the Colonial Society of Massachusetts* 38 (1947–51): 138–214.

73. Gookin, *Historical Collections,* pp. 133–36; Lewis, "Daniel Gookin."

74. Gookin, *Historical Collections,* pp. 77–78; Von Lonkhuyzen, "Reappraisal of the Praying Indians"; Salisbury, "Red Puritans"; Brenner, "To Pray or to Be Prey," pp. 146–49.

75. Gookin, *Historical Collections,* pp. 85–87; John Eliot, *John Eliot's Indian Dialogues: A Study in Cultural Interaction,* ed. James Ronda and Henry Warner Bowden (Westport, Conn., 1980), p. 87.

76. Drake, *Book of Indians,* p. 269; Salisbury, "Social Relationships on a Moving Frontier," p. 94; John Easton, "A Relacion of the Indyan Warre," in Charles H. Lincoln, ed., *Narratives of the Indian Wars, 1675–1699* (New York, 1913), p. 10. On Metacom's or King Philip's War, see Douglas Edward Leach, *Flintlock and Tomahawk: New England in King*

Philip's War (New York, 1966); Leach, *Arms for Empire* (New York, 1973), p. 65. Russell Bourne, *The Red King's Rebellion: Racial Politics in New England, 1675–1678* (New York, 1990); Philip Ranlet, "Another Look at the Causes of King Philip's War," *New England Quarterly* (March 1988): 79–100.

77. Nathaniel B. Shurtleff and David Pulsifer, eds., *Records of the Colony of New Plymouth* (Boston, 1855–61), vol. 5, p. 62; Ranlet, "King Philip's War," pp. 85–90; Virginia DeJohn Anderson, "King Philip's Herds: Indians, Colonists, and the Problem of Livestock in Early New England," *WMQ* 51 (1994): 601–24; Leach, *Flintlock and Tomahawk*, pp. 22–28, 30–33, 36–38; Bourne, *Red King's Rebellion*, pp. 85–95, 99–101, 104–6; Gookin, *Historical Collections*, p. 95; Increase Mather, *A Brief History of the War with the Indians in New-England* (1676), reprinted in Richard Slotkin and James K. Folsom, eds., *So Dreadfull a Judgement: Puritan Responses to King Philip's War, 1676–1677* (Middletown, Conn., 1978), pp. 87–88; Jill Lepore, "Dead Men Tell No Tales: John Sassamon and the Fatal Consequences of Literacy," *American Quarterly* 46 (1994): 479–512.

78. John Eliot to John Winthrop Jr., May 24, 1675, *Coll. Mass. Hist. Soc.*, 5th ser., 1 (1832): 425; Leach, *Flintlock and Tomahawk*, pp. 50–54, 69, 73–74, 78–91, 112–35; Mather, *Brief History of the War*, pp. 89–92, 94–98, 107–9; Gookin, *Historical Account*, pp. 462–63; *Brief and True Narration*, p. 7; Willard, *Willard Memoir*, pp. 283–303; Bourne, *Red King's Rebellion*, pp. 126–29, 146–60, 162–65; Mary Rowlandson, *The Sovereignty and Goodness of God*, 2d ed. (1682), reprinted in Salisbury, *The Sovereignty and Goodness of God* (Boston, 1997), p. 68; Nourse, *Early Records*, pp. 98–99; Hubbard, "The Happiness of a People," quoted in Leach, *Arms for Empire*, p. 61; Patrick M. Malone, *The Skulking Way of War: Technology and Tactics among the Northeastern Indians* (Lanham, Md., 1991), pp. 80–87; John E. Ferling, *A Wilderness of Miseries: War and Warriors in Early America* (Westport, Conn., 1990), pp. 49–50; Leach, *Arms for Empire*, pp. 62–64; William Harris, *A Rhode Islander Reports on King Philip's War: The Second William Harris Letter of August, 1676*, ed. Douglas Leach (Providence, 1963).

79. Leach, *Arms for Empire*, p. 64, and *Flintlock and Tomahawk*, pp. 141, 148–61; Richter, *Ordeal of the Longhouse*, pp. 135; Gookin, *Historical Account*, pp. 450–51, 485, 486–89; Bourne, *Red King's Rebellion*, pp. 160–62; Malone, *Skulking Way of War*, pp. 84–90.

80. Nourse, *Early Records*, pp. 100, 104–6; "James Quanapaug's Information, January 24, 1676," in *Mass. Hist. Soc. Coll.*, 1st ser., 6 (1797): 205–7; Gookin, *Historical Account*, pp. 488–90; Leach, *Flintlock and Tomahawk*, pp. 155–58.

81. Rowlandson, *Sovereignty and Goodness*, pp. 68–69; Leach, *Flintlock and Tomahawk*, pp. 157–58; Bourne, *Red King's Rebellion*, pp. 167–68; Nourse, *Early Records*, pp. 102–6; Lincoln, *Narratives*, pp. 83–84, 113, 116, 118–22.

82. Gookin, *Historical Account*, p. 494; Lancaster petition, March 11, 1676, in Mass. Archives, vol. 68, p. 156, quoted in Nourse, *Early Records*, pp. 107–8; Leach, *Flintlock and Tomahawk*, pp. 164–65; Lincoln, *Narratives*, p. 82; Bourne, *Red King's Rebellion*, pp. 165–68.

83. Lincoln, *Narratives*, pp. 84–87; Leach, *Flintlock and Tomahawk*, pp. 166–70; Melvoin, *Colonial Outpost*, pp. 112–13; Nourse, *Early Records*, p. 108; *Mass. Hist. Soc. Coll.*, 1st ser., 6 (1797): 89.

84. Rowlandson, *Sovereignty and Goodness*, pp. 100–101; Leach, *Flintlock and Tomahawk*, pp. 171–75; Gookin, *Historical Account*, pp. 510–12; Lincoln, *Narratives*, pp. 93–94; Bourne, *Red King's Rebellion*, pp. 178–79.

85. Leach, *Flintlock and Tomahawk*, pp. 201–6, Bourne, *Red King's Rebellion*, pp. 189–93.

86. Benjamin Church, *Entertaining Passages Relating to Philip's War* (1716), reprinted in Slotkin and Folsom, eds., *So Dreadfull a Judgement*, p. 424; Leach, *Flintlock and Tomahawk*, pp. 207–9; Bourne, *Red King's Rebellion*, pp. 195–99, Malone, *Skulking Way of War*, pp. 91–93; Ian K. Steele, *Warpaths* (New York, 1994), pp. 106–7; Axtell, "The Scholastic Philosophy of the Wilderness," in *The European and the Indian*, pp. 145–49.

87. Nourse, *Early Records*, pp. 110–14; Leach, *Flintlock and Tomahawk*, p. 180; Drake, *Book of Indians*, pp. 265, 269.

88. Nourse, *Early Records*, p. 116; Samuel Green, ed., *Diary by Increase Mather* (Cambridge, Mass., 1900), p. 47; Drake, *Book of Indians*, p. 269; Leach, *Flintlock and Tomahawk*, p. 226; Jennings, *Invasion of America*, p. 324.

89. Mitchell Robert Breitwieser, *American Puritanism and the Defense of Mourning* (Madison, 1990), pp. 6, 8.

90. The literature concerned with Mary Rowlandson is voluminous. See Roy Harvey Pearce, "The Significance of the Captivity Narrative," *American Literature* 19 (1947): 1–20; Richard VanDerBeets, *Held Captive by Indians: Selected Narratives, 1642–1836* (Knoxville, 1973); David Minter, "By Dens of Lions: Notes on Stylization in Early Puritan Captivity Narratives," *American Literature* 45 (1973): 335–47; Richard Slotkin, *Regeneration through Violence: The Mythology of the American Frontier, 1600–1860* (Middletown, Conn., 1973); Alden T. Vaughan and Edward W. Clark, eds., *Puritans among the Indians: Accounts of Captivity and Redemption, 1676–1724* (Cambridge, Mass., 1981); Laurel Ulrich, *Good Wives: Image and Reality in the Lives of Women in Northern New England, 1650–1750* (New York, 1982); Tara Fitzpatrick, "The Figure of Captivity: The Cultural Work of the Puritan Captivity Narrative," *American Literary History* 3 (1991): 1–26; David L. Greene, "New Light on Mary Rowlandson," *Early American Literature* 20 (1985): 24–38; Kathryn Zabelle Derounian, "The Publication, Promotion, and Distribution of Mary Rowlandson's Indian Captivity Narrative in the Seventeenth Century," *Early American Literature* 23 (1988): 239–61.

91. Mather, *Brief History of the War*, pp. 179–80; Cotton Mather, *The Short History of New England* (Boston, 1694), pp. 42–43.

92. On the actual experience of captivity, see Alden T. Vaughan and Daniel K. Richter, "Crossing the Cultural Divide: Indians and New Englanders, 1605–1763," *Proceedings of the American Antiquarian Society* 40 (October 1980): 23–99; and James Axtell, "The White Indians of Colonial America," in *The European and the Indian*, pp. 168–206.

93. Breitwieser, *American Puritanism*, p. 53; Sacvan Bercovitch, *The Puritan Origins of the American Self* (New Haven, 1975), p. 5.

94. Rowlandson, *Sovereignty and Goodness*, pp. 71, 78, 91.

95. Breitwieser, *American Puritanism*, p. 53; Rowlandson, *Sovereignty and Goodness*, p. 79.

96. Rowlandson, *Sovereignty and Goodness*, pp. 96–97.

97. Ibid., p. 111.

98. Ibid.

99. Fitzpatrick, "The Figure of Captivity," p. 3.

Chapter 2. "Indian-Fighters" and Town Founders

1. Benjamin Church, *Entertaining Passages Relating to King Philip's War*, reprinted in Richard Slotkin and James K. Folsom, eds., *So Dreadfull a Judgement: Puritan Responses to King Philip's War, 1676–1677* (Middletown, Conn., 1978), p. 396. Biographical details can be found in Ezra Stiles, "The Life of Colonel Church," in Benjamin Church, *The Entertaining History of King Philip's War* (Newport, R.I., 1772); Benjamin Church, *The History of King Philip's War, Commonly Called the Great Indian War of 1675 and 1676: Also of the French and Indian Wars at the Eastward, in 1689, 1690, 1692, 1696, and 1704*, 2d ed., Samuel Gardner Drake (Exeter, N.H., 1829); and Henry Martyn Dexter, "Materials Towards a Memoir," in Benjamin Church, *The History of King Philip's War*, with intro. and notes by Henry Martyn Dexter (Boston, 1865).

2. Church, *Entertaining Passages*, p. 395.

3. Ibid., pp. 371–72; Dexter, "Memoir," p. xviii. See Richard Slotkin, *Regeneration through Violence: The Mythology of the American Frontier* (Middletown, Conn., 1973), p. 152, for a discussion of Church as the first hero of the emerging myth of the frontier.

4. Richard I. Melvoin, *New England Outpost: War and Society in Colonial Deerfield* (New York, 1989), pp. 131–275; Douglas Leach, *The Northern Colonial Frontier, 1607–1763* (New York, 1966), pp. 109–25, and *Arms for Empire: A Military History of the British Colonies in North America, 1607–1763* (New York, 1973); Michael J. Puglisi, *Puritans Besieged: The Legacies of King Philip's War in the Massachusetts Bay Colony* (Lanham, Md., 1991); Colin G. Calloway, *The Western Abenakis of Vermont, 1600–1800: War, Migration, and the Survival of an Indian People* (Norman, Okla., 1990).

5. Subsequent birth and death records show the dispersal: fourteen settlers died in Dorchester, four in Charlestown, and two in Concord; and births were recorded in the coastal towns of Massachusetts Bay with eighteen in Sudbury, Charlestown, and Concord. Henry Stedman Nourse, *The Early Records of Lancaster, Massachusetts, 1643–1725* (Lancaster, Mass., 1884), pp. 313–26; Nourse, ed., *Birth, Marriage, and Death Register, Church Records*

and Epitaphs of Lancaster, Massachusetts, 1643–1850 (Lancaster, Mass., 1890); Puglisi, *Puritans Besieged,* pp. 113–14.

6. Nathaniel Bradstreet Shurtleff, *Records of the Governor and Company of Massachusetts Bay in New England* [hereafter cited as *Mass. Recs.*] (Boston, 1853–54), vol. 5, pp. 170–71, 213–14; William H. Whitmore, ed., *The Colonial Laws of Massachusetts, 1672–1686* (Boston, 1887), pp. 267–68; Massachusetts Archives [hereafter cited as Mass. Archives], vol. 69, p. 238, quoted in Puglisi, *Puritans Besieged,* pp. 86–87; Mass. Archives, vol. 68, pp. 174–75; On Lancaster, see Nourse, *Early Records,* pp. 119–21. See William Pencak, *War, Politics, and Revolution in Provincial Massachusetts* (Boston, 1981), chap. 3.

7. Leach, *Arms for Empire,* pp. 80–111, and *Northern Colonial Frontier,* pp. 109–25.

8. Melvoin, *New England Outpost,* pp. 185–92; W. J. Eccles, *France in America* (New York, 1972), pp. 96–97; Leach, *Arms for Empire,* pp. 80–111, and *Northern Colonial Frontier,* pp. 109–11. On the covenant chain, see Daniel Richter, *The Ordeal of the Longhouse: The Peoples of the Iroquois in the Era of European Colonization* (Chapel Hill, 1992), pp. 162–89; Francis Jennings, *The Ambiguous Iroquois Empire* (New York, 1995); Stephen S. Webb, *1676: The End of American Independence* (New York, 1984). On the Algonquian diaspora, see Calloway, *Western Abenakis,* pp. 86–92, and "Green Mountain Diaspora: Indian Population Movements in Vermont, c. 1600–1800," *Vermont History* 54 (1986): 197–228; Gordon M. Day, *The Identity of the St. Francis Indians* (Ottowa, Ont., 1981), and "The Indian Occupation of Vermont," *Vermont History* 33 (1965): 365–74; Harold E. L. Prins and Bruce J. Bourque, "Norridgewock: Village Translocations on the New England-Acadian Border," *Man in the Northeast* 33 (1987): 137–58; James Spady, "'As If in a Great Darkness': Ancestral Homelands, Diaspora, and the Schaghticokes of Hatfield, Massachusetts, 1677–1697," *Historical Journal of Massachusetts* 23 (1995): 185–97; Kenneth M. Morrison, *The Embattled Northeast: The Elusive Ideal of Alliance in Abenaki-Euramerican Relations* (Berkeley, 1984); Thomas L. Doughton, "Unseen Neighbors: Native Americans of Central Massachusetts, A People Who Had 'Vanished,'" in Colin G. Calloway, ed., *After King Philip's War: Presence and Persistence in Indian New England* (Hanover, N.H., 1997), pp. 207–30; Jean M. O'Brien, *Dispossession by Degrees: Indian and Land and Identity in Natick, Massachusetts, 1650–1790* (New York, 1997).

9. Captain Francis Nicholson, report, Aug. 31, 1688, and Inhabitants of Lancaster, Petition, July 3, 1689, Mass. Archives, vol. 107, pp. 171, and 15, quoted in Nourse, *Early Records,* p. 125–26; Melvoin, *New England Outpost,* p. 189.

10. Thomas Hutchinson, *The History of the Colony and Province of Massachusetts-Bay,* ed. Lawrence Shaw Mayo (1768; Cambridge, 1936), vol. 2, pp. 50, 75. On garrison houses, see Leach, *Northern Colonial Frontier,* pp. 58, 81, 112.

11. Timothy Harrington, *A Century Sermon, Preached at the First Parish in Lancaster* (1753; Clinton, Mass., 1853), pp. 63–64; Abijah R. Marvin, *History of the Town of Lancaster* (Lancaster, Mass., 1879), p. 126; Patrick Malone, *The Skulking Way of War: Technology and Tactics among the New England Indians* (Lanham, Md., 1991), p. 96.

12. Thomas Henchman to General Court, Apr. 12, 1692, Mass. Archives, vol. 37, p. 340, quoted in Nourse, *Early Records,* pp. 129–30; Nourse, *Early Records,* pp. 130–33; Harrington, *A Century Sermon,* p. 64; Marvin, *History of the Town of Lancaster,* pp. 126–27; Jonathan Houghton to General Court, Mar. 3, 1694, in Nourse, *Early Records,* p. 131.

13. Cotton Mather, *Magnalia Christi Americana, Books I and II,* ed. Kenneth B. Murdock (Cambridge, Mass., 1977), vol. 2, p. 639; Mass. Archives, vol. 10, p. 257, quoted in Nourse, *Early Records,* p. 133; Petition of John Houghton to Council and Representatives, Oct. 13, 1697, Mass. Archives, vol. 11, p. 125, quoted in Nourse, *Early Records,* p. 136.

14. Leach, *Arms for Empire,* p. 110; Leach, *Northern Colonial Frontier,* p. 113; Richter, *Ordeal of the Longhouse,* pp. 162–89; Melvoin, *New England Outpost,* pp. 201–4; Puglisi, *Puritans Besieged,* pp. 182–95; Calloway, *Western Abenakis,* pp. 97–98.

15. Samuel Penhallow, *The History of the Wars of New-England with the Eastern Indians* (1824; New York, 1969), pp. 23–27; Leach, *Arms for Empire,* pp. 116–58; Ian K. Steele, *Warpaths: Invasions of North America* (New York, 1994), pp. 151–59; Dale Miquelon, *New France, 1704–1744: "A Supplement to Europe"* (Toronto, 1987), pp. 32–54; Richter, *Ordeal of the Longhouse,* p. 215.

16. Cotton Mather, *Frontiers Well-Defended: An Essay, to Direct the Frontiers of a Countrey Exposed unto the Incursions of a Barbarous Enemy, How to Behave Themselves in Their*

Uneasy Station? (Boston, 1707), p. 4; John Williams to Dudley, Oct. 21, 1703, quoted in George Sheldon, *A History of Deerfield, Massachusetts* (1895–96; Somersworth, N.H., 1972), vol. 2, pp. 288–89; John Williams, *The Redeemed Captive Returning to Zion* (Boston, 1701); John Demos, *The Unredeemed Captive: A Family Story from Early America* (New York, 1994); Melvoin, *New England Outpost*, pp. 211–26.

17. Shy, "A New Look at the Colonial Militia," in *A People Numerous and Armed: Reflections on the Military Struggle for American Independence* (New York, 1976), p. 26; John E. Ferling, *A Wilderness of Miseries: Wars and Warriors in Early America* (Westport, Conn., 1980), pp. 14–15; Jack S. Radabaugh, "The Military System of Colonial Massachusetts, 1690–1740" (Ph.D. diss., University of Southern California, 1967).

18. Hutchinson, *History of Massachusetts-Bay*, vol. 2, p. 108, quoted in Leach, *Arms for Empire*, p. 133; Penhallow, *History of the Wars of New-England*, p. 52; Thomas Church, *The History of the Eastern Expeditions of 1689, 1690, 1692, 1704 against the Indians and French*, ed. Henry Martyn Dexter (Boston, 1867), pp. 128–81.

19. Eyewitness account in *Boston News Letter*, Nov. 20, 1704, quoted in Nourse, *Early Records*, p. 150; Petition of Inhabitants of Lancaster to Dudley and Council, Oct. 25, 1704, Mass. Archives, vol. 113, p. 363, quoted in Nourse, *Early Records*, p. 151; Penhallow, *Indian Wars*, pp. 23–24, 27.

20. Joseph Willard, *An Address in Commemoration of the 200th Anniversary of the Incorporation of Lancaster* (Boston, 1853), pp. 100–101; Marvin, *Lancaster*, p. 156; Mass. Archives, vol. 71, p. 876, quoted in Nourse, *Early Records*, p. 173.

21. Michael Peter Steinitz, "Landmark and Shelter: Domestic Architecture in the Cultural Landscape of the Central Uplands of Massachusetts in the Eighteenth Century" (Ph.D. diss., Clark University, 1988), pp. 38–47; "John White Junior House," Inventory of Historic Assets of the Commonwealth of Massachusetts, Lancaster Form C16, Massachusetts Historic Commission, Boston.

22. Mather, *Magnalia Christi Americana*, vol. 2, p. 639; Nourse, *Early Records*, pp. 131–36; Harrington, *Century Sermon*; James Axtell, *The Invasion Within: The Contest of Cultures in Colonial North America* (New York, 1985), pp. 287–301; Alden T. Vaughan and Daniel K. Richter, "Crossing the Cultural Divide: Indians and New Englanders, 1605–1763," *Proceedings of the American Antiquarian Society* 90 (1980): 52–72; Laurel Thatcher Ulrich, *Good Wives: Image and Reality in the Lives of Women in Northern New England, 1650–1750* (New York, 1982), p. 203.

23. Oct. 15, 1705, *The Diary of Samuel Sewell*, vol. 2, 1709–1729, ed. M. Halsey Thomas (New York, 1973), p. 530; Peter Whitney, *History of Worcester County* (Worcester, 1793), pp. 43–44; Nourse, *Early Records*, p. 155; Marvin, *Lancaster*, p. 145. Emma Lewis Coleman, *New England Captives Carried to Canada* (Portland, Maine, 1925), vol. 1, pp. 310–11; Axtell, *Invasion Within*, pp. 292–93.

24. *A Faithful Narrative, of the many Dangers and Sufferings . . . of Robert Eastburn* (Philadelphia, 1758), quoted in Axtell, *Invasion Within*, p. 292; Vaughan and Richter, "Crossing the Cultural Divide," pp. 52–72; Demos, *Unredeemed Captive*; Nourse, *Early Records*, p. 156; Marvin, *Lancaster*, p. 145.

25. *Boston News Letter*, Aug. 25, 1707, quoted in Nourse, *Early Records*, pp. 165–66; Nourse, *Lancastriana: A Supplement to the Early Records and Military Annals* (Lancaster, Mass., 1900), pp. 30–31; Whitney, *History of Worcester County*, p. 45.

26. Leach, *Arms for Empire*, pp. 155–58.

27. Theodore B. Lewis, "Land Speculation and the Dudley Council of 1686," *William and Mary Quarterly*, 3d ser., 31 (1974): 252–72; Martin, *Profits in the Wilderness*, p. 92; Crane, *Worcester County*, vol. 1, p. 11, quoted in Martin, *Profits in the Wilderness*, p. 92; Francis E. Blake, *History of the Town of Princeton* (Princeton, Mass., 1915), vol. 1, p. 12.

28. Blake, *Princeton*, vol. 1, p. 12; Josiah Temple, *History of Framingham, Massachusetts* (Framingham, 1887), p. 38; Nourse, *Early Records*, pp. 138–39; Frederick L. Weis, "The New England Company of 1649 and Its Missionary Enterprises," *Publications of the Colonial Society of Massachusetts* 38 (1959): 138–39; Doughton, "Unseen Neighbors," in Calloway, ed., *After King Philip's War*.

29. Nourse, *Lancastriana*, p. 28; committee report, Nov. 21–22, 1711, Mass. Archives, vol. 113, p. 633, quoted in Nourse, *Early Records*, pp. 174–75; Martin, *Profits in the Wilderness*, pp. 131–33.

30. "Proprietors of Additional Grant," in Nourse, *Lancastriana*, p. 18; nonresident petition, Town Records, Feb. 4, 1716, in Nourse, *Early Records*, pp. 176–77. On proprietorship, see Richard Bushman, *From Puritan to Yankee: Character and the Social Order in Connecticut* (Cambridge, Mass., 1967), pp. 49–53; Bruce Daniels, *The Connecticut Town: Growth and Development, 1635–1790* (Middletown, Conn., 1979), pp. 119–25; Roy Akagi, *The Town Proprietors in the New England Colonies* (New York, 1924), pp. 55–60; Martin, *Profits in the Wilderness*, pp. 257–80; Hutchinson, *History of Massachusetts-Bay*, vol. 1, p. 289.

31. Martin, *Profits in the Wilderness*, p. 266.

32. "The Proprietors of the Town of Lancaster," meeting report, Mar. 5, 1717, in Nourse, *Early Records*, p. 179; "The Revolution in New England Justified, and the People There Vindicated," testimony of town residents, in W. H. Whitmore, ed., *The Andros Tracts: Being a Collection of Pamphlets and Official Papers* (1868–1874; New York, 1971), vol. 1, pp. 95–96, quoted in Martin, *Profits in the Wilderness*, p. 266.

33. Proprietary meeting, Feb. 4, 1717, and town meeting, Aug. 8, 1718, in Nourse, *Early Records*, pp. 178–79; *Massachusetts Acts and Resolves*, vol. 1, pp. 64–65, 182–83, 704, vol. 2, pp. 30, 407–8, 425–26. See Martin, *Profits in the Wilderness*, pp. 267–69; Akagi, *Town Proprietors of New England*, p. 59; Florence May Woodward, *The Town Proprietors in Vermont: The New England Proprietorship in Decline* (New York, 1936), p. 57.

34. Garrison list, April 20, 1704, in Nourse, *Early Records*, pp. 143–44.

35. "Petition of several of the freeholders Proprietors and Inhabitants of Lancaster [to Governor, Council, and House of Representatives]," 1703, Mass. Archives, vol. 11, pp. 183–84, in Nourse, *Early Records*, pp. 140–41.

36. Inhabitants of Lancaster, Petition, Nov. 29, 1705, Mass. Archives, vol. 11, p. 200, in Nourse, *Early Records*, pp. 155–56; Selectmen, Petition, May 29, 1706, Mass. Archives, vol. 11, p. 209, in Nourse, *Early Records*, pp. 157–58.

37. Petition, Nov. 29, 1705, Mass. Archives, vol. 11, p. 200 in Nourse, *Early Records*, pp. 155–58; Petition, Committee & Inhabitants, May 29, 1706, Mass. Archives, vol. 11, p. 208, in Nourse, *Early Records*, pp. 158–60.

38. Cyprian Stevens, John Prescott, Peter Joslin, Josiah White, and Ephraim Wilder, Petition, May 29, 1706, Mass. Archives, vol. 11, p. 207, in Nourse, *Early Records*, pp. 161–63; John Houghton, Petition [1706], in Nourse, *Early Records*, p. 163; Houghton obituary, in Nourse, *Early Records*, p. 213; Marvin, *History of Lancaster*.

39. Lancaster Church Covenant, Mar. 29, 1708, in Nourse, *Early Records*, pp. 169–70; Harrington, *Century Sermon*; Clifford K. Shipton, "John Prentice," *Biographical Sketches of Harvard Graduates* (Boston, 1951), vol. 8, pp. 529–31.

40. Steele, *Warpaths*, pp. 160–61; Calloway, *Western Abenaki*, pp. 113–31; Leach, *Arms for Empire*, pp. 181–86; Leach, *Northern Colonial Frontier*, pp. 131–33; Morrison, *Embattled Northeast*, pp. 185–90; Miquelon, *New France*, pp. 106–8.

41. *New England Courant*, Aug. 27, 1722, quoted in Nourse, *Lancastriana*, pp. 31–32.

42. Nourse, *Early Records*, pp. 218, 222, 228–30, 236–37; Joseph Willard, *The Willard Memoir, or the Life and Times of Major Simon Willard* (Boston, 1858).

43. Jabez Fairbank to Lt. Gov. Dummer, July 20, 1724, Mass. Archives, vol. 52, p. 16, quoted in Nourse, *Early Records*, p. 218.

44. Edward Hartwell, to Lt. Gov. Dummer, Mar. 18, 1725, Mass. Archives, vol. 72, p. 221; John Houghton to Dummer, Mar. 18, 1725, Mass. Archives, vol. 72, p. 220; Dummer to Col. Eleazer Tyng, Mar. 1724, Mass. Archives, vol. 2, p. 222; Tyng to Dummer, Mass. Archives, vol. 2, p. 223, all reprinted in Nourse, *Early Records*, pp. 222–24.

45. Hartwell to Dummer, Aug. 23, 1725, Mass. Archives, vol. 52, p. 249, in Nourse, *Early Records*, p. 224; Ezra S. Sterns, "Lunenburg," in Duane Hamilton Hurd, ed., *History of Worcester County* (Philadelphia, 1889), vol. 1, p. 766; Willard, *Willard Memoir*.

46. Captain Samuel Willard to Lt. Gov. Dummer, July 25, Aug. 16, Sept. 7, Sept. 9, Sept. 19, Oct. 14, 1725, in Nourse, *Early Records*, pp. 234–36; Willard, "A Journall of My March," July 15–Aug. 12, 1725, Mass. Archives, vol. 38A, pp. 109–10; "A Journal of the March of Capt. Samuel Willard," Sept. 4–Oct. 19, 1725, Mass. Archives, vol. 38A, pp. 119–21; in Nourse, *Early Records*, pp. 239–42; Marvin, *History of Lancaster*, pp. 217–41.

47. Lt. Gov. Dummer to Captains Willard, White, and Blanchard, Mass. Archives, vol. 72, p. 250, in Nourse, *Early Records*, p. 226; Slotkin, *Regeneration through Violence*.

48. John White, "A True Journal of my Travells," Apr. 5–May 6, 1725, Mass. Archives, vol. 38A, pp. 97–98; "A Journal of my March with a Company of Volunteers against the

Indian Enemy, July 6–Aug. 5, 1725," Mass. Archives, vol. 38A, p. 107, reprinted in Nourse, *Early Records*, pp. 231–34; see also *Scout Journals: Journal of Capt. John White*, ed. G. Waldo Browne (Manchester, N.H., 1907); *Massachusetts Acts and Resolves*, vol. 2, pp. 258–59; Hutchinson, *History of Massachusetts-Bay*, vol. 2, p. 238; Leach, *Arms for Empire*, p. 183.

49. On John Lovewell, see Frederic Kidder, *The Expedition of Capt. John Lovewell and his Encounters with the Indians* (Boston, 1865), pp. 12–14; Francis Parkman, *Half-Century of Conflict: France and England in North America* (Boston, 1898), vol. 1, pp. 250–71; Thomas Symmes, *Lovewell Lamented, or a Sermon Occasioned by the Fall of the Brave Capt. Lovewell and Several of his Valiant Company, in the Late Heroic Action at Pigwacket* (Boston, 1725); Hutchinson, *History of Massachusetts-Bay*, vol. 1, p. 238; Nathaniel Bouton, *The Original Account of Capt. John Lovewell's "Great Fight" with the Indians, at Pequawket* (Concord, N.H., 1861); and Penhallow, *The History of the Wars of New-England*.

50. Bouton, *Original Account of Lovewell*, pp. 8–9; Kidder, *Expeditions of Lovewell*, pp. 15–17; [anon], "A True Journal of My Travels . . .," Apr. 1725, in Nourse, *Early Records*, p. 231; Nourse, *Early Records*, pp. 224–26.

51. *Boston Gazette*, May 10–17, 1725, quoted in Leach, *Arms for Empire*, p. 184; Parkman, *Half-Century of Conflict*, vol. 1, p. 254.

52. Kidder, *Expeditions of Lovewell*, pp. 76–78; Dummer, "Orders to Capt White and Wyman, Aug. 7, 1725," Mass. Archives, vol. 52, p. 234, in Nourse, *Early Records*, pp. 226–27; Leach, *Arms for Empire*, p. 186; Morrison, *Embattled Northeast*, pp. 189–90; Calloway, *Western Abenakis*, pp. 129–31.

53. "Song of Lovewell's Fight," reprinted in John Farmer and Jacob Bailey Moore, eds., *Collections, Topographical, Historical, and Biographical, Relating Principally to New-Hampshire*, vol. 4 (1825), pp. 64–66; George Lyman Kittredge offers evidence that "The Voluntier's March" was the original ballad title in his study, *The Ballad of Lovewell's Fight* (Cambridge, Mass., 1925). See also Slotkin, "The Search for a Hero and the Problems of the 'Natural Man,' 1700–1765," chap. 7 of *Regeneration through Violence*, for a literary study of the Indian wars of the early eighteenth century.

54. Symmes, *Lovewell Lamented*, pp. 1, 32. See Bouton, *The Original Account of Lovewell's Fight*; biographical sketch of Symmes in Kidder, *Expeditions of Lovewell*, pp. 21–25.

55. Symmes, *Lovewell Lamented*, pp. 10, 11–15.

56. Ibid., p. xi. Compare with Thomas Prince's edition of John Mason, *A Brief History of the Pequot War* (Boston, 1736), republished in *Collections of the Massachusetts Historical Society*, 2d ser., 8 (1819): 121.

57. Penhallow, *Wars of New England*, pp. 114, 128–29.

58. *New England Courant*, May 31, 1725, in Kittredge, *Ballad of Lovewell's Fight*, pp. 95–97; Farmer and Moore, eds., *Collections, Topographical, Historical*, p. 64.

59. Farmer and Moore, eds., *Collections, Topographical, Historical*, pp. 64–66; Kidder, *Expeditions of Lovewell*, pp. 116–19.

60. Farmer and Moore, eds., *Collections, Topographical, Historical*, pp. 64–66; Farmer and Moore also reprinted the Reverend Symmes's memoirs of the fight.

61. Eunice White, Petition, to Lt. Governor William Dummer, Council, and Representatives, Dec. 23, 1727, Mass. Archives, vol., 72, p. 325, in Nourse, *Early Records*, pp. 227–28.

Chapter 3. Lancaster and Its Offspring

1. John Prentice, *King Jehoshaphat's Charge to the Judges Appointed by him in the Land of Judah . . . A Sermon Preached at Worcester, August 10, 1731, at the Opening of a Court of the General Sessions of the Peace* (Boston, 1731), p. 8. On Prentice, see Clifford K. Shipton, *Biographical Sketches of Graduates of Harvard University, 1726–1730* (Boston, 1951), vol. 8, pp. 529–31.

2. Massachusetts Historical Commission State Survey Team, *Historic and Archaeological Resources of Central Massachusetts* (Boston, 1985), p. 74; Henry S. Nourse, "Lancaster," in Duane Hamilton Hurd, ed., *History of Worcester County* (Philadelphia, 1889), vol. 1, p. 20; John Stilgoe, *Common Landscape of America, 1580 to 1845* (New Haven, 1982), pp. 21–24, 128–32; Donna-Belle Garvin and James L. Garvin, *On the Roads North of Boston: New Hampshire Taverns and Turnpikes, 1700–1900* (Concord, N.H., 1988); Hugh Finlay, *Journal*

Kept by Hugh Finlay, 1773–1774, ed. Frank H. Norton (Brooklyn, N.Y., 1867); Sarah Kemble Knight, *The Journal of Madam Knight* (Boston, 1972).

3. Nathaniel Bradstreet Shurtleff, *Records of the Governor and Company of Massachusetts Bay in New England* (Boston, 1853–54), vol. 2, p. 203; James Axtell, *The School upon a Hill: Education and Society in Colonial New England* (New York, 1976), pp. 169–72; Bernard Bailyn, *Education in the Forming of American Society* (New York, 1972); Lawrence A. Cremin, *American Education: The Colonial Experience, 1607–1783* (New York, 1970), pp. 124, 520–26; Massachusetts Archives [hereafter cited as Mass. Archives], vol. 58, p. 240, quoted in Axtell, *School upon a Hill,* p. 173; Middlesex Court Records, Dec. 12–13, 1715, in Henry Stedman Nourse, *The Early Records of Lancaster, Massachusetts, 1643–1850* (Lancaster, Mass., 1890), p. 175; Mass. Archives, vol. 58, p. 222, quoted in Axtell, *School upon a Hill,* p. 182.

4. Middlesex Court Records, Dec. 12–13, 1715, in Nourse, *Early Records,* p. 175; Wilder account books, March 14, 1722, in Nourse, *Early Records,* pp. 202–3; Abijah P. Marvin, *The History of the Town of Lancaster* (Lancaster, Mass., 1879), p. 189; Bailyn, *Education,* p. 82; Cremin, *American Education.*

5. Francis G. Walett, ed., *The Diary of Ebenezer Parkman, 1703–1782* (Worcester, Mass., 1974), p. 4; Shipton, *Biographical Sketches,* vol. 8, pp. 529–31; Marvin, *History of Lancaster,* pp. 189–91; Robert J. Dinkins, "Seating in the Meeting House in Colonial Massachusetts," *New England Quarterly* 43 (1970): 450–64.

6. Michael Peter Steinitz, "Landmark and Shelter: Domestic Architecture in the Cultural Landscape of the Central Uplands of Massachusetts in the Eighteenth Century" (Ph.D. diss., Clark University, 1988), pp. 79, 138; Captain John Bennet House, "Inventory of Historic Assets of the Commonwealth of Massachusetts," Lancaster Form B37, and Samuel Willard House, "Inventory of Historic Assets of the Commonwealth of Massachusetts," Lancaster Form C3, Massachusetts Historical Commission, Boston; Kevin M. Sweeney, "Mansion People: Kinship, Class, and Architecture in Western Massachusetts in the Mid-Eighteenth Century," *Winterthur Portfolio* 19 (1984): 231–55.

7. *Journal of the House of Representatives of Massachusetts,* vol. 8, *1727–1729* (Boston, 1927), p. 217; vol. 9, *1729–1730* (Boston, 1928), pp. 134, 149, 173, 364, 365, 376, 381–83, quoted in Brooke, *Heart of the Commonwealth,* p. 27; Peter Whitney, *The History of the County of Worcester in the Commonwealth of Massachusetts* (Worcester, 1791), pp. 9–12; Nourse, "Lancaster," in Hurd, *History of Worcester County,* vol. 1, p. 20; Brooke, *Heart of the Commonwealth,* pp. 29–31; Timothy Harrington, "Post Funera Hon. Viri J. Wilder armigeri," manuscript sermon quoted in Nourse, *Early Records,* p. 214; Timothy Harrington, *A Century-Sermon Preached at the First-Parish in Lancaster* (Boston, 1753); John Murrin, "The Legal Transformation: The Bench and Bar of Eighteenth Century Massachusetts," in Stanley Katz, ed., *Colonial America: Essays in Politics and Social Development* (Boston, 1971), pp. 415–49; Kevin McWade, "Worcester County, 1700–1774: A Study of a Provincial Patronage Elite" (Ph.D. diss., Boston University, 1974); Robert Zemsky, *Merchants, Farmers, and River Gods* (Boston, 1971).

8. Henry S. Nourse, *History of the Town of Harvard, Massachusetts, 1732–1893* (Harvard, 1894), pp. 51–60; Nourse, "Lancaster," in Hurd, *History of Worcester County,* vol. 1, pp. 20–24; Robert C. Anderson, *Directions of a Town: A History of Harvard, Massachusetts* (Harvard, 1976), pp. 23–28; Marvin, *History of Lancaster,* pp. 192–95.

9. Nourse, "Lancaster," in Hurd, *History of Worcester County,* vol. 1, pp. 20–24; Marvin, *History of Lancaster,* pp. 199–200; J. D. Miller, "Leominster," in Hurd, *History of Worcester County,* vol. 1, pp. 1200–1202; David Wilder, *The History of Leominster, or the Northern Half of the Lancaster New or Additional Grant* (Fitchburg, Mass., 1853), pp. 16–17; William A. Emerson, *Leominster, Massachusetts, Historical and Picturesque* (Gardner, Mass., 1888).

10. Nourse, "Lancaster," in Hurd, *History of Worcester County,* vol. 1, pp. 20–24; Marvin, *History of Lancaster,* pp. 202–4; J. D. Miller, "Leominster," in Hurd, *History of Worcester County,* pp. 1200–1202; Wilder, *History of Leominster,* pp. 18–19; Emerson, *Leominster, Massachusetts.*

11. Nourse, "Lancaster," in Hurd, *History of Worcester County,* vol. 1, pp. 20–24; Marvin, *History of Lancaster,* pp. 205–10.

12. Douglas Leach, *The Northern Colonial Frontier, 1607–1763* (New York, 1989), pp. 131–33; Colin G. Calloway, *The Western Abenakis of Vermont, 1600–1800: War, Migration, and the Survival of an Indian People* (Norman, Okla., 1990), p. 114; Charles E. Clark,

The Eastern Frontier: The Settlement of Northern New England, 1610–1763 (Hanover, N.H., 1983), pp. 111–20.

13. Doris Kirkpatrick, *The City and the River* (Fitchburg, Mass., 1971), pp. 62–64; Ezra S. Stearns, "Lunenburg," in Hurd, *History of Worcester County*, vol. 1, pp. 761, 766.

14. Walter A. Davis, comp., *The Early Records of the Town of Lunenburg, Including the Part Which Is Now Fitchburg, 1719–1764* (Fitchburg, Mass., 1896), pp. 7–8; Rufus C. Torrey, *History of the Town of Fitchburg* (Fitchburg, Mass., 1836), pp. 24–28; Kirkpatrick, *City and River*, p. 64.

15. List of proprietors, in Davis, *Early Records of Lunenburg*, pp. 14–16. For a discussion of proprietorship and the New England land system, see Roy Hidemachi Akagi, *The Town Proprietors of the New England Colonies* (Philadelphia, 1924); Richard Bushman, *From Puritan to Yankee: Character and Social Order in Connecticut* (Cambridge, Mass., 1967); Florence May Woodard, *The Town Proprietors in Vermont: The New England Town Proprietorship in Decline* (New York, 1936); Davis, *Early Records of Lunenburg*, pp. 13–18.

16. Stearns, "Lunenburg," in Hurd, *History of Worcester County*, vol. 1, pp. 761–62; Kirkpatrick, *City and River*, p. 65.

17. Nourse, *Early Records*, p. 225.

18. Davis, *Early Records of Lunenburg*, pp. 32, 34–36.

19. Stearns, "Lunenburg," in Hurd, *History of Worcester County*, vol. 1, p. 762; Davis, *Early Records of Lunenburg*, p. 64. Kirkpatrick, *City and River*, p. 65; *Proceedings of the Fitchburg Historical Society* 2 (1894–97): 51–52.

20. Gardner's request printed in Davis, *Early Records of Lunenburg*, pp. 75–76. On Gardner, see Torrey, *Fitchburg*, pp. 33–34; Stearns, "Lunenburg," in Hurd, *History of Worcester County*, vol. 1, pp. 774–76.

21. Calloway, *Western Abenakis*; Leach, *Arms for Empire: A Military History of the British Colonies in North America, 1607–1763* (New York, 1973); Henry Hamilton Saunderson, *History of Charlestown, New-Hampshire, the Old No. 4* (Claremont, N.H., 1876).

22. Leach, *Northern Colonial Frontier*, pp. 131–33; Calloway, *Western Abenakis*, pp. 132–42; Clark, *Eastern Frontier*, pp. 176–77; Jere Daniell, *Colonial New Hampshire: A History* (Millwood, N.Y., 1981), pp. 133–64.

23. Stearns, "Lunenburg," in Hurd, *History of Worcester County*, vol. 1, p. 765.

24. On Benjamin Bellows, see Stearns, "Lunenburg," in Hurd, *History of Worcester County*, vol. 1, p. 767; Henry W. Bellows, *Historical Sketch of Col. Benjamin Bellows, Founder of Walpole* (New York, 1855); and Emily Barnes, *Narratives and Traditions of the Bellows Family* (Boston, 1888). On Heywood, see Stearns, "Lunenburg," in Hurd, *History of Worcester County*, vol. 1, p. 764.

25. Kirkpatrick, *City and River*, pp. 74–75; *Proceedings of the Fitchburg Historical Society* 2 (1894–97): 90; William Emerson, *Fireside Legends: Including Anecdotes, Reminiscences, etc., Connected with the Early History of Fitchburg, Massachusetts* (Fitchburg, Mass., 1900).

26. Ezra S. Stearns, "Address at the Dedication of the Fitch Memorial," *Proceedings of the Fitchburg Historical Society* 1 (1892): 245, 235–36.

27. Government Appropriation, Massachusetts Council Records, Nov. 11, 1743; quoted in "Papers relating to the Capture of John Fitch and Defence of the Frontier," *Proceedings of the Fitchburg Historical Society* 1 (1892): 253; Stearns, "Lunenburg," in Hurd, *History of Worcester County*, vol. 1, p. 768; Calloway, *Western Abenakis*, p. 152; Saunderson, *Charlestown, New-Hampshire*; Leach, *Arms for Empire*; Kirkpatrick, *City and River*, p. 68.

28. "Petition of John Fitch," *Proceedings of the Fitchburg Historical Society* 1 (1892): 262–64.

29. *Boston Weekly News Letter*, July 14, 1748, in *Proceedings of the Fitchburg Historical Society* 1 (1892): 253–54.

30. The story of Elizabeth Poole recounted by her great-granddaughter, Mrs. Mary Goff of Jaffrey, New Hampshire, can be found in *Proceedings of the Fitchburg Historical Society* 2 (1894–97): 44–45.

31. Petition of Inhabitants of Lunenburg and Leominster, July 8, 1748, Mass. Archives, vol. 73, p. 187; Letter from the Governor to Samuel Willard, July 18, 1748; and Memorial of Selectmen and Officers of Lunenberg, July 12, 1748, Mass. Archives, vol. 73, p. 189; reprinted in *Proceedings of the Fitchburg Historical Society* 1 (1892): 254–57; Torrey, *History of Fitchburg*, pp. 42–44.

32. "Petition of John Fitch," *Proceedings of the Fitchburg Historical Society* 1 (1892): 262–64; on Fitch's land dealings, see *Proceedings of the Fitchburg Historical Society* 1 (1892): 247.

33. Davis, *Early Records of Lunenburg*, pp. 178, 192–93; *Proceedings of the Fitchburg Historical Society* 2 (1894–97): 63–64, 91. On the Kimballs, see Ebenezer Bailey, "Deacon Ephraim Kimball," *Proceedings of the Fitchburg Historical Society* 5 (1914): 80–94; Davis, *Early Records of Lunenburg*, pp. 178, 192–93; *Proceedings of the Fitchburg Historical Society* 1 (1892): 36–37; Act of Incorporation, Walter A. Davis, *Old Records of the Town of Fitchburg, Massachusetts, 1764–1789* (Fitchburg, Mass., 1890), vol. 1, pp. 1–3; Petition of Kimball and Others, *Proceedings of the Fitchburg Historical Society* 1 (1892): 34; Davis, *Early Records of Lunenburg*, pp. 217–18.

34. Kirkpatrick, *City and River*, pp. 92–93.

35. On Timothy Harrington, see Shipton, *Biographical Sketches*, vol. 8, pp. 188–96; Marvin, *History of Lancaster*, pp. 376–93.

36. Harrington, *Century Sermon* (1733; Clinton, Mass., 1853), pp. 53, 58–68.

37. Ibid., pp. 53, 71.

38. Ibid., p. 73.

39. Timothy Harrington, *A Peaceable Temper and Conduct Divinely Enjoined* (Boston, 1760), pp. 8, 13, 20–21.

Chapter 4. Narragansett No. 2

1. Amicus Patriae [John Wise], *A Word of Comfort to a Melancholy Country* (Boston, 1721), in Andrew McFarland Davis, ed., *Colonial Currency Reprints, 1682–1751* (Boston, 1911), vol. 2, pp. 188–89; Clifford K. Shipton, *Biographical Sketches of Graduates of Harvard University* (Cambridge, Mass., 1881), vol. 2, pp. 428–41.

2. Thomas Hutchinson, *The History of the Colony and Province of Massachusetts-Bay*, ed. Lawrence Shaw Mayo (1765; Cambridge, Mass., 1936), vol. 1, pp. 331–32. Frederick Jackson Turner, "The First Frontier of Massachusetts Bay," in *The Frontier in American History* (New York, 1950), pp. 39–66; Lois K. Mathews [Rosenberry], *The Expansion of New England: The Spread of New England Settlement and Institutions to the Mississippi River, 1620–1865* (New York, 1909), pp. 131–32, 134–35; Roy Hidemachi Akagi, *The Town Proprietors of the New England Colonies* (Philadelphia, 1924), pp. 190–96.

3. The largest body of Westminster materials is stored in the Westminster Town Hall. I consulted Vital Records, 1761–1799; Proprietors' Records, 1728–1756; Town Proceedings, 1759–1793; and Valuations and Taxes, 1763–1830. Proprietors' Records contains the minutes of the proprietors' meetings and details of the division and ownership of the town lands. The long run of tax valuations is unusual for its completeness and contains information on the population along with individual holdings of real estate and livestock. The Westminster Historical Society has assorted accounts and a valuable tax book for the proprietary, Proprietors' Tax Book, 1755–1757, listing the tax and person assessed for each lot of the town's land. The Worcester County Land Deeds are kept in the Worcester County Courthouse, volumes 1–120. These deed books were used to construct an index of about 2,000 deeds that included all the land transactions involving proprietors and settlers from 1737 to 1750. The earliest Westminster tax list is December 17, 1759, and is found in Misc. Bound Mss., 1756–60, Massachusetts Historical Society, Boston. The 1771 provincial valuation is fragmentary, Massachusetts Archives [hereafter cited as Mass. Archives], vol. 134, p. 301, but the town does have a census of families and farms conducted in 1783, "The Number of Inhabitance Distinguishing white from black, the number of acres in the Town of Westminster in the year 1783 as taken by us," Mass. Archives, vol. 233.

Michael Peter Steinitz, "Landmark and Shelter: Domestic Architecture in the Cultural Landscape of the Central Uplands of Massachusetts in the Eighteenth Century" (Ph.D. diss., Clark University, 1988), pp. 98–100; William Francis Galvin, *Historical Data Relating to Counties, Cities, and Towns in Massachusetts*, 5th ed. (Boston, 1997).

4. George M. Bodge, *Soldiers in King Philip's War* (Boston, 1906), pp. 180, 406, 407–500. Bodge reprints many of the documents about the Narragansett townships and grantees (pp. 406–46). Nathaniel Bradstreet Shurtleff, *Records of the Governor and Company of Massachusetts Bay in New England* (Boston, 1853–54), vol. 5, p. 487; Mass. Archives, vol. 112, p. 398; vol. 72, p. 367; William Sweetzer Heywood, *The History of Westminster, Massa-*

chusetts, from the Date of the Original Grant of the Township to the Present Time (Lowell, Mass., 1893), p. 40; *Journal of the House of Representatives of Massachusetts,* vol. 7, 1726–1727 (Boston, 1926), pp. 112, 271–72. On the grant of two townships, June 1728, see Mass. Archives, vol. 115, pp. 760–61; Heywood, *History of Westminster,* p. 41; *Journal of House of Representatives,* vol. 8, 1727–1729 (Boston, 1927), pp. 39, 46, 199, and vol. 9, 1729–1731, pp. 128–29, 221, 344, 358; Bodge, *King Philip's War,* p. 409.

5. Jan. 19, 1731, *Records of Massachusetts Bay,* in William F. Goodwin, comp., *Records of the Proprietors of Narraganset Township, No. 1, Now the Town of Buxton, York County, Maine* (Concord, N.H., 1871), pp. 16–20; Bodge, *King Philip's War,* pp. 410–12; *Journal of House of Representatives,* vol. 10, 1731–1732 (Boston, 1929), p. 18. Heywood, *History of Westminster,* pp. 47–50.

6. Bodge, *King Philip's War,* pp. 411–12; *Journal of House of Representatives,* vol. 10, pp. 18, 31–32, 54, 58, 69–70, 72, 230, 270, 353–54, 356, 372, 416; Goodwin, *Narraganset No. 1,* pp. 21–31; Heywood, *History of Westminster,* pp. 47–49. Town Clerk, Westminster, Massachusetts, Meeting, June 6, 1733, Proprietors' Records [for No. 2], 1728–1756, p. 9; Heywood, *History of Westminster,* pp. 49–52.

7. Proprietary meeting, Dec. 10, 1733, Proprietor's Records, 1728–1756; and Heywood, *History of Westminster,* pp. 53–56. Proprietary meeting, Dec. 17, 24, 28, 1733, Proprietor's Records, 1728–1756; and Heywood, *History of Westminster,* pp. 56–57.

8. Proprietary meeting, June 11, 1734, land divisions, Proprietor's Records, 1728–1756; Heywood, *History of Westminster,* p. 60; Anthony Garvan, *Architecture and Town Planning in Colonial Connecticut* (New Haven, 1951), p. 77; Joseph S. Wood, "Village and Community in Early Colonial New England," *Journal of Historical Geography* 8 (1982): 33–46.

9. See Hutchinson, *History of Massachusetts-Bay,* vol. 2, p. 332; proprietary meetings, Mar. 24, May 13, 1734, June 1736, soprietor's Records, 1728–1756; Heywood, *History of Westminster,* pp. 64–68.

10. Charles Hudson, *A History of Westminster* (Mendon, Mass., 1832), pp. 17–18; Heywood, *History of Westminster,* pp. 213–15. Population estimates are from Heywood, *History of Westminster,* p. 479, until the tax lists beginning in 1759 provide more reliable figures.

11. Christopher M. Jedrey, *The World of John Cleaveland: Family and Community in Eighteenth-Century New England* (New York, 1979), p. 60; Robert A. Gross, *The Minutemen and Their World* (New York, 1976), p. 210; Philip J. Greven, *Four Generations: Population, Land, and Family in Colonial Andover, Massachusetts* (Ithaca, N.Y., 1970), pp. 212–14; Darrett B. Rutman, "People in Process: The New Hampshire Towns of the Eighteenth Century," *Journal of Urban History* 1 (1975): 268–92; Thomas R. Cole, "Family, Settlement, and Migration in Southeastern Massachusetts, 1650–1805: The Case for Regional Analysis," *New England Historical and Genealogical Register* 12 (1978): 171–81; Douglas Lamar Jones, *Village and Seaport: Migration and Society in Eighteenth-Century Massachusetts* (Hanover, N.H., 1981); Virginia DeJohn Anderson, "Migration, Kinship, and the Integration of Colonial New England Society: Three Generations of the Danforth Family," in Robert M. Taylor Jr. and Ralph S. Crandall, eds., *Generations and Change: Genealogical Perspectives in Social History* (Macon, Ga., 1986), pp. 269–90.

12. Nathan Birdsey to Joseph Hawley, Feb. 18, 1767, in Joseph Hawley Papers, vol. 2, n.p., New York Public Library, New York City, quoted in Gregory H. Nobles, *Divisions throughout the Whole: Politics and Society in Hampshire County, Massachusetts, 1740–1777* (New York, 1983), p. 111; John J. Waters, "The Traditional World of the New England Peasants: A View from Seventeenth Century Barnstable," *New England Historical and Genealogical Register* 130 (1976): 3–21; John J. Waters, "Patrimony, Succession, and Social Stability: Guilford, Connecticut, in the Eighteenth Century," *Perspectives in American History* 10 (1976): 131–60; Duane Ball, "Dynamics of Population and Wealth in Eighteenth-Century Chester County, Pennsylvania," *Journal of Interdisciplinary History* 6 (1976): 623; Daniel Vickers, "Competency and Competition: Economic Culture in Early America," *William and Mary Quarterly* [hereafter, cited as *WMQ*] 47 (1990): 3–29; Richard L. Bushman, "Family Security in the Transition from Farm to City, 1750–1850," *Journal of Family History* 6 (1981): 238–56; Linda Auwers Bissell, "From One Generation to Another in Seventeenth-Century Windsor, Connecticut," *WMQ* 31 (1974): 79–110; Jack Goody, Joan Thirsk, and E. P. Thompson, eds., *Family and Inheritance: Rural Society in Western Europe, 1200–1800* (Cambridge, U.K., 1976); David Levine, *Reproducing Families: The Political Economy of English Population History* (Cambridge, 1987); Toby L. Ditz, *Property and Kinship: Inheritance in Early Connecticut, 1750–1820* (Princeton, 1986).

13. Gross, *Minutemen and Their World,* pp. 77–80; Jedrey, *World of John Cleaveland,* p. 61.

14. Westminster Tax Assessment, Dec. 17, 1759, Misc. Bound Mss., 1756–1760. On Bigelow, see Worcester County Land Deeds, Registry of Deeds, Worcester, Massachusetts; Heywood, *History of Westminster;* General Court Visitation, 1751, Mass. Archives, vol. 116, p. 113. Information about proprietary rights comes from an index generated from the following linked sources: List of Proprietors, 1737, Proprietors' Records, 1728–1756; family genealogies in Heywood, *History of Westminster,* pp. 509–953; Worcester County Land Deeds, vols. 1–120; Daniel Vickers, *Farmers and Fishermen: Two Centuries of Work in Essex County, Massachusetts, 1630–1850* (Chapel Hill, N.C., 1994); Charles S. Grant, *Democracy in the Frontier Town of Kent* (New York, 1961).

15. Westminster Tax Assessment, 1759, Misc. Bound Mss., 1756–1760. On Miles, see Worcester County Land Deeds; Heywood, *History of Westminster;* General Court Visitation, 1751, Mass. Archives, vol. 116, p. 113. List of Proprietors, 1737, Proprietors' Records, 1728–1756; family genealogies in Heywood, *History of Westminster,* pp. 509–953; Worcester County Land Deeds, vols. 1–120.

16. On Bellows, see Heywood, *History of Westminster,* pp. 541–42; Henry W. Bellows, *Historical Sketch of Col. Benjamin Bellows, Founder of Walpole* (New York, 1855); Thomas Bellows Peck, *The Bellows Genealogy* (Keene, N.H., 1898). See also Rutman, "People in Process," pp. 268–92; Cole, "Family, Settlement, and Migration," pp. 171–81; Anderson, "Migration, Kinship, and the Integration of Colonial New England Society," pp. 269–90; Jedrey, *World of John Cleaveland.*

17. Turner, "The First Frontier of Massachusetts Bay," p. 54; Jonathan Willard to Benjamin Bellows, Worcester County Land Deeds, vol. 8, p. 417. On the transfer of proprietary shares, see 1741 division recorded in Proprietors' Records, 1728–1756, Dec. 2, 1741, pp. 123–29. (This record gives the name of the person along with the number of the home lot they drew.) The 1751 General Court Visitation listed the settlers' names along with the lot they occupied and the original proprietor (Mass. Archives, vol. 116, p. 113). Sources for ownership of proprietary shares are the List of second-division lots in Proprietors' Records, 1728–1756, Dec. 2, 1741, pp. 123–29; General Court Visitation, 1751, Mass. Archives, vol. 116, p. 113; and Proprietors' Tax Book.

18. General Court Visitation, 1751, Mass. Archives, vol. 116, p. 113.

19. Ibid.; Heywood, *History of Westminster,* pp. 82–84; Steinitz, "Landmark and Shelter."

20. Adams quoted in Howard Russell, *A Long Deep Furrow: Three Centuries of Farming in New England* (Hanover, N.H., 1976), p. 179.

21. Akagi, *Town Proprietors;* John Frederick Martin, *Profits in the Wilderness: Entrepreneurship and the Founding of New England Towns in the Seventeenth Century* (Chapel Hill, N.C., 1991); John Frederick Martin, "Entrepreneurship and the Founding of New England Towns: The Seventeenth Century" (Ph.D. diss., Harvard University, 1985), chap. 16; Nobles, *Divisions throughout the Whole,* chap. 5.

22. June 6, Oct. 31, 1739, Proprietors' Records, 1728–1756, pp. 111–12; Heywood, *History of Westminster,* pp. 71–72. List of second division lots (Proprietors' Records, 1728–1756, Dec. 2, 1741), pp. 123–29; General Court Visitation, 1751, Mass. Archives, vol. 116, p. 113; Proprietors' Tax Book.

23. Shipton, *Biographical Sketches,* vol. 10, pp. 300–301; Heywood, *History of Westminster,* p. 109; William Cooke, *The Great Duty of Ministers, to Take Heed to Themselves and Their Doctrine: A Sermon Preached in a New Township Narragansett No. 2* (Boston, 1742), pp. 22–23.

24. Joseph Tracy, *The Great Awakening: A History of the Revival of Religion in the Time of Edwards and Whitefield* (Boston, 1842), p. 98; Francis G. Walett, ed., *The Diary of Ebenezer Parkman, 1703–1782* (Worcester, Mass., 1974), pp. 84–85; John L. Brooke, *The Heart of the Commonwealth: Society and Political Culture in Worcester County, Massachusetts* (New York, 1989), pp. 67–68, 70–74; Patricia J. Tracy, *Jonathan Edwards, Pastor: Religion and Society in Eighteenth-Century Northampton* (New York, 1979), pp. 109–28. On Whitefield's commercial strategies, see Frank Lambert, *"Pedlar in Divinity": George Whitefield and the Transatlantic Revivals* (Princeton, 1994); John Prentice, *Testimony of an Association of Ministers* (Boston, 1748), p. 4. On Prentice, see Shipton, *Biographical Sketches,* vol. 8, pp. 529–31. On Chauncy, see Harry S. Stout, *The New England Soul: Preaching and Religious Culture in Colonial New England* (New York, 1986), pp. 202–7. On the dissolving of gender

boundaries, see Susan Juster, *Disorderly Women: Sexual Politics and Evangelicalism in Revolutionary New England* (Ithaca, N.Y., 1994). James Walsh, "The Great Awakening in the First Congregational Church of Woodbury, Connecticut," *WMQ* 28 (1971): 543–62; J. M. Bumsted, "Religion, Finance, and Democracy in Massachusetts: The Town of Norton as a Case Study," *Journal of American History* 57 (1971): 830; Harry S. Stout, "Religion, Communications, and the Ideological Origins of the American Revolution," *WMQ* 34 (1977): 525–32; C. C. Goen, *Revivalism and Separatism in New England, 1740–1800: Strict Congregationalists and Separate Baptists in the Great Awakening* (New Haven, 1962), p. 55; Peter Onuf, "New Lights in New London: A Group Portrait of the Separatists," *WMQ* 37 (1980): 627–43; Alan Heimert, *Religion and the American Mind: From the Revival to the Revolution* (Cambridge, Mass., 1966); William McLaughlin, *New England Dissent, 1630–1830* (Cambridge, Mass., 1971). On Marsh, see Shipton, *Biographical Sketches*, vol. 10, pp. 300–306.

25. Heywood, *History of Westminster,* pp. 110–12; Shipton, *Biographical Sketches,* vol. 10, pp. 301–2.

26. William Pratt to Nathan Stone, May 2, 1747, Stone Mss., Massachusetts Historical Society, Boston; "Charges alleged against the Rev. Elisha Marsh," reprinted in Heywood, *History of Westminster,* pp. 111–13; Shipton, *Biographical Sketches,* vol. 10, pp. 301–2.

27. William Baldwin to Nathan Stone, Oct. 12, 1747, Stone Mss.; "Council of five Churches," Oct. 23, 1747, reprinted in Heywood, *History of Westminster,* pp. 111–13; Shipton, *Biographical Sketches,* vol. 10, pp. 301–3; Heywood, *History of Westminster,* pp. 115–19; Feb. 7, 1749, Court of General Sessions of the Peace, Worcester.

28. Petition of Joseph Holden and others, February 1744, Mass. Archives, vol. 115, p. 192; Sept. 10, 1740, Jan. 19, 1742, Sept. 19, 1744, Apr. 16, 1745, Proprietors' Records, 1728–1756, pp. 114, 136, 142, 147; Heywood, *History of Westminster,* pp. 75–76.

29. Mass. Archives, vol. 115, pp. 681–83; Heywood, *History of Westminster,* pp. 79–80; General Court Visitation, 1751, Mass. Archives, vol. 16, pp. 113–15.

30. Petition of several proprietors of land, May 28, 1755, Mass. Archives, vol. 117, p. 127, also reprinted in Heywood, *History of Westminster,* p. 87; Petition of Inhabitants to the General Court, Mar. 23, 1756, Mass. Archives, vol. 117, p. 123; Petition of Inhabitants, May 26, 1756, Mass. Archives, vol. 17, p. 125; Report of Committee, Apr. 20, 1756, Mass. Archives, vol. 117, pp. 128–29.

31. Proprietors' Records, 1728–1756; Heywood, *History of Westminster,* pp. 119–21; Church Council, Nov. 23, 1757, Canton Church Records, quoted in Shipton, *Biographical Sketches,* vol. 10, p. 304.

32. Heywood, *History of Westminster,* p. 122.

33. Petition of Inhabitants, Aug. 15, 1759, Mass. Archives, vol. 117, pp. 510–11, and reprinted in Heywood, *History of Westminster,* p. 89; Act of Incorporation, Mass. Archives, vol. 117, p. 473; Answer of Non-residents to Petition of Inhabitants, Jan. 9, 1760, Mass. Archives, vol. 117, pp. 513–15; Heywood, *History of Westminster,* pp. 90–91.

34. Abner Holden to Nonresidents, Jan. 1760, Mass. Archives, vol. 117, p. 516; Committee Report, Feb. 8, 1760, Mass. Archives, vol. 117, pp. 520–22; Heywood, *History of Westminster,* pp. 129–32, 137–38.

35. Heywood, *History of Westminster,* p. 123; Shipton, *Biographical Sketches,* vol. 10, pp. 305–6; Judson Rich, *Historical Discourse in Westminster* (Springfield, Mass., 1869), p. 85.

36. We can trace the progress of Westminster's farmers, families, and farms through the censuses and town valuations generated by the demands of Boston and London. Robert V. Wells, *The Population of the British Colonies in America before 1776* (Princeton, 1975); Bettye Hobbs Pruitt, ed., *Massachusetts Tax Valuation List of 1771* (Boston, 1978); Susan Geib, "'Changing Works': Agriculture and Society in Brookfield, Massachusetts, 1785–1820" (Ph.D. diss., Boston University, 1981); Bettye Hobbs Pruitt, "Agriculture and Society in Towns of Massachusetts, 1771: A Statistical Analysis" (Ph.D. diss., Boston University, 1981); Evarts B. Greene and Virginia D. Harrington, *American Population before the Federal Census of 1790* (New York, 1932); J. Potter, "The Growth of Population in America, 1700–1860," in D. Glass and D. Eversley, eds., *Population in History* (London, 1965), pp. 631–88; Daniel Scott Smith, "The Demographic History of Colonial New England," *Journal of Economic History* 32 (1972): 165–83; David W. Galenson, "The Settlement and Growth of the Colonies: Population, Labor, and Economic Development," in Stanley L. Engerman and Robert E. Gallman, eds., *The Cambridge Economic History of the United States,* vol. 1, *The Colonial Era* (Cambridge, 1996), pp. 135–208.

37. Greene and Harrington, *American Population*, pp. 21–30; Philip Greven, "The Average Size of Families and Households in the Province of Massachusetts in 1764 and in the United States in 1790," in Peter Laslett and Richard Wall, eds., *Household and Family in Past Time* (Cambridge, 1972), p. 552; Robert V. Wells, "Family Size and Fertility Control in Eighteenth-Century America: A Study of Quaker Families," *Population Studies* 25 (1971): 73–82; Greven, *Four Generations*, p. 177; Robert Gross, "The Problem of Agricultural Crisis in Eighteenth-Century New England: Concord, Massachusetts, as a Test Case" (paper presented at the annual meeting of the American Historical Association, Atlanta, Ga., 1975), p. 7; Jedrey, *World of John Cleaveland*; Greven, "Average Size of Families and Households in the Province of Massachusetts"; on Westminster population estimates, see Heywood, *History of Westminster*, pp. 479–81.

38. Steinitz, "Landmark and Shelter," pp. 124–27, 200–40; "Fairbanks Moore House," Inventory of Historic Assets of the Commonwealth of Massachusetts [hereafter, cited as IHACM], Westminster Form B50; "William Bemis House," IHACM, Westminster Form 144; "Nathan Wood House," National Register of Historic Places Inventory-Nomination Form, Massachusetts Historic Commission, Boston.

39. General Court Visitation, 1751, Mass. Archives, vol. 116, p. 113; Joseph Wood, "Village and Community in Early Colonial New England," *Journal of Historical Geography* 8 (1982): 333–46; David Grayson Allen, *In English Ways: The Movement of Societies and the Transferal of English Local Law and Custom to Massachusetts Bay in the Seventeenth Century* (Chapel Hill, N.C., 1981). Westminster Tax Assessment, Dec. 17, 1759, Misc. Bound Mss., 1756–1760; Gross, "Agricultural Crisis in Eighteenth Century New England." Farmers are defined here as individuals with taxable real estate and livestock holdings.

40. Westminster Tax Assessment, Dec. 17, 1759, Misc. Bound Mss., 1756–1760. On Hoar, see Worcester County Land Deeds; Heywood, *History of Westminster*; General Court Visitation, 1751, Mass. Archives, vol. 116, p. 113.

41. Diary of Abijah Bigelow, folder 3, box 1, Bigelow Family Papers, American Antiquarian Society, Worcester, Massachusetts; Westminster Tax Assessment, Dec. 17, 1759, Misc. Bound Mss., 1756–1760; Heywood, *History of Westminster*, pp. 548–52.

42. Westminster Valuation, 1771, incomplete, Mass. Archives, vol. 134, p. 301, also reprinted in Pruitt, ed., *Massachusetts Tax Valuation List of 1771*. Percy Wells Bidwell and John I. Falconer, *History of Agriculture in the Northern United States, 1620–1860* (Washington, D.C., 1925); Russell, *A Long Deep Furrow*; Carolyn Merchant, *Ecological Revolutions: Nature, Gender, and Science in New England* (Chapel Hill, N.C., 1989); Pruitt, "Agriculture and Society in the Towns of Massachusetts"; Geib, "'Changing Works'"; Max George Schumacher, *The Northern Farmer and His Markets during the Late Colonial Period* (New York, 1975); Winifred B. Rothenberg, "The Emergence of Farm Labor Markets and the Transformation of the Rural Economy: Massachusetts, 1750–1855," *Journal of Economic History* 48 (1988): 544–63; Winifred Barr Rothenberg, *From Market Places to a Market Economy: The Transformation of Rural Massachusetts, 1750–1850* (Chicago, 1992).

43. Westminster Valuation, 1771, incomplete, Mass. Archives, vol. 134, p. 301; Pruitt, "Agriculture and Society in the Towns of Massachusetts"; Gross, "Problem of Agricultural Crisis in Eighteenth-Century New England"; J. Ritchie Garrison, "Farm Dynamics and Regional Exchange: The Connecticut Valley Beef Trade, 1670–1850," *Agricultural History* 61 (1987): 1–17. Bettye Hobbs Pruitt, "Self-Sufficiency and the Agricultural Economy of Eighteenth-Century Massachusetts," *WMQ* 41 (1984): 33–64; James A. Henretta, "Families and Farms: *Mentalité* in Pre-Industrial America," *WMQ* 35 (1978): 3–22; Vickers, "Competency and Competition"; Michael Merrill, "'Cash is Good to Eat': Self-Sufficiency in the Rural Economy of the United States," *Radical History Review* 4 (1977): 52–64; Christopher Clark, *The Roots of Rural Capitalism: Western Massachusetts, 1780–1860* (Ithaca, N.Y., 1990).

44. All data is taken from the following sources: "The Number of Inhabitance Distinguishing white from black, the number of acres in the Town of Westminster in the year 1783 as taken by us," Mass. Archives, vol. 233; "Valuation and Rate Bill for 1783," State Library, Boston; On the 1784 Valuation, see "A List of the Polls and of the Estates, Real and Personal . . . Westminster, Dec. 9, 1784," Assessments, General Court, Mass. Archives; John Demos, "Families in Colonial Bristol, Rhode Island: An Exercise in Historical Demography," *WMQ* 25 (1968): 40–57; Clark, *Roots of Rural Capitalism*; Thomas Dublin, *Transforming Women's Work: New England Lives in the Industrial Revolution* (Ithaca, N.Y., 1994); Allan Kulikoff, *The Agrarian Origins of American Capitalism* (Charlottesville, Va., 1992).

45. On Cowee, see Heywood, *History of Westminster,* pp. 591–92; Esther Moore, *History of Gardner, Massachusetts* (Gardner, Mass., n.d.).

46. Heywood, *History of Westminster,* pp. 520, 521, 591–92; Waters, "Family, Inheritance, and Migration in Colonial New England"; Jedrey, *World of John Cleaveland;* Fred Anderson, "A People's Army: Provincial Military Service in Massachusetts during the Seven Years' War," *WMQ* 40 (1983): 499–527; Douglas Lamar Jones, "The Strolling Poor: Transiency in Eighteenth-Century Massachusetts," *Journal of Social History* 8 (1975): 28–54; Pruitt, "Self-Sufficiency and the Agricultural Economy"; Vickers, "Competency and Competition."

47. Heywood, *History of Westminster,* pp. 548–50; Geib, "Changing Works," p. 49.

48. Virginia DeJohn Anderson, *New England's Generation: The Great Migration and the Formation of Society and Culture in the Seventeenth Century* (New York, 1991); Heywood, *History of Westminster,* pp. 522–28.

49. Heywood, *History of Westminster,* pp. 697–702; Gross, *Minutemen and Their World.*

50. Heywood, *History of Westminster,* pp. 590–92, 904–6; Thomas C. Thompson, "The Life Course and Labour of a Colonial Farmer," *Historical New Hampshire* 40 (1985): 135–55; Paul G. E. Clemens and Lucy Simler, "Rural Labor and the Farm Household in Chester County, Pennsylvania, 1750–1820," in Stephen Innes, ed., *Work and Labor in Early America* (Chapel Hill, N.C., 1988), pp. 106–43.

51. Grant, *Democracy in the Frontier Town of Kent,* p. 53.

52. Charles E. Clark, *The Eastern Frontier: The Settlement of Northern New England, 1610–1763* (Hanover, N.H., 1983).

53. Charles Hudson, *A History of the Town of Westminster, from its First Settlement to the Present Time* (Mendon, Mass., 1832), pp. 20–21.

54. Peter Whitney, *History of Worcester County* (Worcester, Mass., 1793), pp. v–vi.

55. David D. Hall, "Reassessing the Local History of New England," in Roger Parks, ed., *New England: A Bibliography of Its History* (Hanover, N.H., 1989), vol. 7, pp. xx–xxi; Lawrence Buell, *New England Literary Culture: From Revolution through Renaissance* (New York, 1986), pp. 195–96; Nina Baym, *American Women Writers and the Work of History, 1790–1860* (New Brunswick, N.J., 1995); George Calcott, *History in the United States, 1800–1860: Its Practice and Purpose* (Baltimore, 1970).

56. Hudson, *History of Westminster;* Patricia Cline Cohen, *A Calculating People: The Spread of Numeracy in Early America* (Chicago, 1982).

57. Hudson, *History of Westminster,* pp. 11, 17.

58. Ibid., pp. 19–21.

59. Ibid.

60. Ibid., pp. 34–41.

Part 3. The Creation of Greater New England

1. Bernard Bailyn, *Voyagers to the West: A Passage in the Peopling of America on the Eve of the Revolution* (New York, 1986), pp. 9–10; D. W. Meinig, *Atlantic America, 1492–1800* (New Haven, 1986), p. 289.

Chapter 5. New England Moves North

1. *Cornwallis Township Records, MG 9, B-9, Public Archives of Canada, Ottawa* [hereafter, cited as PAC], quoted in Gordon T. Stewart, ed., *Documents Relating to the Great Awakening in Nova Scotia, 1760–1791* (Toronto, 1982), p. xv. J. B. Brebner, *The Neutral Yankees of Nova Scotia: A Marginal Colony during the Revolutionary Years* (New York, 1937); Ian MacKinnon, *Settlements and Churches in Nova Scotia* (Montreal, 1930); W. S. MacNutt, *The Atlantic Provinces* (Toronto, 1965); George A. Rawlyk, *Nova Scotia's Massachusetts: A Study of Massachusetts–Nova Scotia Relations, 1630–1784* (Montreal, 1973); Graeme Wynn, "A Province Too Much Dependent on New England," *Canadian Geographer* 31 (1987): 98–113; D. W. Meinig, *Atlantic America, 1492–1800* (New Haven, 1986), p. 274; Margaret Conrad, ed., *They Planted Well: New England Planters in Maritime Canada* (Fredericton, N.B., 1988); David C. Harvey, "The Struggle for the New England Form of Town Government," *Canadian Historical Association Annual Report* (1933): 15–22.

2. Orderly Book of Captain Abijah Willard, reprinted in Henry Stedman Nourse, ed., *The Military Annals of Lancaster, Massachusetts* (Lancaster, Mass., 1889), p. 48; also reprinted, "Journal of Abijah Willard," *Collections of the New Brunswick Historical Society* 13 (1930): 1–75; Andrew Hill Clark, *Acadia: The Geography of Early Nova Scotia to 1760* (Madison, 1968); Naomi E. S. Griffiths, *The Contexts of Acadian History, 1686–1784* (Montreal, 1992); J. Diagle, "Acadian Marshland Settlement," in R. C. Harris, ed., *The Historical Atlas of Canada* (Toronto, 1987), plate 29; Dale Miguelon, *New France, 1701–1744: A Supplement to Europe* (Toronto, 1987); John Robert McNeill, *Atlantic Empires of France and Spain: Louisbourg and Havana, 1700–1763* (Chapel Hill, 1983); L. F. S. Upton, *Micmacs and Colonists: Indian-White Relations in the Maritimes, 1713–1760* (Vancouver, 1979); Olive Patricia Dickason, "Amerindians between French and English in Nova Scotia, 1713–1763," *American Indian Culture and Research Journal* 10 (1986): 31–56; Brebner, *New England's Outpost* (New York, 1927); Wynn, "Province Too Much Dependent," pp. 98–101; Stephen E. Patterson, "1744–1763: Colonial Wars and Aboriginal Peoples," in Phillip A. Bucker and John G. Reid, eds., *The Atlantic Region to Confederation: A History* (Toronto, 1994), pp. 125–55; Winthrop Bell, *The "Foreign Protestants" and the Settlement of Nova Scotia* (Toronto, 1961).

3. Governor Charles Lawrence, in Executive Council Minutes, Oct. 12, 1758, vol. 9, p. 103, PAC; Lawrence Proclamation, *Boston News-Letter*, Nov. 2, 1758, quoted in Rawlyk, *Nova Scotia's Massachusetts*, p. 218; Governor Charles Lawrence, *A Proclamation: Whereas since the issuing of the proclamation dated the twelfth day of October 1758 . . .* (Boston, 1759); Meinig, *Atlantic America*, pp. 270–74.

4. Lawrence, *Proclamation;* Harvey, "Struggle for the New England Form," pp. 15–22; Executive Council Minutes, Jan. 11, 1759, vol. 9, p. 129; Colonial Office Papers, Feb 5, 1759, vol. 63, p. 1, PAC; Elizabeth Mancke, "Corporate Structure and Private Interest: The Mid-Eighteenth Century Expansion of New England," in Conrad, *They Planted Well*, pp. 163–64.

5. MacKinnon, *Settlements and Churches*, p. 2; R. S. Longley, "The Coming of the New England Planters to the Annapolis Valley," in Conrad, *They Planted Well*, pp. 14–28; Stewart, *Great Awakening*, p. xiv; A. W. H. Eaton, "The Settling of Colchester County, Nova Scotia, by New England Puritans and Ulster Scotsmen," *Royal Society of Canada Transactions* 6 (1912): 221–65; Colonial Office Papers, Apr. 20, Sept. 20, Dec. 20, 1759, vol. 63, pp. 1, 80–81, 160, PAC; Executive Council Minutes, Jan. 11, Feb. 18, July 16, 1759, Aug. 15, 1760, vol. 9, pp. 129, 150, 208, vol. 10, p. 246; Genealogical data from Wynn, "Province Too Much Dependent," p. 102; J. S. Martell, "Pre-Loyalist Settlements around the Minas Basin" (M.A. thesis, Dalhousie University, 1933); Esther Wright, *Planters and Pioneers: Nova Scotia, 1749–1775* (Hantsport, N.S., 1982); *Boston News-Letter*, Jan. 31, 1760; C. B. Fergusson, "Pre-Revolutionary Settlements in Nova Scotia," *Collections of the Nova Scotia Historical Society* 37 (1970), p. 17; Debra McNabb, "Land and Families in Horton Township, Nova Scotia, 1760–1830" (M.A. thesis, University of British Columbia, 1986), pp. 19–21; McNabb, "The Role of the Land in the Development of Horton Township, 1760–1775," in Conrad, *They Planted Well*, p. 152. Also, on land systems, see Carol Campbell, "A Scots-Irish Plantation in Nova Scotia: Truro, 1760–1775," pp. 153–64; Barry Moody, "Land, Kinship, and Inheritance in Granville Township, 1760–1800," pp. 165–79, in Margaret Conrad, ed., *Making Adjustments: Change and Continuity in Planter Nova Scotia, 1759–1800* (Fredericton, N.B., 1991).

6. D. M. Brown, "From Yankee to Nova Scotian: Simeon Perkins of Liverpool, Nova Scotia, 1762–1796" (M.A. thesis, Queen's University, 1978); Mancke, "Corporate Structure and Private Interest," p. 167; Mancke, "Two Patterns of Transformation: Machias, Maine, and Liverpool, Nova Scotia, 1760–1820" (Ph.D. diss., Johns Hopkins University, 1989); Charles Morris, "State and Condition of the Province of Nova Scotia, 29th October, 1763," *Report of the Public Archives of Nova Scotia, 1933* (Halifax, 1934), app. B, p. 25; Wynn, "Province Too Much Dependent," pp. 101–4.

7. Chester Branch of the Women's Institute of Nova Scotia, *History of Chester* (Lunenburg, 1967), pp. 51–61; Chester Township Records, MG 100, vol. 120, file 39g, Public Archives of Nova Scotia, Halifax [hereafter, cited as PANS]; John Seccombe, "Journal," Family Papers: Seccombe, MG 1, vol. 797C, #1, p. 13, PANS (typescript in Seccombe Family Papers, American Antiquarian Society, Worcester; reprinted in *Report of the Public Archives of Nova Scotia* [Halifax, 1959], app. B, pp. 18–47); "Memoranda of leading events by a member of the Seccombe family, Harvard and Chester, Nova Scotia, 1755 to 1770, by Miss Seccombe daughter of Rev. John Seccombe," Family Papers: Seccombe, MG 1, vol. 797C, #2, p. 3;

Gwendolyn Davies, "Poet to Pulpit to Planter: The Peregrinations of the Reverend John Seccombe," in Conrad, *Making Adjustments,* pp. 189–97.

8. Women's Institute, History of Chester, p. 51; Mary Byers, *Atlantic Hearth: Early Homes and Families of Nova Scotia* (Toronto, 1994), pp. 91–96; Mather DesBrisay, *History of the County of Lunenburg* (Toronto, 1895); Catherine Fitch et. al., *Chester: A Pictorial History of a Nova Scotia Village* (Halifax, 1983); Everett M. Backman, *225 Years in Chester Basin, 1760–1985* (Halifax, 1986); Clifford Oxner and Ruth Oxner, *Chester Basin Memories, 1749–1989* (Chester Basin, 1989).

9. On Prescott: *History of Chester,* pp. 26, 61; DesBrisay, *History of County of Lunenburg;* Thomas Haliburton, *A General Description of Nova Scotia* (Halifax, 1823), p. 90.

10. Shoreham Township Grant, Chester Township Records, MG 100, vol. 120, file 39g, PANS; Mancke, "Corporate Structure and Private Interest," p. 165.

11. Ernest P. Webber, *Genealogy of the Houghton Family* (Halifax, 1896), Charles Edward Church, *History and Genealogy of the Houghton Family* (Halifax, 1896); in vertical file, V. 100, #21, PANS; "Genealogy of Houghton," manuscript, MG 100, vol. 31, 43, p. 49, PANS; Micro: Biography: "Smith, Cottnam," Papers, #4, PANS; Robert Anderson, *Directions of a Town* (Harvard, 1976), p. 36.

12. Women's Institute, *History of Chester,* p. 28; DesBrisay, *History of the County of Lunenburg;* Chester Township Book, MG 100, vol. 120, PANS; Executive Council Minutes, June 6, 1761, Mar. 3, 1762, vol. 10, p. 213, vol. 12, p. 10, PAC.

13. Belcher to Board of Trade, June 16 and Dec. 12, 1760, Colonial Office Papers, MG 11, vol. 64, pp. 178, 196, 262, 268; Belcher to Lords of Trade, Apr. 10, 1761, vol. 65, p. 180, PAC; John Collier, Charles Morris, Henry Newton, and Michael Francklin to Governor-elect Henry Ellis, Nov. 23, 1762, Nova Scotia State Papers A, vol. 69, p. 184, PAC, quoted in Brebner, *Neutral Yankees,* p. 50.

14. Seccombe, "Journal," pp. 1–6; Davies, "Gendered Responses," pp. 132–40; Bell, "Foreign Protestants," pp. 401–86; DesBrisay, *History of the County of Lunenburg;* Grant Wanzel, *Lunenburg Memories: Buildings, Places, Events* (Halifax, 1989); Richard Henning Field, "Claiming Rank: The Display of Wealth and Status by Eighteenth-Century Lunenburg, Nova Scotia, Merchants," *Material History Review* 35 (1992): 1–3; Kenneth Paulsen, "Land, Family, and Inheritance in Lunenburg Township, Nova Scotia, 1760–1800," in *Intimate Relations,* pp. 110–21.

15. Seccombe, "Diary," pp. 1, 7–8.

16. Ibid., pp. 16–19; Susan Buggey, "John Seccombe," *Dictionary of Canadian Biography* (Toronto, 1979), vol. 4, pp. 704–5; Clifford Shipton, *Biographical Sketches of Graduates of Harvard University* (Boston, Mass., 1951), vol. 8, pp. 485–88; Davies, "Poet to Pulpit to Planter."

17. Shipton, *Biographical Sketches,* vol. 8, pp. 485–88; Anderson, *Directions of a Town,* pp. 41–43, 58–59; Henry Stedman Nourse, *History of the Town of Harvard, Massachusetts* (Harvard, Mass., 1892), pp. 182–89; Davies, "From Poet to Pulpit to Planter," p. 191.

18. Shipton, *Biographical Sketches,* vol. 8, pp. 485–88; Anderson, *Directions of a Town,* pp. 41–43, 58–59; Nourse, *History of the Town of Harvard,* pp. 182–94; Davies, "From Poet to Pulpit to Planter," pp. 191–93; *Christian History* 2 (1744), pp. 13–21; Francis G. Walett, ed., *The Diary of Ebenezer Parkman: 1703–1782* (Worcester, Mass., 1974), pp. 60–62, 156.

19. Executive Council Minutes, May 4, 1762, vol. 11, p. 91; regulations for settlers, Aug. 15, 1761, vol. 10, p. 246, PAC; "Plan of the Townships of New Dublin, Lunenburg, and Chester," V. 7/230, Map Collection, PANS; Joan Dawson, "The Mapping of the Planter Settlements in Nova Scotia," in Conrad, *Making Adjustments,* p. 214; Mancke, "Corporate Structure and Private Interest," p. 164; Harvey, "Struggle for the New England Form," p. 18.

20. Memorial, Liverpool Township, July 24, 1762, Executive Council Minutes, vol. 12, p. 43, PAC; Harvey, "Struggle for the New England Form," pp. 20–21; Brebner, *Neutral Yankees,* p. 215.

21. "State and Condition of Nova Scotia, 1763," *Report of the Public Archives of Nova Scotia,* 1933, app. B, p. 23.

22. Brebner, *Neutral Yankees,* pp. 214–16.

23. Belcher to Lords of Trade, Jan. 11, 1762, Colonial Office Papers, vol. 67, pp. 25–26, PAC; Charles Morris, "State and Condition of Nova Scotia, 1763," *Report of the Public Archives of Nova Scotia,* 1933, app. B, pp. 21–28.

24. Morris, "State and Condition of Nova Scotia, 1763," pp. 21–28; Brebner, *Neutral Yankees,* p. 64.

25. J. M. Bumsted, "1763–1783: Resettlement and Rebellion," in *Atlantic Region to Confederation,* p. 159; Wynn, "Province Too Much Dependent," p. 103.

26. Brebner, *Neutral Yankees,* chap. 5; Bernard Bailyn, *Voyagers to the West* (New York, 1986), chap. 11; Wynn, "Province Too Much Dependent," p. 103; Bumsted, "1763–1783: Resettlement and Rebellion," pp. 157–59.

27. Wynn, "Province Too Much Dependent," p. 104 (graphical mapping of 1767 returns); "A General Return of the Several Townships in the Province of Nova Scotia, the first of January 1767," RG 1, vol. 443, doc. 1, PANS; Return of Proprietors, Chester, Jan. 1764, RG 20, ser. C, vol. 90a, #4, PANS; vertical file, V. 58, #3, PANS; DesBrisay, *History of the County of Lunenburg,* pp. 264–65; Brebner, *Neutral Yankees,* p. 81; Robert V. Wells, *The Population of the British Colonies in America before 1776: A Survey of the Census Data* (Princeton, 1975), pp. 60–63; Meinig, *Atlantic America,* p. 274; Clark, *Acadia,* pp. 364–67; M. Wade, "After the Grand Derangement: The Acadians Return to the Gulf of St. Lawrence and to Nova Scotia," *American Review of Canadian Studies* 5 (1975): 42–65; Griffiths, *Contexts of Acadian History;* Wynn, "Pre-Loyalist Nova Scotia," *Historical Atlas of Canada,* plate 31.

28. Lewis R. Fischer, "Revolution without Independence: The Canadian Colonies, 1749–1775," in Ronald Hoffman et al., eds., *The Economy of Early America: The Revolutionary Period, 1763–1790* (Charlottesville, Va., 1988), pp. 112–13; Wynn, "Province Too Much Dependent," pp. 107–8; John J. McCusker and Russell R. Menard, *The Economy of British North America, 1607–1789* (Chapel Hill, 1985), pp. 111–16; John Reid, "Change and Continuity in Nova Scotia, 1758–1775," in Conrad, *Making Adjustments,* pp. 45–69; Julian Gwyn, "Economic Fluctuations in Wartime Nova Scotia, 1755–1815," in Conrad, *Making Adjustments,* pp. 72–81.

29. Francklin to Lords of Trade, Sept. 30, 1766, Colonial Office Papers, vol. 78, pp. 112–15; Wynn, "Province Too Much Dependent," p. 107; McNabb, "Land and Families in Horton," pp. 69–70; Brebner, *Neutral Yankees,* p. 109; A. R. Macneill, "Early American Communities on the Fundy: A Case Study of Annapolis and Amherst Townships, 1767–1827," *Agricultural History* 62 (1989): 101–18; Graeme Wynn, "Late Eighteenth Century Agriculture on the Bay of Fundy Marshlands," *Acadiensis* 8 (1979): 80–89; A. R. Macneill, "The Acadian Legacy and Agricultural Development in Nova Scotia, 1760–1861," in Kris Inwood, ed., *Farm and Factory* (Fredericton, N.B., 1995), pp. 1–16.

30. DesBrisay, *History of the County of Lunenburg,* pp. 264–65; Wynn, "Province Too Much Dependent," pp. 107–8; Rawlyk, *Nova Scotia's Massachusetts,* pp. 224–25; Fischer, "Revolution without Independence," pp. 112–13; on sawmills, see "List of Sawmills Built in 1786 and 1787," RG 1, vol. 223, no. 156, PANS.

31. Benjamin Gerrish and Malachy Salter to Reverend Andrew Elliot, Jan. 18, 1770, *Proceedings of the Massachusetts Historical Society,* 2d ser., 4 (1888): 68; John Seccombe quoted in J. C. L. Clark, "Interesting Facts Regarding Rev. John Seccombe," *Acadiensis* 4 (1907): 339; Davies, "Poet to Pulpit to Planter," p. 194; Fred Crowell, "New Englanders in Nova Scotia," Micro, Biography: Crowell, Fred: Scrapbook; No. 89, "Seccombe," p. 97, PANS; on Seccombe Land grants, see Chester Township Records, MG 100, vol. 120, file 39g; Chester Proprietors, MG 100, vol. 120, file 39k–m, PANS.

32. Chester Township Records, MG 100, vol. 120, file 39–39r, PANS. On Horton, see Wynn, "Province Much Too Dependent," p. 102; Liverpool, McNabb, "Corporate Structure," p. 167; Winthrop Bell, Register of Lunenburg, MG 1, vol. 2, sec. 2, p. 23, PANS; Esther Wright, *Planters and Pioneers* (Hansport, N.S., 1978), p. 166; Land Grant in Return of Proprietors of Chester, 1784, MG 100, vol. 120, file 39m; Bell, *"Foreign Protestants,"* p. 416 (for Wiederholt), pp. 539–40 (for Knaut); DesBrisay, *History of the County of Lunenburg,* p. 110; Field, "Claiming Status," p. 2.

33. Walter Murray, "History of St. Matthew's Church, Halifax, N.S.," *Nova Scotia Historical Society Collections* 16 (1912), quoted in Bell, *Foreign Protestants,* pp. 599–600; John Seccombe, *A Sermon Preached at Halifax, July 3rd 1770, at the Ordination of the Rev. Bruin Romcas Comingoe, to the Dutch Calvinistic Presbyterian Church at Lunenburg* (Halifax, 1770); Ronald Rompkey, "Bruin Romkes Comingo," *Dictionary of Canadian Biography,* vol. 4, p. 199; Buggey, "Seccombe," p. 705; DesBrisay, *History of County of Lunenburg,* pp. 90–91; Bell, *Foreign Protestants,* pp. 598–600, 606; Seccombe-Comingo Correspondence, Mss., MG 100, vol. 219, #9–10; Micro: Biography, 1771–86, PANS.

34. P. Ennals and D. Holdsworth, "Vernacular Architecture and the Cultural Landscape of the Maritime Provinces: A Reconnaissance," *Acadiensis* 10 (1981): 86–106; Wynn, "A Region of Scattered Settlements," p. 331; Ronald McDonald, *Report on Selected Buildings in Mahone Bay, Nova Scotia* (Ottawa, 1977); Heritage Trust of Nova Scotia, *Seasoned Timbers* (Halifax, 1972); Blackman, *225 Years in Chester Basin*.

35. Francis Legge, Proclamation against Unlawful Meetings and Assemblies, Sept. 19, 1774, vol. 1, p. 177, PAC; Legge, Proclamation, Aug. 26, 1775, Executive Council Minutes, RG 1, vol. 189, p. 345, PANS; Houghton, "Extracts from Book Kept by Timothy Houghton," mss., Dal MS 2.135, Dalhousie University Archives, Halifax; Barry Cahill, "The Sedition Trial of Timothy Houghton: Repression in a Marginal Township during the Revolutionary Years," *Acadiensis* 24 (1994): 35–58; Bumsted, "1763–1783: Resettlement and Rebellion," pp. 168–72; Brebner, *Neutral Yankees*; George Rawlyk, "J. B. Brebner and Some Recent Trends in Eighteenth-Century Maritime Historiography," in Conrad, *They Planted Well*, pp. 97–119; Wilfred Brenton Kerr, *The Maritime Provinces of British North America and the American Revolution* (Sackville, N.B., 1942); Stewart and Rawlyk, *Nova Scotia's Massachusetts*; Ernest Clarke, *The Siege of Fort Cumberland, 1776: An Episode in the American Revolution* (Montreal, 1995).

36. Memorial of the Inhabitants of Yarmouth, Dec. 8, 1775, Colonial Office Papers, vol. 94, p. 300, PAC; on the Council, see Enclosure in letter of William Legge to Lord Dartmouth, Dec. 20, 1775, Dartmouth Papers, PANS; Fergusson, "Life of Jonathan Scott," p. 51; Gordon Stewart and George Rawlyk, *A People Highly Favoured of God* (Toronto, 1972), pp. 45–76.

37. Cumberland Remonstrance, quoted in Clarke, *Siege of Fort Cumberland*, p. 15; Bumstead, "1763–1783: Resettlement and Rebellion," p. 170.

38. Executive Council Minutes, Dec. 23, 1776, Jan. 6, 1777, MG 100, vol. 212, no. 39C, PANS; Cahill, "Trial of Timothy Houghton," p. 39; Davies, "Poet to Pulpit to Planter," p. 195; Brebner, *Neutral Yankees*, p. 340.

39. William Harrison deposition, Dec. 19, 1776, RG 1, vol. 342, no. 60, PANS; Cahill, "Trial of Timothy Houghton," pp. 44–45.

40. Depositions of William Negus, John Imlach, and Charles Adams, Jan. 10, 1777, RG 1, vol. 342, no. 61–63, PANS; Grand Jury, Jan. 28, 1777, no. 64, PANS; King versus Timothy Houghton, Esq., Supreme Court, Hilary Term, RG 1, vol. 342, no. 65, PANS; Cahill, "Trial of Timothy Houghton," p. 45.

41. Brebner, *Neutral Yankees*, p. 342; Cahill, "Trial of Timothy Houghton," pp. 45–46, 53–58.

42. H. A. Innis, ed., *Diary of Simeon Perkins, 1766–1780* (Toronto, 1948), p. xx; Bumstead, "1763–1783: Resettlement and Rebellion," pp. 170–72; Women's Institute, *History of Chester*, pp. 46–47; DesBrisay, *History of County of Lunenburg*, pp. 268–70; Stewart and Rawlyk, *A People Highly Favoured of God*, pp. 66–70.

43. Graeme Wynn, "A Region of Scattered Settlements and Bounded Possibilities: Northeastern America, 1775–1800," *Canadian Geographer* 31 (1987): 319–38; Ann Condon, "1783–1800: Loyalist Arrival, Acadian Return, Imperial Reform," in *Atlantic Region to Confederation*, pp. 184–209; Neil MacKinnon, *This Unfriendly Soil: The Loyalist Experience in Nova Scotia 1783–1791* (Kingston and Montreal, 1986); Gerald S. Graham, *Sea Power and British North America, 1783–1820: A Study on British Colonial Policy* (Cambridge, Mass., 1941).

44. *London Chronicle*, Dec. 4–7, 1784, quoted in Wynn, "A Region of Scattered Settlements," p. 323; Jacob Bailey to Dr. Morice, Nov. 3, 1784, M 23, D(1), vol. 72, PAC, quoted in MacKinnon, *This Unfriendly Soil*, pp. 40–41; Haliburton, *General Description of Nova Scotia*, p. 90; Marion Robertson, *King's Bounty: A History of Early Shelburne, Nova Scotia* (Halifax, 1983), pp. 51–82; Bumsted, "1763–1783: Resettlement and Rebellion," pp. 181–83; Condon, "Loyalist Arrival, Acadian Return, Imperial Reform," pp. 186–87.

45. S. Hollingsworth, *An Account of the Present State of Nova Scotia* (Edinburgh, 1786), pp. 18, 36, 133; Graham, *Sea Power and British North America*, pp. 28–40; MacKinnon, *This Unfriendly Soil*, pp. 140–50; Harold Hampden Robertson, "The Common Relationship between Nova Scotia and the British West Indies, 1788–1822: The Twilight of Mercantalism in the British Empire" (M.A. thesis, Dalhousie University, 1975); Condon, "Loyalist Arrival, Acadian Return, Imperial Reform," pp. 194–96.

46. Petition of Shelburne Merchants, enclosure, Parr to Granville, June 28, 1791, quoted in Graham, *Sea Power and British North America*, p. 43; Beamish Murdoch, *A History of Nova-Scotia or Acadie* (Halifax, 1865), p. 244; Barbara R. Robertson, *Sawpower: Making Lumber in the Sawmills of Nova Scotia* (Halifax, 1986), p. 30; "List of Sawmills Built in 1786

and 1787," RG 1, vol. 223, #156, PANS; Condon, "Loyalist Arrival, Acadian Return, Imperial Reform," pp. 194–96; Wynn, "A Region of Scattered Settlements," pp. 325–29; Gwyn, "Economic Fluctuations in Wartime Nova Scotia, 1755–1815," pp. 82–83; D. A. Sutherland, "Halifax Merchants and the Pursuit of Development, 1783–1850," *Canadian Historical Review* 59 (1978): 1–17.

47. Robertson, "Common Relationship, 1788–1822," p. 152; Graham, *Sea Power and British North America,* pp. 154–56; Wynn, "A Region of Scattered Settlements," pp. 326–27; MacKinnon, *This Unfriendly Soil,* pp. 150–54.

48. Condon, "Loyalist Arrival, Acadian Return, Imperial Reform," pp. 194, 206; Wynn, "A Region of Scattered Settlements," pp. 325–27; Howard K. Temperly, "Frontierism, Capital, and the American Loyalists in Canada," *Journal of American Studies* 13 (1979): 5–27; MacKinnon, *This Unfriendly Soil,* p. 169; Gwyn, "Economic Fluctuations in Wartime Nova Scotia," p. 88.

49. 1783 Assessment, reprinted in DesBrisay, *History of County of Lunenburg,* pp. 265–66. "Assessment on the Inhabitants of Chester for the Year 1794, Collected for Alexander Stuart," RG 1, vol. 444 1/2, #23; Chester Township Poll Tax List 1793, RG 1, vol. 444, #62; Chester Township Poll Tax 1791, RG 1, vol. 444, #4–5; Chester Township Poll Tax 1795, RG 444 1/2, #59; Chester Township Land Holdings, n.d., RG 20, 'C', vol. 90, #70; Chester Allotment Books, Micro# 18455, RG 47, 1761–1768; Chester Proprietors Lists, n.d., RG 20, 'C', vol. 90, #76; Proprietors List, 1780, RG 20, 'C', vol. 90, # 38; Proprietors List, RG 20, 'C', vol. 90, #48; all of the preceding archival sources are in PANS. Terrence M. Punch, "Lunenburg County, Nova Scotia: Poll Taxes of the 1790s," *Canadian Genealogist* 1 (1979): 103–14; B. L. Anderson, "The 1793 Capitation Assessment for Nova Scotia," *Nova Scotia Historical Review* 9 (1989): 18–32; Titus Smith, *Rambles at the Eastern and Northern Parts of the Province in the Years 1801 and 1802* (Halifax, 1857), pp. 139–40; Wynn, "A Region of Scattered Settlements," pp. 325–27.

50. 1783 Assessment; "Assessment for the year 1794"; Anderson, "The 1793 Capitation Assessment," pp. 18–32; Wynn "A Region of Scattered Settlements," pp. 325–27; Charles Morris, Map of Lunenburg County, 1785, PANS.

51. "Copy of Town Records," mss., Dal. MS 2.135, Dalhousie University Archives, Halifax; Women's Institute, *History of Chester,* pp. 46–47; Petition about Road Costs, 1791, RG 5, 'A', vol. 4, #37, PANS.

52. Peter Zinck, "Reminiscences," *Chronicle-Herald,* Mar. 30, 1964, quoted in B. A. Balcom, *History of the Lunenburg Fishing Industry* (Lunenburg, N.S., 1977), p. 2.

53. W. Paine to John Wentworth, Mar. 1, 1788, Wentworth Papers, MG 1, vol. 940, PANS, quoted in Wynn, "A Region of Scattered Settlements," p. 331.

54. I use the following editions of Scott's and Alline's works: Henry Scott Jr., ed., *The Journal of the Reverend Jonathan Scott* (Boston, 1980); Stewart, *Documents Relating to the Great Awakening,* pp. 4–199, which contains the entire "Records of the Church of Jebogue in Yarmouth" along with other materials on Yarmouth and Alline; see also C. B. Fergusson, ed., "The Life of Jonathan Scott," in *Bulletin of the Public Archives of Nova Scotia* (1960). The most recent edition of the Yarmouth church records is Gwen G. Trask et al., ed., *The Records of the Church of Jebogue, 1766–1851* (Yarmouth, N.S., 1992); Gwen Guiou Trask and F. Stuart Trask, "The Reverend Jonathan Scott, Planter, Preacher, and Patriarch," in Conrad, *Intimate Relations,* pp. 258–73.

55. Scott, *Journal of the Reverend Jonathan Scott,* pp. 8–10; Fergusson, "Life of Jonathan Scott," p. 8–9; Guiou and Trask, "The Reverend Jonathan Scott," pp. 268–71.

56. On Yarmouth, see Fergusson, "Life of Jonathan Scott," pp. 5–6; Stewart, *Documents Relating to the Great Awakening,* p. xxx; "Return of the Settlers with Their Stock of the Township of Yarmouth, June 1764," RG 1, vol. 222, #23, PANS; Gordon Stewart, "Socio-Economic Factors in the Great Awakening: The Case of Yarmouth, Nova Scotia," *Acadiensis* 3 (1973): 18–34.

57. Stewart, *Documents Relating to the Great Awakening,* p. 20; Daniel C. Goodwin, "From Disunity to Integration: Evangelical Religion and Society in Yarmouth, Nova Scotia, 1761–1830," in Conrad, *They Planted Well,* p. 191; Stewart and Rawlyk, *A People Highly Favoured of God,* pp. 98–120; Stewart, *Documents Relating to the Great Awakening,* pp. 13–20, 22–28; Scott, *Journal of the Reverend Jonathan Scott,* pp. 20–22.

58. Scott, *Journal of the Reverend Jonathan Scott,* pp. 10–22, 27–29; Stewart and Rawlyk, *A People Highly Favoured of God,* pp. 103–5; Stewart, *Documents Relating to the Great Awakening,* pp. 28–31.

59. Stewart, *Documents Relating to the Great Awakening*, pp. 45–64, 80, 86; "Androscoggin [Maine] Church Records," quoted in Trask, "The Reverend Jonathan Scott," p. 263; Daniel Goodwin, "Advancing Light: Evangelicalism in Yarmouth Township, 1761–1830" (M.A. thesis, Acadia University, 1986), p. 193.

60. Alline, "The Rev. Mr. Henry Alline's Life &C. (1741–1784)," reprinted in Stewart, *Documents Relating to the Great Awakening*, p. 225; on Henry Alline, see George Rawlyk, *Ravished by the Spirit: Religious Revivals, Baptists, and Henry Alline* (Montreal, 1984); Steven Marini, *Revolutionary Sects of Revolutionary New England* (Cambridge, Mass., 1982); J. M. Bumsted, *Henry Alline, 1748–1784* (Toronto, 1971); Stewart and Rawlyk, *A People Highly Favoured of God;* D. G. Bell, *Henry Alline and Maritime Religion,* Canadian Historical Association, Historical Booklet No. 51 (Ottawa, 1993).

61. Alline, "The Rev. Mr. Henry Alline's Life," in *Documents Relating to the Great Awakening*, pp. 223–79; D. C. Harvey, ed., *The Diary of Simeon Perkins, 1780–1789* (Toronto, 1958), p. 177; Bell, *Henry Alline*, pp. 9–10; Stewart and Rawlyk, *A People Highly Favoured of God*, p. 125; Rawlyk, *Ravished by the Spirit*, pp. 29–34.

62. Alline, *Two Mites on the Most Important and Much Disputed Points of Divinity, Cast into the Treasury for the Welfare of the Poor and Needy* (Halifax, N.S., 1781), pp. 150–51; Nancy Christie, "'In These Times of Democratic Rage and Delusion': Popular Religion and the Challenge to the Established Order, 1760–1815," in George A. Rawlyk, ed., *The Canadian Protestant Experience, 1760–1990* (Burlington, Ont., 1990), p. 34; Alline, quoted in George A. Rawlyk, *The Canada Fire: Radical Evangelicalism in British North America, 1775–1812* (Montreal, 1995), p. 13; Trask, *Jebogue Church Records*, p. 141; Stewart, *Documents Relating to the Great Awakening*, p. xi; Stewart and Rawlyk, *A People Highly Favoured of God*, p. 125; Rawlyk, *Ravished by the Spirit*, pp. 29–34; Bell, *Henry Alline*, pp. 13–14, Marini, *Radical Sects of Revolutionary New England*, pp. 139–44.

63. Stewart, *Documents Relating to the Great Awakening*, pp. 119–20; Goodwin, "From Disunity to Integration," p. 194.

64. Stewart, *Documents Relating to the Great Awakening*, pp. 120–23.

65. Trask, *Yarmouth Church Records*, p. 140; Christie, "'In These Times of Democratic Rage,'" p. 34; Rawlyk, *A People Highly Favoured of God*, p. 95; Bell, *Henry Alline*.

66. Jonathan Scott, *A Brief View of the Religious Tenets And Sentiments Lately Published and Spread in the Province of Nova Scotia* (Halifax, N.S., 1784), pp. 84, 162, 206–7, 255, 330; Alline, *Two Mites;* Stewart, *Documents Relating to the Great Awakening*, pp. 119–20, 142; Maurice Armstrong, "Jonathan Scott's 'Brief View,'" *Harvard Theological Review* 40 (1947): 120–36; Goodwin, "Advancing Light: Evangelicalism in Yarmouth Township"; Trask, "The Reverend Jonathan Scott," pp. 264–65.

67. Stewart, *Documents Relating to the Great Awakening*, pp. 138, 144–45; Scott, *A Brief View*, pp. 168, 256; Christie, "'In These Times of Democratic Rage,'" p. 34; Goodwin, "Advancing Light"; Stewart and Rawlyk, *A People Highly Favoured of God*, pp. 98–120; Bell, *Henry Alline*.

68. Alline, *Two Mites*, pp. 264–65, quoted in Stewart and Rawlyk, *A People Highly Favoured of God*, pp. 159–61.

69. Henry Alline, "A Sermon on a Day of Thanksgiving Preached at Liverpool, November 21, 1782," reprinted in George A. Rawlyk, ed., *Henry Alline: Selected Writings* (New York, 1987), pp. 126, 130; Alline, "The Rev. Mr. Henry Alline's Life," in *Documents Relating to the Great Awakening*, p. 245; George A. Rawlyk, "'A Total Revolution in Religious and Civil Government': The Maritimes, New England, and the Evolving Evangelical Ethos, 1776–1812," in Mark A. Noll, David W. Bebbington, and George A. Rawlyk, eds., *Evangelicalism: Comparative Studies of Popular Protestantism in North America, the British Isles, and Beyond, 1700–1900* (New York, 1994), pp. 137–55.

70. Marini, *Revolutionary Sects*, p. 43; Stewart, *Documents Relating to the Great Awakening*, pp. 144–45; Stewart and Rawlyk, *A People Highly Favoured of God*, pp. 98–120; Goodwin, "Advancing Light"; Trask, "The Reverend Jonathan Scott," p. 267; Scott, *Journal of the Reverend Jonathan Scott*, p. xvii.

71. Henry Alline, "Life and Journal," in Stewart, *Documents Relating to the Great Awakening*, pp. 281–85; Rawlyk, *Ravished by the Spirit*, pp. 41, 57–58, 68; Marini, *Radical Sects of Revolutionary New England*, pp. 41–43, 158–62; Bell, *Henry Alline*, pp. 16–17; Alline, *Selected Hymns and Spiritual Songs of Henry Alline,* ed. Thomas Vincent (Kingston, Ont.,

1982); Thomas B. Vincent, "Henry Alline: Problems of Approach and Reading the Hymns as Poetry," in Conrad, *They Planted Well,* pp. 201–10.

72. Scott, *Journal of the Reverend Jonathan Scott,* pp. xviii–xxii; Trask, "The Reverend Jonathan Scott," pp. 267–68; Rawlyk, *Ravished by the Spirit,* pp. 86–105; Rawlyk, *Canada Fire,* p. 134; Goodwin, "From Disunity to Integration"; George E. Levy, ed., *Diary and Related Writings of the Reverend Joseph Dimock* (Hantsport, 1979); George A. Rawlyk, "From New Light to Baptist: Harris Harding and the Second Great Awakening in Nova Scotia," in Barry Moody, ed., *Repent and Believe: The Baptist Experience in Maritime Canada* (Hantsport, 1990), pp. 1–26; Christie, "'In These Times of Democratic Rage.'"

Chapter 6. Town Founding and the Village Enlightenment

1. Jeremy Belknap, *The History of New-Hampshire* (1792; New York, 1970), vol. 3, p. 251.
2. Charles E. Clark, *The Eastern Frontier: The Settlement of Northern New England, 1610–1763* (Hanover, N.H., 1983), pp. 169–79; Jere Daniell, *Colonial New Hampshire: A History* (Millwood, N.Y., 1981), pp. 133–64; Douglas Leach, *The Northern Colonial Frontier, 1607–1765* (New York, 1966), pp. 125–27; Roy Hidemachi Akagi, *The Town Proprietors of the New England Colonies* (Philadelphia, 1924); Lois Kimball Mathews [Rosenberry], *The Expansion of New England* (Boston, 1909).
3. Leach, *Northern Colonial Frontier,* pp. 125–27, 133; Daniell, *Colonial New Hampshire,* p. 108; Belknap, *History of New-Hampshire,* pp. 188–90; Douglas Leach, *Arms for Empire* (New York, 1973), pp. 133–36; *Cheshire County, N.H., 1753–1816: The Early Maps with a Narrative History of the Town Grants* (West Chesterfield, N.H., 1983), p. 3; Colin Calloway, *The Western Abenakis of Vermont, 1600–1800* (Norman, Okla., 1990), p. 26; *Cheshire County,* pp. 3–4; Akagi, *Town Proprietors,* pp. 190–96; Clark, *Eastern Frontier,* pp. 176–77; Daniell, *Colonial New Hampshire,* pp. 146–47; Matthews, *Expansion of New England,* pp. 82–83; *Acts and Resolves Passed by the Massachusetts General Court,* vol. 12, pp. 225, 232, 234, 292–93, 306–7, 342; Belknap, *History of New-Hampshire,* vol. 1, pp. 218–19. For a study of proprietors in the 1730s, see Samuel E. Morison, *Proprietors of Peterborough, N.H.* (Peterborough, N.H., 1930).
4. Daniell, *Colonial New Hampshire,* p. 157; Morison, *Proprietors of Peterborough.*
5. Henry H. Saunderson, *History of Charlestown, New-Hampshire, the Old No. 4* (Claremont, N.H., 1876), pp. 335–41, 619–20; Susannah Johnson, *A Narrative of the Captivity of Mrs. Johnson* (Bowie, Md., 1990), pp. 4–5; Doris Kirkpatrick, *The City and the River* (Fitchburg, Mass., 1971), pp. 76–77; George S. Roberts, *Historic Towns of the Connecticut River Valley* (Schenectady, N.Y., 1906); George I. Putnam, *Old Number Four* (Oxford, N.H., 1965); Ezra S. Stearns, "The Offering of Lunenburg, Mass., to Cheshire County," *Proceedings of New Hampshire Historical Society* 2 (1888–95): 95–100; Joseph Willard, *Willard Memoir, or the Life and Times of Major Simon Willard* (Boston, 1858).
6. Saunderson, *History of Charlestown,* pp. 24–32; Jaazaniah Crosby, *History of Charlestown in New-Hampshire* (Concord, N.H., 1833); Belknap, *History of New-Hampshire,* vol. 1, pp. 286–89; Rev. Benjamin Doolittle, "A Short Narrative of Mischief Done by the French and Indian Enemy on the Western Frontiers of the Province of Massachusetts Bay," *Magazine of History with Notes and Queries* 2, extra no. 7 (1909), pp. 7–11; Leach, *Northern Colonial Frontier,* pp. 92–95; Leach, *Arms for Empire,* p. 247; Johnson, *Captivity of Mrs. Johnson,* pp. 7–12; Calloway, *Western Abenaki,* pp. 3–26.
7. Daniell, *Colonial New Hampshire,* p. 135; Belknap, *History of New-Hampshire,* pp. 91, 237–39, 256–60; Thomas Hutchinson, *The History of the Colony and Province of Massachusetts Bay* (1768; Cambridge, Mass., 1936), vol. 2, p. 397; Jonathan Smith, "The Massachusetts and New Hampshire Boundary Controversy, 1693–1740," *Proceedings of the Massachusetts Historical Society* 43 (1909–10): 77–88; George Aldrich, *Walpole as It Was and as It Is* (Claremont, N.H., 1880), pp. 16–17; Henry W. Bellows, *Historical Sketch of Col. Benjamin Bellows* (New York, 1855), pp. 14–15; Dorothy A. Pettit, "Walpole, New Hampshire, as an Example of a Frontier Town in the Connecticut River Valley prior to 1800" (unpublished paper, University of New Hampshire, January 1968, in author's possession), pp. 9–10; John F. Looney, "Benning Wentworth's Land Grant Policy: A Reappraisal," *Historical New Hampshire* 13 (1968): 3–13.
8. Albert Stillman Batchellor, ed., *New Hampshire Provincial and State Papers* (Concord, N.H., 1867–1919), vol. 26, pp. 593–96; Bellows, *Historical Sketch,* pp. 16–18; Aldrich, *Walpole as It Was,* pp. 16–19.

9. "Proprietors Records, 1735–74, No. 3," New Hampshire Land Registry, Concord, N.H.; *New Hampshire State Papers,* vol. 6, pp. 25–28, 236, 264–65, 291, vol. 13, pp. 592–97; Emily Barnes, *Narratives, Traditions and Personal Reminiscences* (Boston, 1888), p. 384; Payne Kenyon Kilbourne, *The History and Antiquities of the Name and Family of Kilbourn* (New Haven, 1856), pp. 44, 81; Thomas Fessenden, "Letter," *Collections of the New Hampshire Historical Society* 2 (1825): 290; Aldrich, *Walpole as It Was,* p. 21; *New York Colonial Documents,* vol. 10, pp. 252–54; Leach, *Northern Colonial Frontier,* pp. 197–99; on Shirley, see Newcastle Papers, L, 129, Add. Mss. 32735, British Museum, quoted in Leach, *Northern Colonial Frontier,* p. 198; Charles Lincoln, *Correspondence of William Shirley, Governor of Massachusetts* (New York, 1912), vol. 2, pp. 33–39.

10. Colonel Israel Williams's letter, Sept. 12, 1754, Israel Williams Papers, vol. 1, p. 80, Massachusetts Historical Society, quoted in Lincoln, *Correspondence of William Shirley,* vol. 2, pp. 86–89; Johnson, *Captivity of Mrs. Johnson,* pp. 27–33; Calloway, *Western Abenakis,* pp. 162–65; Benjamin Bellows to Colonel Joseph Blanchard, letter of Aug. 31, 1754, quoted in Bellows, *Historical Sketch,* pp. 24–25; George Aldrich, "History of Walpole," in D. Hamilton Hurd, ed., *The History of Cheshire County, New Hampshire* (Philadelphia, 1886), pp. 412, 419. Bellows, *Historical Sketch,* pp. 24–25, 29–30; Aldrich, *Walpole as It Was,* pp. 18–30; *New Hampshire State Papers,* vol. 6, p. 313; Saunderson, *History of Charlestown,* pp. 59–61.

11. Calloway, *Western Abenakis,* pp. 170–71; Leach, *Northern Colonial Frontier,* pp. 200–201; Leach, *Arms for Empire,* pp. 351–404; Chase, *Gathered Sketches,* pp. 65–70; Saunderson, *Charlestown,* pp. 71–75; Belknap, *History of New-Hampshire,* vol. 1, p. 314.

12. Mayhew quoted in Leach, *Northern Colonial Frontier,* pp. 204–5; Calloway, *Western Abenakis,* pp. 174–87; Robert Rogers, *The Journals of Major Robert Rogers* (Ann Arbor, 1966), pp. 144–46; J. R. Brodhead and E. B. O'Callaghan, eds., *Documents Relative to the Colonial History of New York* (Albany, 1855–61), vol. 10, pp. 1033, 1042; Leach, *Arms for Empire,* pp. 415–77; Clark, *Northern Frontier,* pp. 352–55.

13. Province Deeds, *New Hampshire State Papers,* vol. 71, p. 41, vol. 77, pp. 11, 13–15, 17, 19–21; Bellows, *Historical Sketch,* pp. 21–22.

14. Province Deeds, *New Hampshire State Papers,* vol. 77, p. 21, vol. 100, p. 197; Martha McDanolds Frizzell, *A History of Walpole, New Hampshire* (Walpole, 1963), pp. 112–14.

15. Aldrich, *Walpole as It Was,* pp. 19–20; Pruitt, "Walpole, New Hampshire," p. 13; Bellows, *Historical Sketch,* p. 20.

16. On Cheshire County land records, see Bellows to Kilburn, Jan. 20, 1755, vol. 6, p. 141, Cheshire County Courthouse, Keene, N.H.; Aldrich, *Walpole as It Was,* pp. 21–24; Bellows, *Historical Sketch,* pp. 31–32; Shipton, *Biographical Sketches of Graduates of Harvard University* (Boston, 1960), vol. 11, pp. 561–62.

17. Province Deeds, *New Hampshire State Papers,* vol. 61, p. 447, vol. 65, pp. 207, 447, vol. 69, pp. 91, 99, vol. 70, p. 198, vol. 80, pp. 32, 531, vol. 86, p. 510, vol. 89, p. 283, vol. 90, p. 230; Cheshire County land records, vol. 1, pp. 10, 31, 34, 59, 62, 76, 90, 116, 142, 174, vol. 2, p. 141, vol. 3, pp. 135, 424, 427–28, 430, 446, 448, 450, 453–54, 492, vol. 4, p. 182, vol. 5, pp. 3, 6, 8, vol. 6, pp. 42, 59, 88–90, 103, 120, 139, 141, 144, 165, 179, 187, 242, 360, 434–36, 453; Frizzell, *History of Walpole,* pp. 6–8, 114.

18. Harry J. Carman, ed., *American Husbandry* (1775; New York, 1939), p. 36; Aldrich, "History of Walpole," p. 427; Barnes, *Narratives,* p. 354; Fanning account in *Cheshire Gazette* (1826), reprinted in Bellows, *Historical Sketch,* pp. 38–39.

19. Barnes, *Narratives,* p. 354; Bellows, *Historical Sketch,* pp. 36–37; Aldrich, *Walpole as It Was;* Shipton, *Biographical Sketches* (Boston, 1960), vol. 11, pp. 561–62.

20. Fanning in Bellows, *Historical Sketch,* pp. 38–39; Aldrich, "History of Walpole," pp. 421–22.

21. Shipton, *Biographical Sketches* (Boston, 1968), vol. 14, pp. 257–58; Aldrich, *Walpole as It Was,* pp. 36–37.

22. Bellows, *Historical Sketch;* Emily Barnes, *Narratives, Traditions and Personal Reminiscences* (Boston, 1888); Thomas Bellows Peck, *The Bellows Genealogy* (Keene, N.H., 1898); Aldrich, *Walpole As It Was;* Frizzell, *History of Walpole;* Bellows Mss., New Hampshire Historical Society, Concord, N. H.; Looney, "Benning Wentworth's Land Grant Policy"; Jere Daniell, *Experiment in Republicanism: New Hampshire Politics and the American Revolution* (Cambridge, Mass., 1970).

23. Aldrich, "History of Walpole," pp. 446–47, *Walpole as It Was,* pp. 50–51, 159–62; Bellows, *Historical Sketch,* pp. 43–44, 54–55, 68–69.

24. On the Green Mountain struggle against New York, see Michael A. Bellesiles, *Revolutionary Outlaws: Ethan Allen and the Struggle for Independence on the Early American Frontier* (Charlottesville, 1993), pp. 105–11; Benjamin Hall, *History of Eastern Vermont* (New York, 1858), pp. 209–37; E. P. Walton, *Records of the Governor and Council of the State of Vermont* (Montpelier, 1874), vol. 1, pp. 332–38; *Documentary History of New York*, vol. 4, pp. 905–14. On the struggle between Vermont and New Hampshire, see Belknap, *History of New-Hampshire*, vol. 1, pp. 385–95; Jere Daniell, *Experiment in Republicanism: New Hampshire Politics and the American Revolution* (Cambridge, Mass., 1970), pp. 145–63; *New Hampshire State Papers*, vol. 10, pp. 228–500; Frederick Chase, *A History of Dartmouth College,* ed. John K. Lord (Cambridge, Mass., 1891), pp. 443–507; Saunderson, *History of Charlestown*, pp. 123–205; Walton, *Records of the Governor*, vol. 2, pp. 238–395. G. A. Rawlyk, *The Canada Fire: Radical Evangelicalism in British North America, 1775–1812* (Kingston, Ont., 1994); Stephen A. Marini, *Radical Sects of Revolutionary New England* (Cambridge, Mass., 1982); Nathan O. Hatch, *The Democratization of American Christianity* (New Haven, 1989); Randolph A. Roth, *The Democratic Dilemma: Religion, Reform, and the Social Order in the Connecticut River Valley of Vermont, 1791–1850* (New York, 1987).

25. Bellesiles, *Revolutionary Outlaws*, pp. 28–32, 42–45; Belknap, *History of New-Hampshire*, vol. 1, pp. 322–26; Hall, *Eastern Vermont*, pp. 30–32, 79–80; Looney, "Benning Wentworth's Land Grant Policy," pp. 10–12; Calloway, *Western Abenakis*, pp. 183–87; Bailyn, *Voyagers to the West*, p. 10; Clark, *Eastern Frontier*, pp. 352–59; Florence M. Woodward, *The Town Proprietors in Vermont: The New England Proprietorship in Decline* (New York, 1936); Daniell, *Experiment in Republicanism*, pp. 15–16.

26. Reuben Jones, "Relation of the Proceedings," Mar. 23, 1775, and Thomas Chandler, "State of the Facts," Mar. 1775, in Walton, *Records of the Governor and Council*, vol. 1, pp. 33–38; Hall, *Eastern Vermont*, pp. 223–27; *Documentary History of New York*, vol. 4, pp. 905–6; Bellows, *Historical Sketch*, pp. 47–48; Bellesiles, *Revolutionary Outlaws*, pp. 108–9.

27. Lynn Warner Turner, *The Ninth State: New Hampshire's Formative Years* (Chapel Hill, 1983), p. 9; Daniell, *Experiment in Republicanism*, pp. 144–45, 155–56; Chase, *History of Dartmouth College*, pp. 444–45, 449–54; *New Hampshire State Papers*, vol. 10, pp. 233, 272–95, 311–13, 320–21; Walton, *Records of the Governor and Council*, vol. 1, pp. 405–46; Belknap, *History of New-Hampshire*, vol. 12, pp. 287–89, 383–87.

28. *New Hampshire State Papers*, vol. 10, pp. 325–41, 381–401; Williams, *History of Eastern Vermont*, pp. 400–401; Saunderson, *History of Charlestown*, pp. 141–555; Daniell, *Experiment in Republicanism*, pp. 156–60; Chase, *History of Dartmouth College*, pp. 463–71, 490–96; General Bellows to Weare, Feb. 1781, Weare Papers, Massachusetts Historical Society, Boston; Walton, *Records of the Governor and Council*, vol. 2, pp. 107, 115–31; Belknap, *History of New-Hampshire*, vol. 1, p. 391.

29. Belknap, *History of New-Hampshire*, vol. 1, pp. 391–93; *New Hampshire State Papers*, vol. 10, pp. 401–49, 466–67, 479–83; vol. 13. pp. 527, 664; Saunderson, *History of Charlestown*, pp. 168–203; Daniell, *Experiment in Republicanism*, pp. 160–62; Walton, *Records of the Governor and Council*, vol. 2, pp. 335–50, 379–83; Washington to Chittenden, Jan. 1, 1782, quoted in *New Hampshire State Papers*, vol. 10, pp. 463, 481–85; Chase, *History of Dartmouth College*, pp. 503–27; Bellesiles, *Revolutionary Outlaws*, p. 207.

30. Rawlyk, *Canada Fire*; Marini, *Radical Sects of Revolutionary New England;* Hatch, *Democratization of American Christianity*; Gordon S. Wood, *The Radicalism of the American Revolution* (New York, 1992); John L. Brooke, *The Heart of the Commonwealth: Society and Political Culture in Worcester County, Massachusetts, 1713–1861* (New York, 1989); Roth, *The Democratic Dilemma*.

31. Shipton, *Biographical Sketches*, vol. 14, pp. 256–62; Pliny Dickinson, *A Discourse Delivered at the Funeral of Thomas Fessenden* (Brattleborough, Vt., 1812); Thomas Fessenden, *A Theoretic Explanation of the Science of Sanctity* (Brattleborough, Vt., 1804); Fessenden, Sermons, Fessenden Ms., American Antiquarian Society (AAS).

32. Shipton, *Biographical Sketches*, vol. 14, pp. 256–62; *New-Hampshire Gazette*, Sept. 7, 1764; Aldrich, *Walpole as It Was*, pp. 36–37; Ebenezer Parkman Diary, Dec. 16, 1766, AAS; Marini, *Radical Sects of Revolutionary New England;* Roth, *Democratic Dilemma;* Hatch, *Democratization of American Christianity;* Bellesiles, *Revolutionary Outlaws*.

33. Thomas Fessenden, Sermons, Jan. 21, Mar. 17, 1776, Fessenden Ms., AAS.

34. Ibid., June 22, 1777, Sept. 4, 1775; Fessenden, *A Theoretic Explanation*, p. xx.

35. Thomas Fessenden, *A Luminous Shining Character* (Keene, 1789), pp. 13–15; Shipton, *Biographical Sketches*, vol. 14, p. 258; Aldrich, *Walpole as It Was*, pp. 131, 250–51; Bellows, *Historical Sketch*, p. 60.

36. Fessenden, Sermons, Nov. 22, 1778, Fessenden Ms., AAS; Aldrich, *Walpole as It Was*, p. 131; Roth, *Democratic Dilemma*, pp. 64–65; Thomas Whittemore, *The Modern History of Universalism* (Boston, 1830), p. 388.

37. Jeremiah Mason, *Memoirs and Correspondence of Jeremiah Mason*, ed. George Stillman Hillard (Cambridge, Mass., 1873), p. 29; David Jaffee, "The Village Enlightenment in New England," *William and Mary Quarterly* [hereafter, cited as WMQ] 47 (July 1990): 327–46; Christopher Clark, *The Roots of Rural Capitalism: Western Massachusetts, 1780–1860* (Ithaca, N.Y., 1990); Jack Larkin, "The Merriams of Brookfield: Printing in the Economy and Culture of Rural Massachusetts in the Early Nineteenth Century," *Proceedings of the American Antiquarian Society* 96 (1986): 42; Wood, *Radicalism of the American Revolution;* Joseph Wood, "Elaboration of a Settlement System: The New England Village in the Federal Period," *Journal of Historical Geography* 10 (1984): 331–56; Richard D. Brown, *Knowledge is Power: The Diffusion of Information in Early America, 1700–1865* (New York, 1989).

38. Wood, "Elaboration of a Settlement System," pp. 332–56.

39. Aldrich, *Walpole as It Was*, pp. 75–79.

40. John Lambert, *Travels through Canada and the United States of North America* (London, 1813), vol. 2, pp. 497–98; Aldrich, *Walpole as It Was*, p. 97; Donna-Belle and James L. Garvin, *On the Road North of Boston: New Hampshire Taverns and Turnpikes, 1700–1900* (Concord, N.H., 1988), pp. 84–92; Belknap, *History of New-Hampshire*, vol. 3, pp. 61, 106; Timothy Dwight, *Travels in New England and New York*, ed. Barbara Miller Solomon (Cambridge, Mass., 1968), vol. 4, p. 117; Ledger, Allen, and Weld, store account book, 1790, Walpole, N.H., Manuscripts Collection, Baker Library, Harvard University, Cambridge.

41. Wood, "Elaboration of a Settlement System," pp. 331–56; Fisher Ames quoted in Roger N. Parks, *Roads and Travel in New England, 1790–1840* (Sturbridge, Mass., 1966), p. 17; Frederic Wood, *The Turnpikes of New England and the Evolution of the Same through England, Virginia, and Maryland* (Boston, 1919), pp. 215–48; Garvin, *Road North of Boston*, pp. 48–52; Frizzell, *History of Walpole*, vol. 1, pp. 25, 34–35.

42. Aldrich, *Walpole as It Was*, p. 73; Garvin, *Road North of Boston*, pp. 55–56; Dwight, *Travels in New England*, vol. 2, pp. 62–64; Robert Fletcher and Jonathan P. Snow, "A History of the Development of Wooden Bridges," in *American Wooden Bridges* (New York, 1976); P. H. Gobie, *Bellows Falls and Vicinity Illustrated* (Bellows Falls, Vt., 1908).

43. Larkin, "Merriams of Brookfield," p. 42; Advertisements from *Farmers Weekly Museum*, 1793–1798, reprinted in Frizzell, *History of Walpole*, pp. 23–24; Ledger, Allen, and Weld, 1790; David Jaffee, "Peddlers of Progress and the Transformation of the Rural North, 1760–1860," *Journal of American History* (1991): 514–16; Gregory Nobles, "The Rise of Merchants in Rural Market Towns: A Case Study of Eighteenth-Century Northampton, Massachusetts," *Journal of Social History* 24 (1990): 5–23; Clark, *Roots of Rural Capitalism*, chap. 5; Thomas Dublin, *Transforming Women's Work: New England Lives in the Industrial Revolution* (Ithaca, N.Y., 1994).

44. Dublin, *Transforming Women's Work*, pp. 29–33; Barnes, *Narratives*, pp. 105–10; Frizzell, *History of Walpole*, pp. 561–63; *Farmer's Weekly Museum*, Aug. 21, 1797.

45. Zadock Thompson, *History of Vermont, Natural, Civil, and Statistical: In Three Parts* (Burlington, Vt., 1853), pp. 213–14; Wood, *Radicalism of the American Revolution*, p. 300; Richard Bushman, *The Refinement of America* (New York, 1992); Jaffee, "Peddlers of Progress."

46. Philip Zea and Robert C. Cheney, *Clock Making in New England: An Interpretation of the Old Sturbridge Village Collection* (Sturbridge, Mass., 1992), pp. 108–12; Frizzell, *History of Walpole*, pp. 151–52, 301–13; Chris H. Bailey, *Two Hundred Years of American Clocks and Watches* (Englewood Cliffs, N.J., 1975), pp. 22, 61–64, 87; Philip Zea, "Clockmaking and Society at the River and the Bay: Jedidiah and Jabez Baldwin, 1790–1820," in Peter Benes, ed., *The Bay and the River Dublin Seminar for New England Folklife, 1981* (Boston, 1982), pp. 45–53; Charles S. Parsons, *New Hampshire Clocks and Clockmaking* (Exeter, N.H., 1976), pp. 55, 100–101, 318–19; Jedediah Baldwin Account Books and Daybooks, 1799–1809, Papers, Baker Library, Dartmouth College Library, Hanover, N.H.

47. New Hampshire Historical Society, *Plain and Elegant, Rich and Common: Documented New Hampshire Furniture, 1780–1880* (Concord, N.H., 1979), pp. 124–27, 146; Kenneth Joel Zogry, *The Best the Country Affords: Vermont Furniture* (Bennington, Vt., 1995), pp. 110–11; *Farmer's Weekly Museum,* Aug. 21, Dec. 5, 1797; William N. Hosley Jr., "Vermont Furniture, 1790–1830," in Brock Jobe, ed., *New England Furniture: Essays in Memory of Benno Forman* (Boston, 1987), pp. 245–86; Charles A. Robinson, *Vermont Cabinetmakers and Chairmakers before 1855: A Checklist* (Shelburne, Vt., 1994); Donna-Belle Garvin, "Concord, New Hampshire: A Furniture-Making Capital," *Historical New Hampshire* 45 (1990): 8–87; Philip Zea, "The Emergence of Neoclassical Furniture Making in Rural Western Massachusetts," *Antiques* 142 (1992): 842–51; William N. Hosley, "Architecture and Society of the Urban Frontier: Windsor, Vermont, in 1800," in Benes, *The Bay and the River,* pp. 73–86.

48. William J. Gilmore, *Reading Becomes a Necessity of Life: Material and Cultural Life in Rural New England, 1780–1835* (Knoxville, Tenn., 1989), p. 24; David Carlisle and Isaiah Thomas, Memorandum of Agreement, Feb. 12, 1798, Isaiah Thomas Papers, AAS; Aldrich, *Walpole as It Was,* p. 81; Milton Ellis, *Joseph Dennie and His Circle* (Austin, Tx., 1915); Lawrence Buell, *New England Literary Culture: From Revolution through Renaissance* (New York, 1986), pp. 27–28; Robert A. Ferguson, *Law and Letters in American Culture* (Cambridge, Mass., 1984), p. 98; Joseph Buckingham, *Specimens of Newspaper Literature* (Boston, 1852), vol. 2, p. 199; Isaiah Thomas, *The History of Printing in America* (New York, 1970), p. 182; Richard John, *Spreading the News: The American Postal System from Franklin to Morse* (Cambridge, Mass., 1995); Jaffee, "Village Enlightenment in New England"; Richard D. Brown, "The Emergence of Urban Society in Rural Massachusetts, 1760–1820," *Journal of American History* 61 (1974): 43–44; Frizzell, *History of Walpole.*

49. Isaiah Thomas, *Catalogue of Books for Sale by Thomas and Thomas at Their Bookstore in Walpole* (Walpole, N.H., 1803); Account of Stock, 1796–1818, Walpole, Thomas Papers, AAS; Gilmore, *Reading Becomes a Necessity of Life,* p. 59; Larkin, "Merriams of Brookfield," pp. 39–72.

50. Joseph Buckingham, *Boston Courier,* Apr. 9, 1849 (semiweekly edition), quoted in Gilmore, *Reading Becomes a Necessity,* p. 266; Buckingham, *Personal Memoirs and Recollections of Editorial Life* (Boston, 1853), vol. 2, pp. 19–20; David D. Hall, "Introduction: The Uses of Literacy in New England, 1600–1850," in William L. Joyce et al., eds., *Printing and Society in Early America* (Worcester, Mass., 1983), pp. 1–47; Cathy N. Davidson, *Revolution and the Word: The Rise of the Novel in America* (New York, 1986), p. 22; Jaffee, "Village Enlightenment in New England."

51. Gilmore, "Reading Becomes a Necessity," p. 57; Lambert, *Travels through Canada, and the United States,* vol. 2, pp. 497–98; John, *Spreading the News;* Ellis, *Joseph Dennie and His Circle,* pp. 81–85; Mason, *Memoirs,* p. 28; David Paul Nord, "Newspapers and American Nationhood, 1776–1826," in *Three Hundred Years of American Newspapers,* ed. John B. Hench (Worcester, Mass., 1991).

52. Joseph Dennie to Mary Green Dennie, Walpole, Apr. 26, 1797, in *The Letters of Joseph Dennie,* ed. Laura G. Pedder (Orono, Maine, 1936), p. 158; Aldrich, *Walpole as It Was,* pp. 79–83; Ellis, *Joseph Dennie and His Circle; Farmer's Weekly Museum,* Apr. 5, 1796, Mar. 14, 1797; Buell, *New England Literary Culture,* pp. 26–27; Michael T. Gilmore, "The Literature of the Revolutionary and Early National Periods," in Sacvan Bercovitch, ed., *The Cambridge History of American Literature* (New York, 1994), vol. 1, pp. 567–69; Joseph Dennie, "Advertisement," in Milton Ellis, ed., *The Lay Preacher* (New York, 1943), p. 3; Christopher Grasso, "Print, Poetry, and Politics: John Trumbull and the Transformation of Public Discourse in Revolutionary America," *Early American Literature* 30 (1995): 5–31.

53. Aldrich, *Walpole as It Was,* p. 81; Ellis, *Joseph Dennie and His Circle,* pp. 9–83; Buell, *New England Literary Culture,* pp. 26–27; Gilmore, "Revolutionary and Early National Periods," pp. 567–69; Joseph Dennie, *The Farrago,* ed. Bruce Granger (Delmar, N.Y., 1985); Buckingham, *Specimens of Newspaper Literature,* vol. 2, p. 99; Frizzell, *History of Walpole,* pp. 19–21; Pedder, *Letters of Joseph Dennie,* pp. 141–55; Sidney E. Berger, "Innovation and Diversity among the Green Family of Printers," *Printing History* 23 (1990); see Joseph Dennie, Papers 1783–1815, Houghton Library, Harvard University, Cambridge, for Dennie's editorial correspondence with various New England literary figures.

54. Ellis, *Joseph Dennie and His Circle,* pp. 85–88; Buell, *New England Literary Culture,* pp. 26–27; Gilmore, "Revolutionary and Early National Periods," pp. 567–69; Buckingham,

Specimens of Newspaper Literature, vol. 2, p. 199; Buckingham, *Personal Recollections,* vol. 2, p. 24; Frizzell, *History of Walpole,* pp. 19–21; Dennie, *The Lay Preacher;* Royall Tyler, *New England Galaxy,* July 24, 1818; Pedder, *Letters of Joseph Dennie,* pp. 153–60.

55. See Dennie's fascinating correspondence with Boston literati in Joseph Dennie Papers, 1783–1815, Houghton Library, Harvard University, Cambridge; Gilmore, "Revolutionary and Early National Periods," pp. 558–72; Benjamin Franklin V, "Joseph Dennie, the Farmer's Museum, and the Promotion of Early American Literature," *Historical New Hampshire* 33(1978): 297–307; Louis Leary, "The Literary Opinions of Joseph Dennie," *Soundings* (Athens, Ga., 1970), pp. 253–70; Grasso, "Print, Poetry, and Politics," pp. 5–31; William Charvat, *The Profession of Authorship in America, 1800–1870* (Columbus, Ohio, 1968), pp. 14–18; Lewis P. Simpson, *The Federalist Literary Mind* (Boston, 1962); Lewis P. Simpson, "Federalism and the Crisis of Literary Order," *American Literature* 32 (1960): 253–66; William L. Hedges, "The Old World Yet: Writers and Writing in Post-Revolutionary America," *Early American Literature* 16 (1981): 3–19; Michael Warner, *The Letters of the Republic: Publication and the Public Sphere in Eighteenth-Century America* (Cambridge, Mass., 1990); Larzer Ziff, *Writing in the New Nation: Prose, Print, and Politics in the Early National United States* (New Haven, 1991), pp. 95–98.

56. Mason, *Memoirs,* pp. 28–32; Ferguson, *Law and Letters,* pp. 68–72; *Farmer's Weekly Museum,* Apr. 24, 1798; Dennie, *The Spirit of the Farmers' Museum, and Lay Preacher's Gazette* (Walpole, N.H., 1801); Marius Péladeau, ed., *The Verse of Royall Tyler* (Charlottesville, Va., 1968), and *The Prose of Royall Tyler* (Charlottesville, Va., 1972); G. Thomas Tanselle, *Royall Tyler* (Cambridge, Mass., 1967); Ada Lou Carson and Harry Carson, *Royall Tyler* (Boston, 1979); Royall Tyler, *The Algerine Captive* (New Haven, Ct., 1970); Robert A. Gross, "The Confidence Man and the Preacher: The Cultural Politics of Shay's Rebellion," in Robert Gross, ed., *In Debt to Shays: The Bicentennial of an Agrarian Rebellion* (Charlottesville, Va., 1993), p. 316; Kenneth Silverman, *A Cultural History of the American Revolution* (New York, 1976); Mary Hunt Tyler, *Grandmother Tyler's Book: The Recollections of Mary Palmer Tyler,* ed., Frederick Tupper and Helen Tyler Brown (New York, 1925); Gordon Wood, *The Radicalism of the American Revolution* (New York, 1992), pp. 347–50; Joseph Dennie, "Miscellany," *Port Folio,* n.s., 3 (Apr. 25, 1807): 259, and "Legal Character," *Port Folio,* n.s., 5 (Apr. 20, 1805): 112–13; Linda Kerber, *Federalists in Dissent: Imagery and Ideology in Jeffersonian America* (Ithaca, N.Y., 1970), pp. 13–17, 174–77.

57. *Farmer's Weekly Museum,* Apr. 5, 1796, July 24, 1797; Ellis, *Joseph Dennie and His Circle,* pp. 90–93.

58. *Farmer's Weekly Museum,* Sept. 16, 1796, July 27, 1798; Kerber, *Federalists in Dissent,* p. 178; Gilmore, "Revolutionary and Early National Periods," pp. 558–72; Buell, *New England Literary Culture;* Lewis P. Simpson, "The Satiric Mode: The Early National Wits," in Louis D. Rubin, ed., *The Comic Imagination in America* (New Brunswick, N.J., 1973), pp. 49–61; George L. Roth, "American Theory of Satire, 1790–1820," *American Literature* 29 (1958): 399–407; Roger B. Stein, "Royall Tyler and the Question of Our Speech," *New England Quarterly* 38 (1965): 454–74; Joyce Appleby, *Liberalism and Republicanism in the Historical Imagination* (Cambridge, Mass., 1992).

59. Joseph Dennie, "The Farrago No. 1," Feb. 14, 1792, reprinted in Bruce Granger, ed., *The Farrago* (Delmar, N.Y., 1985), p. 10; *Farmers' Weekly Museum,* Oct. 13, 1795 (moral monitor), Apr. 5, Sept. 13, 1796; Gilmore, "Revolutionary and Early National Periods," p. 569; Joseph Dennie, "Advertisement," *Lay Preacher,* p. 3; Gross, "The Confidence Man and the Preacher," p. 316.

60. *Farmer's Weekly Museum,* Oct. 13, Dec. 1, 1795, Jan. 12, Mar. 15, May 10, Oct. 25, 1796; Dennie, *Lay Preacher,* pp. 3, 29–31; Kerber, *Federalists in Dissent,* p. 186; Gross, "The Confidence Man and the Preacher," p. 316; Leo Marx, *The Machine in the Garden: Technology and the Pastoral Ideal in America* (New York, 1964), p. 127; Wood, *Radicalism of the American Revolution;* Gilmore, "Revolutionary and Early National Periods," p. 553.

61. *Farmer's Weekly Museum,* July 19, 1796; Kerber, *Federalists in Dissent,* pp. 174–77; Buell, *New England Literary Culture,* pp. 307–12; Cameron Nickels, *New England Humor: From the Revolutionary War to the Civil War* (Knoxville, Tenn., 1993), pp. 48–50.

62. *Farmer's Weekly Museum,* Aug. 16, 1796, Feb. 18, Apr. 11, May 27, 1799; Péladeau, *Verse of Royall Tyler,* p. 249; Gilmore, "Revolutionary and Early National Periods"; Ferguson, *Law and Letters,* pp. 97–99; Kerber, *Federalists in Dissent,* p. 17; Simpson, *Federalist Literary Mind.*

63. Joseph Dennie and Royall Tyler, *Farmer's Weekly Museum*, Apr. 5, Aug. 16, 1796, Apr. 11, 1797, Feb. 18, 1799 ("The Pap of Science"); Henry David Thoreau, *Walden*, quoted in Robert A. Gross, "Much Instruction from Little Reading: Books and Libraries in Thoreau's Concord," *Proceedings of the American Antiquarian Society* 97 (1988): 130; Ferguson, *Law and Letters*, pp. 98–99; Gross, "Confidence Man and Preacher"; Gilmore, "Revolutionary and Early National Periods," p. 570.

64. Thomas Green Fessenden, *Jonathan's Courtship* ([New Haven], 1795?), broadside, *Original Poems* (London, 1804), pp. vi–xii; Porter Gale Perrin, *The Life and Works of Thomas Green Fessenden* (Orono, Maine, 1925), pp. 186–92; Marcus A. McCorison, "Thomas Green Fessenden, 1771–1837: Not in BAL," *Publications of the Bibliographical Society of America* 89 (1995): 5–59; Nathaniel Hawthorne, *Fanshawe and Other Pieces* (Boston, 1876), pp. 216–17; Buell, *New England Literary Culture*, pp. 343–44; Nickels, *New England Humor*, pp. 42–56; Judith Yaross Lee, "Republican Rhymes: Constitutional Controversy and the Democratization of the Verse Satire, 1786–1799," *Studies in American Humor* 6 (1988): 30–39.

65. *Farmer's Weekly Museum*, Aug. 20, 1798; Nichols, *New England Humor*, pp. 46–47.

66. "Simon Spunkey's Irregular Ode to Colonel Candidate of Fair Haven," *Farmer's Weekly Museum*, Feb. 18, 1797; "'Love's Labour Lost' Peter Pumpkin-head defeated by Tabitha Towzer," *Original Poems*, pp. 130–39.

67. Thomas Fessenden, *A Sermon, Preached in Walpole* (Walpole, 1795), pp. 6–7, 10.

68. Thomas Fessenden, *A Sermon, Delivered July 4th, 1802* (Walpole, 1802), pp. 12–14, 15, 17, 23, 30–31.

69. "A Town," *Farmer's Weekly Museum*, Mar. 15, 1795, July 21, 1797; Buell, *New England Literary Culture*, p. 312; Darrett Rutman, "Assessing the Little Communities of Early America," *WMQ* 43 (1986): 163–78; Gilmore, "Revolutionary and Early National Periods," pp. 591–95; Grasso, "Print, Poetry, and Politics"; John, *Spreading the News*; Brown, *Knowledge is Power*; Jaffee, "Village Enlightenment in New England"; Joseph S. Wood, "'Build, Therefore, Your Own World': The New England Village as Settlement Ideal," *Annals of the Association of American Geographers* 81 (1991): 32–50; Benedict Anderson, *Imagined Communities* (New York, 1991).

70. Tyler, *The Contrast* (1787), in Edwin H. Cady, ed., *Literature of the Early Republic* (San Francisco, 1969), pp. 595–653; Buell, *New England Literary Culture*; Gilmore, "Revolutionary and Early National Periods," pp. 591–95; Hawthorne, *Fanshawe*, p. 247; Grasso, "Print, Poetry, and Politics"; Ferguson, *Law and Letters*, pp. 114–19; Gross, "Confidence Man and the Preacher," pp. 316–19; Leary, "Literary Opinions of Joseph Dennie"; Franklin, "Joseph Dennie."

71. Ellis, *Joseph Dennie and His Circle*, pp. 134–52; Gilmore, "Revolutionary and Early National Periods," pp. 570–71; on problems of rural publishing, see Dennie to Tyler, Aug. 30, 1797, in Pedder, *Letters of Joseph Dennie*, p. 165; Jaffee, "Village Enlightenment in New England"; Clark, *Roots of Rural Capitalism*; Wood, *Radicalism of the American Revolution*.

72. Christie, "'In These Times of Democratic Rage,'" p. 38; Jaffee, "Peddlers of Progress"; Wood, *Radicalism of the American Revolution*; Bellesiles, *Revolutionary Outlaws*; Alan Taylor, *Liberty Men and Great Proprietors: The Revolutionary Settlement on the Northern Frontier* (Chapel Hill, 1990); Randolph A. Roth, *The Democratic Dilemma: Religion, Reform, and the Social Order in the Connecticut River Valley of Vermont, 1791–1850* (Cambridge, 1987); Gregory H. Nobles, "Breaking into the Backcountry: New Approaches to the Early American Frontier," *WMQ* 46 (1989): 641–70; Rawlyk, *Canada Fire*; George L. Parker, *The Beginnings of the Book Trade in Canada* (Toronto, 1985), p. 29; Daniel C. Goodwin, "From Disunity to Integration: Evangelical Religion and Society in Yarmouth, Nova Scotia, 1761–1830," in Conrad, *They Planted Well*.

Epilogue: The Myth of Town Settlement

1. John M. Stowe, *An Address in Commemoration of the One Hundredth Anniversary of the Incorporation of the Town of Hubbardston, Mass., Delivered June 13th, 1867* (Worcester, 1867), p. 88; Charles Hudson, *Celebration of the One Hundredth Anniversary of the Incorporation of Westminster, Mass.* (Boston, 1859), p. 5; Charles Theodore Russell, *Celebration of the One Hundredth Anniversary of the Incorporation of Princeton, Mass., October 20th, 1859* (Worcester, 1860); Charles H. B. Snow, *Address at the Centennial Celebration of the Town of*

Fitchburg, June 30, 1864 (Fitchburg, 1876); E. B. Willson, *An Address Delivered In Petersham, Massachusetts, July 4, 1854, in Commemoration of the One Hundredth Anniversary of the Incorporation of that Town* (Boston, 1855); A. H. Bullock, *A Commemorative Address at Royalson, August 23d, 1865: The Hundredth Anniversary of Its Incorporation* (Winchendon, Mass., 1865); Lucius R. Paige, *An Address at the Centennial Celebration in Hardwick, Mass., November 15, 1838* (Cambridge, Mass., 1838); Joseph Willard, *An Address in Commemoration of the Two-Hundredth Anniversary of the Incorporation of Lancaster, Massachusetts* (Boston, 1853).

2. John R. Gillis, "Memory and Identity: The History of a Relationship," in John Gillis, ed., *Commemorations* (Princeton, 1994), pp. 3–24; also see the essays in that volume by Richard Handler, "Is 'Identity' A Useful Cross-Cultural Concept," pp. 27–40, and David Lowenthal, "Identity, Heritage, and History," pp. 41–57; Jonathan Arac, "Establishing National Narrative," in Sacvan Bercovitch, ed., *The Cambridge History of American Literature* (New York, 1994), vol. 2, p. 608.

On collective memory, see Maurice Halbwachs, *The Collective Memory,* trans. F. J. Ditter (New York, 1980); Paul Connerton, *How Societies Remember* (Cambridge, U.K., 1989); James Fentress and Chris Wickham, *Social Memory* (Cambridge, Mass., 1992); Patrick H. Hutton, *History as an Art of Memory* (Hanover, N.H., 1993); Peter Burke, "History as Social Memory," in Thomas Butler, ed., *Memory: History, Culture, and the Mind* (Oxford, U.K., 1989), pp. 97–113; David Lowenthal, *The Past is a Foreign Country* (Cambridge, U.K., 1985); Pierre Nora, "Between Memory and History: Les Lieux de Mémoire," *Representations* 26 (1989): 7–25; "AHR Forum," *American Historical Review* 102 (1997): 1371–1412, with essays by Susan A. Crane, "Writing the Individual Back into Collective Memory," Alon Confino, "Collective Memory and Cultural History: Problems of Method," and Daniel James, "Meatpackers, Peronists, and Collective Memory: A View from the South."

For individual case studies, see Yael Zerubavel, *Recovered Roots: Collective Memory and the Making of Israeli National Tradition* (Chicago, 1995); Gillis, *Commemorations;* Michael Kammen, *Mystic Chords of Memory: The Transformation of Tradition in American Culture* (New York, 1991); Joanne Rappaport, *The Politics of Memory: Native Historical Interpretation in the Columbian Andes* (New York, 1990); Popular Memory Group, "Popular Memory: Theory, Politics, Method," in Richard Johnson, ed., *Making Histories: Studies in History Writing and Politics* (Minneapolis, 1982), pp. 205–52; Alon Confino, *The Nation as Local Metaphor: Württenberg, Imperial Germany, and National Memory, 1871–1918* (Chapel Hill, 1997).

3. *Litchfield County Centennial Celebration, Held at Litchfield, Conn., 13th and 14th of August, 1851* (Hartford, 1851); Ralph Waldo Emerson, "Historical Discourse Delivered before the Citizens of Concord, on the Second Centennial Anniversary of the Incorporation of the Town, September 12, 1835," in *Selected Essays and Addresses* (New York, 1905), pp. 433–75. On twentieth-century celebrations in Newburyport, Massachusetts, see W. Lloyd Warner, *The Living and the Dead: A Study of the Symbolic Life of Americans* (New Haven, 1959), pp. 101–226.

4. Willson, *Address Delivered in Petersham, Massachusetts,* pp. 123–33.

5. Zerubavel, *Recovered Roots;* Gillis, *Commemorations;* Stephen Eddy Snow, *Performing the Pilgrims: A Study of Ethnohistorical Role Playing at Plimoth Plantation* (Jackson, Miss., 1993); Hayden White, *The Content of the Form: Narrative Discourse and Historical Representation* (Baltimore, 1987), pp. 1–25; David Carr, *Time, Narrative, and History* (Bloomington, 1986); William Cronon, "A Place for Stories: Nature, History, and Narrative," *Journal of American History* 78 (1992): 1347–76; Robert Berkhofer, *Beyond the Great Story* (Cambridge, Mass., 1995). On tradition, see Eric Hobsbawm and Terence Ranger, *The Invention of Tradition* (Cambridge, 1983); Marilyn Ivy, *Discourses of the Vanishing: Modernity, Phantasm, Japan* (Chicago, 1995); Daniel Walker Howe, *The Political Culture of the American Whigs* (Chicago, 1979), pp. 69–83.

6. Willard, *Centennial Address at Lancaster, Massachusetts,* pp. 137, 139; Snow, *Address at Centennial Celebration of Fitchburg,* p. 10; Hudson, *Celebration at Westminster,* pp. 66–68; Bushnell, "The Age of Homespun," *Litchfield County Centennial Celebration,* pp. 107–30; Howe, *Political Culture of Whigs,* pp. 234–35; Peter Burke, *The Origins of Popular Culture in Europe* (New York, 1978); Ian McKay, *The Quest of the Folk* (Montreal, 1994); David Whisnant, *All That Is Native and Fine: The Politics of Culture in an American Region* (Chapel Hill, 1983); Ivy, *Discourses of the Vanishing,* p. 100.

7. Jeremiah Lyford Hanaford, *History of Princeton, Worcester County, Massachusetts: Civil and Ecclesiastical* (Worcester, Mass., 1852), p. iv; Hudson, *Celebration of Westminster,*

pp. 12–40 (family histories); Willard, *Centennial Address at Lancaster, Massachusetts,* p. 139; Stowe, *Address at Hubbardston,* p. 5.

8. Bushnell, "Age of Homespun," pp. 114, 118, 120, 121, 126; Snow, *Address at Centennial Celebration of Fitchburg,* p. 9; Laurel Thatcher Ulrich delivered a wonderful analysis of Bushnell's presentation and the construction of the "colonial," in "A Centennial of Homespun," 1996 Anson G. Phelps Lectures, "New England's Age of Homespun," Feb. 26, 1996, New York University, New York.

9. Russell, *Celebration of One Hundredth Anniversary of Princeton,* p. 75; Snow, *Address at Centennial Celebration of Fitchburg,* p. 10; Stowe, *Address in Commemoration of Hubbardston,* p. 77; Willson, *Address Delivered at Petersham, Massachusetts,* pp. 75, 131; Joseph Wood, "'Build, Therefore, Your Own Village': The New England Village as Settlement Ideal," *Annals of the Association of American Geographers* 81 (1991): 32–50; Donald W. Meinig, "Symbolic Landscapes," in *The Interpretation of Ordinary Landscapes* (New York, 1979), pp. 164–92.

10. George B. Emerson, Letter, in Willard *Address in Commemoration of Lancaster, Massachusetts,* p. 226; Snow, *Address at Centennial Celebration of Fitchburg,* pp. 24, 118–19 (letters); Hudson, *Celebration of One Hundredth Anniversary of Westminster,* p. 5 (opening), 107–8, 112–15 (letters); Nora, "Between Memory and History," p. 18; Bushnell, "Age of Homespun"; Nina Baym, *American Women Writers and the Work of History* (New Brunswick, N.J., 1995).

11. Buell, *New England Literary Culture,* p. 305; Wood, "'Build, Therefore, Your Own World,'" pp. 32, 36; Snow, *Address at Centennial Celebration of Fitchburg,* p. 42; Raymond Williams, *The Country and the City* (London, 1973), p. 12; Jennifer Robertson, *Native and Newcomer: Making and Remaking a Japanese City* (Berkeley, 1991); Warner, *Living and Dead.* Orators performed cultural work similar to the work of Japan's modernizers analyzed by Carol Gluck: "Confronted with a modernity that threatened to shake the social foundations of the nation, ideologues turned to the verities of the past—village and family, social harmony and communal custom—to cure civilization of its fevers so that society as they envisioned it could yet survive" (Carol Gluck, *Japan's Modern Myths: Ideology in the Late Meiji Period* [Princeton, 1985], pp. 177–78).

12. Willard, *Address in Commemoration of Lancaster, Massachusetts,* pp. 60–63; Hudson, *Celebration of One Hundredth Anniversary of Westminster,* p. xx; Klaus Lubbers, "Reinventing Native Americans in Fourth of July Orations," *Studies in the American Literary Imagination* 27 (1994): 47–69; Robert Berkhofer, *The White Man's Indian* (New York, 1978); Eric Sundquist, "The Literature of Expansion and Race," in Bercovitch, *Cambridge History of American Literature,* vol. 2, pp. 175–238.

13. Hudson, *Celebration of One Hundredth Anniversary of Westminster,* pp. 66–67.

14. Russell, *Celebration of One Hundredth Anniversary of Princeton,* pp. 92–95.

15. Thoreau, *Journals,* vol. 1, p. 417, quoted in Buel, *New England Literary Culture,* p. 206; Hudson, *Celebration of One Hundredth Anniversary of Westminster,* pp. x, 5; Stowe, *Address in Commemoration of Hubbardston,* p. 6; Snow, *Address at Centennial Celebration of Fitchburg,* p. xx.

16. *Address Delivered in Petersham,* p. 129; Emerson, "Historical Discourse at Second Centennial of Concord," p. 474; Willard, *Address in Commemoration of Lancaster, Massachusetts,* p. 136; Stowe, *Address in Commemoration of Hubbardston,* p. xx; Ivy, *Visions of the Vanishing,* pp. 16–17; David D. Hall, "Reassessing the Local History of New England," in Roger Parks, ed., *New England: A Bibliography of Its History* (Hanover, N.H., 1989), vol. 7, p. xxvii; Sandra A. Zagarell, "'America' as Community in Three Antebellum Village Sketches," in Joyce Warren, ed., *The (Other) American Traditions: Nineteenth-Century Women Writers* (New Brunswick, N.J., 1993), pp. 143–59.

17. Arac, "Establishing National Narrative," p. 608; White, "Value of Narrativity," in *The Content of the Form: Narrative Discourse and Historical Representation* (Baltimore, 1987), p. 1–25; John M. Murrin, "A Roof without Walls: The Dilemma of American National Identity," in Richard Beeman, Stephen Botein, and Edward Carter, eds., *Beyond Confederation: Origins of the Constitution and American National Identity* (Chapel Hill, 1987), pp. 346–47; Angela Miller, *The Empire of the Eye: Landscape Representation and American Cultural Politics, 1825–1875* (Ithaca, N.Y., 1993), p. 7.

18. Susan G. Davis, *Parades and Power: Street Theatre in Nineteenth-Century Philadelphia* (Philadelphia, 1994), p. 17; Mary P. Ryan, *Women in Public: Between Banners and Ballots:*

1825–1880 (Berkeley, 1990); Alessandro Falassi, *Time Out of Time: Essays on the Festival* (Albuquerque, N.M., 1987); Howe, *Political Culture of Whigs,* pp. 69–95; Buell, *New England Literary Culture,* pp. 206–8; Choate, *Addresses and Orations,* p. 29; Burke, *Popular Culture in Early Modern Europe,* chap. 4; Ivy, *Visions of the Vanishing,* pp. 12–13, 66–97; Partha Chatterjee, *The Nation and Its Fragments: Colonial and Postcolonial Histories* (Princeton, 1993).

19. Hanaford, *History of Princeton,* p. iv; Hudson, *Celebration of One Hundredth Anniversary of Westminster,* p. 5.

Bibliographical Essay

This work began many years ago with the study of the town of Westminster and its rich lode of records in the town clerk's office vaults. Westminster figured prominently in the accounts of the Massachusetts frontier inspired by Frederick Jackson Turner, where the eighteenth-century settlers battle the eastern speculators. These works include Turner's own "The First Frontier of Massachusetts Bay," in *The Frontier in American History* (New York: Henry Holt, 1920), as well as the studies of Lois Kimball Matthews [Rosenberry], *The Expansion of New England: The Spread of New England Settlement and Institutions to the Mississippi River, 1620–1865* (Boston: Houghton Mifflin, 1909), and Roy Hidemachi Akagi, *The Town Proprietors of the New England Colonies: A Study of Their Development, Organization, Activities, and Controversies, 1620–1770* (Philadelphia: University of Pennsylvania Press, 1924). Later studies of New England expansion include Alan Heimert, "Puritanism, the Wilderness, and the Frontier," *New England Quarterly* 26 (1953): 361–82; Douglas Edward Leach, *The Northern Colonial Frontier, 1607–1763* (New York: Henry Holt and Company, 1966); Charles E. Clark, *The Eastern Frontier: The Settlement of Northern New England, 1610–1763* (New York: Knopf, 1970); and Bernard Bailyn, *Voyagers to the West: A Passage in the Peopling of America on the Eve of the Revolution* (New York: Knopf, 1986).

All social historians of New England rely upon the "classic" town studies: Philip J. Greven, *Four Generations: Population, Land, and Family in Colonial Andover, Massachusetts* (Ithaca, N.Y.: Cornell University Press, 1970); Kenneth Lockridge, *A New England Town: The First Hundred Years, Dedham, Massachusetts, 1636–1736* (New York: W. W. Norton, 1970); Michael Zuckerman, *Peaceable Kingdoms: New England Towns in the Eighteenth Century* (New York: Knopf, 1970); and John Demos, *A Little Commonwealth: Family Life in Plymouth Colony* (New York: Oxford University

Press, 1970). Significant later eighteenth-century studies include Richard L. Bushman, *From Puritan to Yankee: Character and the Social Order in Connecticut, 1690–1765* (Cambridge: Harvard University Press, 1967); Robert A. Gross, *The Minutemen and their World* (New York: Hill and Wang, 1976); Bruce C. Daniels, *The Connecticut Town: Growth and Development, 1635–1790* (Middletown, Conn.: Wesleyan University Press, 1979); Gregory Nobles, *Divisions through the Whole: Politics and Society in Hampshire County, Massachusetts, 1740–1775* (New York: Cambridge University Press, 1983); John L. Brooke, *The Heart of the Commonwealth: Society and Political Culture in Worcester County, Massachusetts, 1713–1861* (New York: Cambridge University Press, 1991); Edward Byers, *The Nation of Nantucket: Society and Politics in an Early American Commercial Center, 1660–1820* (Boston: Northeastern University Press, 1989); and Christine Leigh Heyrman, *Commerce and Culture: The Maritime Communities of Colonial Massachusetts, 1690–1750* (New York: W.W. Norton, 1984).

When I looked back from eighteenth-century Westminster to its roots in the Wachusett, among those works I found important for understanding the Great Migration and seventeenth-century New England were Bernard Bailyn, *The New England Merchants in the Seventeenth Century* (Cambridge: Harvard University Press, 1955); Virginia DeJohn Anderson, *New England's Generation: The Great Migration and the Formation of Society and Culture* (New York: Cambridge University Press, 1991); David Grayson Allen, *In English Ways: The Movement of Societies and the Transferal of English Local Law and Custom to Massachusetts Bay in the Seventeenth Century* (Chapel Hill: University of North Carolina Press, 1981); Sumner Chilton Powell, *Puritan Village: The Formation of a New England Town* (Middletown, Conn., 1963); T. H. Breen, *Puritans and Adventurers: Change and Persistence in Early America* (New York: W. W. Norton, 1980); David D. Hall, *Worlds of Wonder, Days of Judgement: Popular Religious Belief in Early New England* (New York: Knopf, 1989); and Andrew Delbanco, *The Puritan Ordeal* (Cambridge: Harvard University Press, 1989). And indispensable for reconceiving the role of town proprietors in New England economic life were those of John Frederick Martin, *Profits in the Wilderness: Entrepreneurship and the Founding of New England Towns in the Seventeenth Century* (Chapel Hill: University of North Carolina Press, 1991), and Stephen Innes, *Creating the Commonwealth: The Economic Culture of Puritan New England* (New York: W. W. Norton, 1995).

The studies critical for rethinking the Turnerian view of eighteenth-century settlements as a "speculative" declension from seventeenth-century foundations were Christopher Jedrey, *The World of John Cleaveland: Family and Community in Eighteenth-Century New England* (New York: W. W. Norton, 1979), and Charles S. Grant, *Democracy in the Connecticut Frontier Town of Kent* (New York: Columbia University Press, 1961). The rich body of work on the maintenance of the goals of family and settlement within the changing structure of economic and social life include James Henretta, "Families and Farms: Mentalité in Pre-Industrial America," *William and Mary Quarterly* 35 (1978): 3–32; Christopher Clark, *The Roots of Rural Capitalism: Western Massachusetts, 1780–1860* (Ithaca, N.Y.: Cornell University Press, 1990); and Daniel Vickers, *Farmers and Fisherman: Two Centuries of Work in Essex County, Massachusetts, 1630–1830* (Chapel Hill: University Press of North Carolina, 1994). For the spatial patterns of settlement two works stand out: Joseph S. Wood, *The New England Village* (Baltimore: Johns Hopkins University Press, 1997), and Michael Peter Steinitz, "Landmark and Shelter: Domestic Architecture in the Cultural Landscape of the Central Uplands of Massachusetts in the Eighteenth Century" (Ph.D. diss., Clark University, 1988). For understanding the roles of artisans and entrepreneurs, I looked at Robert St. George, "'Set Thine House in Order': The Domestication of the Yeomanry in Seventeenth Century New England," in Jonathan Fairbanks, ed., *New England Begins,* (Boston: Museum of Fine Arts, 1982), and William Gilmore, *Reading Becomes a Necessity of Life: Material and Cultural Life in Rural New England, 1780–1835* (Knoxville: University of Tennessee Press, 1989)

The powerful body of ethnohistory writing on Native Americans also forced me to rethink my original premises about New England settlement; of especial importance were Neal Salisbury, *Manitou and Providence: Indians, Europeans, and the Making of New England, 1500–1643* (New York: Oxford University Press, 1982); his article "Social Relationships on a Moving Frontier: Natives and Settlers in Southern New England, 1638–1675," *Man in the Northeast* 33 (1987): 89–99; James Axtell, *The Invasion Within: The Contest of Cultures in Colonial North America* (New York: Oxford University Press, 1985); William Cronon, *Changes in the Land: Indians, Colonists, and the Ecology of New England* (New York: Hill and Wang, 1983); Colin G. Calloway, *The Western Abenakis of Vermont, 1600–1800: War, Migration, and the Survival of an Indian People* (Norman: University Press of Oklahoma, 1990); James Merrell, *The Indians' New World: Catawbas and their Neighbors from First Contact through the Era of Removal* (Chapel Hill: University of North Carolina Press, 1989); Patrick Malone, *The Skulking Way of War: Technology and Tactics among the New England Indians* (Lanham, Md.: Masdon Books, 1991); and William S. Simmons, *Spirit of the New England Tribes: Indian History and Folklore, 1620–1984* (Hanover: University Press of New England, 1984). James Clifford, *The Predicament of Culture: Twentieth-Century Ethnography, Literature, and Culture* (Cambridge: Harvard University Press, 1988); Rhys Isaac, *The Transformation of Virginia, 1740–1790* (Chapel Hill: University of North Carolina Press, 1982); and Greg Dening, *Performances* (Chicago: University of Chicago Press, 1996), spurred my rethinking about identity and cultural change.

For an understanding of the relationship between war and colonization, a different and important perspective on New England town settlement, see the work of Douglas Leach, *Arms for Empire: A Military History of the British Colonies in North America, 1607–1763* (New York: Macmillan, 1973), and Fred Anderson, *A People's Army: Massachusetts Soldiers and Society in the Seven Year's War* (Chapel Hill: University of North Carolina Press, 1984), both which discuss the social history of military life. Richard I. Melvoin, *New England's Outpost: War and Society in Colonial Deerfield* (New York: W. W. Norton, 1989), is a community study integrating war and settlement, and Ian K. Steele, *Warpaths: Invasions of North America* (New York: Oxford University Press, 1994), presents the imperial perspective.

Another impetus for rethinking Massachusetts town settlement came by looking north. Supplementing Clark on the Massachusetts colonial system and Calloway on the northern borderlands, works on northern New England include Michael Bellesiles, *Revolutionary Outlaws: Ethan Allen and the Struggle for Independence on the Early American Frontier* (Charlottesville: University Press of Virginia, 1993); Alan Taylor, *Liberty Men and Great Proprietors: The Revolutionary Settlement on the Maine Frontier* (Chapel Hill: University of North Carolina Press, 1990); Laurel Ulrich, *Good Wives: Image and Reality in the Lives of Women in Northern New England, 1650–1750* (New York: Knopf, 1983); Stephen A. Marini, *Radical Sects of Revolutionary New England* (Cambridge: Harvard University Press, 1982); Jere Daniell, *Colonial New Hampshire: A History* (Millwood: KTO Press, 1981).

My first foray to the Public Archives of Nova Scotia opened up an entirely new body of scholarship as well as a different perspective on "Greater New England." I located the first of the Planter Studies Conference volumes, *They Planted Well: New England Planters in Maritime Canada*, ed. Margaret Conrad (Fredericton, N.B.: Acadiensis Press, 1988); later volumes include *Making Adjustments: Change and Continuity in Planter Nova Scotia, 1759–1800* (Fredericton, N.B.: Acadiensis Press, 1991) and *Intimate Relations: Family and Community in Planter Nova Scotia, 1759–1800* (Fredericton, N.B.: Acadiensis, 1995), both ed. Margaret Conrad. The dominant figures in Planter studies about New England in Nova Scotia are John Bartlet Brebner, *The Neutral Yankees of Nova Scotia: A Marginal Colony during the Revolutionary Years* (New York: Columbia University Press, 1937), and George A. Rawlyk, *Nova Scotia's Massachusetts: A Study of Nova Scotia–Massachusetts Relations, 1610–1783* (Montreal: McGill-Queens University Press, 1973). Graeme Wynne's essays "A Province Too Much Dependent on New England," *Canadian Geographer* 31 (1987): 98–113, and "A Region of Scattered Settlements and Bounded Possibilities: Northeastern America, 1775–1800," *Canadian Geographer* 31 (1987): 319–38, contain an important geographical perspective on Nova Scotia settlement. Rawlyk continued to focus on the cause and consequences of the Allinite New Birth revival: *Ravished by the Spirit: Religious Revivals, Baptists, and Henry Alline* (Montreal: McGill-Queens University Press, 1984). J. M. Bumsted, *Land, Settlement, and Politics on Eighteenth-Century Prince Edward Island* (Montreal: McGill-Queens University Press, 1987), concerns the larger maritime settlement; valuable material about this also can be found in Bailyn, *Voyagers*. All the world is not New England, and during many years of reading and revising, I found European social historians of local life to be essential, including Margaret Spufford, *Contrasting Communities: English Villagers in the Sixteenth and Seventeenth Centuries* (Cambridge, U.K.: Cambridge University Press, 1974); the work of the Cambridge Group for Population and Social Structure, especially E. A. Wrigley *Population and History* (New York: McGraw-Hill, 1969); Emmanuel LeRoy Ladurie, *Montaillou: The Promised Land of Error* (New York: G. Braziller, 1978); and Pierre Goubert, *The Ancient Régime: French Society, 1600–1750* (New York: Harper and Row, 1973). Also, David Weber, *The Spanish Frontier in North America* (New Haven: Yale University Press, 1987), expands our view into the southwestern borderlands, as does W. J. Eccles, *Essays on New France* (Toronto: University of Toronto Press, 1987).

Finally, for incorporating local history as an integral part of New England colonization, the following cultural studies were critical: Richard Slotkin, *Regeneration through Violence: The Mythology of the American Frontier, 1600–1860* (Middletown: Wesleyan University Press, 1973); Sacvan Bercovitch, ed., *The Cambridge History of American Literature*, vol. 1, *1590–1820* (New York: Cambridge University Press, 1994); Stephen Arch, *Authorizing the Past: The Rhetoric of History in Seventeenth-Century New England* (DeKalb: Northern Illinois Press, 1994); Jill Lepore, *The Name of War: King Philip's War and the Origins of American Identity* (New York: Knopf, 1998). About history and memory, see Patrick Hutton, *History as an Art of Memory* (Hanover: University Press of New England, 1993); Yael Zerubavel, *Recovered Roots: Collective Memory and the Making of Israeli National Tradition* (Chicago: University of Chicago Press, 1994); John R. Gillis, ed., *Commemorations: The Politics of National Identity* (Princeton: Princeton University Press, 1994). Finally, a series of works helped me think about the relation between history and narrative: Alan Taylor, *William Cooper's Town: Power and Persuasion on the Frontiers of the Early Republic* (New York: Knopf, 1995); John Demos, *The Unredeemed Captive: A Family Story from Early America* (New York: Knopf, 1994); Laurel Ulrich, *A Midwife's Tale: The Life of Martha Ballard, Based on Her Diary, 1785–1812* (New York: Knopf, 1990); William Cronon, "A Place for Stories: Nature, History, and Narrative," *Journal of American History* 78 (1992): 1347–76.

Index

Abenaki people ("Eastern Indians"), 35; as French allies, 92, 114; Mohawk wars against, 58; war against, 94, 96, 98, 202, 206–7
Acadia: British control of, 78, 86, 164; expulsion of French from, 165, 167; housing in, 182; recolonization of, 167, 171, 179, 180. *See also* Nova Scotia
An Account of the Present State of Nova Scotia (Hollingsworth), 187
Act for Encouraging Mines (1641), 33
Adams, George, 56, 57
Adams, John, 138–39
agriculture: centennial depictions of, 243; concerns about, 160–61; and early New England towns, 5, 19; and family farms, 146–47, 149–50, 152–57; goals of, 153, 154; of Nashaways, 35, 38; in New Brunswick, 187; in Nova Scotia, 165, 168, 170, 179, 180, 188, 190. *See also* competency; livestock; proprietors: and family farms
Akagi, Roy, 128
The Algerine Captive (Tyler), 233
Algonquian peoples: language of, 44, 45; Puritan pressures on, 61, 63; as residents of contested land, 4, 58–59, 109, 204; on wilderness, 25–29. *See also* Nashaway people; Nipmuc people; *names of other Algonquian tribes*
Allen, Ethan, 212, 213, 215
Allen, Ira, 215
Alline, Henry, 191–92, 194–99, 237–38. *See also* New Birth revival
American Antiquarian Society, 241
American Husbandry, 209
American Revolution. *See* War for Independence
Ames, Fisher, 221
Amherst, Jeffrey, 206
Andenoy, John, 221
Anderson, Virginia DeJohn, 14, 155
Andover (Massachusetts), 135, 147
Andros, Edmund, 89
Annapolis County (Nova Scotia), 175
Appalachian Mountains, 178
Arac, Jonathan, 248
Arch, Stephen, 19
Argyle (Nova Scotia), 196
Arlington (New Hampshire), 115, 204
artisans: encouragement of, in town settlement, 13, 135; in Fitchburg, Massachusetts, 121; as landless

men, 156; and market economies, 5; scarcity of, in Canada, 85–86, 190; in Walpole, New Hampshire, 200, 209, 219, 220, 222–23. *See also* commercialization; wage labor
Ashburnham (Massachusetts), 119, 129, 138
Atkinson, Theodore, 207–8
Axtell, James, 86

Bacon, Edward, Sr., 154
Bacon, Edward, Jr., 154
Bacon, Edward, III, 154
Bailey, Jacob, 187
Bailyn, Bernard, 163
Baker, Joel, 155
Baker, John, 155
Baker, Mary Sawyer, 155
Baker, Richard, 155, 156
Baker, Robert, 155
Bakers-Town (Maine), 199
Baldwin, Jedediah, 223
Baldwin, Susannah, 154
Baldwin, William, 142
Baptist religion, 198–99
Bare Hill village, 107
Barre (Massachusetts), 129
Barrett, Benjamin, 136
Barrett, Humphrey, 136
Barrett, James, 136
Barrett, Joseph, 136
Barrett, Thomas, 136
Beaman, Gamalial, 107, 109
Belcher, Jonathan (Massachusetts governor), 132
Belcher, Jonathan (Nova Scotian governor), 172–74, 177
Belknap, Jeremy, 200, 202, 235
Bell, John, 42
Bellows, Abigail Stearns, 137
Bellows, "Aunt Colonel," 222
Bellows, Benjamin, Sr., 117, 138; as Lunenburg town founder, 137
Bellows, Benjamin, Jr. ("Colonel"), 137; as Westminster and Walpole town founder, 5, 142, 145, 163, 165, 201, 202, 205–11, 219, 221, 227, 237, 247
Bellows, Benjamin, III ("General"), 208, 209, 211–13, 215–16, 219–21, 237
Bellows, Dorcus Cutter Willard, 137

Bellows, John (English emigrant), 137–38
Bellows, John (General Benjamin Bellows' brother), 212, 221
Bellows, John, Jr., 221
Bellows, Judith, 137
Bellows, Phoebe Strong, 212
Bellows, Thomas, 212
Bellows Falls Canal, 221
Bemis, Philip, 142
Bemis, William, 147
Bennet, John, 105
Bercovitch, Sacvan, 70
Berkeley, William, 60
Bethel, Robert, 190
Bible, 226
Bigelow, Abijah, 152
Bigelow, Eliezer, 136, 150, 152, 154–55
Bigelow, Elisha, 136, 150, 152
Bigelow, Jabez, 155
Bigelow, John, 85
Bigelow, Joshua (Eliezer Bigelow's father), 136, 154, 155, 205
Bigelow, Joshua (Eliezer Bigelow's son), 155
Birdsey, Nathan, 135
blacklead mines, 33–34
blacksmiths. *See* artisans
Blanchard, Jonathan, 205, 207
Bliss, Thomas, 223
Block House (Nova Scotia), 182
Bolton (Massachusetts), 40, 107, 109, 146, 172
books, 225–27
Borgard house (Nova Scotia), 182
Boston (Massachusetts), 8, 216, 221; frontier settlement interest in, 42, 69; migration from, 132; and Nova Scotia, 178–80, 237
Boston Gazette, 96
Boston Weekly News Letter, 120
Bowman, William, 160
Boynton, Priscilla, 117
Bradford, William, 17, 21
Braintree (Massachusetts), 34
Brattle, William, 134, 159
Brattleboro (Vermont), 225
Breck, Edward, 51, 93
Breen, T. H., 12
bridges, 43, 221
A Brief History of the War with the Indians in New England (Mather), 69
A Brief View of the Religious Tenets and Sentiments Lately Published and Spread in the Province of Nova Scotia (Scott), 191, 196
Brookfield (Massachusetts), 65, 129
Broughton, Edward, 105
Brown, Edmund, 9
Brown, John, 247
Browne, Richard, 8
Buckingham, Joseph, 226
"budding" (as form of town expansion), 2, 3, 104–9, 123, 219
Buell, Lawrence, 235, 236, 244
Bulkeley, Richard, 177
Bushnell, Horace, 240, 242–43
Bute, Lord, 185

cabinetmakers, 223, 237
Calloway, Colin, 206–7
Cambridge (Massachusetts), 8, 60, 132, 134, 154, 216–17

Canada: captives of French and Indian War in, 83, 85–86; as English possession, 207; French parts of, 202. *See also* Acadia; Quebec; *specific Canadian provinces, towns, and sites*
Canada Expedition (1690), 117
Canada townships (Wachusett territory), 128
canals, 221
Cape Ann (Massachusetts), 191
Cape Forchu, 192
capitalism: New England towns' role in transition to, 2, 5, 221–22, 249. *See also* artisans; commercialization; land speculation; manufacturing; wage labor
Carlisle, David, 225–28
Carter, Thomas, 20
Catholic religion, 179, 185, 247
chairmakers, 223
Champlain, Samuel de, 38
Chandler, Thomas, 213
Charles River, 8
Charlestown (Massachusetts), 215; as early settlement, 8, 202, 204–7; expansion of, 8, 20; migration from, 132, 155; roads from, 204
Charlestown (New Hampshire) (also called No. 4), 114, 223, 228
Chauncey, Charles, 141
Chebacco (Massachusetts), 134
Chebogue (Nova Scotia). *See* Jebogue (Nova Scotia)
Cheever, Israel, 170
Chelmsford (Massachusetts), 55, 56
Cheshire County (New Hampshire), 213, 215–16
Cheshire Turnpike, 221
Chester (Nova Scotia), 165, 170–81, 184–88, 190
Child, Robert, 32–34, 42–44, 47
Chocksett (Massachusetts), 107, 109
Chocksett River, 104
Christianity: conversion of Indians to, 4, 29, 44–47, 60–66, 87, 245. *See also* religion; *specific Christian denominations*
Christie, Nancy, 194–95, 197
Church, Benjamin, 67–68, 73–74, 81, 95, 97
Church, Samuel, 74
churches. *See* Congregational Church; meetinghouses
Clark, Charles, 157
class divisions, 8; and democracy, 244–45; and housing, 5, 105–6, 147–49; in older towns, 3, 5, 48, 88–89, 105–6; and settler "quality," 51, 173; through industrialization, 247. *See also* life cycle
Clinton (Massachusetts), 40
clockmakers, 222–23, 237
Cohen, Patricia Cline, 159
Collections, Historical and Miscellaneous (Farmer and Moore), 99
Colman, Benjamin, 98
colonial authorities: challenges to, regarding religious toleration, 43; colonists' dependence on, 29; licensing of proprietors by, 13; role of, in New England serial town settlement, 1, 91; and sachem selection, 53. *See also* General Court of Massachusetts; ministers; *specific governors and colonial figures*
colonization: and colonial boundary disputes, 200, 205, 212, 213; and commercialization, 6, 55–57, 72, 113–14, 121–23, 200–204; 18th century characteristics of, 109–10; legitimacy of, 97–100; Metacom's War's effects on, 23, 67, 68; of New Hampshire, 200–238; of northern New England, 5, 163–99; of Nova Scotia, 5, 163–99; of town centennials' celebration of, 249; of the Wachusett, 1–161; and war, 4, 6, 23–24, 74–86, 92–97,

colonization (*cont.*)
  113–15, 119–20, 124–26, 128, 160; of wilderness,
  1–2, 4, 17–19. *See also* colonial authorities; frontier; land; migration; militia; towns; wilderness
Comingo, Bruin, 181
commercialization: and colonization, 6, 55–57, 72,
  113–14, 121–23, 200–204; and culture, 200, 201,
  219–27; difficulties of, in Nova Scotia, 164,
  179–80, 237; of fur trade, 38–40; among Indians,
  70–71; infrastructure needed for, 48, 113, 115,
  117, 202, 204, 209, 220–21; and law, 106; in New
  England town history, 1, 2, 5, 6, 239; in postrevolutionary villages, 200–238, 249; in Watertown, 8.
  See also artisans; capitalism; fur traders; land speculation; manufacturing; monopolies; town
  founders: as entrepreneurs; wage labor
Committee of Correspondence, 213
competency: as colonial goal, 135, 153, 157, 242; definition of, 13; efforts to secure, 4, 5, 13, 14, 20, 136
Concord (Massachusetts), 104; agriculture in, 153;
  artisans in, 156; bicentennial celebration in, 240,
  247; founding and settlement of, 19–20, 55; in
  Metacom's War, 65, 66; migration from, 111, 132,
  134, 136, 137; migration to, 155, 171; population
  density of, 147; removal of Indians from, 65; residents of, 156; War for Independence in, 182
Concord (New Hampshire), 55
Congregational Church: challenges to, 43, 216–18; as
  element of New England town life, 4, 160; in
  Nova Scotia, 164, 174, 181, 184, 191, 192–93,
  199. *See also* Great Awakening; meetinghouses;
  ministers; New Light movement
Connecticut, 157, 168, 209. *See also* Connecticut
  River valley; *specific towns*
Connecticut River valley, 30; agriculture in, 153;
  commercialization of, 6, 55; Indian wars in, 78,
  115, 119; settlement of, 4, 92, 113, 114, 117, 122,
  124, 163, 201, 202, 204
"Connecticut Wits," 227
Continental Congress, 215
The Contrast (Royall), 236
conversion: of Indians, 4, 29, 44–47, 60–66, 87, 245;
  Puritans' experience of, 69–70
Cooke, William, 140–41
Cornwallis (Nova Scotia), 168
"The Country Lovers, or Jonathan Jolthead's
  Courtship with Miss Sally Snapper" (Fessenden),
  233–34
county courts, 106
Court. *See* General Court
"Covenant Chain," 78
Cowee, David, 154
Cowee, James, Sr., 154
Cowee, James, Jr., 154, 156
Cowee, John, 154
Cowee, Mary Pearson, 154
Cowee, Persis, 154
Cowee, Susannah Baldwin, 154
craftsmen. *See* artisans
Crafts Tavern (Walpole, New Hampshire), 218, 219
Crawley (squire), 196
Creating the Commonwealth (Innes), 7
Cronon, William, 35
Crown Point, 114, 172, 207
cultural mediators: elites as, 106, 219, 226; fur
  traders as, 5, 94; missionaries as, 2, 44–46, 53, 55,
  59–64, 66, 68, 87, 94, 98, 245, 248. *See also*
  sachems
Cumberland County (Nova Scotia), 184

Danforth, Thomas, 52
Daniell, Jere, 204
Davis, Susan, 248
Day, Stephen, 33–34, 48, 54, 56, 57
Declaration of Independence, 215
Deerfield (Massachusetts), 78, 80
Deer Island, 65, 68
deism, 216, 235
democracy: as facet of New England towns, 242,
  244–45; frontier seen as contributor to, 3; opposi-
  tion to, among Walpole Wits, 7, 225–27, 231; and
  religious pluralism, 212–16; War for Indepen-
  dence's impetus toward, 164, 212. *See also* town
  meetings; town offices; towns: government of
Dennie, Joseph, 227–37, 249
distilling, 57
division of labor (among Nashaway), 38
Dominion of New England, 87, 89
Dorchester (Massachusetts), 8, 51, 110, 129
Dudley, Joseph, 87
Dudley, Thomas, 32
Dummer, William, 94–96, 112. *See also* Dummer's War
Dummer's War, 92–100, 111–12, 114, 202
Dunstable (Massachusetts), 217
Dutch Reformed religion, 181
Dutch trade, 58
Dwight, Timothy, 1, 16, 202

Eastern Indians. *See* Abenaki people
Eddy, Jonathan, 184
Edwards, Jonathan, 141
Eliot, Andrew, 180
Eliot, John: as cultural mediator, 44–46, 53, 55, 87,
  94, 98; and Gookin, 60, 61; on Indian policy, 53,
  65, 245; and Metacom, 65
Emerson, George B., 244
Emerson, Ralph Waldo, 240, 247
England: and French and Indian War, 76, 78; revolu-
  tion in, 32–33. *See also* colonization; Puritans;
  War for Independence
English. *See* Puritans
Entertaining Passages Relating to Metacom's War
  (Church), 73–74
entrepreneurs. *See* town founders: as entrepreneurs
Ernst-Emms house (Nova Scotia), 182
Essex County (Massachusetts), 147
ethnic diversity: and industrialization, 247; in Nova
  Scotia, 167, 170, 179, 181, 184. *See also* identity;
  Indians; slavery
Everett, Edward, 244

Fairbank, Jabez, 93
Falmouth (Nova Scotia), 194
Fanning family, 209–11
Farmer, John, 99
The Farmer's Museum (newspaper), 201, 223,
  225–29, 233, 234, 236
*The Farmer's Museum and the New Hampshire and
  Vermont Journal. See Farmer's Museum*
Farmers' Weekly Museum (newspaper). *See Farmer's
  Museum*
Farnsworth brothers, 204
"Father Abbey's Will" (Seccombe), 174
federalists, 7, 227–39
fence viewers, 14
Ferguson, Robert, 229
Fessenden, Reverend Thomas, 211, 212, 216–19,
  227, 234–35
Fessenden, Thomas Green ("Simon Spunky"),
  233–34, 236

Firmin, Giles, 13

fishing, 8, 164, 165, 167, 170, 171, 178–80, 186, 187; trade in, 188, 190–91

Fitch, John, 117, 119–23

Fitchburg (Massachusetts): development of, 103, 119, 121, 127, 129; housing in, 147; manufacturing in, 161, 243–44, 247

Fitzpatrick, Tara, 72

flax, 222

Fort Cumberland (Nova Scotia), 184, 185

Fort Dummer, 114, 117, 202, 204, 205, 209

France. *See* Acadia; French; French and Indian War; Quebec

Francklin, Michael, 180

Franklin, Benjamin, 226

Franklin, James, 98–99

Free Will Baptist religion, 199

French: end of threats from, 163; as holders of British captives in French and Indian Wars, 83, 85; as residents of contested land, 4, 23, 76, 78, 80, 81, 109, 113–14, 128, 204, 207; threats from, 206. *See also* French and Indian War

French and Indian War, 76–86, 92, 163, 201, 206–7. *See also* King George's War; King William's War; Queen Anne's War; Seven Years War

Frontenac, Louis de Buade, comte de, 78

frontier: as alternative to land morselization, 3, 14; changes in contemporaries' perception of, 72; changes in historians' views of, 2, 3, 6; military on, 81; opening of, by scouts, 94, 96–97; as protection for eastern towns, 72, 90–91, 110; Worcester County as, 4. *See also* French; Indians; land; scouting; wilderness

Frontier townships (Wachusett territory), 128

Frost, John, 192–93

furniture makers, 223

fur traders, 33; as cultural mediators, 5, 94; economic rather than reciprocal relationships among, 38–40; among Nashaway, 34–35, 38–40, 54–57, 64; in Nova Scotia, 181, 187; Prescott as, 5, 44, 54; regulation of, 55. *See also* traders; trading posts

Gardner, Andrew (of Lancaster), 82, 90

Gardner, Andrew (of Lunenburg, Massachusetts), 114, 121–22, 204

Gardner (Massachusetts), 247

Gardner Mountain (New Hampshire), 114

Garfield, Benjamin, 147

garrison housing: in New Hampshire, 206–7; in Nova Scotia, 182; in Wachusett, 24, 66–67, 78–81, 83, 87, 90, 92, 93, 100, 105, 111, 117. *See also* garrisons; *specific forts*

garrisons, 113–15, 119–21. *See also* garrison housing

Gates, Asa C., 239, 244

Gates, Mary, 52

Gay, Ebenezer, 143–44

General Court of Massachusetts: and fur trade regulation, 55, 56; and Indians, 41, 78, 80, 87, 245; land office business of, 128, 129; members of, 60; memorialization of Indian fighters by, 97; models of town founding set by, 3, 110, 114, 127; and monopolies, 54, 56; and Nashaway Company, 42–44; as supervisor of early towns, 8, 10, 12, 16, 23, 47, 48, 67, 76, 78, 80, 81, 90, 92, 104, 107, 112, 113, 119, 121, 129, 136, 142–43, 146; and town government, 59; township grants by, 5, 9, 12, 20, 51, 52, 57, 60, 88, 92, 101, 103, 109–11, 127, 129, 145, 202; town visitations by, 138, 143, 147. *See also* colonial authorities; cultural mediators; land allocation; proprietors; town founders

generations: assistance between, 113, 128, 135–37; conflicts between, 10, 14, 101, 139, 145–46. *See also* lifecycle

George II (king of England), 112

George III (king of England), 175, 177, 185

German immigrants, 167, 181

Gill, Moses, 149

Gillis, John, 240

Gilmore, William, 225, 226

Gluscap ["Glooscap"] (mythical character), 25–29

Goodwin, Daniel, 193

Gookin, Daniel: as cultural mediator with Indians, 59–64, 66, 68, 94, 245, 248; on Indian policy, 46, 65, 245; as town founder, 59–60, 63, 122; as town officer, 60

Governor Dummer's War, 92–100, 111–12, 114, 202

Governor's Council. *See* Nova Scotia Council

Grafton (Massachusetts), 136

Grafton County (New Hampshire), 215–16

Grant, Charles, 157

graphite mines, 33–34

Great Awakening, 139–42, 174. *See also* Congregational Church; New Light movement

Greater New England, 163–99

Great Migration, 3, 7, 14, 32

"Green Mountain boys," 212, 213, 215

gristmills. *See* mills

Gross, Robert, 152

Groton (Massachusetts), 66, 67, 104, 111, 117

Hale, Enoch, 215–16, 221

Halifax (Nova Scotia), 167, 178, 179; vs. outsettlements, 188, 190–91

Hall, Donald, 158

Hall, Elizabeth, 47

Hallowell, Irving, 27

Hancock, John, 124

Hanover (New Hampshire), 202, 223, 225

Harding, Elisha, 210

Harland, Thomas, 223

Harrington, Timothy, 123–26, 245, 248

Harrison, William, 184–85

Hartford (Connnecticut), 202

Hartwell, Edward, 93, 94, 109, 112, 113, 119

Harvard (Massachusetts): agriculture in, 152, 153; establishment of, 107; land for, purchased from Indians, 40; migration from, 165; ministers in, 174–75, 180, 181; population of, 146; soldiers from, 167; surveyors of, 172

Hawthorne, Nathaniel, 233

Hayes, Allen, 223

hedge vs. wilderness metaphor, 69, 72, 74, 196

Henchman, Thomas, 79

Henretta, James, 135

Heywood, Ezra, 246–47

Heywood, Levi, 247

Heywood, Nathan, 117

Hilton, Amos, 196

Hingham (Massachusetts), 51

An Historical Account of the Doings and Sufferings of the Christian Indians of New England (Gookin), 64, 245

Historical Collections of the Indians in New England (Gookin), 60, 61

A History of New England (Johnson), 6

History of New-Hampshire (Belknap), 200

A History of the Town of Westminster (Hudson), 157–61

The History of the Wars of New-England with the
    Eastern Indians (Penhallow), 98
History of Worcester County (Whitney), 158
Hoar, Daniel, 150, 155–56
Hoar, James, 150
Hoar, John, Sr., 156
Hoar, John, Jr., 156
Hoar, Samuel, 156
Hoar, Stephen, 156
Hoar, Timothy, Sr., 156
Hoar, Timothy, Jr., 156
hogreeves, 14
Holden, Abner, 134, 160
Holden, Joseph, 142, 143, 160
Hollingsworth, S., 187
"hometown," 243–44
Horswell, John, 223
Horton (Nova Scotia), 168, 170, 173, 178, 180, 181
Houghton, John, 48, 87, 89, 91–92, 94, 104, 172
Houghton, Jonas, 172
Houghton, Jonathan, 79
Houghton, Mary, 172
Houghton, Ralph, 48, 52
Houghton, Robert, 91–92
Houghton, Timothy, 163, 165, 181; as town founder,
    170–73, 175, 177, 199; and War for Indepen-
    dence, 182, 184–86
House of Representatives (Massachusetts), 129,
    131–32
housing: and class divisions, 5, 105–6, 147–49; of
    Colonel Benjamin Bellows, 210, 219; of early set-
    tlers, 138; garrison, in New Hampshire, 206–7;
    garrison, in Nova Scotia, 182; garrison, in
    Wachusett, 24, 66–67, 78–81, 83, 87, 90, 92, 93,
    100, 105, 111, 117; of the Nashaways, 38; in
    Nova Scotia, 182; of Simon Willard, 56
Howe, Elizabeth, 83
Howe, Peter, 83
Hubbard, William, 65
Hubbardston (Massachusetts), 239, 244
Hudson, Charles, 157–61, 245, 246, 248
Hudson, Daniel, 48
Hudson Bay, 86
Hudson (Massachusetts), 159
Hudson River, 163
Hull, Isaac, 138–39
Hunt, Hannah, 121
Hunt, John, 144
Hunt, Samuel, 121
Huntington, Gordon, 222
Hutchinson (Massachusetts), 129
Hutchinson, Thomas, 78–79, 128
Hymns and Spiritual Songs (Alline), 199

identity: New England historical, 239–49; Nova Sco-
    tia's sense of, 164, 167, 186, 191–92, 197–99,
    237–38; Yankee, 227, 231–37, 241–49. See also
    Puritans
immigrants, 136, 167, 181, 202, 243, 247. See also
    Puritans
Indian Dialogues (Eliot), 63
Indian fighters, 73–86, 92–97; memorialization of, 6,
    72, 97–100, 102; as protectors of frontier towns,
    111–12; as scouting new land for town foundings,
    94, 96–97, 207. See also land allocation: for mili-
    tary service; specific Indian fighters
Indians: authority among, 35, 41; bounties for scalps
    of, 81, 92, 95–96, 99, 119; captives of, 67, 68–72,
    76, 79, 80, 83, 84–86, 93, 119–21; Christian, 4, 29,
    44–47, 60–66, 87, 245; coastal vs. inland, 29, 33,

41, 72; colonists' hatred of, 6, 65–66, 86, 94–95;
    conflicts among, 41, 46, 58, 65, 67–68, 204; cooper-
    ation and reciprocity among, 26, 29, 34–35, 38, 41,
    59, 64; as depicted in centennial celebrations of New
    England towns, 241, 245–46; growing dependence
    of, on Europeans, 39–41, 57, 58, 64; interdepen-
    dence of early English settlers and, 29, 72, 94, 124,
    125–26; internment of, 65, 68; joint villages of, with
    English, 3–4, 23, 29, 30, 32–48, 57–61, 66, 68, 72;
    land obtained from, 40, 57, 64, 65, 87, 101, 122,
    124, 128, 136, 245; land views of, 28–29, 40, 57;
    seasonal locales of, 35, 38, 46; as slaves, 68, 245;
    "superintendents" of, 4, 60–64; trade of, in Nova
    Scotia, 173; trade of, with English, 3–4, 23, 29,
    34–35, 38–40, 54–57, 119; villages among, 2, 3–4,
    35, 38, 51, 57, 58, 63, 86, 87, 204, 207; war
    against, 6, 17, 23, 41, 64–65, 74–86, 92–97,
    119–20, 124–26, 159, 201, 204, 206–7. See also
    Indian fighters; powwows; sachems; wampum trade;
    specific tribes and individuals
Indians Converted (Gookin), 61
industry (in Wachusett), 3, 32–34, 42, 44. See also
    manufacturing
Innes, Stephen, 7
inns. See taverns
Ipswich Canada (Massachusetts). See Ashburnham
Irish immigrants, 167, 247
ironworks, 34, 42, 44
Iroquois Indians, 78, 80, 204, 206. See also Mohawk
    people
itinerant revivalists, 141–42, 192–93, 198, 237–38.
    See also Alline, Henry; Whitefield, George

Jay's Treaty, 188
Jebogue (Nova Scotia), 192–95
Jethro (Christian Nipmuc), 63, 68
John (Indian). See "One-eyed John"
Johnson, Edward, 8, 23, 61; as Lancaster commis-
    sioner, 52; as local historian, 6, 16–22, 98, 102,
    124, 159, 198, 248; as town founder, 16–22
Johnson, Moses, 221–22
Joslin, Peter, 79

Keene (New Hampshire), 225
Kerley, Henry, 66
Kerley, William, 52
Keyes, William, 171, 172
Kilburn, John, 206–9
Kimball, Amos, 121
Kimball, Ephraim, 121
King, Thomas: fur trading post of, 40–42, 44, 53–55;
    land bought from Indians by, 33, 57, 124; mining
    interests of, 33–34
King George's War, 113, 119–20, 204–5, 207
King Philip's War. See Metacom's War
Kings County (Nova Scotia), 175, 177, 178
King William's War, 76, 78, 80, 81, 83, 123–24
kinship ties: and family landholdings, 146–47,
    149–50, 152–57; and migration, 13, 117, 128,
    137, 157, 168
Knaut, Philip, 173, 181
Knight, Philip, 48

Lancaster (Massachusetts): abandonment of, 67, 68;
    "Additional Grant" of, 88–89, 107; agriculture in,
    152, 154; artisans in, 156; bicentennial celebration
    of, 239, 241–42, 244; centennial of, 6, 123–26,
    245–46, 248; as early inland Wachusett settlement,
    4, 72; founding of, 2–3, 16, 72, 134, 205; govern-

ment of, 52–53, 59, 89–90; growth of, 48–54, 59, 82, 104–5; housing in, 78–79, 147; Indian raids on, 65–69, 76, 78–83, 92–93, 124–25, 245; land for, purchased from Indians, 40, 88; meetinghouses in, 90–92, 104, 105, 107, 109; in Metacom's War, 65, 66–68, 82; migration from, 109–17, 126, 134, 160; names for, 38, 47–48; partition of, 104–9, 121; population of, 146; resettlement of, 2, 76, 87; soldiers from, 167; town form of, 219; towns around, 128–29; towns spawned from, 106–7; Willard in, 55, 56. *See also* Nashaway Plantation

Lancaster (New Hampshire), 122

land: clearing of, 138–39; Indian vs. European views of, 28–29, 40, 57; lack of, 156; obtained from Indians, 40, 57, 64, 65, 87, 101, 122, 124, 128, 136, 245; pressures of, and Nova Scotian settlement, 168, 170; pressures of, and serial town development, 8, 14, 127, 134–36, 157. *See also* frontier; land allocation; land speculation; scouting; surveying; towns

land allocation: colonial supplies for, 12; generational conflicts regarding, 10, 14, 101, 139, 145–46; for industrial uses, 42–44; methods of, 7, 12, 14, 16, 20, 43, 88–89; for military service, 95, 97, 100, 117, 128–29, 131–32, 135, 136, 145, 202; in Nashaway Plantation, 43, 48, 51, 57; in New Brunswick, 187; in New Hampshire, 207–9; in Nova Scotia, 168, 170, 175, 177, 179, 180; to proprietors, 4, 5, 12–13, 110–11; restrictions on, 9–10, 51; in Watertown, 8–9; in Westminster, 133–34. *See also* townships: grants for

landholdings: claims of, by New Yorkers, 212, 213; family, 146–47, 149–50, 152–57

land morselization, 3, 14, 131

land speculation, 3, 102, 112; factors in promotion of, 128; fears of disorder associated with, 128, 131; as means of accumulating land and capital, 5, 8, 136, 138–39; in Nova Scotia, 179; in Walpole, New Hampshire, 207–8; in Watertown, 8

Larkin, Jack, 221

law, 106

Law, William, 195

Lawrence, Charles, 165, 167–68, 171, 175

"Lay Preacher." *See* Dennie, Joseph

The Lay Preacher, or Short Sermons for Idle Readers (Dennie), 228

Leavitt, Jonathan, 209, 210–11, 217

Lebanon (Connecticut), 202

Legge, Francis, 182

Leominster (Massachusetts), 107, 109, 120, 146

Leverett, John, 53

Lexington (Massachusetts), 124, 156, 159, 182

life cycle: as status factor in agrarian towns, 14. *See also* generations

Linton, Richard, 42

Litchfield County (Connecticut), 240, 242–43

Liverpool (Nova Scotia), 170, 173, 177, 178, 194–96

livestock, 149–50, 152–53, 177, 178, 180, 190

Lloyd, Thomas, 190

local historians: on captivity by Indians, 68–72; on Christian Indians, 59–64; as connecting generations, 125–26, 158, 159; efforts of, to restore lost sense of community, 247; on Indian fighting, 73, 97–99; on Nova Scotian religious conflicts, 191–99; as organizers of memory into coherent patterns, 6–7, 17, 22, 198, 227–37; popularity of works by, 158; on town founding, 1, 3, 6–7, 73, 157–61, 239–49; on Walpole, New Hampshire, 200, 227–37; on wilderness, 29. *See also* Walpole Wits; *specific historians*

Loring, Deborah, 141

Lothrop, Thomas, 141

Louisbourg (Canada), 119, 167

"Love's Labour Lost: Peter Pumpkinhead defeated by Tabitha Towzer" (Fessenden), 234

Lovewell, John, 95–100, 122, 129

Lovewell's Fight, 95–100

Lowden, James, 132

Lowell, James Russell, 233

Lowell (Massachusetts), 161

Loyalists, 182–86, 191, 212–16

lumber (in Nova Scotia), 170, 171, 177–78, 180, 187, 188, 190; importation of, 182, 188

Lunenburg (Massachusetts), 126; entrepreneurs from, 115, 204; founding of, 103, 112, 127; land in, 208; migrants from, to Nova Scotia, 167, 191; migrants from, to Walpole, New Hampshire, 205–6; roads from, 204; settlers of, 114, 117, 119–23, 137, 247; soldiers from, 167. *See also* Turkey Hills

Lunenburg (New Hampshire), 122

Lunenburg (Nova Scotia): agriculture in, 190; ethnic diversity in, 167, 170, 184; migration from, 181; occupations in, 190; population of, 178; privateers' raid on, 186; reasons for establishing, 173; trade in, 180

Lunenburg County (Nova Scotia), 175

Maine, 80, 92, 94, 127, 163, 199

Maine Missionary Society, 199

Malden (Massachusetts), 132

Maliseet Indians, 184

Mancke, Elizabeth, 175

"manitou," 26

manufacturing, 160–61, 222, 243–44, 247. *See also* industry

Marblehead (Massachusetts), 191

Marini, Stephen, 199, 216

market economy. *See* capitalism

Marlborough (Massachusetts): founding of, 10, 12, 134; histories of, 159; Indian attacks on, 66, 86; residents of, 137, 155. *See also* Marlborough Association

Marlborough Association, 141, 142, 174

Marsh, Deborah Loring Lothrop, 141

Marsh, Elisha, 140–45, 154, 249

Martin, John, 12–13, 88

Masasoit (Wampanoag sachem), 64

Mason, Jeremiah, 218–19, 229

Massachusett language, 61

Massachusett people, 35, 41

Massachusetts Bay Company, 7, 8

Massachusetts Colony: boundary disputes of, 202, 205, 213; early settlements in, 8; migration to Nova Scotia from, 165, 168. *See also* General Court of Massachusetts; *specific towns and individuals in*

Massachusetts Council (legislative house), 129, 131–33

Massachusetts General Court. *See* General Court of Massachusetts

Massachusetts Historical Society, 158

Massachusetts House of Representatives, 4, 129, 131

Massachusetts Magazine, 228

Massachusetts Turnpike, 221

Mather, Cotton, 69, 72, 74, 80–81, 124, 125, 196

Mather, Increase, 68, 69, 74, 124, 125

Matthew (Nashaway sachem), 53, 57, 63, 64

Matthews, Lois, 128

Maushop (mythical character), 26

Mayhew, Jonathan, 207
McClure, David, 199
Medfield (Massachusetts), 66, 67
Medford (Massachusetts), 8, 132, 139, 174
meetinghouses (churches): centrality of, in New
    England towns, 8, 14, 16, 20, 51, 111, 132,
    139–40, 143; in Lancaster, 90–92, 104, 105, 107,
    109; in Nova Scotia, 170; in Walpole, New Hamp-
    shire, 209, 220. *See also* ministers
merchants (storekeepers), 5, 200, 219–22. *See also*
    fur traders
Merrimack River valley, 23, 30, 46, 54, 55, 67, 92,
    163, 202
Metacom's War (King Philip's War), 6, 78, 87, 101,
    204; Benjamin Church's account of, 73–74; and
    Christian Indians, 64–68; effects of, on Daniel
    Gookin, 60; effects of, on Lancaster, 2, 65–69, 76,
    79, 82, 104, 120, 124, 245; goals of, 23; land
    claims by veterans of, 129, 136, 145; lessons
    learned in, 80; ministers' interpretations of, 69
Micmac people, 173, 184, 192
Middlesex County (Massachusetts), 29
migration: as component of English settlement, 4,
    111, 113; as depicted in centennial celebrations,
    243; factors in, 8–13, 48, 132–36, 154; kinship
    ties in, 13, 117, 128, 137, 157, 168; to New
    Hampshire, 200–201; to Nova Scotia, 165–68,
    172–75, 177–81, 186–87, 191–92; of Wachusett
    residents, 109–61, 164, 165, 167, 172, 173–75,
    201, 202, 204. *See also* "budding"; transportation
Miles, John, Jr., 137, 152
Miles, John, Sr., 137, 152
Miles, Noah, 137, 152
Miles, Reuben, 137, 152
militia: British acts regarding, 182–84; farming duties
    combined with, 79, 93–94, 111–12; leaders of, 5;
    musters of, 14, 54; requirements for, 81; warfare
    engaged in by, 86, 93–95, 206. *See also* Indian
    fighters; land allocation: for military service; scout-
    ing; soldiers
Miller, Joseph, 144
millers, 85–86, 104, 181. *See also* mills
mills, 8, 57, 121, 209; importance of, 13, 53–54, 85,
    134, 140, 159, 170. *See also* millers
mining, 32–33, 72
ministers: attempts by Boston, to control frontier set-
    tlers, 69; authority of, 138, 141; as cultural media-
    tors, 2; hiring of, 20, 140, 209, 216, 217; on Lan-
    caster's centennial, 6; in Nova Scotia, 170–71,
    173–75, 180–81, 184, 185, 191–99. *See also*
    Great Awakening; missionaries; *specific ministers*
missionaries: as cultural mediators, 2, 45, 59–64, 94;
    knowledge of Indian languages by, 44, 61; in
    Nashaway Plantation, 44–46, 59–64, 245; in
    Nova Scotia, 190. *See also* Christianity; *specific
    missionaries*
Mohawk people, 58–59, 65
Mohawk River, 163
Mohegan Indians, 41, 46
monadnocks, 30
Monoco (Nipmuc warrior), 66–67
monopolies (given to town founders), 54, 56, 163
Montcalm, Louis-Joseph de, 206
Montesquieu, Baron de La Brède et de, 231
Moor, Fairbanks, 134, 137, 140, 142, 147, 160
Moor, Judith Bellows, 137
Moore, Jacob, 99
Morison, Samuel Eliot, 33
Morning Ray (Windsor, Vermont paper), 228

Morris, Charles, 168, 171, 177, 178
Morton, Thomas, 38
Moulton, Ebenezer, 192–93
Mount Wachusett, 26, 29, 65, 149; centennial cele-
    bration depictions of, 243; Indians near, 35, 79,
    93; as monadnock, 30
Mount Wataquidock, 26
"mourning wars," 58

Narragansett Indians, 46, 65, 67, 87
Narragansett No. 2. *See* Westminster (Massachusetts)
Narragansett townships, 128, 159
Nashaway Company, 42–44. *See also* Nashaway
    Plantation
Nashaway people: conflicts of, with other Indians,
    58–59; dispossession of, 76; and English settle-
    ment, 48, 51, 72, 87; joint villages of, with
    English, 3–4, 23, 29, 30, 32–48, 57–61, 66, 68,
    72; and Metacom's War, 64–68, 204; sachems of,
    32, 34, 35, 38, 53, 57, 63–68, 124; stories about,
    245; stories of, 26, 28, 29; trade with, 54–57, 94.
    See also Algonquian peoples; Nipmuc people
Nashaway Plantation, 23, 32–48, 88. *See also* Lan-
    caster (Massachusetts)
Nashaway village (of Indians), 35, 38, 63
Nashobah (praying town), 61
Nashua River valley, 30, 32, 53
Natick (praying town), 61
national culture: town settlement's role in creation of,
    1, 2, 158
natural religion, 216–18
New Birth revival, 167, 191–99, 237–38. *See also*
    New Light movement
New Brunswick, 187
New England: commercial ties of, with Nova Scotia,
    167, 179, 180, 237; interdependence of Indians and
    early English settlers in, 29, 72, 94, 124, 125–26;
    local governing traditions of, 175, 177; and Meta-
    com's War, 65, 67; mythic constructions of, 5, 7,
    17–22, 70, 239–49; serial town development's role
    in creation of, 1, 4, 12–14, 16, 22, 122, 128, 157,
    227–39; as story of America, 248; towns of, as liter-
    ary subject, 227. *See also* Greater New England;
    specific New England states and cities
New England Courant, 93, 98–99
Newfoundland, 180, 188
New Hampshire: boundary disputes of, 202, 205;
    exploration of, 94; land available in, 127; migra-
    tion to, 155, 212, 213; roads in, 221; settlement
    of, 92, 163, 165, 237; Vermont's break with, 212.
    See also Walpole (New Hampshire)
New-Hampshire Journal, 225, 226. *See also Farmer's
    Museum*
New Hampshire Turnpikes, 221
New Light movement, 186, 216. *See also* Great
    Awakening; New Birth revival
New London (Connecticut), 55
newspapers, 220, 226–36. *See also specific newspapers*
Newton (Massachusetts), 132
New York City, 187
New York State: landholders' claims from, 212, 213;
    migration to, 155, 163
Nicholson, Francis, 78
Nipmuc people (Nipnett people): attempts to "civi-
    lize," 4, 60–64, 245; land of, 87, 92, 109; Nash-
    aways as part of, 35; Puritan dealings with, 33–34,
    59–64; in Wachusett, 32; war with, 64–68. *See
    also* Nashaway people
Nipnett (region), 26

Nipnett people. *See* Nipmuc people
Nissenbaum, Stephen, 5
Nora, Pierra, 244
Norcross, Nathaniel, 42–44
Northfield (Massachusetts), 202, 204
Northfield Road, 115, 119, 121
North Nashua River, 32, 104
North Town Plantation, 110
Norwich (Connecticut), 202
Nova Scotia: as British military colony, 7, 165, 167, 171, 199, 237; commercialization in, 164, 167, 178–80, 237; diversity of population in, 167, 170, 179, 181, 184; in French and Indian Wars, 78, 81; governing of, 164, 168, 172, 175, 177, 178, 182, 184–85, 199, 237–38; imperial neglect of, 187; incentives for settling in, 164, 165, 167–68, 172, 177; infrastructure problems in, 164, 179–80, 188, 190, 193; New Englanders in, 3, 5, 163–65, 167–87; outsettlements in, 164, 168, 178, 180–82, 188, 190, 193, 194, 198, 237; religious issues in, 168, 191–99, 237–38; schools in, 191, 193; sense of identity of, 164, 167, 186, 191–92, 197–99, 237–38; War for Independence's effects on, 171, 182–86. *See also* Acadia
Nova Scotia Council, 168, 172, 175, 177
Nowell, Increase, 53
Noyes, Peter, 9
No. 1 (Massachusetts), 202
No. 2 (Massachusetts), 202
No. 3 (Massachusetts), 202, 206
No. 4. *See* Charlestown (New Hampshire)

"Ode Composed for the Fourth of July" (Tyler), 231–33
Of Plymouth Plantation (Bradford), 17, 20
Ohio, 178
Oldham, John, 9
Oliver, Peter, 193
"One-eyed John" (Nipmuc warrior), 66, 68
outsettlements (in Nova Scotia), 164, 168, 178, 180–82, 188, 190, 193, 194, 198, 237

Page, David, 117, 119, 121–22, 247
Page, David, Jr., 122
Page, Joseph, 111
Page, Martha, 110
Page, Priscilla Poynton, 117
Page, Samuel, 110, 111, 113
Paine, Tom, 235
Paine, William, 191
Pakachoog village, 63
Parkman, Ebenezer, 105, 141, 174, 217
Parkman, Francis, 96
Parr (Nova Scotian governor), 187
Passaconoway (Pennecook sachem), 53
Patriots, 182–86
Pawtucket people, 57
Paxton (Massachusetts), 136
A Peaceable Temper and Conduct Divinely Enjoined (Harrington), 123–26
Peace of Aix-la-Chapelle, 120
Peace of Utrecht. *See* Treaty of Utrecht
Pearson, Mary, 154
Pendleton, Brian, 9
Penhallow, Samuel, 98, 100, 124
Pennacook confederation, 35, 41, 53
Penobscott Indians, 96
Pequot War (1637), 41, 44
Perkins, Simeon, 185, 194
Peterborough (New Hampshire), 136, 171

"Peter Periwinkle, to Tabitha Towzer" (Fessenden), 234
Petersham (Massachusetts), 122, 129, 240–41, 244
Philip (Abenaki Indian), 207
Philip (King). *See* Metacom's War
Phillips, George, 8
Phillips, Jonathan, 156
Phillips, Samuel, 47
Phips, William, 78
Pierpont (schoolmaster), 104
Pigwacket fight, 95–100
Planters: definition of, 165
Plymouth Colony, 64, 67, 73–74, 137
Pocumtuck people, 59
Pokanoket people, 64
Poole, Elizabeth, 120
Poole, James, 117, 120
Poole, Samuel, 117
population: dispersal of, in eighteenth-century settlement, 200, 205; diversity of, in New Hampshire borderlands, 201; diversity of, in Nova Scotia, 167, 170, 179, 181, 184; growth of, in 18th century, 146; of New Hampshire, 209; pressures of, and serial town development, 8–10, 12, 18, 82, 101, 128, 134–35, 157, 161
Porter, Nehemiah, 192
The Portfolio, 237
Port Royal (Nova Scotia), 78
Portsmouth (New Hampshire), 98, 155
postal routes, 220
Pownall, Thomas, 144
powwows, 45, 46, 63
Pratt, Noah, 142
"praying Indians." *See* Indians: Christian
"praying towns," 46–47, 60–63
Prentice, John, 91, 92, 103, 105, 141
Prentiss, Stephen, 223
Prescott (proposed town), 47, 122
Prescott, John, 93, 121, 122; as blacksmith, 44, 53–54; as fur trader, 5, 44, 54–57; house of, 79; and Indians, 57–58, 94; as Lancaster founder, 52, 76, 171, 205; land granted to, 57; as miller, 53–54, 119; as Nashaway Company settler, 43, 44, 47, 48, 155; as pioneer, 46
Prescott, Jonathan (John Prescott's great-great-grandson): in Nova Scotia, 171, 174, 182, 184, 186, 188, 190
Prescott, Jonathan (John Prescott's son), 171
Prescott, Joseph, 171
Prescott, Mary, 48
Prescott, Peter, 171
Prescott, William, 244
Prince, Thomas, 38
Princeton (Massachusetts), 38, 123, 126, 148–49, 243, 246–47
print culture: in transmission of New England ideology, 7; in Walpole, New Hampshire, 164, 201–2, 223, 225–37. *See also specific newspapers, books, and writers*
privateers (in Nova Scotia), 185–86
Profits in the Wilderness (Martin), 12–13
proprietors ("undertakers"), 42; family-based, 4, 5, 107, 132, 136–37, 154–57; and family farms, 128, 138–39, 149–50, 152, 155–57; Gookin as, 60; land grants to, 4, 5, 12–13, 110–11; mixed private and public powers of, 43, 89; as monopolists, 54, 163; New England meaning of, 168; in Nova Scotia, 173, 175, 177, 199; requirements of, 16, 89, 132, 133, 138–40, 205; rewards offered to settlers by, 133–34, 209; sole, in Walpole, New Hampshire, 201, 207–8, 211; suing of, 142, 144; in 18th

proprietors (*cont.*)
century, 110–11, 127–28, 159, 202, 204; as town founders, 87–89, 101–2, 201, 205; vs. town inhabitants, 14, 51, 89, 112–13, 139–46, 149; veterans as, 128. *See also* General Court of Massachusetts: township grants by; land allocation; land speculation; town founders; towns
"prudential" men, 51, 52
Puritans: communalism among, 13, 72; divisions among, 2, 6, 8, 17, 23, 42–43, 47, 69, 246; expectations of, 7, 51; expectations of Indians among, 60–64, 246; Great Migration of, 3, 7, 14, 32; on nature, 28–29, 32–34; typological histories of, 68–72; villages of, 3–4, 7–9. *See also* Congregational Church; missionaries; Yankee identity
Pynchon, John, 53, 54
Pynchon, William, 55, 56

Quanapohit, James, 57, 66
Quebec, 185; sieges against, 78, 81, 86, 168, 207
Queen Anne's War, 76, 80, 81, 86, 88

Rand, Silas Tertias, 25
Randell, Benjamin, 199
Rawlyk, George, 186, 216
Reading (Massachusetts), 132
The Redeemed Captive (Williams), 80, 86
regional culture: town settlement's role in creating, 1, 4, 12–14, 16, 122, 128, 157, 227–39
religion: increasing pluralism in, 212, 216–18, 246; in Nova Scotia, 179, 191–99. *See also* Christianity; Congregational Church; Great Awakening; New Light movement; Puritans; *specific denominations*
Remonstrance of 1646, 43, 44
Revolutionary War. *See* War for Independence
Rhode Island Colony, 67, 165, 168
Ring, George, 192
Ring, Lucy, 192, 194
roads: development of, and commercialization, 5, 113, 115, 117, 202, 204, 207, 220–21; lack of, in Nova Scotia, 164, 179, 180, 188, 190, 193; and town settlement, 13, 47, 111, 115, 117, 119, 121, 140, 143; in Wachusett, 30, 71, 103, 104
Robins (ensign), 96
Roper, Ephraim, Jr., 83
Roper, Ephraim, Sr., 83
Rowlandson, Joseph, 51–52, 66, 68, 76, 79, 93
Rowlandson, Mary White, 83, 93; background of, 51–52; as local historian, 3, 6, 68–72, 102, 119, 121, 125; on Metacom's War, 66–72, 76
Rowley (Massachusetts), 117
Roxbury (Massachusetts), 8
Royal Proclamation of 1763, 178
Ruddock, John, 10
Russell, John, 139
Rutman, Darrett, 235

sachems: authority of, 35, 41; missionaries' attempts to convert, to Christianity, 44–46, 63; of Nashaway people, 32, 34, 35, 38, 53, 57, 63–68, 124; Rowlandson's depiction of, 71. *See also* Matthew; Shoshanim; Showanon
Saco (Maine), 80
Sagamore (Indian chief), 47
"Sagamore Sam." *See* Shoshanim
St. Francis (Abenaki village), 207
Salem (Massachusetts), 8, 191
Salisbury, Neal, 35, 64
Saltonstall, Richard, 8

saltworks, 33
"Sam" (Nashaway leader). *See* Shoshanim
Sassamon, John, 65
sawmills, 54, 85, 121, 134, 173, 180, 181, 185, 190; Nova Scotian incentives for, 187–88
Sawyer, Caleb, 83
Sawyer, Elias, 85, 86
Sawyer, Mary, 155
Sawyer, Thomas, 48, 76, 85
scalping, 81, 92, 95–96, 99, 119
schools: depictions of, in centennial celebrations, 243; in Lancaster, 104–5, 109; in Lunenburg, Massachusetts, 114; in Nova Scotia, 191, 193; quality of, 160; and town settlement, 13, 111, 132, 140; in Walpole, New Hampshire, 211
The Science of Sanctity (Fessenden), 218
Scotland, 179, 192. *See also* Scots-Irish immigrants
Scots-Irish immigrants, 136, 202
Scott, John, 192
Scott, Jonathan, 167, 191–99
Scott, Lucy Ring, 192, 194
Scott, Moses, 192
scouting, 113, 115, 117, 119; by Indian fighters, 94, 96–97, 207
Seasonable Thoughts on the State of Religion (Chauncey), 141
Seavey, Ormond, 18
Seccombe, John, 163, 165; as Nova Scotian town founder, 170–71, 173–75, 180–81; in War for Independence, 184, 185
Seccombe, Mercy Williams, 174
Sedgwick, Captain John, 20
"serial town development": definition of, 1; and social change, 3, 9, 90. *See also* town founders; town founding; towns
Seven Years War, 167
Sewall, Samuel, 85
shamans, 46
Shelburne (New Brunswick), 187, 188
shipbuilding, 187, 188
Shirley, William, 206
Shoreham (Nova Scotia), 171. *See also* Chester (Nova Scotia)
Shoshanim (Nashaway sachem, also called "Sam"), 53, 63, 64–68
Showanon (Nashaway sachem), 32, 34, 35, 38, 40, 44–46, 48, 54, 245; death of, 53; land sold by, 57; portrayed as town founder, 124, 125–26
Shy, John, 81
Sibley, Asa, 223
silver, 33, 34
Simmons, William, 26, 28
"Simon Spunkey's Irregular Ode to Colonel Candidate Fair Haven" (Fessenden), 234
slavery: colonial, 137, 211; controversies concerning, 246; of Indians, 68, 245
social change: local historians' legitimation of, 6, 22; and serial town development, 3, 9, 90
Society for the Propagation of the Gospel, 190
Sogkonate, 73
soldiers: as precursors of settlers, 204, 205; as settlers, 173. *See also* Indian fighters; militia; scouting; war
The Song of Lovewell's Fight, 99
South Town Plantation, 110. *See also* Lunenburg (Massachusetts); Turkey Hills (Massachusetts)
The Sovereignty and Goodness of God (Rowlandson), 68–72
Sparks, Jared, 244
The Spirit of the Laws (Montesquieu), 231

Sprague, John, 148
Springfield (Massachusetts), 55
Spunkey, Simon. *See* Fessenden, Thomas Green
Squakeag village, 58
stagecoaches, 220
Stearns, Abigail, 137
Stearns, John, 137
Stearns, Thomas, 137
Sterling (Massachusetts), 40. *See also* Weshakim
Stevens, Cyprian, 56
Stevens, Mary Willard, 56
Stevens, Phineas, 207
Stewart, Gordon, 186
Still River, 82, 90, 104, 105
Still River village, 107
Stoddard, Solomon, 174
Stone, Nathan, 142
Stoneham (Massachusetts), 117
storekeepers. *See* merchants
Stoughton, William, 87
Stow, Samuel, 104
Strong, Phoebe, 212
Sudbury (Massachusetts), 110; bridges from, 43; founding of, 9, 16; in Metacom's War, 66, 67; migration from, 12, 14, 51, 132, 134; town officers in, 14
"superintendents" (of Indians), 4, 60–64
surveying, 5, 114, 115, 168, 172, 204, 205
Swansea (Massachusetts), 65
Swanzey (New Hampshire), 123–24
Swiss, 167
Symmes, Thomas, 97–98, 100
Symond, Henry, 40–42

Tahanto, George, 87–88
Tantiusques (near Sturbridge, Massachusetts), 33–34
taverns (inns), 103–5, 113, 115, 117, 119, 121, 155
taxes: abatements of, 13, 54; controversies concerning, 90, 139, 140, 143, 144–45; for ministers and meetinghouses, 209; in Nova Scotia, 182; for schools, 104
Templeton (Massachusetts), 129
Thomas, Isaiah, 219, 225–28, 236
Thoreau, Henry David, 233
timber. *See* lumber
Tinker, John, 52, 54–57
Tocqueville, Alexis de, 248
town founders, 3; backgrounds of, 12, 44, 60, 73–74, 92, 95, 99–100, 115, 117, 199, 201, 204; as creators of local institutions, 6; as cultural mediators, 59–64; as entrepreneurs, 5, 12–13, 32–34, 44, 53–55, 72, 95, 114, 121–22, 237; Indians as, 124, 125–26; memorialization of, 102, 241–42; monopolies given to, 54, 56; new interpretations of, 6; in Nova Scotia, 165, 167; religious unorthodoxy among, 43; Wachusett migrants as, 114–15, 165, 167; of Watertown, 8. *See also* proprietors; soldiers; surveying; town founding; *specific towns and town founders*
town founding: centennial celebrations of, 6, 123–26, 161, 239–49; methods of, 3, 4–5, 12, 88; motivations for, 150, 154; number of, 163; process of, 16–22, 109–13, 200; seasonal character of, 138–39. *See also* local historians; town founders
town grants. *See* townships: grants for
town meetings, 112–13, 121, 143
town offices, 14, 17, 20, 52–53, 55, 60, 89–91, 113, 150; in Nova Scotia, 175, 177; in Walpole, New Hampshire, 201, 208
towns: authority in, 91–92, 139; compact settlement of, 78–79, 87, 92, 128; competition for settlers by, 134; dispersed settlement of, 8, 14, 16; expansion of, 1–2, 4–5, 9, 96–97, 101–2, 104–23, 219; expectations of, 4–5, 7, 51, 109, 110; government of, 52–53, 59, 89–90, 128, 139–46, 157, 159, 208, 211–13, 215–16; infrastructure for, 103, 140; institutions associated with, 13–14, 20, 29, 47, 51, 81, 102, 132, 164; land limits in, 5, 8, 9; life cycle of early, 14; Metacom's War's effects on, 67, 68; model for establishing, in 18th century, 110, 114; modification of, in 18th century, 102, 121; as necessary for economic development, 34; partitioning of, 104–9, 121; "praying," 60–64; religious divisions in, 8, 216–18; rituals associated with, 14; settlement of, 1, 4–9; social divisions within, 14, 51, 88–89; variations among, 12, 23. *See also* agriculture; "budding"; class divisions; colonization; commercialization; local historians; mills; "serial town development"; town founders; town founding; town meetings; town offices; villages; *specific towns and town institutions*
townships: grants for, 5, 9, 12, 20, 51, 52, 57, 60, 88, 92, 101, 103, 109–11, 127, 129, 145, 202; Nova Scotian contention over term, 168, 172, 175, 177
traders: in Nova Scotia, 167, 171, 173. *See also* fishing; fur traders
trading posts, 40–42, 44, 53–55, 113. *See also* commercialization
transportation. *See* bridges; canals; roads; *specific rivers and river valleys*
Treaty of Fort Stanwyx, 178
Treaty of Paris, 207
Treaty of Ryswick, 79
Treaty of Utrecht, 86, 92, 101, 103, 109, 110, 127
Turkey Hills (Massachusetts), 93, 110–13, 122. *See also* Lunenburg (Massachusetts)
Turner, Frederick Jackson, 3, 6, 128, 138
Turner, William, 67
turnpikes, 5, 221. *See also* roads
Tyler, Royall, 228, 231–33, 236
Tyng, Eleazer, 94

"undertakers," 42. *See also* proprietors
Universalism, 216, 218

Vaudreuil, Philippe de Rigaud de, 85
Vermont: creation of, 212, 213, 215–16; land available in, 127; migration to, 155; settlement of, 92
Vickers, David, 135
"Village Enlightenment," 218–36
villages: English, as New England model, 7; among Indians, 2, 3–4, 35, 38, 51, 57, 58, 63, 86, 87, 204, 207; joint Indian and English, in Wachusett, 3–4, 23, 29, 30, 32–48, 57–61, 66, 68, 72; Nova Scotia outsettlements as, 164, 168, 178, 180–82, 188, 190, 193, 194, 198, 237; postrevolutionary commercial, 5, 164, 200–238, 249. *See also* towns; *names of specific villages*
Virgina Company, 7
Virginia Colony, 60
The Voluntier's March (ballad), 97, 99

Waban (sachem), 45
Wachusett (central Massachusetts): centennial celebrations of towns in, 6, 123–26, 161, 239–49; as inland part of New England, 2, 29–32; meaning of, 38. *See also* colonization; commercialization; Indians; migration; towns; war; *specific towns*
wage labor, 3, 135, 139, 160–61, 222. *See also* artisans; capitalism; manufacturing

Wakeley, "Old," 69
Walpole (New Hampshire), 7, 145, 200–238; as commercial village, 218–27; founding of, 137, 204; growth of, 164, 209–12; print culture in, 227–38; religious innovation in, 212, 216–18. *See also* Walpole Wits
Walpole Wits, 7, 201–2, 223, 225–39
Wampanoag people, 64–65, 67, 71
wampum trade, 35, 39–40, 58
Wamsutta (Alexander), 64
war: against Indians, 6, 17, 23, 41, 64–65, 74–86, 92–97, 119–20, 124–26, 159, 201, 204, 206–7; metaphors of, in settlement history, 18; "mourning," 58; as part of colonial life, 2, 4, 6, 23–24, 74–86, 113–15, 119–20, 128, 160
War for Independence: Alline on, 197, 198; and regional self-definition, 7, 246–47; sympathies regarding, in Nova Scotia, 171, 182–86; Westminster's involvement in, 160. *See also* Loyalists
War of the League of Augsburg, 76
Washington, George, 216
Wassamegon (Nipmuc sachem), 40
Wataquadock (Massachusetts), 105
Waters, Lawrence, 42, 48, 56
Watertown (Massachusetts): commercial activities in, 8, 40; as home of Nashaway Company investors, 42, 44; migration from, 12, 132, 134, 154; settlement and expansion of, 7–9, 14
Watkins, Alexander, 222
Wattasacompanum (Nipmuc ruler), 63
Weathersfield (Connecticut), 9, 76
Weetamoo (Wampanoag sachem), 71
Wells (Maine), 80
Wentworth, Benning, 122, 163, 201, 205, 207–9, 212, 213
Wentworth, John, 201
Weshakim (Indian village near Sterling, Massachusetts), 35, 38, 51, 57, 63, 86, 87
Wesley, John, 195
West, Benjamin, 228
West, Sophia, 223
West Indies, 86; North American Indians shipped to, 68; Nova Scotian trade with, 170, 180, 187–88
Westminster (Massachusetts) (also known as Narragansett No. 2), 128; centennial of, 161, 245–46, 248; family farms in, 146–57; founding of, 128, 132–39, 205, 245; government of, 139–46; local histories of, 157–61; "massacre" in, 212; migrants from, 201
Weston (Massachusetts), 132
Wetherbee, Ephraim, 156
Wetherbee, Nathan, 156
Whaley, George, 47
Wheeler, Abraham, 79
White, Eunice, 100
White, John (Lancaster landowner), 51–52, 93
White, John (soldier), 93, 95, 96, 99, 122, 129
White, John, Jr., 82
White, Josiah, 90
White, Mary, 51–52
Whitefield, George, 141, 174, 199
Whiting, John, 80
Whitney, Peter, 7, 158
Wiederholt, Adolph, 181
Wilder, Joseph, 89, 106
Wilder, Nathaniel, 87
Wilder, Thomas, Sr., 92
Wilder, Thomas, Jr., 92
wilderness: captives' survival in, 69–72; colonization of, 1–2, 4, 17–19; descriptions of, 134, 160; vs.

hedge metaphor, 69, 72, 74, 196; Indian vs. English views of, 25–29, 40; as spiritual metaphor, 18–22, 69–72, 102; transformation of, into garden, 124–26, 159, 248. *See also* colonization; frontier; migration; towns
Willard, Abijah, 167
Willard, Benjamin, 82–83
Willard, Dorcas Cutter, 137
Willard, Henry, 82, 138
Willard, Joseph, 241–42, 245
Willard, Josiah, 93–96, 99–100, 111–13; and Arlington, New Hampshire, 204; land granted to, 115, 117, 202; and Lunenburg, Massachusetts, 111–13; and Walpole, New Hampshire, 208
Willard, Levi, 148
Willard, Mary, 56
Willard, Samuel, 93–96, 99–100, 119, 121–22, 172; house of, 105–6, 147, 148
Willard, Simon, 19, 93; death of, 67; descendants of, 172; as fur trader, 55–57, 94; house of, 90; on Indian conflicts, 58, 65; as Lancaster commissioner, 52; as Nashaway Plantation commissioner, 43, 107; as town founder, 5, 54–56, 82, 122
William of Orange (king of England), 76
Williams, Eunice, 86
Williams, Israel, 206
Williams, Mercy, 174
Williams, Roger, 26, 34
Williams, William, 174
Winchendon (Massachusetts), 129. *See also* Dorchester
Windsor (Nova Scotia), 190
Windsor (Vermont), 225, 228
Winthrop, John, 13; as General Court administrator, 41; and land allotments, 16, 28–29; as local historian, 6, 17, 21, 25, 245; as pioneer, 26, 32; on religious divisions in Puritanism, 43; and Showanon, 44; Watertown visits of, 8
Winthrop, John, Jr., 32–34, 67
Wise, John, 127
Wiser, James, 87
Wiser, John, 87
Woburn (Massachusetts), 17, 20–21, 110, 117
Wolfe, James, 206
women: and captivity narrative genre, 71–72; as defense against privateers, 186; depictions of, in centennial celebrations, 243; as domestic manufacturers, 200, 222; as Indian fighters, 111–12; work of Nashaway, 38
The Wonder-Working Providence of Zion's Saviour in New England (Johnson), 16–22, 198
Wood, Joseph, 219, 245
Wood, Nathan, 147
Wood, William, 38, 41
wool, 222
Worcester (Massachusetts), 104, 106, 136, 155
Worcester (New York), 155
Worcester County (Massachusetts), 29–30, 38; class divisions in, 148; establishment of, 103; household sizes in, 146; land available in, 127. *See also* Wachusett; *specific towns in*
Worcester Plateau. *See* Wachusett
Wynn, Graeme, 179

Yankee identity, 227, 231–37, 241–49
Yarmouth (Nova Scotia), 165, 167, 179, 183, 191–92, 195–96
yeoman. *See* identity: Yankee
Yorkshire (England), 179